Sliding to the Right

D1569875

Sliding to the Right

The Contest for the Future
of American Jewish Orthodoxy

Samuel C. Heilman

UNIVERSITY OF CALIFORNIA PRESS

Berkeley / Los Angeles / London

TAO

The publisher gratefully acknowledges the generous contribution to
this book provided by the Lucius N. Littauer Foundation Jewish Studies
Endowment Fund of the University of California Press Foundation.

University of California Press, one of the most distinguished university
presses in the United States, enriches lives around the world by advancing
scholarship in the humanities, social sciences, and natural sciences.
Its activities are supported by the UC Press Foundation and by philanthropic
contributions from individuals and institutions. For more information,
visit www.ucpress.edu.

University of California Press
Berkeley and Los Angeles, California

University of California Press, Ltd.
London, England

© 2006 by The Regents of the University of California

Library of Congress Cataloging-in-Publication Data
Heilman, Samuel C.
    Sliding to the right : the contest for the future of American Jewish
Orthodoxy / Samuel C. Heilman.
        p.   cm.
    Includes bibliographical references and index.
    ISBN 13: 978-0-520-23136-8 (cloth : alk. paper), ISBN 10: 0-520-23136-8
(cloth : alk. paper)
    ISBN 13: 978-0-520-24763-5 (pbk. : alk. paper), ISBN 10: 0-520-24763-9
(pbk. : alk. paper)
    1. Orthodox Judaism—United States.   2. Ultra-Orthodox Jews—
United States.   3. Jewish religious education—United States.   4. Jews—
Cultural assimilation—United States.   I. Title.
BM205.H439   2006
296.8'32'0973—dc22   2005020670

Manufactured in the United States of America

15   14   13   12   11   10   09   08   07
10   9   8   7   6   5   4   3   2

This book is printed on Natures Book, which contains 50% post-consumer
waste and meets the minimum requirements of ANSI/NISO Z39.48–1992 (R
1997) (*Permanence of Paper*).

*For Yoni and Gabrielle upon the occasion
of their building a new orthodox home*

Contents

Acknowledgments

I have benefited from the assistance of many people while writing this book. The Institute for Advanced Study in Jerusalem provided an intellectual atmosphere and material support, augmented by a scholar-incentive award from Queens College, my academic home. I drew invaluable insight and advice from the members of my working group at the institute: Steven M. Cohen, Lynn Davidman, Shlomo Fisher, Menachem Friedman, Harvey Goldberg, Theodore Sasson, Yaakov Yadgar, and Yael Zerubavel. Two anonymous readers at the University of California Press helped me reorganize my thoughts in useful and important ways. Sergio Della Pergola and Uzi Rebhun helped me muddle my way through the demographic details, as did Jack Ukeles, director of the 2002 New York Jewish Community Study. Shalom Berger, Haym Soloveitchik, and Marvin Schick (with whom I argued endlessly) were generous and helpful with their knowledge. I have also benefited over the years from discussions about Orthodoxy with the late Charles Liebman and with Lawrence Kaplan, Chaim I. Waxman, and William Helmreich. As always, my wife, Ellin, who enabled me to escape many responsibilities at home and spend the time in Jerusalem working on this manuscript, deserves the highest praise. Without her, I would be lost.

Jerusalem, Shvat 5765/January 2005

Introduction

What the son wishes to forget the grandson wishes to remember.

Marcus Hansen, "The Third Generation in America"

Although once characterized as a "residual category" by one sociologist and a "case study in institutional decay" by another, who considered it likely to disappear in contemporary secular society and the American "melting pot," Orthodox Judaism at the dawn of the twenty-first century has decidedly not melted completely away.[1] As Marshall Sklare, who had predicted its demise in the mid-1950s, admitted by the early 1970s, "Orthodoxy has refused to assume the role of invalid. Rather, it has transformed itself into a growing force in American Jewish life."[2]

But what exactly is American Orthodoxy? In their end-of-the-twentieth-century study of American Jewry, and in particular the large segment of it that they characterize as the "moderately affiliated," Steven M. Cohen and Arnold M. Eisen describe a population who consider their faith a private matter, shy away from Jewish institutional and organizational life, and see Judaism as offering "no final answers, no irrevocable commitments." These are Jews who are ready to revise and amend their Judaism, to "decide week by week, year by year, which rituals they will observe and how they will observe them." With what Cohen and Eisen call a "profound individualism," these exquisitely American Jews, whose "principal authority" has become "the sovereign self," chart their own personal paths "to Jewish attitudes and behaviors with which they feel comfortable," utterly

I

convinced "that one need not take on any rituals with which one is un-comfortable" or that one does not find meaningful. Moreover, even the most religiously observant and active among them express "discomfort with the idea of commandment, all the more so with the notion of particular commandments issued by God to Jews alone," what Jewish tradition defines as the "Torah covenant at Sinai."[3]

Compared to these people, who Cohen and Eisen claim "make up the bulk" of contemporary Jewish America, Orthodox Jews, who number only at most about 12 percent of that same population and with whom this book is concerned, stand in sharpest contrast. They are highly affiliated to all things Jewish. For them, Judaism is *not* primarily a personal matter. On the contrary, it is a series of mandates: requirements whose origins are con-sidered to be part of a venerated tradition that sets definite criteria for how each person must act and live, regardless of personal wishes and inclina-tions. Moreover, for the Orthodox, Judaism's authority is in principle not situated in the self but remains determined by law and tradition and is sit-uated in the community, through shared patterns and standards of behavior as well as powerful attachments to institutions that these Jews have been assiduous in building during the last half of the twentieth century.[4] This is a life with people who are rooted in obligations to what some of them have come to call "Torah-true Judaism," a Judaism linked inextricably to a way of life defined by the Halacha (Jewish law) and in common parlance referred to as *frum*.[5] Elsewhere I have written that "*frum* or *frumkeit* (the state of being *frum*) is a Yiddish expression referring both to the actual practice of Halachic [Judeo-legal] Judaism and to the religious outlook associated with it." In practice it is simply what the Orthodox use to define what they consider an acceptable "Jewish way of behaving."[6] This is a path and way of life whose followers claim begins with divine revelation at Sinai and leads to final answers and demands, irrevocable commitments to rules, codes, and a series of ultimate rabbinic authorities both dead and living whose interpretations of the sacred obligations of the Torah carry the weight of law and the ultimate authority of the normative. In fact, *frum* has come to mean acting in conformity with other like-minded Orthodox Jews in one's community. But the Orthodox do not live in an undifferen-tiated community. *Frum* now confronts *frum*mer (more *frum*).

Two Types of Orthodoxy

From nearly its beginnings as a movement in nineteenth-century Europe to its present manifestations in America, Orthodox Judaism has been accused of asserting that there was only *one* way to be a Jew and that this way was the Orthodox one. Yet if that was the view from the outside, within the world of the Orthodox there was by no means unanimity as to what was legitimately Orthodox. When we examine American Orthodoxy today, we discover that still there is no agreement on this point. While there are internal Orthodox debates over a variety of details—from how Jews should dress to what they can properly eat, the rightful demands of ritual, the appropriate style of life, and even religious ideology and leadership—all these can be subsumed under the two essential and often oppositional orientations that have evolved in American Orthodoxy and that are now engaged in a struggle to define the essence of the movement authoritatively. That contest is the starting point for this book.

On the one side are Jews for whom the real meaning of Orthodoxy is the ability to live in and be embraced by several cultures and worldviews at once. These are Jews for whom the key to Jewish survival is, borrowing a term from Mary Douglas, "contrapuntal belonging."[7] In the contrapuntal, pluralist model, competing loyalties to potentially rivalrous institutions and cultures are permitted, even encouraged. This is because the people involved believe that they have much to gain by living in what Peter Berger once called "plural life-worlds." Contrapuntalism not only allows people to belong to multiple institutions and cultures simultaneously, but also grants them some modicum of autonomy in making and establishing those affiliations. If in contrapuntalism plural life-worlds and associated institutions engender dissonant and competing loyalties, the individual handles them either by redefining the rivalries as substantively insignificant and "merely symbolic" or by treating the loyalties as provisional and situational, subject to modification as the need arises. This accommodationist stance has been the approach of the majority of American Orthodox Jews, those who for most of the twentieth century have been called "modern Orthodox."

In general, the accommodationist approach allowed Orthodox Jews to feel that they were not all that different from the surrounding society, even while they remained steadfastly loyal to Jewish traditions, law, and custom. An acculturative contrapuntalist Orthodoxy was most popular in milieus where features that characterized the surrounding civilization were attractive to religiously observant Jews and where they had some hope of access to that culture. In nineteenth- and early-twentieth-century Germany, with its high culture, this often became the case, especially for Jews who lived in the cities. And such an approach was even more conformable to America, with its open culture and beckoning democratic society and meritocratic ethos.

4 INTRODUCTION

In the last half of the American twentieth century, the cosmopolitan attitudes and desires to illumine and deepen Jewish commitments through the prism of general education that characterized modern Orthodoxy created a population of religiously observant Jews who entered the ranks of the professions and achieved political power and some wealth—all apparently without sacrificing their Orthodoxy. The existence of modern Orthodox physicians, lawyers, politicians, CEOs, successful entrepreneurs, and distinguished university professors is no longer astonishing. By the last decade of the twentieth century, 32 percent of Orthodox Jews were professionals and about 11 percent managers. According to most recent polls, about 52 percent of American Orthodox Jews had at least one to three years of college. Among those Orthodox Jews who came to America after 1950, the number with college training was even higher, a whopping 81 percent.

But these are not the only Orthodox Jews who have thrived in America. A second type, which views the surrounding modern world not as an opportunity but as a threat and seeks instead to keep it at arm's length, has also emerged and multiplied. I call this type of Orthodoxy contra-acculturative and "enclavist."[8] In this approach, the emphasis is on the Jewish minority remaining protected within its parochial cultural enclaves. Here the goal is not to fit Orthodoxy to the surrounding culture but rather to ensure that all insiders conform to the religious behavior and worldview that predominate within the enclave culture, no matter how retrograde it may seem. Here the received wisdom is that yesterday is superior to today and that only those who remain totally committed to and enclosed within the "four cubits of Jewish life" are truly Orthodox.

In the enclave the individual does not count as much as the group. Unlike the contrapuntalists, who believe individuals can autonomously divide themselves, their time, and their loyalties and shift among various parochial and cosmopolitan involvements, the enclavists are certain that anything less than complete engagement in and domination by the parochial life of the enclave is culturally destructive. This sectarian stance is the approach of an increasingly visible Orthodox Jewish group, those who have been called Haredi, from the indigenous Hebrew word that means "anxiously and fervently religious."[9]

The Haredim are divided into at least three groups. The Hasidim, the most enclavist of the lot, are a pietistic movement that traces its origins back to Israel ben Eliezer, the Baal Shem Tov, in the eighteenth century in Eastern Europe. The Mitnagdim, insular but less so than most Hasidim, trace their origins to the yeshiva world that reached its apex in Lithuania in the same period; originally they followed Elijah of Vilna and opposed much of the early pietistic excesses of Hasidism. A third group consists of Jews of Middle East origins who emerged in modern Israel in the latter half of the twentieth century, who are often identified with the Israeli Shas party, and whose enclave culture tends to be more ethnically oriented and less insular than that of other Haredim.[10] Important in Israel, they play a relatively negligible role in American Orthodox life for now. However, in some communities, where Israeli expatriates have settled, the impact of these Jews has increased significantly.

In general, sectarian enclavist approaches emerge where the outside world is not attractive or where it remains closed to minorities, as was the case for observant Jews in much of eastern Europe. But they also emerge when a minority feels that it is threatened with assimilation or defilement by contact with the outside world. This is the fear that many of the Haredim express vis-à-vis America. They encourage a consciousness that, in the words of one contemporary Haredi, demands *galus hanefesh*, a moral and spiritual "sense of separateness and estrangement" from the contemporary, often enticing, westernized, materialistic world that they believe "devours those who seek to embrace it."[11]

The overarching question this book seeks to answer is which of these kinds of Orthodoxy today dominates the movement in America. For much of the past fifty years, the period in which Orthodoxy firmly established itself in an American community that in 2004 marked its 350th anniversary, the contrapuntalists were on the rise, winning most hearts and minds. During the past decade and a half, however, that dominance has been thrown into doubt as the Orthodox in America have increasingly considered contrapuntalism to be destructive to Judaism rather than enriching and have moved to champion what one of their rabbis has called "the heroic retreat from . . . fragmentation"—from engagement in plural life-worlds—seeking instead the haven of religious insularity in their enclaves.[12] In so doing they have argued the Haredi line that so-called modern Orthodoxy and its contrapuntalism have been anomalies, that they represent merely a brief interlude in Jewish history and a reaction to the dizzying succession of historical changes that the Jews experienced through much of the twentieth century. The true purpose and character of Orthodoxy, these Jews argue, is to preserve and make certain that "only the ancient, unadulterated Jewish heritage with its honest motto '*Moshe emes v'toraso emes*' [Moses is true and his Torah is true] can be accepted as Jewish."[13] Anything else is counterfeit.

The Triumph of Orthodoxy

Whether enclavist or contrapuntalist, Orthodox Jews have demonstrated in a number of ways that they have found their place in America. Contrary to the attitudes and patterns of Jewish behavior particular to the moderately affiliated, who today constitute about 60 percent of American Jewry and who, according to Cohen and Eisen, may "contribute to the dissolution of communal institutions and intergenerational commitment, thereby weakening the very sources of [their] own Jewish fulfillment and making them far less available to succeeding generations," the Orthodox have built many institutions in America and have much more hope in their future and their ability to hold onto their young and pass on to them their way of life and type of religion.[14] As Rabbi Zvi Holland, director of the Phoenix Community Kollel of the Aish HaTorah Yeshiva, articulated this point of view, "With the intermarriage rate as it stands, Orthodox Jewry is likely to emerge in a mere handful of generations as the only viable Jewish movement left."[15] About nine in ten American Orthodox Jews are married to Jews, and of the relative few who have intermarried, a quarter have spouses who have converted to Judaism. In their family life they maintain a high degree of stability, with a divorce rate that, although rising, remains far lower than the approximately 30 percent among other Jews and than much of the rest of America. Their birthrate remains somewhere between three and eight children per family.[16] In other words, barring a far-reaching and rapid exodus from Orthodoxy, concrete factors will lead to its demographic growth that may offset generations of decline.[17]

Once predominantly working class or immigrant and located among the poorest neighborhoods of the inner cities, throughout the last decades Orthodox Jews have become overwhelmingly native born and have moved in large numbers to the suburbs. Indeed, even among the Hasidim, so many of whom made their way to the United States just before and after the Holocaust, a majority are now native born.[18] Although overwhelmingly found in and around the cities of the Northeast, particularly New York City (where by one estimate they may as of 2002 actually constitute the largest Jewish denomination), Orthodox Jews have established a significant presence in parts of the South, Midwest, and West.[19]

The Orthodox commonly live in the areas of highest Jewish density. However, when they move to the periphery of the Jewish community, they manage to do something that few other Jews achieve: they change the communities into which they have moved rather than becoming changed by them. Thus, because they will not acquiesce to a diminished level of Jewish life, no matter where they live, the entry of Orthodox Jews into small Jewish communities has frequently promoted greater religious and ethnic participation in these places. Simply put: American Orthodox Jews have been able to make Jewish life in such communities flourish.

In the political domain, Orthodox Jews have risen to unprecedented levels of political power and influence in both local and national government, all without hiding their Jewish and religious commitments. The nomination of openly Orthodox Jewish Joseph Lieberman as vice-president of the United States on the 2000 national Democrat ticket (and his serious bid for the presidential nomination four years later) and the role that a yarmulke-clad, Jewishly observant Ari Weiss played as House Speaker Tip O'Neill's chief legislative aide in the ninety-fifth through the ninety-ninth Congresses are among the most dramatic examples of American national political involvement among individual Orthodox Jews, and the ascension of the Orthodox Jewish Sheldon Silver to the high-ranking position of Assembly Speaker in the New York State Legislature and perhaps the most powerful Democrat in the state is no less impressive.

As a group, the Orthodox know their way around a variety of political institutions and corridors of power, exerting political influence both within the Jewish community and in all levels of government where they have interests at stake. Lobbying in Congress by Orthodox groups, including such organizations as the National Council of Young Israel, the Union of Orthodox Jewish Congregations of America, Lubavitcher Hasidim, and the Agudath Israel is today routine. At the local and state levels, this activity is even more pronounced, particularly in and around metropolitan New York, where Orthodox Jews constitute approximately a fifth of the Jewish population. Lubavitcher Hasidim have been in the Oval Office in every administration since Jimmy Carter's. Moreover, it is not surprising to see politicians courting the American Jewish vote by having their pictures taken with some Hasidic rebbe or donning a yarmulke, as if Orthodoxy were emblematic of American Jewry. While the Orthodox in America are not as broadly engaged in the political life of the nation as they are in Israel, their engagement in the politics and government of the United States is quite remarkable when one considers that America is not a Jewish state or one where there is a Jewish majority but rather one in which the Jews constitute between 2 and 3 percent of the population and the Orthodox somewhere around 10 to 12 percent of that tiny fraction.

The Orthodox have been successful in building institutions. According to one survey, almost 40 percent of the synagogues in America are Orthodox, and in the New York metropolitan area that proportion rises to 57 percent.[20] They have several national rabbinic organizations, nationwide synagogue associations, day school and yeshiva organizations representing a growing network of such institutions, lay and professional organizations, advocacy groups, youth associations, a plethora of kashruth-certifying associations, groups built around coordinated Jewish study—the list seems endless. Moreover, the Orthodox increasingly have taken positions of leadership in many of the major Jewish organizations and serve as executives or in primary staff positions in such varied organizations as the Conference of Presidents of Major Jewish Organizations, the American Jewish Committee, the Memorial Foundation for Jewish Culture, and the Association for Jewish Studies, to name just a few, as well as a number of large federations. The Orthodox are at the hub of activity in Jewish organizations and federations, and their share of leadership positions is growing.

Throughout the last decades of the twentieth century, Orthodox Jews, although still the Jewish group with the lowest per capita average income and the highest Jewish bill (costs paid to Jewish institutions and for Jewish needs), a result of their greater involvement in Jewish life, including most prominently full-time, private Jewish education for their children, have become wealthier and far better educated than during most of their past, although more careful scrutiny and analysis reveal that those commonly referred to as Haredim account for much of the lower income and higher costs (as well as most of the greater fertility).

The Orthodox overwhelmingly provide their offspring with full-time religious education in day schools and yeshivas, which they view as key to continuity. What was once viewed as optional is now a sine qua non for those who would call themselves members of the movement. Not only have Orthodox girls and women now universally joined the ranks of Jews who are given a solid Jewish education from the primary grades through high school, but especially in the past twenty years there has been a rapid proliferation of advanced Torah learning institutions and study circles that serve Orthodox women, many of whom now consider such study as an obligatory element of their lives. In some neighborhoods yeshivas, and particularly those that cater to adult married men, are not only educating but also sustaining whole communities (made up of large families), often at enormous expense.

Not altogether unrelated to these developments, the Orthodox today publish (and own) more sacred Jewish books (many in translation as well as in the original) than ever before in their history. The Mesorah Foundation has just marked the completion of its Schottenstein Babylonian Talmud with its English translation and commentary. The private library of the average Orthodox Jew today probably rivals, if it does not exceed, those found in some of the renowned yeshivas of Europe. And increasingly, even Jews who do not pursue Torah learning as a vocation are reviewing these books, whether in the context of a national movement of Jewish study—the *daf yomi,* a program in which Jews the world over each day review the same page of the Babylonian Talmud in a seven-and-a-half-year cycle that allows them to complete all sixty volumes, being perhaps the best known—or in the myriad study circles in synagogues, boardrooms, private homes, and other places where Orthodox Jews gather. The idea of every Jew—male and female alike—having a *chavruta* (study partner) is an increasingly popular feature in the web of relationships that tie Orthodox Jews to one another.

In popular culture, Orthodoxy no longer remains in the shadows. On television and in the movies Orthodox Jews figure in plots, and not always in the classic guise of immigrants, old Jews, or some other stereotype. Even the hugely popular series *The Sopranos* presented some Hasidim and a young man in a yarmulke who figured in several episodes. In newspapers and magazines, stories about Orthodox Jews are far from rare.

Kosher food, the staple of the Orthodox diet, is no longer an unusual item on the American dietary scene. Once a dietary mandate that served to circumscribe the Jews' ability to move freely outside the tribal domains of their parochial universe, the restrictions of a kosher diet are now far less limiting than at any time in American Jewish history. Orthodox Jewish institutions, both nonprofit and for-profit, have made kosher food widely available. The kosher food industry is booming. Kosher food specialty firms like Aron Streit and Manischewitz now constitute a $200 million industry.[21] There are today over 41,000 kosher-certified products in the U.S. retail food market, including everything from Oreo Cookies and M&M's to fake bacon as well as gourmet foods and wines.[22] By the last decade of the twentieth century over 180,000 cases of kosher wines per year were being sold in the United States. Five years later this number had more than doubled to 365,000.[23] The 2001 International Kosher Food trade show was held in the huge Meadowlands Arena in New Jersey, and the one the previous year had filled the equally large Javits Center across the Hudson River in Manhattan. In part this happened because kosher food has become a very big business, growing from $3.5 billion in sales in 1997 to about $4.3 billion at century's end. In 2002, after a decade of growth in the neighborhood of 12 to 15 percent, estimates put the number of American shoppers who bought products because of their kosher certification at ten and a half million, with sales of approximately $6.65 billion.[24] To be sure, the so-called core market, dedicated consumers of a kosher diet, is a much smaller group (being made up primarily of Jews, Muslims, and Seventh Day Adventists).[25] Strict standards of dietary law observance are taken increasingly for granted. Indeed, even so-called *glatt* kosher, originally a more stringent and rarely invoked standard of kosher meat but today generally defining food subject to greater supervisory costs, is now almost as widely available as any other kosher food standard. There is, moreover, no airline flight leaving from or destined for anywhere in North America where one cannot order a kosher meal in lieu of the standard refreshment.[26]

The emergence of a rich cultural life among Orthodox Jews is another aspect of a triumphalist contemporary American Jewish scene. This is an Orthodoxy that has a contemporary literature in English, some of it in common with American literature of the day and some of it particularistic, religiously inspirational, and quite distinct. It is an Orthodoxy that makes use of music and arts to further its way of life. It has its own cultural heroes and even a growing array of distinctively Jewish leisure activities and venues, including fast-food and fancy restaurants as well as indigenous "vacation villages" in which all the occupants are Orthodox. Even such relatively exotic trips as a luxury cruise to Alaska can be taken under the auspices of a group calling itself Kosherica Tours, and excursions deep inside China, Japan, and other "exotic" destinations are available to and increasingly taken by the well-to-do Orthodox and other kosher food–eating fellow travelers.

In cyberspace, the Orthodox are well represented. In chat rooms and weblogs as well on the World Wide Web, the Orthodox are easily found. From sites that assist romance to those that help find apartments and those that provide religious instruction, locations of synagogues and communities, or advice about the Messiah, there is almost no realm of Orthodox existence that is not represented on the Internet.

All this has led to an infusion of confidence and assertiveness in American Orthodoxy, in contrast to the timidity that often characterized it in the past. And it has led to a conviction that the rest of American Jewry is not going to be nearly as successful in maintaining itself. Much of this constitutes the triumphalist "big picture" of American Orthodoxy.

Orthodoxy, however, has not remained static. While celebrating its ability to survive and even thrive in America, it has found itself pulled increasingly toward the religious right. To some, this trend is simply an intensification of its character, an inevitable return to its true incarnation that in the years of its renewal in America was temporarily compromised. To others, this move to the right is a consequence of social and structural developments within Orthodoxy, a sign of the growing institutional and cultural dominance of the Haredi wing and of Orthodox rabbinic authority, which has become less comfortable with contemporary American mores. Still others see it as a reflection of the changing nature of ethnicity and the role of religion in America, which has encouraged diversity and greater public expression of distinctiveness and matters of faith, making it easier for Orthodox Jews to come out into the public square, even in their Haredi incarnation. Finally, there are those who see in the emerging assertiveness of the Haredim a reflection of a general American tilt toward the religious right, arguing that, as Eliot Cohen, the first editor of *Commentary* magazine, once put it, "[T]he Jews are like everyone else, only more so."[27]

Thus, while the crisis of Orthodox survival in America seems to have passed, the version of that Orthodoxy that has survived is increasingly not the modernist, contrapuntalist, acculturative variety, the movement peopled by Jews who do not want to remain untouched by or remote from the general culture and who instead seek to accommodate themselves to the host society. That modern Orthodoxy, which appeared to promise a new way of being linked both to the strict demands of Jewish tradition and to the changing vicissitudes of contemporary culture, and which seemed to attract the bulk of the Orthodox in America, has been increasingly supplanted by a variant of Judaism that eschews too much accommodation to non-Orthodox ways. This is an Orthodoxy that devalues American acculturation and continues to raise the ante for those who want to consider themselves truly bound to Jewish tradition. Moreover, it stresses its difference from all other American Jewry, putting on the defensive those of its number who have for more than a generation tried to stress the continuities with their non-Orthodox co-religionists and fellow Americans. Gone is the attitude expressed by one of the prominent and best-known Orthodox rabbis in New York during the 1950s, Joseph Lookstein, who "publicly called on his camp to drop the word 'Orthodox' since it had Old World connotations that were unacceptable to young American Jews." And the integrationist efforts of his son, Rabbi Haskell Lookstein, who once headed the now defunct Synagogue Council of America, an organization founded in 1926 to provide most congregationally affiliated Jews (regardless of individual differences) with a common voice in activities in which the Orthodox joined with Jews from other denominations, were weakened.[28] After nearly two generations of a dominating modernism in American Orthodoxy, the assertion by Nathan Glazer in the same decade that the future of American Orthodoxy lay with a "particularly backward and archaic group of Jews" may turn out to be true after all.[29]

To the modernists within the Orthodox universe, the replacement of many of their culturally accommodationist assumptions and goals by contra-acculturationist ones characteristic of the Haredi Jewish options constitutes a new crisis. For the Haredim, however, this development emerging out of the competition between these two trends represents vindication and triumph—the end of a period of crisis. To them what others call backward is veneration for ancient truths and traditions and the archaic is the time-honored. These competing views constitute this book's central concern.

A Guide for What Follows

This book commences with a review of the situation of Orthodoxy in America in the aftermath of the Holocaust, a period during which those who had been most steadfast in their Orthodoxy were at last forced to abandon what had for generations been the heartland of their culture and to come to America in large numbers. This chapter will trace the development of the competing trends in Orthodoxy during the ensuing fifty years. Next follows a brief demographic profile of today's American Orthodox, who are divided between these two inclinations. Following this, the book explores Jewish education as a field of contest between the two Orthodoxies, finding there some origins of the forces that have pulled Orthodoxy toward the religious right. Next it looks at a result of that struggle, the way that many of today's Orthodox Jews have reinvented tradition in America, and what this tells us about a gradual but seemingly inexorable shift of the population toward the religious right. The chapter explores such matters as the increasing dependence on "going by the book" in place of following naturally evolving customs and behaviors that are part of community life. While these chapters lead to the belief that the religiously right-wing tendencies within Orthodoxy appear to be ascendant, the next chapter shows how economic forces are drawing some in the religious right wing out of their enclave culture and into engagement with the culture of America in ways that may be transformative. The chapter examines this new engagement by looking at an alternative educational institution that has emerged within that community and what it tells us about the ability of the Haredim to maintain their enclave culture. The book then explores how some young modern Orthodox Jews are responding to the changing demands of their religious identity. It does this through a close reading of an Internet Web site putatively organized by young Orthodox Jews around humor but in fact offering a window on the resistance, or at the very least the ambivalence, among some of them regarding the move toward the Haredi right. These chapters are followed by an ethnographic look at four New York Orthodox neighborhoods through the placards and broadsides that residents post in their public spaces. Through these posters we discover what is on the mind of today's Orthodoxy and how these various versions of what its constituents consider important contend with one another for the hearts and minds of the population. Here we can watch the contest between the two versions of Orthodoxy in the writing on the walls. A concluding chapter pulls together what we have learned and speculates briefly about the future of American Orthodoxy.

The purpose of this volume, then, is to examine these developments and the contest within American Orthodoxy at the beginning of the new century. In particular, I seek to understand how what was thought once to be the type of Jewish life and practice most ill-suited to and at odds with America—Haredi Orthodoxy—has managed to secure itself here and how the trend of Orthodoxy once believed to be best fitted to survive here—modern Orthodoxy—now finds itself losing the ideological battle for survival. *Frum* is giving way to *frum*mer.

One last point: this book is part of an ongoing examination in the sociology of religion that seeks to explain how what Hent de Vries has called "the uncontested and often self-congratulatory narrative of Western 'secularist' modernity" has turned out to be something less than a complete cultural triumph.[30] Those who claim that old traditions can be rehabilitated and reinvigorated even in the capitals of the West are often demanding hegemony over matters of faith, replacing those who tried to make peace with secularist modernity. The radical traditionalists eschew compromise and often demand that both individual and collective identities that were once adapted to modern secular society be rejected and "restored" to what they consider their original character. This has put modernist variants of religion on the defensive. Or, more precisely, traditionalism has usurped the dominance of the secular and cosmopolitan in the definition of modernity, especially in the public sphere. Some have called this development a postmodernist deconstruction of what is normative religion; others call it the rise of religious fundamentalisms.[31] Still others have been quick to point out that the so-called return to tradition is nothing of the sort; it is rather a modern movement masquerading as a restoration.

The struggle between modern and Haredi Orthodoxy must be seen within this context. In the cultural atmosphere of the mid–twentieth century modernism was the prevailing trend, and, not surprisingly, this was also the period when modern Orthodoxy thrived and grew. But with the new millennium in America, the forces of the right found the temper of the times far more hospitable to their outlook. Often unnoticed, yet relentlessly, those who had not made their peace with the dominant transformations of the earlier period took steps to change the reality. Trends within Orthodoxy, the changing nature of the rabbinate, generational changes, institutional developments, and demographic factors all played a part in this. In an astonishing confluence of events, some internal to Orthodoxy and some taking place in the larger cultural climate in America and the West, the balance shifted from the modernists to those who claimed to champion the hoariest of traditions. Among the Orthodox Jews in America, this shift has had significant consequences. Such consequences are the main focus of this book.

CHAPTER I

Orthodoxy in America
after the Holocaust

Let us put aside our pain and bitter experiences and demonstrate
for all the world to see that we are the people of the Torah,
blessed with eternal life.

Eliezer Gershon Friedenson,
Beth Jacob Journal, June 27, 1938

The branch that may be bare will bloom again—
The flowers, once fallen, never rejoin the bough

Hua-Pen, "Song of the Forsaken Wife"

In his analysis of what he calls "The Third Great Cycle in Jewish History," an epoch that begins in the last half of the twentieth century, Irving Greenberg defines the Holocaust as an "orienting event," one that
changes the way Jews view the world. While this analysis may or may
not be true for other Jews, for the Orthodox—particularly in America—
the Holocaust undoubtedly not only set their future direction but also
ex post facto reconsecrated and even more importantly *reframed* and redefined their past. After the Holocaust, much of that Jewish past was
sentimentally perceived, anachronistically understood, and nostalgically
recollected in often inaccurate ways. In part this was because the new
post-Holocaust reality confronted Orthodoxy most dramatically with the
question of whether its past strategies for survival had been correct,
whether in light of its massive losses in the Nazi firestorm it could continue to exist, and, if so, what would be its best future course for survival. Nowhere were these questions more urgent than in the Diaspora,
which according to a worldview promoted particularly by Zionists (including the "religious" among them) *ineluctably* led to persecution and
ultimately genocide—the inevitable consequences, for the Jews, of being a people bereft of their homeland and dependent on the hospitality,
protection, and tolerance of others. All Jewish life in societies not their

own, these Jewish nationalists (who now had a state of their own) asserted, must end in maltreatment and banishment.[1] The Holocaust, the
argument ran, simply carried this process to its logical and fateful extreme.
The facts seemed obvious. In Europe, yeshivas, synagogues, Hasidic
courts, and indeed whole communities of the Orthodox (who were eas-
iest to identify and slowest to flee) and many of their leaders had been
destroyed or at best decimated by the Nazis and their supporters. The
question therefore was whether the fate of the European Jewish Diaspora was a template for the remaining Diaspora Jewish communities—
including America—or whether lessons could be learned from Europe
to help prevent another disaster.

Orthodoxy in what would become its new major Diaspora, America,
had to answer this question and to deal with the human and institutional
reality of its extraordinary losses. The influx of Holocaust refugees and
survivors just before (many through the efforts of the Orthodox-sponsored
Hatzalah program) and in the aftermath of World War II, which gave
American Orthodoxy an important infusion of new blood, made this
question even more consequential.[2] Indeed, the proportion of Holocaust
survivors who remained Orthodox after arrival in America is twice as high
as the proportion of the Orthodox in the American population overall,
a figure confirmed in every National Jewish Population Survey since
1970.[3] Postwar Orthodoxy, after all, had to face the question of its own
responsibility for those deaths—in great measure because so many of its
leaders had urged their followers not to leave Europe's Jewish communities for what they described as the impurities of the cultural melting
pot that was America or the heresies of a largely secular and socialist Israel, places in which they argued individual Jews might physically survive but genuine Judaism would not. Finally, as it grew by virtue of the
flow of refugees and survivors, American Orthodoxy became overwhelmingly populated by those in its midst who had been traumatized
by and survived the events in Europe.[4] One might argue that much of
what Orthodoxy has become after the war, particularly in the new American Diaspora, is in some way a reflection of how it came to terms with
these issues. In all this, one might argue, Orthodoxy evolved a post-
Holocaust ideology and sociology that have played a role in its persistence and character in the ensuing years. In effect, American Orthodox
Jews, during most of the years since the end of the Holocaust, have asked
themselves, either explicitly or implicitly, if what they have done justifies
their survival. Hence this is where the analysis of today's American Orthodoxy must begin.

The Last 150 Years

However tragic the Nazi era was for Orthodox Jews and Judaism, it would be a misreading of history to suggest that only the Holocaust affected them. The late nineteenth and twentieth centuries were periods of social flux and cultural change. While a review of this era is far beyond the scope of this chapter, one can recall—albeit telegraphically—that through much of this period Jews experienced the dislocations of mass migration, during which a majority moved (or were chased) from places in which they had lived for generations. They also lived through processes of rapid urbanization, during which the last vestiges of rural Jewry disappeared; then, by the end of the era, at least in America, many would experience the new realities of suburbanization, when whole communities had to be invented from scratch. During the years leading up to the Holocaust, Jews also felt the impact of the sweeping, almost relentless forces of what appeared to many to be the ineluctable imperatives of secularization, when large numbers of people abandoned and often actively spurned the traditional and religious ways of life that had been dominant in favor of something else, mostly shaped by non-Jewish cultural norms. This was a time when Jews became increasingly assimilated into the host cultures around them, at least insofar as they were accepted (the Holocaust, of course, demonstrated the limits of this acceptance). All of this inevitably left the Orthodox who disdained assimilation with a sense of their fragility as a people, along with a cultural fixation on the matter of Jewish survival.

Uprootedness and change, the basic elements of what Erik Erikson calls "transmigrations," were the essential components of this sense of fragility. The vicissitudes of transmigration and of surviving a variety of assimilationist waves as well as persecutions culminating in the Holocaust made a feeling of "uprootedness" an abiding part of Orthodox identity. Put differently, one might say that for many of these Jews the experiences of the last 150 years fostered a consciousness in which an expectation of change rather than stability became the governing element of life. In varying ways this history seemed repeatedly to force breaks with the past. If previous generations of the Orthodox had shared (at least for a time) a general sense that their future would essentially be no different from their past—barring some miraculous messianic redemption—the Orthodox at the midpoint of the twentieth century, on the contrary, were increasingly convinced that the future was less and less prone to be anything at all like the past. The line between yesterday, today, and tomorrow seemed always to be broken.

Like all those who undergo such repeated migrations, these Jews found that they often had to suddenly assume "new and often transitory identities" whose purpose was to help them navigate the traumatic passage from one world or way of life to another without feeling as if they have been completely set adrift.[5] Jews therefore often found themselves looking for new ways of defining who they were, a quest for identity that was often indistinguishable from the process of their migration. To be sure, many of the identities they adopted tended to be "liminal" or transitional.[6] The Orthodox, although they wanted to remain true to tradition, albeit in a sometimes purely reactive way, found that doing so was increasingly difficult as the cultural and social contexts in which they tried to do it changed.[7] The Orthodox movement, itself a product of the ferment and change that marked the era, and by no means monolithic, therefore kept trying to redefine what it meant to be Orthodox. Moreover, they were not always successful in holding onto their members. Even in their most hallowed institutions like the yeshivas, interests in the world outside and Zionism and changes in those who were students moved significant numbers out of the confines of Orthodoxy and in the direction of the modern culture.[8] Many sensed what most Jews were coming to believe: the advantage was to those who chose *verbesserung*, the German-Jewish term for naturalization or acculturation, or at the very least were willing to engage in religious adaptation and reform and break the restraints of traditional Jewish life.[9]

In response, some of the Orthodox leaders railed against those who broke with tradition, warning loyalists that in such an era of transition it was mandatory to avoid even minor accommodations and to stay within the religious confines of European Orthodoxy. In the face of change, the only possible response was to embrace a more stringent insularity and parochialism that would enable one to avoid or perhaps deny the dislocations of change. Change had to be actively rejected and yesterday frozen in the imagination; no accommodation to local conditions was acceptable, lest it lead to drift. The Orthodox opposition to accommodation and reform came from the belief that any effort to blend Jewish identity with *verbesserung* was cultural suicide. Moreover, even when they did something new, the Orthodox had to persuade themselves that they were not really changing.

The so-called neo-Orthodox, who traced their origins to German-speaking Jewry, disagreed. They strove to respond to the experience of transmigration and change by fashioning a life that eschewed the rejectionist approach to accommodation or change and included a sense of belonging to both the host and Jewish cultures in which they found themselves. Theirs was an Orthodoxy that endowed the general civilization that so many of their co-religionists wanted to be part of with ontological meaning and cultural value, even as they remained powerfully loyal and profoundly attached to Jewish tradition and law (Halacha). This was what some called *Torah-im-derech-eretz* (Torah Judaism combined with the surrounding culture), in terminology that German Rabbi Samson Raphael Hirsch made famous.[10] Such Jews, seeking to participate in civil society, were convinced that, if mined carefully, the surrounding civilization could ultimately contribute positively to their humanity and their Judaism. As such, they became the ideological predecessors of those who later in America came to be called "modern Orthodox" and defined themselves as Jews who grappled "with the issues involved in both civilizations," understanding "their points of conflict and tension."[11] To be sure, to add the adjective *modern* to the identity "Orthodox" is somehow "to invite the inference that this implies modification in the attachment to tradition."[12] But the neo-Orthodox believed that they could have the associations of the first without fundamentally undermining the associations of the second, something their more tradition-minded opponents would always challenge.

In general, as noted in the previous chapter, the accommodationist approach was most popular in cultural milieus where features that characterized the surrounding civilization were attractive to Jews and where they had some hope of access to that culture. In nineteenth- and early-twentieth-century Germany, with its high culture, this often became the case, especially for Jews who lived in the cities. In eastern Europe and Poland this was less likely. Here Orthodox Jews more often sought to emphasize their parochialism and sectarian rejection of non-Jewish culture. Looking at their surroundings in the shtetls and pale of settlement where they most frequently found themselves, these Orthodox Jews saw peasants and those whose culture presented little they found attractive or superior to what they had within their own precincts. In practice, therefore, sectarianism for these shtetl Jews was no great sacrifice. Compared to what they saw on the other side of the cultural divide, these Jews could genuinely believe, as a popular maxim put it, that *toyreh ist di beste schoyre* (the Torah offers us the best goods). But those surrounded by the high culture of Western Europe were not quite as certain.

The border between the culturally pluralist Hirschian approach and the more sectarian eastern European one was somewhere in central Europe, in the remnants of the Austro-Hungarian empire. Here both types of Orthodoxy could be found. Indeed the conflicts along this frontline in the Jewish ideological battleground were probably the sharpest—which is why the Hungarian region is one to which both the most insular Orthodox sects as well as the most assimilated of modern Jewries can trace their origins. Those on one side of the divide were attracted by the European "high culture" around them more than the Jewish one, while those on the other were repelled by what they saw as the surrounding "low culture," preferring what they viewed as the superiority of Jewish life and tradition.[13]

The ideological successors of these highly sectarian Jews are today's Haredim, particularly (but not exclusively) those who trace their origins to Hungary and parts of Romania where the Jewish culture wars were most sharply defined.[14] The sectarians encouraged, as noted in our introduction, a purposeful sense of alienation from the contemporary, often enticing, westernized, materialistic world that they believed would lead ultimately to assimilation and the end of true Orthodox Judaism, which was to them the only true Judaism.

Yet whatever their differences from one another, insofar as they were Orthodox these prewar Jews were clearly steadfastly holding onto a way of life that ran against the rest of Jewish stream. While no one can be certain what would have happened had the Nazis not extinguished European Jewry, it was nevertheless already clear by the eve of the war that Orthodoxy, whatever its orientation, was destined to be at best a minority orientation among Ashkenazic Jews. Certainly that was the case in America, where the Nazi horror did not reach; American Orthodox Jews—those who had been willing to come to the Jewish frontier in the New World—were and continued through most of the twentieth century to be an ever-shrinking minority.

After the Holocaust, however, the relatively few Orthodox survivors looked around in the ashes of their European Jewish life. Notwithstanding all the erosion of their numbers before the war, the Nazi regime seemed more than anything else to strike the deathblow to Orthodoxy. Or at least so it might have looked in the war's immediate aftermath. The Orthodox Jews were particularly bewildered to discover that proportionately they had been hardest hit and that their strategies for survival had on their face been a terrible mistake, nowhere more so than among those who had been most uncompromising in their Orthodoxy. In the summer of 1945, writing in *Diglenu,* a publication of the Tzeiray Agudat Yisrael, Moshe Sheinfeld captured the reality that many Jews like him could not help but perceive at the time.[15]

What do the numbers tell us? In Poland . . . about thirty thousand Jews remained, broken in body and spirit. And the proportion of observant Jews among them was totally negligible, since it was those who spoke fluent Polish and were able to pass themselves off as Poles who were saved. In the labor camps it was the master craftsmen and the most robust who survived [and many Orthodox yeshiva boys or elderly rabbinic sages belonged to neither category]. . . . [T]he fact is that religious Jewry in Poland and the Baltic states was effectively annihilated and no longer exists. . . . The Jews in Slovakia, who were for the most part organized in independent Orthodox communities and excelled in piousness and the pure belief in the sages . . . , were also nearly all wiped out. And in Romania it was still more forcefully apparent that the Holocaust had singled out Orthodox Jewry in particular. One hundred and forty thousand Jews from Carpathian Russia, all of them followers of popular Hasidim, were deported to the crematoria in Poland. The same holds for the myriads of village Jews from Marmaros [Hungary] who worshipped God with ardent joy and were wonderfully devoted to their spiritual leaders.

To Sheinfeld the facts were incontrovertible: "[W]hoever was more pious was more utterly destroyed."[16] To drive his point about the greater vulnerability of the Orthodox, he added: "Saloniki, the Greek [Jewish] community famous for its Sabbath rest in its port, was destroyed. Assimilated Athens, with God's help, emerged alive. In Belgium there were two large communities: the liberal Brussels community which was almost completely saved thanks be to God, and the Antwerp community, a great Jewish center unexampled in Western Europe—of its forty thousand Jews, fewer than two thousand survived."[17]

In effect, those who had been expert in parochial Jewish crafts and scholarship and nothing more were lost in great numbers, as were those sectarians who had remained totally within the precincts of Judaism. Loyalty to the Orthodox community and its ways had turned out to be a recipe for disaster. If other Jews had also been unlucky, the Orthodox Jews were nevertheless even more unfortunate.

Sheinfeld, who found himself living and writing in a Jewish state, was not alone in his perceptions. Many of those who ended up in yet another Diaspora in America saw things the same way. They also asked themselves, "Why did this happen to us?" and "What must we do now?"[18] These questions and the answers that people formulated for themselves were particularly compelling in America because that society, particularly in the 1950s and the decades that followed, offered so much opportunity for Jews, as indeed for everyone, to "start over" anew after the war.[19]

American Orthodox Jews could not help but share in this sense of the new. They could also not be blind to the fact that life here was not like life in Europe. American culture and society were welcoming, particularly to the survivors, refugees, and displaced persons who were brought to this country just at the time that it was about to renew itself and prosper after nearly a half-century of war and economic depression. But the question that lingered somewhere in the minds of many of these new Orthodox immigrants, survivors and children of survivors, was: Would this Diaspora be better for them, or would it end as had the previous one, in tragedy?

First, however, was the question of regeneration. The Orthodox community that was going to try to reconstitute itself in America had lost some of the most remarkable flowers of European Orthodoxy. Now they would see if the branch that was nearly bare could be made to bloom again. Although the Orthodox went to the cities, particularly in the Northeast and especially in and around New York, they came in the 1950s, just as Americans were about to begin the great suburban migration. The trends of suburbanization and its capacity for reinvention would emerge along with a new version of the Jewish local community. Jews, like everyone else in these suburbs, could gain access to the community (such as it was) and become something new. While the Orthodox were slower than others of their co-religionists in coming to suburbia, both because they were among the poorest of all Jews and because they remained bonded to the established Jewish institutions that were reluctant to leave the city, they would in time come in increasing numbers to the new suburban frontier. Here and also in the cities they would endeavor to transform their "uprootedness" into "transplantedness."

Implicit in this effort at transplantation were two different and often competing assumptions about the character of America. The first was the modernist and accommodationist one, which asserted that America was "different," a place in which Jews were not now or ever excluded legally from full-fledged citizenship. Consequently, the proper Jewish response was to become a *new kind of Jew* who instead of being identified with the old ways was ready to start over. This called for affirmative acculturation, a rerooting that acknowledged that America was a good place to be and be part of. This attitude provided a comforting psychosocial response to the deeply unsettling experience of uprootedness and stigmatization that was Jewish life during the first half of this century.[20] Only thus, by rejecting old places and ways and embracing the new, could Jews feel fully "at home in America."[21] Taking advantage of American opportunities, education, and mobility, Jews were increasingly inclined to speak in "new languages," mostly English, albeit with a newcomer's accent, rather than in the old languages without one. They often changed their physical appearance, making their clothes and grooming indistinguishable from what was standard in contemporary Western civilization. And they actively pursued education, occupations, and lifestyles that made it possible for them to pass unnoticed into the mainstream cultures around them.[22] This was the strategy of most Jews, and it was also that of modern Orthodoxy, even as it tried to maintain allegiance to the tradition.

At the other extreme was what would become the Haredi assumption, which avowed that if America was different a greater vigilance and more powerful strategies would be necessary to prevent its undoing of tradition and Orthodoxy. They worried that attractive new American identities would come at the expense of Jewish ones. And if America was not different, then the best course of action was to revert to the old patterns of behavior, the ways that some called *Yisrael sabbah,* meaning a kind of tribalist attachment to the paradigmatic old-worldly ways of the "Jewish grandfather," in which any change from the past (or the past as those after the Holocaust imagined it) was proscribed.[23] Yet because the sentiments and doubts expressed by Sheinfeld were common (if not always as explicit) among these Jews, at least in the immediate aftermath of the war, they were slow in coming back to those ways or at least soft-pedaled their arguments in favor of it. Particularly in America in the late 1940s and early 1950s many Orthodox survivors, including some of the most prominent rabbis and Hasidic leaders, seemed broken and unsure of themselves and their future.[24] Indeed, there was an insecurity and stillness in many Orthodox quarters during what might best be called the "aftershock years," a time when the Orthodox (and certainly the Haredim among them) in America were almost invisible. Trying to fathom the meaning of what had happened, some actually counseled survivors to "sit in loneliness and be silent" and suggested that they would do best by "not asking questions but contemplating our condition."[25] *Dor sheh tov lo ha shetika* (a generation that would do well to be silent) was the emblematic phrase used by a preeminent Orthodox religious leader in Israel, the Hazon Ish, Rabbi Avraham Yishayahu Karelitz (1878–1953). The advice was taken up in America as well. Those who, in spite of their "shame, embarrassment and guilt over their utter failure to save their communities," wanted nevertheless to maintain a steadfast attachment to the traditions of Orthodoxy settled their questions of faith at the outset with the modest theological conclusion that "[m]ysterious are the ways of the Lord and who can fathom their purpose."[26] Thus, as American Orthodoxy began the second half of the twentieth century with a combination of immigrants, refugees, and those who had been trying to make traditional Judaism take root in what had for a long time been an Orthodox periphery but was about to become a major center of it, the question that took up its attention was less the classic "Who is a truly Orthodox Jew?" than "What is to be the nature of an American Orthodox Jew?" and "How is the Jewish tradition to be expressed, if at all?"

To Compensate and Continue:
The Orthodox as Survivors

American Orthodox Jews of all sorts who reflected on these questions and wondered about their future could see themselves as survivors in a double sense: first, they had survived the social ferment, waves of assimilation, and religious reform that had marked the end of the nineteenth and the beginning of the twentieth century; and second, however decimated and dislocated as a community, they had survived the Holocaust. But in the late 1940s and the early years of the next decade, the aftereffects of this twofold onslaught surely left them feeling like a shadow of what they once had been and beset by doubts and anxiety about their continued survival. Was Sheinfeld right? Was the very strategy they had used for surviving the first onslaught—holding fast to the ways of *Yisrael sabbah*—that which had exacerbated the damage of the second? Was Orthodox reinvention the only hope for continued survival?

In this light, the possibility that Orthodox refugees might see themselves as relics of a bygone era and way of life, becoming ready either to abandon that old way or to see themselves as its final incarnation, would not be surprising. That, as we have seen, was what some sociologists believed to be the likely outcome. This sort of denouement would not be unusual in America, with its collective tendency to forget the past and focus on the future, and it surely would have been in tune with suburbanization. While we do not know how many survivors abandoned their attachments to Orthodoxy, through most of the twentieth century more American Jews left the ranks of the Orthodox than entered them. We must conclude that some Holocaust survivors also chose that option, though, as noted, many of the refugees did not.

What of those who kept the faith? Some still saw Orthodoxy as the "right answer" and therefore explained both their decimation and survival by reverting to the "ancient response to persecution: *mipnei chatoenu* 'because of our sins,' we have been punished" but also shifting the blame of the sinning to others.[27] Fingers were pointed in a variety of directions. To some postwar Orthodox, the sins were those of their generation who had gone too far in their religious reform or assimilation. Others argued that heretical secular Zionists had angered and agitated God, by rebelling against an exile that they had sought to end before its God-appointed time, and had aroused the ire of enemies of the Jews (judged to be instruments of Divine anger) who saw activities in favor of a Jewish homeland as signs of Jewish disloyalty to and denigration of their citizenship in the lands of their domicile. For the most part, however, these arguments were not heard very clearly and did not stand out until years after the war.[28]

There was also in some quarters an effort to perceive the Holocaust not as somehow preventable but rather as part of an ineluctable, ongoing historic Jewish experience of persecution, part of the endless tests of faith that were the destiny of the faithful. In line with this, certain Orthodox Jews rejected the idea of the Holocaust's uniqueness and shunned the Hebrew term *sho'ah,* that was used by some Jews, referring instead to *churban,* the Hebrew word used to describe Jewish destruction and ruin since the days of the Holy Temple. They therefore claimed to commemorate the loss not on Yom HaSho'ah, the special anniversary of the Warsaw Ghetto uprising that the Israeli government had established as the official memorial day, but rather on Tisha B'Av, the fast day in the Jewish calendar that already was used to mark the destruction of both the first and second Holy Temples in Jerusalem and the paradigm from which all Jewish mourning emerged.[29] Thus this suffering was to be seen as part of an ongoing "Divine retribution" and not as an "isolated catastrophe."[30]

"Jews have always been beaten by Gentiles," this argument ran — in this case in the words of Rabbi Yitzhak Hutner, the postwar head of the major Orthodox Chaim Berlin Yeshiva in America. Pursuing the theme of ongoing Jewish persecution, Hutner concluded that "only the means and instruments of torment have varied." Then, with a xenophobic flourish, he added that the latest destruction — what we call the Holocaust — had been more traumatizing because before it "Jews were deluded into trust in the Gentiles by a series of laws and regulations in their behalf, only to have that trust shattered by the rescission of those very laws."[31] "Trust in the Gentiles" was the way the rabbi, along with many of the most sectarian and insular Orthodox, understood any and all acculturationist movements and motivations. Hence, for the faithful, the only response to the Holocaust was to turn powerfully against modern Western culture ("trust in the Gentiles"). The lesson, these Orthodox concluded, was that the Holocaust proved the worthlessness of "the values of Western society. After all, the horrendous outrages were perpetrated not by some primitive tribes but by one of the most 'civilized' nations." "[H]ow can one respect modern culture, if a Martin Heidegger, one of the most celebrated German philosophers, could turn into a Nazi and enthusiastically endorse Hitler's policies"?[32] For Jews like Hutner and those who shared his outlook, the lesson of the Holocaust was that no culture, however attractive or open, could be trusted. Judaism, especially Judaism in its most traditional forms, was the only reliable treasure. This argument was directed toward the modern Orthodox in America who *did* trust American culture.

"A man with a conviction," say the authors of *When Prophecy Fails*, the classic study of the persistence of faith in the face of disconfirming evidence, "is a hard man to change. Tell him you disagree and he turns away. Show him facts or figures and he questions your sources. Appeal to logic and he fails to see your point."[33] Indeed, they tell us that confronted by facts that might be imagined to undermine their beliefs or the behaviors they have established to support them, believers "may even show a new fervor about convincing and converting other people to [their] view."[34] This is particularly true when beliefs are specific and deeply held; when they demand certain definite or concrete commitments, and when there is a social framework that supports both the beliefs and practices. Such was and remains the case with Orthodox Jews and Judaism. Hutner and other Orthodox who held similar viewpoints demonstrated this sort of fervor. Accordingly, rather than withering away or atrophying in a frozen and shocked silence, their Orthodoxy came back, and did so with an astonishing vitality and remarkable speed—Sheinfeld's questions notwithstanding.

At the start, the resistance took the form of a quiet but unyielding commitment to remain faithful and attached to Jewish tradition and Orthodox practice, even in America. This took the form of building yeshivas and other Orthodox institutions. The commitment was striking, particularly to the young. Netty Gross, for example, describes how struck she was by watching the religious devotion of "my grandparents, ultra-Orthodox survivors, and not quite being able to understand why, after God failed such righteous people, my grandparents went on adhering to their way of life."[35] Moreover, the Orthodox were not content simply to hold onto the old ways; rather they sought to grow even more vigorously than before the war and even to reach beyond their natural constituency—the survivors, their spouses, and their offspring—in order to bring back and reconvert as well the "wayward" non-Orthodox Jews to Orthodox ways. The silence that the Hazon Ish had advocated was short-lived, and the "new fervor" that the authors of *When Prophecy Fails* describe was undeniable. As the twentieth century drew to a close, these Jews would not be

satisfied with simply holding onto their own; many of them would be focusing increasing attention on what came to be called *kiruv,* the bringing
of outsiders nearer to the tradition.[36]

Part of this Orthodox resurgence is explained by the fact that many
post-Holocaust Orthodox Jews saw their survival as a sacred religious and
moral challenge and defined their continued existence as a way to demonstrate to themselves and others that, despite the realities as Sheinfeld had
summarized them, they had definitely *not* been abandoned by God or Jewish history. Closely related to this theme was the notion, also commonly
found in Orthodox Jewish responses to the Holocaust, of survivors feeling a "responsibility [to act] as God's witnesses in history."[37] The Orthodox renewal was thus a way of giving content and meaning to the
words spoken by the believers when in the dark days of recent history
they swore, *Mir velen sie iberleben, Avinu shebashomayim* (We will outlive
them, O Father in Heaven).[38] While the "them" were the Nazis and their
supporters, the line could also be understood after the war as referring to
Jews who assimilated. Hence continuing to live as Orthodox Jews and
doing so uncompromisingly became a means of proving that the advice
they and their forebears had followed to remain steadfast was in the longer
view historically correct. This would mean being able, as one postwar Orthodox theologian put it, "to see again the finger of God in the fate of
the Jewish people."[39]

"Let us put aside our pain and bitter experiences and demonstrate for
all the world to see that we are the people of the Torah, blessed with eternal life." These words, quoted as the epigraph to this chapter, come from
Eliezer Gershon Friedenson in the *Beth Jacob Journal* on the eve of the
second Siyum Ha Shas (completion of the review of the entire Talmud),
June 27, 1938, as the Holocaust was looming frighteningly close, but they
were echoed again and again after the war, most recently in 1990 at the
Ninth Siyum Ha Shas, the great mass celebration of Haredi Orthodoxy
in New York's Madison Square Garden that marked the coordinated completion by thousands of mostly Orthodox Jews the world over of the entire Talmud in a seven-and-a-half-year cycle.[40] In their sentiment, they capture what became the essential response of most of those who remained
Orthodox after the Holocaust: surviving and doing so visibly.

Michael Wyschograd, a contemporary Orthodox philosopher, writing
in *Tradition,* the journal of the (Orthodox) Rabbinical Council of America, elaborated the reasoning behind this attitude thus: "[E]very time a Jew
encounters the holocaust and loses his faith, the holocaust has claimed one
more Jewish victim."[41] The requirement to maintain Jewish life and faith

in its *most* intense form becomes for each practicing Orthodox Jew whose people suffered so at the hands of Nazis a way to at once defeat Hitler and carry on the legacy of the dead. It also tries to undo the decimation by in a sense replacing it with a kind of Orthodox resurrection. Ensuring the continuity of Orthodoxy was therefore the point of survival. "On our shoulders was placed the historic duty to mend the torn Sefer Torah and put on it a new beautiful mantle," was how in 1976 Rabbi Yaakov Perlow, the American-born Novominsker Rebbe and a leader of the Haredi Agudath Israel of America, put it, suggesting that the restoration of the damaged scroll of all that is Jewish tradition was the responsibility of Orthodox Jewry and that "if we succeed in our task we shall look back to the Churban and proclaim to the entire world . . . 'Do not rejoice enemies of Yisroel [Israel]! Indeed I have fallen but I have arisen again.'"[42]

The imperative to remain Orthodox is affirmed by the conviction among the survivors that "those who perished at the hands of the Nazi murderers did not wish the demise of Judaism."[43] Many in the Orthodox audience that Perlow addressed saw themselves as the true heirs of the ancients—if not their reincarnation—and as being so *only because they had chosen to stay the course.* That was why they had survived, the rabbi assured them, and why they needed to believe that Jews who in these days did not maintain the traditions of the past had somehow forfeited the moral justification for their survival. To have survived and thrived was also an inversion of the common accusation that the Orthodox victims were like lambs led to the slaughter, easy targets, doing nothing to fight for their survival.[44]

This requirement to defy death by bearing witness through one's existence as an Orthodox Jew was a theme not only reiterated in words but also echoed in the Orthodox commemorations of the Holocaust, which were often symbolically blended with the re-creation of a vital Orthodox life. Describing one such typical ceremony in which the names of the *kidoshim,* the [holy] Jewish martyrs, were publicly inscribed by Orthodox day school children on shattered glass that was then ceremonially placed in a mosaic on a memorial tablet on the school wall to spell out a message, the principal of this New York institution concluded: "We had taken the broken pieces of the lives of the '*Kidoshim*' and created 'Am Yisroel Chai' [the Jewish people lives]."[45] In other words, the presence of Orthodox children in an Orthodox Jewish day school symbolically and practically transformed the shards of an Orthodoxy broken by the Holocaust into a living testament to Jewish continuity. Their continuing Orthodoxy became nothing less than an existential response to the Holocaust. By twenty years after the war, as the resurgence of Orthodoxy grew in intensity, this survivor attitude had become firmly established in the Orthodox community of America. "We, today, are all children of the Holocaust," as Rabbi Mordechai Gifter, a yeshiva head at the famous Telshe Yeshiva in Wickliffe, Ohio, explained in 1974 to a conference of teachers of the Orthodox young.[46]

The end result was a post-Holocaust Orthodoxy that not only sought to give a second life to its predecessors but also determined, as part of the survival of its members, no less so than for the survivors whom Freud describes in *Totem and Taboo*, "not to repeat the deed[s] which had brought destruction" to their forbears.[47] In this way, the survivors who made up a resurgent postwar Orthodoxy could—to borrow again from Freud's analysis—"smooth things over and make it possible to forget the event[s] to which it owed its origin."[48] In a sense, Orthodox Jews ideologically and sociologically endorsed the idea of rebirth and rebuilding because it shifted the focus from the question of their guilt for not having found ways to survive previously to an argument about how to survive in the present. That is why the question that people like Sheinfeld raised about who was responsible for the Holocaust gave way to the issue of how to give new vitality to Orthodox life in the Diaspora and what lessons needed to be learned in order not to end Diaspora once again with Holocaust.

One might thus argue that psychologically a part of the drive behind the imperative of robust Orthodox continuity was a combination of guilt that more had not survived and survivor guilt among those who had, a felt need to prove the religious and existential significance of their having survived. This survivor guilt was not necessarily felt at a personal level by all Orthodox Jews; rather, it was a kind of institutionalized survivor guilt built into their ideology and the institutions or behavior patterns that supported it.

Incorporated in this institutionalized, collective Orthodox survivor guilt, however, was also an anger at the dead for having, through their demise, left the survivors alone, along with a longing for these very same people, whose absence was keenly felt and often recalled.[49] One way to deal with these complicated feelings, as Freud suggests, is to endow the dead with an enhanced power, making them "stronger than the living."[50] Hence after the war the European Orthodoxy that had suffered death and destruction became "stronger" in the imagined memory of the survivors. Rather than recalling how it had been losing so many of its adherents to assimilation and reform or how its strategies had led to decimation, survivors portrayed it in idealized form. They also made it in imagined retrospect more religiously demanding and developed, more loyal to the recreated past. To enhance the ingeniously resurrected dead even more, the living Orthodox (particularly the Haredim, who perhaps felt most guilty about the part they might have played in the Orthodox past) always claimed to defer to them as somehow superior. As one Haredi rabbinic head of a yeshiva put it: "Modern people . . . believe that today we're much more advanced, superior human beings . . . and we haredim believe we're going downhill."[51]

This attitude led to an effort to stop the slide down the slippery slope by creating more and more powerful orthodoxies and orthopraxies. "As surviving witnesses we are charged with an awesome responsibility," one Orthodox writer stated in the *Jewish Observer*, an American monthly published by the Haredi Agudath Israel of America.[52] That responsibility was not only to hold onto traditional beliefs and maintain an uncompromising ideological commitment to an invigorated Orthodoxy, as part of the consciousness of the *churban*. For many Orthodox Jews, it meant also joining an ideological battle, which was best won by becoming *even more* punctilious in religious and ritual practices to slow down the inevitable decline and corrosion of Judaism that modern life had wrought.

If American Orthodox Jews needed proof that they were engaged in a rebuilding effort whose success would justify their survival—and remove any feelings of guilt—they found it in the surprising renaissance of their institutions—from the growth of their families to the multiplicity of their congregations and schools—all in places and times that many had once thought impossible. That renaissance, in full swing by the 1980s, was what one Orthodox writer, in reflection at the World Gathering of Holocaust Survivors in 1982, called "compensation." As he put it, "[F]ollowing the vast losses of the Holocaust 'answers' and 'replacements' were not forthcoming, but compensations were: new spouses, new children . . . new yeshivot, Jewish reawakening in Russia and elsewhere."[53] In this thinking Orthodox Jewish expansion and growth took on theological and ideological dimensions.

The schools were perhaps the most important expression of rebirth and resurrection. These themes still reverberate in many of the appeals that Orthodox institutions make even today to their supporters, as seen in the following text from a fairly typical fund-raising flyer for a rabbinic training institute in Brooklyn, New York, named Asei Lecho Rav (Make for Yourself a Teacher), after the famous imperative in the Talmudic *Pirke Avot* (Ethics of the Fathers). The organization defines itself (somewhat hyperbolically) as "dedicated to nothing less than building the Torah leadership of the future," and in the leaflet justifies the need for this as follows: "Less than fifty years ago, one third of our people and most of our greatest Talmidei Chachomim [scholars] were barbarically destroyed, ה"יד [May God avenge their blood]. In spite of this indescribable tragedy, our generation has witnessed a tremendous resurgence of Yiddishkeit [Jewishness] in America ב"ה [Praise the Lord]."

Implicit, but hardly hidden, in this brochure are at least two important and repeated themes (with proof texts in Scripture) connecting the continuity of contemporary Orthodoxy with the Holocaust. One is the theme of miraculous survival against all odds and in the face of "indescribable tragedy." That survival is presented as a gift from God; the survivors are "a brand snatched from the fire," in the words of the prophet.[54] The second theme is the responsibility to "reinstate as far as possible, that which was lost," in order to ensure the continuity of the institutions of Jewish life and law that were destroyed.[55]

In this newly created Orthodox American culture that was both institutionally rich and religiously demanding, names resonated with resurrection themes. Synagogues were, for example, named *Zichron* (memorial of) this or that. Hasidic courts that came from Europe and reestablished themselves in America resurrected the names of the towns from which they had come. If Chabad Hasidim had once lived in the White Russian village of Lubavitch, now that their headquarters had moved to Crown Heights, Brooklyn, they would still call themselves Lubavitchers—so too with other Hasidic groups who rerooted themselves here with names and histories that came from there. The same happened to many of the yeshivas whose origins had been in Lithuania and elsewhere in eastern Europe.

The participants in the new resurrected Orthodoxy would have to stand up against the twin threats of assimilation and anti-Semitism by being *haredi,* constantly fretful, anxious, and vigilant about their attachment to tradition, and by stressing the continuing importance of remaining behind the wall of virtue they had created around their insular enclave cultures. They would demonstrate, moreover, that they, and no other group of Jews, were doing the most to reinstate that which had been lost.[56]

The Modern Orthodox Choice

If Orthodox Jews share a psychological, ideological, and social sense of their responsibility for Orthodox continuity after the Holocaust as well as a determination not to repeat the mistakes of their forebears, they do not agree on the best way to ensure it. Indeed, the differences that had emerged among Orthodox Jews prior to the Holocaust appeared again after the war—except that in the aftermath of the Holocaust they seemed affectively sharper. Surrounded even more than before by a majority of Jews who were not Orthodox, post-Holocaust American Orthodox Jews, like their European predecessors, had to deal with the question of whether they should become like most American Jews—acculturated to or assimilated by the host Gentile society—or whether they should try to transform that society with a reborn Orthodoxy. Given the moral and psychological burden they carried as survivors, while some decided to try to blend into America (as had most of the earlier Orthodox immigrants) and maintain a kind of nominal, almost nostalgic or ethnic attachment to their Jewish traditions, most Orthodox Jews—and in particular those who arrived in America after the war—chose the second alternative. But because Orthodox Jews were not alike, they tried to rebuild their Orthodoxy in their varying images, simultaneously reflecting their differing interpretations of the lessons of the Holocaust.

The Haredim by and large increasingly took the position that had crystallized by the 1970s that, in the words of Rabbi Yaakov Weinberg, head of the Ner Israel Yeshiva in Baltimore, "there is an 'otherness' to us, a gulf of strangeness that cannot be bridged, separating us from our compatriots."[57] The modernists rejected this sort of purposive estrangement and the ritual punctiliousness that help enforce it. Both were certain, however, that their approaches were based on lessons learned from the European Jewish experience.

As insistent as the Haredim were, the modernists were no less so, but unlike the former they embraced the idea of America and its promise of new beginnings. This was an Orthodoxy ever more powerfully committed to a positive attitude toward what they saw as "healthy Americanism."[58] They urged one another—in the words of Professor Lawrence Kaplan, one of their most articulate contemporary writers—to "be wary of separatist groups."[59] In post–World War II America they would, as Rabbi Norman Lamm, president of Yeshiva University through most of this period, put it, see their "religious duty" and "sacred responsibility to live the whole Torah tradition *in the* world instead of retreated from the world."[60] Only by turning their Orthodoxy into a component of engagement with the modern world of America, they believed, could they succeed in surviving. For them, the lesson to be learned from the recent past was that Judaism was "not identified with ghetto conditions"; "the Torah commanded man . . . to exercise his authority as an intelligent be-

ing whose task consists in engaging the objective order in a cognitive contest" and, through constructive "conflict and intellectual performance,"
to rebuild attachments to Jewish law and tradition in a way that engaged
them with contemporary culture.[61] As Rabbi Walter Wurzburger, one of
the champions of this new Orthodoxy, put it, they of course had to examine "each part of the modern ethos as to its compatibility with Halakhic Judaism." But informed by their open inquiry and engagement,
they would, most of the modernists believed, discover it unnecessary to
reject *all* of modern America. If properly educated, they would discover
the power of "tolerance, democracy, and human initiative in creating cultural values" and would see that these were far from "contaminating," as
the Haredim or "right-wing Orthodoxy" might suggest.[62]

To such modern Orthodox Jews post-Holocaust Orthodoxy had to be
adaptive, based both ideologically and sociologically on an "equally firm
commitment to Torah on the one hand, and to the values of World Culture on the other."[63] Mirroring the emergent and increasingly dominant
late-twentieth-century American ethos of pluralism, these modern Orthodox aimed also to foster "an awareness and respect for a diversity of
views among ourselves and in American society, and an understanding
of the equality and dignity of all people."[64]

This line of behavior and thinking was to be distinguished from the
more popular strategy of American Conservative Judaism, with its more
compromisingly accommodationist approach, which seemed to give
modern American culture *priority* over Jewish law and in practice gave
equal authority to representatives of the laity to decide along with ordained
Conservative rabbis what in Judaism was subject to change and compromise.[65] Some of the modern Orthodox feared that the attractiveness of
Conservative Judaism, along with the American ethos of do-it-yourself-
ism that allowed individuals to choose for themselves how to live their
lives, would lead to the slow demise of Orthodoxy, especially if the latter
remained insular, stultified, and unbending.[66] Hence, while they embraced cultural accommodations, these had to be far more controlled,
subject to rabbinic approval. The modern Orthodox Jew might make autonomous choices, but these would always be subject to rabbinic sanction and authorization.

RABBINIC DEPENDENCE AND LEGITIMATION

Essential to the modern Orthodox approach of seeking rabbinic approval
was dependence by the laity, who lived in both the Jewish and general

societies at once, on a rabbinate that embraced its religious commitments as well as the value these Jews placed on engagement with the general culture of America and who could act as a legitimating authority for the accommodations that the modernists sought. Without such outward-looking bicultural rabbis, the modern Orthodox would be forced to allow the laity the authority to choose what was permissible and what crossed the line. If they did that, the modern Orthodox would as such become indistinguishable from the Conservative Jews. Indeed, during the mid–twentieth century in America one could find many formerly Orthodox Jews who had made the transition to Conservative Jewish synagogues and from there to the Conservative movement, people who could not find Orthodox rabbis that were sufficiently adaptive for them or who did not want to bother checking with the rabbis because they found them too parochial and culturally limited. This danger of slippage always stood behind the adaptations of the modern Orthodox, who worked very hard to keep the distinctions between them and the Conservatives clear, with varying degrees of success.[67]

Many of the modern Orthodox rabbis who dominated the scene and who fulfilled these roles during the late 1940s, the 1950s, and much of the 1960s were influenced by German neo-Orthodoxy or associated with Yeshiva University.[68] Almost all of the first generation of these twentieth-century leaders were European born. Foremost among them was Joseph B. Soloveitchik, originally from eastern Europe (born in Poland but from a well-known Lithuanian rabbinic family). Ordained by his father, and scion of the Brisk and Volozhin Yeshiva world, he had also received a doctorate in philosophy from Berlin in 1932 and ultimately became the towering rabbinic head of the seminary at Yeshiva University, a post he took over from his father Moses in 1941 and held for more than forty years. But there were others (most of whom were both rabbis and holders of university doctorates) like Dov Revel, Samuel Belkin, Joseph Lookstein, Leo Jung, Eliezer Berkovits, and Walter Wurzburger.[69] These were men who wanted to ease the transition to America and not close themselves off from it, who embraced the value inherent in non-Jewish culture (as their university degrees testified) but who also believed that in so doing there was no need to compromise Jewish attachment and fidelity to Jewish law and practice. The second generation of American modern Orthodox rabbinic leaders was also American born and even more comfortable forming attachments to American culture. These were men like Norman Lamm and Israel Miller (who became respectively president and vice-president of Yeshiva University), Haskell Lookstein (head of the Ramaz School, pulpit rabbi in New York, and a leader of the Synagogue Council of America), Emanuel Rackman (a former practicing attorney, pulpit rabbi in New York City, provost at Yeshiva University of New York, and later president and chancellor of Israel's Bar Ilan University), Irving Greenberg (Harvard graduate, pulpit rabbi, professor of history at the City University of New York, and head of a variety of outreach Jewish organizations), Shlomo Riskin (pulpit rabbi, Yeshiva College teacher, and later modern Orthodox leader in Efrat, Israel), David Hartman (pulpit rabbi in Canada and later in Israel founder of the Shalom Hartman Institute), Jacob J. Schachter (Harvard PhD, professor at Yeshiva University, for many years pulpit rabbi at New York's Jewish Center, and later head of the Soloveitchik Institute at Maimonides School in Brookline, Massachusetts). These were rabbis who through their lives and philosophies, which were very much influenced by the overarching model of Rabbi Soloveitchik, acted as legitimating authorities for modern Orthodoxy's engagement with American culture and modern society, an engagement that did not gainsay their fidelity to the demands of Jewish law and tradition. More importantly, perhaps, they all had held pulpits for a time and thus had learned to speak to and serve the needs of Orthodox laity—something that the Haredi rabbis who were often yeshiva heads did not need to do.[70] Typical of the attitude of this second generation of modern Orthodox rabbis was the assertion by Rabbi David Hartman that modern Orthodoxy requires training young Jews to believe—as the medieval philosopher and rabbi Moses Maimonides did (these rabbis were always invoking this physician and traditional authority)—"that experiential and intellectual encounter with modern values and insights can help deepen and illuminate one's commitment to the tradition."[71]

Such encounters required nuanced and vigilant engagement. Soloveitchik suggested that Orthodox Jews could "cooperate with the members of other faith communities in all fields of constructive human endeavor," but at the same time he cautioned that that they should be wary of the risks of such cooperation. They needed to keep in mind that, "simultaneously with [their] integration into the general social framework," they would have to "engage in a movement of recoil" and be ready, where and when the attraction led to an undermining of Jewish attachments, to "retrace [their] steps": the same accommodators to American culture had to be prepared also to "feel as strangers and outsiders."[72] For the modern Orthodox, as for all the Orthodox, the rabbis were there both to sanction engagements with the larger culture and to signal the necessary retreats.

In practice this required sophisticated and sometimes complex cognitive leadership as well as nuanced instrumental adjustments, intellectual skills that few rabbis were taught as part of their training. Elsewhere I have defined these modern Orthodox strategies at greater length as involving reinterpretation, in which the contradictions between Judaism and American cultural belonging were interpretively reconstructed so as to diminish the sense of dissonance created by their combination.[73] Old meanings were ascribed to new elements, making modernity seem to be in tune with tradition, and old elements were understood in new ways, making tradition seem to be at home in modern life. In this approach there was nothing so old that it could not be made new and nothing so new that it had not been foreseen by the ancient law and Torah, although at times to some Orthodox who resisted accommodation these interpretations seemed forced.[74] In the modern Orthodox Jewish milieu this process was supported by an ethos that prescribed, as Grand Rabbi Abraham Isaac Kook (viewed by many Orthodox Jews as a precursor of this modernist ideology) once put it, that "the old must be made new; the new must be made holy." Or, to use the more sociological language of Peter Berger and Thomas Luckmann in *The Social Construction of Reality*, "[T]he present is interpreted so as to stand in a continuous relationship with the past, with a tendency to minimize such transformations as have actually taken place."[75] These processes, which respectively I call *contemporization* and *traditioning,* required ideological virtuosi, comfortable in and committed to both the modern and traditional Jewish worlds. That was precisely the role that many of those modern Orthodox rabbis tried to fill.

With the death or decline of the first generation of postwar rabbis, whose stature and connection to traditional Orthodoxy gave them an authority that the next generation did not have, there arose a new generation of rabbinic leaders, trained increasingly by Haredim (for most modernists completed their almost universal university education and chose *not* to be rabbis, instead pursuing other more cosmopolitan vocations and leaving their more parochial kin to be teachers in the yeshivas and seminaries). These new Orthodox rabbis emerged with a greater attachment to Jewish parochialism and wariness of American culture. They often considered the yeshiva the ideal environment and the modern world and university education a necessary evil or distraction—perhaps even an obstacle to Orthodoxy. More to the point, they did not see the skills of contemporization and traditioning as essential to their rabbinic vocation. These men's capacity to serve as reinterpreters and guides for sometimes perplexed modern Orthodox Jews was accordingly both less developed and less persuasive than had been the case among their earlier counterparts.

Ironically, the decline of rabbinic concern with contemporization and traditioning came just at a time when the challenges to integrate Orthodox Judaism and American contemporary culture became greater. By the turn of the millennium the need to find a way to harmonize Orthodoxy with such thorny issues as feminism, homosexuality, messianism, nationalist Zionism, large-scale pluralism, and intermarriage—among the matters that rose to prominence as time passed—required Orthodox reinterpretations of an unprecedented complexity. But the emerging Orthodox rabbis who might offer a modern Orthodox approach to navigating these issues were more interested in reviewing ancient texts and embedding themselves in traditional yeshiva study or values than in providing direction through the changing currents of American life. Others became caught up with right-wing political movements, messianism, and settlement in Israeli territories.

STABILIZED DUALISM

While most American modern Orthodox Jews wanted to remain planted in two worlds at once, ideologically anchored in Jewish law and tradition and culturally attached to contemporary America, they began to depend less and less on rabbis (who were becoming more and more parochial by the last quarter of the twentieth century) to help maintain their dualistic stance. Instead they focused on acquiring a profession, achieving economic security, and anchoring themselves in modern Orthodox communities. There they could find places where people shared lifestyles and a number of instrumental and institutional ties with Jews of similar outlooks and attachments. They did not really partake fully in the high culture of Western civilization, even though they paid lip service to it. Rather, they were embracing American popular culture and middle-class values. This lifestyle of modern Orthodoxy might be characterized as "stabilized dualism." Cynics might call it "stabilized duplicity." This was the twentieth-century American version of *Torah-im-derech-eretz.*[76] When it succeeded, the modern Orthodox community stood with its feet firmly planted in two very different worlds at once, living with and even embracing the tensions caused by this dualism. The repeated patterns of engagement in religious life and with the world outside it became second nature. It was as if they were putting weight first on one foot, the one planted in the tribal community, and then on the other, the secular American one. So adept were they in their shifting stances and involvements that they seemed to go on almost automatically. They lacked a powerful ideological drive and were instead what David Reisman called "other-directed," an orientation normative during America's midcentury. Other-directedness, as Reisman explained, was a way of life in which people looked to "their contemporaries . . . [as] the source of direction for the individual"; it was less an ideology and more a commitment to being like one's contemporaries.[77] Modern Orthodox Jews became either diffident and often ideologically bankrupt or increasingly concerned with being as or no more or less *frum* than others in their community and thereby generally unthinkingly validated and sustained one another's beliefs and behaviors. That was why they tended increasingly to stress practical behavior rather than ideology. That was also why creating community, usually through a synagogue and a school, was so important to these people, as was keeping tabs on community standards. Their leaders became lay, and their rabbis increasingly defined a separate cultural order.

To the modern Orthodox these other-directed choices may have *seemed* autonomous because they leaned less and less on rabbinic authority. To the rabbis who were not being obeyed they may have also seemed that way. But as Reisman makes clear, other-directedness masquerades as individual choice.

Ironically, in so emphasizing the importance of their communities for helping them articulate what it meant to be contrapuntalist modern Orthodox, these Jews were creating a kind of enclave culture. Indeed, in their conformist nature many modern Orthodox Jewish neighborhoods began to take on the characteristics of more traditionalist, even Haredi, orthodoxy.[78] To be sure, these were Jews who left their enclaves readily and continued to embrace life beyond them. Yet increasingly they were finding that they needed to be with other like-minded Jews, where they felt more secure and directed in their Judaism. The modern Orthodox Jews became no less ghettoized than the Haredim, and when those ghettoes began to swing to the religious right, the individuals and families living within them fell like dominoes all in the same direction. But this did not happen right away; it came at the end of a process that started out with the desire to remain culturally dualistic and in tune with others who shared this desire.

Seeing that one could be serious about one's commitments to Judaism but that one did not therefore have to spend life either in a yeshiva or completely and always within the boundaries of the traditional Orthodox enclave, many modern Orthodox Jews had gone on after the 1950s to pursue lives very much rooted in American professions, dependent on extended American (secular) education (often at campuses far beyond the orbit of Orthodoxy), and outward-looking. In these places, they often had to extrapolate for themselves what they could or should do as Orthodox Jews. In the early days of this outward movement, Jewish campus organizations like Hillel were dominated by the non-Orthodox, and although an Orthodox campus organization called Yavneh was formed, it never had more than about thirty-five chapters, with a handful of members in most.[79] That made college among the most difficult places for modern Orthodox Jews to use a community-belonging strategy, something that would have consequences later as the modern Orthodox began to worry about the religious price tag of being on campus. Because of their enhanced Jewish education, many felt able to make some Halachic (i.e., traditional-Judaic legal) judgments for themselves, at least at the level of practical knowledge. Yet this was generally not a strategy they trumpeted as an ideology; they still looked to rabbis as the ultimate authorities, even though there were fewer and fewer such rabbis who could speak to their needs. By the end of the twentieth century, young Orthodox Jews on campus were increasingly huddling together in enclaves of like-minded Jews who had similar experiences and biographies, hoping thereby to maintain their particular way of life; in this regard they were no different from the adult communities.

In addition to anchoring themselves in modern Orthodox communities and other-directedly guiding themselves by community norms and behaviors, the modern Orthodox laity also often turned toward *compartmentalization*. In this ad hoc strategy, one accepted contradiction by ignoring it. This approach required of modern Orthodox Jews a kind of conceptual looking away from the inherent conflicts built into their competing beliefs and practices as well as their dissonant cultural stances. Here two possibilities exist: inattention and disattention. The former involves a kind of conceptual dimming of the lights, while the latter requires an active withdrawal of attention from contradiction. In compartmentalizing, people assign a *temporarily* inferior ontological status, and thereby a not-to-be-taken-seriously cognitive status, to elements that contradict their conviction that one can be truly Orthodox and also engaged in the American society and culture or vice versa. Thus modern Orthodox Jews either ignored those laws and observances that did not fit into the modern world when the occasion seemed to demand it or actively blotted them out. Such action did not presume an ideological or legalistic repudiation whereby the inappropriate was wiped off the books—the approach of Conservative and Reform Judaism. Nor did it even require a well-thought-out ideological virtuosity, as had been offered by people like

Rabbi Soloveitchik. On the contrary, in the compartmentalist approach, the same matters that might be blotted out or ignored on one occasion could be honored on another. Moreover, when pressed to account for their inattention to Jewish laws and practice — skipping afternoon prayers, for example, because they were busy at work — the compartmentalizing modern Orthodox would likely admit the error of their ways. That is, to use terminology Robert Merton made famous, they saw themselves as criminals rather than revolutionaries, the latter being the status of non-Orthodox religious reformers.[80]

Alternatively, compartmentalization led Orthodox Jews to engage in avoidance behavior, so that they simply did not carry on behaviors that seemed to undermine their religious commitments. "Don't put yourself in a situation where you'll have a conflict." Thus they might avoid living in suburbs where there were no Orthodox synagogues, choose only those careers that would let them observe Jewish law and tradition, travel only to places where permissible food was available, and so on. In short, they might stay anchored in modern Orthodox ghettoes, the strategy previously outlined. Here people knew what they could or could not do — and learned not to challenge the inconsistencies or accommodations of their neighbors.

But this sort of anchoring was not the same as remaining strictly within the Orthodox enclave in an assertively sectarian existence, a strategy characteristic of Haredi Orthodoxy. The modern Orthodox enclaves tended to function more like bedroom or weekend communities, allowing their members to wander culturally and socially far afield much of the rest of the time. They offered a longer and more flexible tether than did Haredi ones. Both the compartmentalization and the avoidance behavior so characteristic of the modern Orthodox required a kind of endless cultural and instrumental shifting. I have called this dynamic of belonging "contrapuntal."

CONTRAPUNTALISM

The dynamic belonging or contrapuntalism that was at the heart of the modern Orthodox ideology, such as it was before it devolved into other-directedness, was not simply a disguised effort to ease the restrictions of Orthodox practice or compromise the Jewish traditions to which the Orthodox were expected to hold fast. It was, as at least some of the adherents believed, driven at least through the late 1970s by a desire to expand the nature of what it meant to be Orthodox and Jewish in the modern age. As one thinker who espoused this attitude, Professor Lawrence J. Kaplan, put it in an article in *Commentary Magazine* in which he tried to mark the differences of this movement from even the most moderate Conservative Jewish approaches, "It is possible and necessary, to live with the dissonance and tension between halachic values and modern ones."[81] Indeed, Kaplan and other contrapuntal modernists like him saw that tension as creative, even a particular source of strength, because it allowed people to intellectually stretch, innovate, and develop both their Judaism and their manner of engagement in the modern world. Even compartmentalization and avoidance required creativity.

Although its ideological virtuosi were declining in number and its emphasis was more on lifestyle by the 1980s, for at least thirty years after the Second World War modern Orthodox contrapuntalism seemed to flourish. It represented a new engaged-with-the-world flexible kind of Orthodox Judaism that could live with contradiction and build upon it. As such, it also wanted to demonstrate to itself and the rest of the Jewish world that one did not need to abandon commitments to Jewish law (Halacha) and traditional observance in order to live this way. To these Jews not only was their way of life possible; it was, they increasingly believed, also the most desirable way to live Jewishly. As such, some of these Jews perceived themselves to be engaged in "a cognitive contest" with all other forms of Jewish adaptation to contemporary realities and were convinced they were bound to win.[82]

While modern Orthodoxy held to this notion that it was living according to Halacha and, unlike the non-Orthodox, not according to some temporal choice, this did not mean that its adherents believed that there was no room for change or variation in what they did. Indeed, just as they sought to distinguish themselves from the non-Orthodox, they also wanted to be set apart from the Haredim. Thus, unlike the Haredim, the modern Orthodox accepted the idea that "the definition of 'right and good' changed from generation to generation," as Rabbi Walter S. Wurzburger put it. "In other words," he continued, "religious behavior need not be totally stagnant; there can be an evolution here as well."[83]

Being in the middle, however, was not easy. Too strong a contestation with the non-Orthodox would lead to the modernists' being defined as hopelessly parochial, and too enthusiastic an embrace of change would result in their Orthodox legitimacy being questioned by the growing Haredi sector, which was quietly building itself up, particularly in the rabbinic ranks. The modern Orthodox laity handled this by trying to keep its faith in Orthodox standards but to do so in as understated a way as possible. After all, for all of Soloveitchik's desire to draw the line sharply and engage in a cognitive contest, there was, as most rank-and-file modern Orthodox Jews realized, something quite comparable between their own aims and those among their non-Orthodox counterparts who tried seriously to adapt their Judaism to America. The latter might go too far in abandoning tradition and embracing reform, as far as the modern Orthodox were concerned, by declaring core matters peripheral or outdated. However, the modern Orthodox did *not* believe that their non-Orthodox counterparts were completely wrongheaded in their outward-looking Americanism (which may have been why Soloveitchik, afraid of the blurring of boundaries, tried so hard to draw the line).

The modern Orthodox enthusiasm of the postwar period in America did not last forever. Compartmentalization, which had worked for at least a generation as a supportive mechanism for contrapuntalism, was by the last quarter of the twentieth century beginning to wear thin. The challenges of a changing American society and culture that was increasingly permissive and radical were progressively more difficult to disattend. Moreover, many of the next generation of modern Orthodox were looking at the dualism of their parents' generation with disdain and seeing it rather as duplicity. Without the distinguished rabbis to lead the way and offer it legitimacy, they saw the actions of the modern Orthodox laity as driven more by habit or inertia and convenience than by an inspiring ideology. Once again, they needed ideological virtuosi to help navigate through the cultural narrows without taking them either toward the Scylla of Haredism or the Charybdis of Conservative and Reform Jewish reformulations. But, as noted, their movement into that outside world also led to a decline in the number of them who chose to be rabbis.

At the same time, as we have seen, those who opted to be rabbis increasingly found themselves trained by those who had chosen *not* to embrace the contrapuntalism of modern Orthodoxy but had instead remained within the framework of yeshiva studies and tended to be both more insular and parochial as well as religiously right wing. With the disappearance of the generation of those trained by and modeling themselves after the outward-looking Soloveitchik, men who sought an impressive secular education to combine with their Jewish learning; this became even more the case. As a result, the number of rabbis who were prepared to act as legitimating authorities for the approach of modern Orthodoxy diminished radically. Those who remained were unable to stand up to the challenges increasingly thrown at modern Orthodoxy by the rabbis of the Haredi world. In addition, there emerged a kind of revisionism in

defining exactly who Rabbi Soloveitchik was and where he stood on matters relating to modernist tendencies, with increasing numbers of people
arguing that he genuinely embraced the Haredi point of view and took
modernist stances only under duress and in limited circumstances.[84] By
the end of the twentieth century, and increasingly following Soloveitchik's
death in 1993, newly minted rabbis would emerge with viewpoints that
were far more retrograde and parochial.[85] Without modernist rabbinic
champions to guide their way, the center of gravity within modern Orthodoxy moved even more toward the laity or toward a few rabbis who were
increasingly treated as marginal by their Orthodox rabbinic peers (many
of whom were becoming increasingly Haredi) and who lacked the cultural stature of the first and second generations after the Holocaust. This
left the modern Orthodox struggling to stabilize their dualism. The frac-
ture lines among them became clearer and began to shift.

VARIETIES OF MODERN ORTHODOXY

To follow these developments it is necessary to understand that the group
I have been calling modern Orthodox was never monolithic. In 1989, in
our book *Cosmopolitans and Parochials: Modern Orthodox Jews in America*,
Steven M. Cohen and I tried to describe the variations that existed within
this group that was generally characterized by contrapuntalism.[86] We
found then that modern Orthodox Jews in America were essentially clus-
tered in three general orientations. At one end, we found those we called
the "nominally Orthodox." These were people who, while they chose to
call themselves Orthodox and were in many of their social affiliations undoubtedly within the Orthodox realm of influence, nevertheless spent
their lives in the outermost reaches of that realm, in great measure because they were drawn ever more powerfully to the society and culture
of America. They sought to reduce the tension between their Orthodoxy
and the demands of modern America by embedding themselves as much
as possible in the latter but still not abandoning the Orthodox label, which
many held onto at best out of family history or nostalgic connections.
Toward that end they maintained relatively few ritual practices, were the
least fervent in and most uncertain about their religious beliefs, were the
most flexible in their cultural outlook, and were far more pluralist in their
affiliations than other Orthodox Jews, who tended to be more exclusively
bonded to an Orthodox social community and cultural enclave. At one
point they were perhaps as much as a third of the population who were
identified as Orthodox. In a well-worn reference to these Jews, pundits

often jokingly typified them by noting that "the synagogue they don't regularly attend is an Orthodox one." In the era of 1950s and well into the 1960s they turned up in the sanctuary occasionally, especially on the High Holy Days, when, as Haym Soloveitchik describes them, "most didn't know what they were saying, and bored, wandered in and out. Yet, at the closing service of Yom Kippur, the Ne'ilah, the synagogue filled and a hush set in upon the crowd. The tension was palpable and tears were shed."[87] Although they might send their offspring to a yeshiva, they were satisfied with sending their children to afternoon Hebrew schools (commonly those affiliated with Orthodox synagogues) rather than the emerging day schools. Until the beginning of the 1970s most of these Jews found it possible to be minimally involved in their Orthodox Judaism without somehow disqualifying themselves from inclusion in it. By the last quarter of the twentieth century, however, as we shall see, as the ante for being considered Orthodox was raised more and more by many within the movement, these Jews found it more and more difficult and ultimately inapt to call themselves Orthodox. Unwilling to go beyond their symbolic religiosity, these Jews often dropped out, no longer choosing to identify themselves as Orthodox.[88] The nostalgia and inertia that had sustained their attachments were simply no longer sufficient, while the growing demands of Orthodox affiliation were becoming too great.

At the opposite extreme were those Cohen and I called the "traditionally Orthodox," people who were far more powerfully drawn toward old school Orthodoxies, more stringent in their practices, traditionally oriented in their religious beliefs, ready to take a confrontational stance vis-à-vis non-Orthodoxy (although in an understated way), relatively monochromatic in their cultural outlook, and tending toward the proudly insular in their social affiliations. They were not the purely enclavist and actively confrontational Haredim, a term Cohen and I did not use, but they were certainly sympathetic to the Haredi way. In practice the traditionally Orthodox were distinguished from Haredim by their tacit acceptance (and often reluctant embrace) of the cultural legitimacy of the world beyond Orthodoxy and a feeling that one could find a place in that world for tradition. Yet one sensed that as that outside world became increasingly debased in their eyes throughout the radically permissive social revolution of the 1960s and 1970s or began to undermine the values and practices of Judaism that they considered paramount they would tend to adopt the ethos of insularity and aggressive cultural opposition characteristic of Haredi Orthodoxy—and if not, they might have children who would. In effect, to reduce the tension between their Orthodoxy and the demands of a modern America by which they were becoming increasingly disturbed, they chose to shift toward the Haredi orbit. They trusted in the religious right more than in the liberal left.

Ironically, part of this repositioning came from a growing self-confidence of Orthodoxy that it *could* find a place in an America that had gradually grown more pluralist and cognizant, if not always respectful, of the social and cultural requirements of minority communities. When therefore the traditionally Orthodox felt they were not always getting what they needed to maintain their way of life and guarantee their future because American popular culture or social trends were threatening to absorb or otherwise undo their Jewish life and values, increasing numbers of them embraced what the late Charles Liebman called "extremism as a religious norm" and the demands of Haredi enclave culture as *"an irreducible basis for communal and personal identity."*[89] In other words, the Haredi option of being *in* but not *of* American culture became both more attractive and more conceivable in America than it had been in the previous decades. Even among the American born it became acceptable to stress reservations about liberal, popular American culture and to choose an alternative identity. Over the course of the last twenty years of the twentieth century and into the twenty-first, many of these traditionalists in the mainstream of modern Orthodoxy came to have doubts about modernism and to believe that only Haredism and identities rooted in it could ensure that Orthodox Judaism (which they considered the only legitimate expression of Judaism) would remain free from religious and cultural erosion, immune to substantial destructive change, and protected from the vicissitudes of history and social change until the time of divine redemption. They believed that only thus were they honoring the memory of those whom the Holocaust had incinerated.

Finally, between these extremes Cohen and I described were those who tried to maintain an equal balance in their dualism, who worked for its stabilization so that they could keep one foot inside the world of Orthodox commitments and the other in the mainstream of modern American culture, society, practices, and values. These were the bulk of Orthodox Jews, and they bridged the gap between the traditionalists at one extreme and members of the Orthodox movement in little more than name only at the other. We called them "centrists."[90] At the time of our survey in the mid-1980s, the forces pulling the nominally Orthodox further toward the religious left and the traditionally Orthodox further toward the right were not yet as powerful or at least as obvious as they would later become.[91]

The term *centrist* was both analytically descriptive—these Orthodox

Jews were in the middle of all our scales on belief, religious practices, communal solidarity, and cultural outlook, doing "more" and scoring "higher" than those to the religious left of them and "less" than those to the religious right—and symbolic. These were people who *chose* to be in the middle, who eschewed extremism as a religious norm but also disdained excessive religious laxity. As such, centrism and its adherents were for us the most powerful exemplars—the heart—of modern Orthodoxy, which we believed had purposefully staked out a broad middle ground in religion and culture. We thought that the centrists' numbers also gave them dominance in defining American Orthodoxy.

These assumptions about the centrist mainstream were based not only on their numbers but also on their successes in creating institutions, primarily the day school—about which more later in this volume—but also a web of synagogues (many of them in the burgeoning suburban communities that were also dominated by them) to which modern Orthodox families gravitated, as well as other organizations, from youth movements to kashruth-certifying agencies. The centrists were largely a cadre of college-educated but religiously observant young people, most of whom appeared willing to follow the modern Orthodox cultural norm of stabilized dualism. Indeed, "the encounter with American culture was considered desirable, providing an opportunity for engagement, challenge, and ultimately integration, and was not merely an economically driven pragmatic middle-class value."[92] As Seth Farber has argued in his description of a community of such modern Orthodox Jews as they began to take shape in Boston (a community dominated by Rabbi Joseph Soloveitchik) in the 1950s and early 1960s: "What held this group together was a shared belief that American societal norms and Orthodox Jewish life could be integrated seamlessly. They did not see any conflict between the two. Attendance at Fenway Park (the home field of the Boston Red Sox), barbecues, theater outings, ski trips, and trips to the Boston Museum of Fine Arts were frequent activities as were synagogue participation and public study convocations."[93] As Rabbi Aharon Lichtenstein, son-in-law and student of Soloveitchik, celebrated this sort of Orthodoxy, "Centrism at its best encourages a sense of complexity and integration . . . . [I]nasmuch as a person of this orientation looks to the right and to the left, he is more likely to reject the kind of black-and-white solutions appealing to others . . . , relates to more areas of human life . . . , [and is] more inclined to perceive shadings and nuances, differences between areas and levels of moral and spiritual reality."[94]

To be sure, as noted, there were limits to the integration possible, and centrist Orthodox Jews understood that because of their irrevocable attachments to Jewish tradition and the particular demands that their commitments to Jewish law and ritual made on them their lot in life was always to be "both citizen and stranger," as Rabbi Soloveitchik put it.[95] They were content to know that the multiple worlds they inhabited could not always be perfectly harmonized, and in the final analysis above all else they remained committed to Orthodoxy. That knowledge was behind Rabbi Soloveitchik's belief that even under the best conditions there remained for all Orthodox Jews in America a necessary level of estrangement that limited their complete absorption in America. (This belief was what the Haredim used as evidence that Soloveitchik was one of them.) But in the heyday of American modern Orthodoxy, the twenty years between 1945 and 1965, most of its advocates believed that the necessary estrangement and cultural distance from America would be mitigated in culturally wholesome mid-twentieth-century America, where being religiously observant was neither shameful nor a recipe for exclusion and intolerance. After all, in 1954, the time when this sort of Orthodoxy was carving out its middle ground, America added the words "under God" into its national pledge of allegiance, and the motto "The family that prays together, stays together" was on billboards throughout the land. Adherents to modern Orthodoxy did believe that "America was different" and that here a true modern Orthodoxy could find a home. There would be nothing in America from which they would have to really run—or so they believed in those early years.

From Modernism to Haredism

With the radicalization of that once culturally wholesome America by the late 1960s and into the next decade, Orthodox estrangement seemed to grow, and modernism gave way to a centrism that was more reticent in its Americanism, was doubtful about the wholesomeness of America, and looked more for continuity with its traditionalist right wing. The Orthodox community, though largely on the periphery of this radicalization, was not untouched by it. By the end of the 1970s, in the wake of racial turmoil, often violent anti–Vietnam War protests, growing radicalism on campus, polarization in the political process, the excesses of the sexual revolution, freethinking in lifestyle choices, and increasing signs of a decline in Jewish affiliation and involvement among young college graduates, the American dream seemed to growing numbers of Orthodox Jews to have become a nightmare. This was when the once wholesome culture to which the modernists had aspired to integrate themselves, and which they saw as a source of personal improvement and a vehicle for the social betterment of their children, increasingly became instead a destructive, radicalized, *unhealthy* Americanism. Most disturbing was the fact that its most radical, antireligious, and destructive elements were in the universities where the modern Orthodox had been sending those children. Indeed, the most elite schools to which many of the modern Orthodox had aspired were often the most radicalized and countercultural— Columbia University being perhaps the archetype. Now the strategy that modern Orthodoxy had enabled of keeping a foot in that world began to look less attractive and more dangerous. It could become a destabilizing element. The thought that a modern Orthodox childhood might not ensure adolescent or even adult Jewish continuity was now increasingly reasonable. As if to underscore this, Jewish population surveys (whose results were widely disseminated) made clear that the number of Orthodox Jews in America was not growing.

All this led at least some among the traditionalist right wing of modern Orthodoxy, for whom the level of estrangement from American society and culture had always been higher, to suspect that the nascent Haredi sector (whose estrangement was highest) might be correct: that the encounter with the modern world, even and perhaps especially in the United States, was a propaedeutic to assimilation, a recipe for disaster. These traditionalists began to look anew at both the integrative goals of modern Orthodoxy and the separatist ideology of Haredi Orthodoxy. As the former looked more worrisome, the latter looked more appealing. A careful observer could see these changes in the evolving terminology of the times. By the late 1980s and 1990s, our analytically descriptive term *centrist* was, within Orthodox circles, supplanting the adjective *modern*, which had for a long time named the major stream of contemporary Orthodoxy. In some measure this was because in the preceding fifteen years *modern* had acquired a kind of ignominy in an America that increasingly valued the traditional over the modern and where those on the nominal periphery were slipping out of the Orthodox orbit by way of their attachments to America. Moreover, in the atmosphere of postmodernism that was part of the emerging American scene, where being a little of this *and* that rather than choosing to be this *or* that was acceptable, the need to label oneself as unambiguously modern was no longer viewed as essential.

Centrist was no longer just a description of a group in the middle; it was the title for a group that did *not* want to be associated with the liberalism that was correlated with modernism. By the 1980s the idea of an

Orthodox centrism that was culturally conservative and uncomfortable with some American excesses (for the center is always dependent on where the extremes happen to be) had eroded the enthusiasm for Orthodox modernism. While some people conflated the term *centrist Orthodox* with *modern Orthodox*, the two labels were less and less cognate. As the extremes moved further apart, the strain on those standing in the center with a foot in each world grew exponentially.

Centrist Orthodoxy had always been a kind of ambivalent Orthodoxy. Groups in the center generally are always torn, particularly if they are contrapuntal in character, as this one was. This was not, however, simply a psychological ambivalence. "So-called sectarian behavior has little to do with personal psychology."[96] It was in part anchored in the competing and not always harmonious expectations of centrists' position in the Orthodox world. This resulted in what Robert Merton and Elinor Barber have called "sociological ambivalence," ambivalence indigenous to those who are forced to accept and adapt to the contradictory values attached to a plurality of contradictory cultures.[97]

With the gradual evaporation of the nominally Orthodox, the movement had become far more hard-core by the end of the 1980s. The traditionalists were being pulled gradually so close to Haredism that at times it was difficult to see the line of separation. As for the centrists, they found themselves no longer inhabiting a middle ground where they had staked out their ideological and behavioral place. Instead, they now represented the liberal outer edge, a position they found unnerving. They were concerned that from their new position at the liberal edge they would be outcast by the Orthodox rabbis and those to their right, and there was some of that going on. They retreated further and turned their modernist suburbs into increasingly parochial cultural enclaves. Their communities were transformed "from suburb to shtetl," as Egon Mayer put it in his eponymous book on an Orthodox neighborhood in New York.[98]

Indeed, the absence of the nominally Orthodox, whose presence within the movement had served to offset the Haredi tendencies on the other extreme of Orthodoxy, allowed the latter become a stronger force within the movement. So when they exerted their influence and made their case for a more stringent and parochial Orthodoxy, those who had once been in the center felt rightly that the Haredi criticisms were now directed at them and not at the nominally Orthodox who had once been on their liberal left. They looked to the left and saw no Orthodoxy there. They had themselves become the left. These Jews were therefore distressed that their sort of Orthodoxy might be accused of threatening the continuity of observant Judaism and that as such they would fail those who had died in the Holocaust but who had not wavered in their religious observance (or at least were reputed in retrospect to have been religious stalwarts). They had two choices now: to become more traditionalist like the Haredim or to move out of the movement as their nominally Orthodox counterparts had.

Those who chose to move out, who threw off the increasingly heavy yoke of Orthodoxy with its Haredi mandates, looked at the movement they left behind and saw it becoming more religiously right wing, a perception that reconfirmed them in their conclusion that they were correct to leave, since the contrapuntal dualism they had once found attractive in modern Orthodoxy was giving way to the monotones of Haredism. Those who remained found that their contrapuntalism was too dissonant and their ambiguity too threatening for a movement that increasingly standardized its behavior and beliefs in favor of the stringencies of Haredism. If they tried to make the case for greater autonomy and personal style, the rabbis and the Haredi world reminded them how dangerous and duplicitous this stance was, pulling back from the edge. Whereas modern Orthodoxy had recognized, at least implicitly, that the multiple worlds in which they lived were never going to be completely harmonized, Haredism was in favor of a single world, all Jewish, and allowed for neither dissonance nor contrapuntalism. Anyone who did not follow this tune, or who was slightly off-key, was silenced or dismissed. Orthodoxy in America became harder core.

There was yet another basis for the centrists' discomfort: the liturgy, which impressed on those who recited it daily, as did these Orthodox Jews, that they needed to "be forgiven for we have sinned and be absolved for we have transgressed." Multiple times a day and in a variety of prayers they recited the words that reminded them that wrongdoing and desire for exculpation were an inevitable part of their lives. In other words, feelings of guilt were built into their expressions of religiousness, on top of the post-Holocaust and Haredi-induced sense of guilt that was part of the late-twentieth-century experience. Thus, if there was something structural that might tip the balance in their increasingly ambivalent cultural stance away from engagement in the modern world—as indeed happened during these years with the growing influence and confidence of Haredi outcasting and enclavism—their liturgy was ready to give expression to underlying feelings of culpability that were in any event part of their post-Holocaust Orthodoxy. The words of the liturgy began to take on new meanings at least for some (especially when their children came back from school with a renewed fervor for prayer that they injected into Orthodox life).[99] To mitigate the feelings of blame that they were told they deserved for wandering into the "defiling" world beyond the Orthodox enclaves, some centrists began to draw back from that world.

This was at a time that an ever more vigorous and outspoken Haredi enclavist Orthodoxy, exercising "its own distinctive power of exclusion," was willing to declare that "Orthodox independence from the organized community was the ideal."[100] By and large, Haredim had for many years remained content to build their own religious institutions, live in their separate communities, and eschew the acculturative and educational aspirations of the majority of Jewry. They did this not only by emphasizing the superiority of their *orach chayim* (way of life) but also by devaluing the *chukos hagoyim* (the ways of Gentiles) and defining those rewards as counterfeit *(goyim nachas)*. Throughout the twentieth century and more aggressively in its final quarter, Haredim increasingly turned away from the American dream and engaged in what Mary Douglas has called "outcasting" and "downgrading" those outside their enclaves. They extended the "power of exclusion" so that what was different was essentially defined as "abhorrent."[101] Outcasting was a key instrument by which enclavist Orthodoxy helped maintain the boundaries of their community. While these Jews did not long to feel beleaguered or attacked, they sensed that when Jews did feel this way Judaism as a way of life was somehow protected from the smothering embrace and dangers of easy assimilation. Hence it was not unusual to find voices in the Haredi world that not only stressed distrust of Gentiles but reminded Jews that they were forever subject to attacks from these "others." "Esau hates Jacob" was the way they articulated this "truth."[102] As Rabbi Yitzhak Hutner of the Chaim Berlin Yeshiva and the Rabbinic Council of Sages of Agudath Israel asserted, it was and remained "a sin to trust other nations from which will follow רעות רבות," many evils. Indeed, he added, "[W]e have seen, the 'great evils and troubles' did indeed come upon us from those very Gentile nations who had gained our confidence and trust."[103]

So powerful was this belief that even dialogue with Gentiles was viewed as corrupting and prohibited. No less a rabbinic authority than Rabbi Moshe Feinstein, in an opinion issued in March 1967, asserted that dialogue with Catholics and Protestants was prohibited because "all contact and discussion with them, even on worldly matters, is forbidden, for the act of 'drawing near' is in and of itself forbidden, as it falls under the category of the grave prohibition against "rapprochement with idolatry—*hitkarvut 'im 'avodah zarah.*' "[104] Nothing could be a clearer expression of outcasting.

As this enclavist approach aligned people with Haredi cultural biases, the spirit of cooperation that had once been a hallmark of modern Orthodoxy began to weaken, particularly in the closing years of the twentieth century. Not only did the Synagogue Council fall apart in 1994, as mentioned in the Introduction, but also intra-Jewish organizations that included the Orthodox were declining in number.[105] In a statement typical of the time, the traditionalist Orthodox rabbinic organization Agudath Harabonim, taking a position to the religious right of the more moderate Rabbinical Council of America, declared in 1997 that Conservative and Reform Judaism, with which up to two-thirds of American Jewry affiliated, were "not Judaism." In part, this attitude among the Haredim and those within the Orthodox world who sympathized with them was driven by the typical preoccupation and fear of enclave cultures: "the leakage of members."[106] Ironically, all this activity of raising the barriers and outcasting aimed at stemming this only helped accelerate the exodus of the nominally Orthodox from the movement. All this pushing and pulling in the meantime was pulling the centrists apart.

The stress on the center was not unique to Orthodoxy. American society in general was becoming bifurcated—more liberal in some respects and more conservative in others. The moderate center was shrinking. While the Christian and conservative as well as ethnic forces grew more aggressive in setting their agenda to become the American one, other Americans were also increasingly willing to legitimate new and often radical lifestyles and values and to allow for the end of WASP cultural hegemony.

Among American Jews too there was a shrinking of the middle. A minority was becoming actively Jewish and producing a richer and more complex Jewish culture than America had ever seen, while the majority of American Jewry were interested in maintaining little more than a positive attitude toward the Jewish heritage.[107] On the right, full-time Jewish education grew while supplementary Jewish education waned. On the left, the declining affiliation of young Jews was leading to increased intermarriage and growing numbers of Jews who were largely divorced from Jewish life. In denominational life among the affiliated, the increasing liberalism of non-Orthodox Jewish groups was creating an ever-wider chasm separating them from an increasingly conservative Orthodoxy. The decisions of the Reform movement to ordain women as rabbis in the 1970s and a parallel one among Conservative Jews in 1983, the same year Reform Jews resolved to accept patrilineal descent as a basis for Jewish belonging no less legitimate than the traditional matrilineal descent that

Orthodox Jewish law considered the exclusive basis for Jewish continuity, and later permissive stances on a variety of personal status issues were only the most prominent moves that widened the gap between the Orthodox and everyone else.

The ambivalence of the Orthodox centrists had mirrored something that already in 1976 Charles Liebman saw in all of those who took their Judaism seriously in America. He described this ambivalence as coming out of a Jewry that "desperately sought to participate in the society and rejected sectarianism as a survival strategy, yet at the same time refused to make [their] own Jewishness irrelevant."[108] When they thought of themselves as simply "modern Orthodox," the emphasis was on modernity, which in practice signified participation in the larger society. But when this sector of Orthodoxy began to have doubts and anxieties about the value of its participation in American society and culture, its ambivalence crumbled and what remained nudged those who had been in the center, at first slightly and then more vigorously, in the direction of sectarianism.

While the Orthodox were by the closing years of the twentieth century moving toward greater sectarianism and retreating to an enclave culture behind what they viewed as a Jewish wall of virtue, American society was rapidly moving toward more flexible definitions of religious boundaries. The old notions that one must be either one religion or another gave way to the postmodern conception that one could be more than one at a time—in part a reflection of increasing intermarriage rates. The increasingly dominant attitude in America was that "the intermingling of peoples of a variety of backgrounds strengthens the national culture."[109] In this view, intermarriage and other crossing of old social and cultural boundaries was not only a sign that a person had transcended segregation, either coerced or self-imposed, but also the most potent illustration of the extent to which Americans did *not* encourage sectarian separation from one from another. This attitude, particularly powerful among those who had received a liberal arts education, which the modern Orthodox had embraced as an ideal, these same Orthodox Jews saw as a sure pathway to the disappearance of Judaism and betrayal of the post-Holocaust pledge to survive. Such cultural conflicts their contrapuntalism could not handle. If indeed the university educated were more likely to think of themselves as having multiple identities, then maybe the Orthodox needed to rethink and better arm themselves before entering college.[110] The university environment was of course the most fertile setting for spawning encounters across religious boundaries, interdating, intermarriage, and multiple or shifting identities.

Transcultural encounters had for much of the last quarter of a century acquired a positive valence for America, since by crossing boundaries and interdating and intermarrying, individuals would lose the negative attitudes they had toward other groups, becoming more integrated and thus creating a more harmonious society—something necessary for the multiracial, multicutural, and multiethnic society that the United States had increasingly become since 1965, the year the immigration law was changed to remove most of the national origin quotas and allow more newcomers from non-European sources. It was, however, problematic for Jews, and particularly for Orthodox Jews, who despite their desire to be integrated into American society and culture placed a high premium on continued Orthodox Jewish survival. They understood well that intermarriage decreases the salience of cultural distinctions in future generations, since the children of mixed marriages are less likely to identify themselves with a single group. Only outcasting could prevent the Orthodox from following this path.

As for matters of gender, the growing American trend of offering equality to women, the result of a new wave of feminism (sometimes called "radical") that began in the 1970s on the heels of civil rights reform, changed the way American society and culture looked at the separation of the sexes. As modern Americans, the modern Orthodox were moved in this direction as well, but in their Orthodox Jewish character they were reluctant to breach traditional distinctions between the sexes that Jewish law held to be sacrosanct.

Together, these trends toward postmodern attitudes of religious identity, changing views regarding gender equality, and in general the breaking down of all sorts of barriers to integration created a dilemma for the modern Orthodox. They could not, or perhaps did not want to, keep up with the pace of postmodernity. Traditionalism and centrism were their response.

This was a striking turnaround. At midcentury, modern Orthodoxy, with its emergent day schools and soon to be suburban synagogues, had seemed to be the face of the future. It was happy to hold multiple contrapuntal identities and participate in several worlds. It made the center a place that was both modern and traditional. It created institutions—mostly day schools, synagogues, and communities—that reflected this. It had rabbis who encouraged and even celebrated this stance. Barely thirty years later, it was retreating toward sectarianism, if at first with only a slight shift in emphasis that would show itself most clearly in the way people identified themselves, educational choices, and decisions about the sorts of experiences they wanted their children to have. Most of these choices turned out to be, as we shall see in greater detail later, in a contra-acculturative and sectarian direction.

By 1996, those who still wanted to hold onto modern Orthodoxy needed to create a new organization in order "to refresh the spirit of the Orthodox Jewish community." That organization, calling itself Edah, had as its motto "the courage to be modern and Orthodox," for by this time those who wanted to be modern felt they needed moral courage.[111]

This Orthodox shift to the right could be seen in all sorts of ways. It was in the changing Orthodox position on intra-Jewish cooperation and dialogue in favor of outcasting. During the first half of the twentieth century, modern American Orthodox Jews tended to engage in interdenominational collaboration, whether in education or community concerns from kashruth supervision to institution building.[112] While some have suggested that this sort of collaboration was a result of Orthodox institutional weakness and necessity rather than ideological commitment, there is no doubt that for some of the modernists necessity morphed into an attitudinal tendency to accept the idea of cooperation as a positive development. But by forty years later Orthodox cooperation with other Jews was increasingly overwhelmed by the Haredi attitude of outcasting that argued that no cooperation was possible. To be sure, this was not unprecedented. Already among nineteenth-century German Jewry controversy had erupted in 1845 over whether Orthodox Jews should be included in the *Gemeinde* (community) or whether they should be a separate community *(Austrits Gemeinde)*.[113] The latter point of view stressed the need of the Orthodox to distinguish themselves from and confront their non-Orthodox co-religionists and hence avoid being swallowed up by them in theory and practice.[114]

Orthodoxy thus had always been wary of intra-Jewish relations because they were reluctant to legitimate non-Orthodox Judaism and were wary of being indistinguishable from Jews in the Conservative movement. Even such a centrist Orthodox rabbi as Shubert Spero argued in the early 1980s that with regard to relations between Orthodox and non-Orthodox Jews "our dealings with the other cannot always be reciprocal." Although Spero tried to hold back the increasingly exclusionary and outcasting tendencies of Orthodoxy when he suggested what he called a "de-denominationalized zone" in which the Orthodox and all other sorts of Jews could meet in mutual respect and cooperation while suspending judgments of one another's Jewish legitimacy, he also asserted that Orthodox Jews could not "affirm that each branch of Judaism is an equally valid version of Judaism, an equally correct approach to God, an equally legitimate Jewish way of life."[115] That rightward-tilting centrist position ever more dominated the Orthodox perspective and led gradually and inexorably to an increasing level of American Orthodox sectarianism.

While the modern Orthodox went through these realignments, seeking a variety of means to gain access to the world beyond the boundaries of their religious and cultural enclaves, the Haredim, and increasingly the traditionalists and some of the centrists (those on centrism's religious right wing), were warning that this was not necessarily a primary goal for Orthodoxy.[116] The Haredi Orthodox Jews looked anew at the lessons of the Holocaust in light of developments in late-twentieth-century America and concluded with growing vehemence that the best way to turn was away from an increasingly debased and debasing American cultural life. This required a growing consensus within the Haredi enclave that the world outside was not only dangerous for Jewish survival but polluting. They had to return to the conclusion that despite their losses in the Holocaust their sectarianism and insularity were after all the right strategy for survival. The remarks of Rabbi Yitzchok Hutner are typical of this reassessment. He combined the lessons he believed should be learned from the Holocaust and from the developments in America in the late 1970s, both which moved him to urge Orthodox Jews (and in particular the hundred Jewish school principals gathered in 1977 at the Chaim Berlin Yeshiva) to turn away from "illusions," "infatuations," and "misplaced trust" in the "Gentile ways" of secularity and non-Orthodox Judaism.[117] The Orthodox society that these Jews should build needed to be an *alternative* one inside a protected enclave culture, behind a Jewish wall of virtue, rather than one that was free of these boundaries and sought integration. In this Orthodox Jewish countersociety and culture, which had a distinctive pattern of claims of what was necessary to life, those who wanted to survive as Jews committed to Orthodox Judaism had to get away from thinking that they were like or belonged anywhere near the mainstream. To these sectarian Orthodox, as Rabbi Yaakov Weinberg, dean of the Ner Israel Rabbinical College in Baltimore, put it in 1978, "there is no way that we can become totally assimilated in our adopted countries," so the lesson of the Holocaust and of American life was to remind Jews, especially those looking to become part of modern America: "Do not assume their values or their lives. You are not part of them. You are not in your proper place; while there, you are not living your lives."[118] The Haredim believed, as Menachem Friedman has put it, that Orthodox Jewry was "obligated to close in on itself and to differentiate itself from the world around it (both the non-Jewish world and the modern Jewish secular world), to see itself as being 'on one side' with 'all the rest of the world on the other.'"[119] Understood as well was the notion that those who were not in their proper place had transgressed and ran the risk of becoming themselves outcast. Indeed, in this view, to relate positively to either the non-Orthodox or the non-Jew was to flirt with sin and exclusion.

While once these sorts of messages would have fallen on deaf ears among the modern Orthodox, by the last quarter of the twentieth century more of them were giving heed. This was also abetted by the absence of alternative rabbinic voices of consequence that espoused the dualistic or dialectic cultural approach. And it was all happening just at the time that modern Orthodoxy was having doubts about what it had stepped into—even with only one foot—when it walked toward American society and culture. Haredi thinking that Judaism and Jewish life were totalistic in its character was finding a receptive audience even among the centrists. Contrapuntalism was in retreat.

Thus an ever more exclusive enclave culture developed that marked people as either insiders or outsiders, defining outsiders as at worst defiled outcasts and at best people of a "lower order." This led to hostility or at least disdain toward popular culture, especially as it had emerged in contemporary America, to rejection of the ideal of the melting pot and mobility, and to downgrading of the Jewish bona fides of all those who were not Haredi in their Judaism. As well, it led to an embrace, among other things, of the ideal of separate but equal, a standard that of course had been repudiated in the United States, where integration had been the goal for at least fifty years.

The American Haredim who argued this point understood (or at least their ideological leaders did) that this turning away from American society and culture and its promises was difficult, since America was a beckoning, open society that did not want its citizens to feel a sense of exile—the very sense of exile that the Haredim were demanding as a propaedeutic to redemption—but rather encouraged acculturation in the salad-bowl multicultural United States, or even assimilation in its melting-pot precursor.[120] Accordingly, to these Orthodox Jews the *golus* or exile mentality, the embrace of estrangement from all other ways of life, became the key to survival, the sure way to avoid another Holocaust and wholesale Jewish destruction. In short, they argued that "it is imperative that we impress upon American Jews that we are, have been, and always will be, different."[121] Modern Orthodoxy had rejected that idea, but there were signs by the end of the century that their rejection was beginning to erode.

The counterarguments of the Haredim that were repeated continuously began to be heard, particularly among the young who were in a variety of educational institutions where they were exposed to them.[122] When the temptation to assimilate or even adapt grew, the battle against those tendencies had to be joined. Hence the success that the modern Orthodox had had in the first thirty years after the Holocaust in modern American society called forth an equally powerful counterforce. In 1953 Rabbi Elya Meir Bloch, the head of the Yeshiva of Telshe, was said to have explained: "We no longer have to fear [the movement of Jewish] Conservatism—that is no longer the danger. Everyone knows that it is *avoda zara* [idol worship]. What we have to fear is Modern Orthodoxy."[123] By the 1970s, that warning was being publicly repeated, but by a Haredi Orthodoxy ready to be far more outcasting of the modernists.

In what has become a struggle to determine the character and direction of American Orthodoxy, the question is who will lead in the future. If the early aftermath of the Holocaust made it seem that the modernists would come out ascendant, the trends now seem to have switched. Evidence abounds. Typical of the turn toward outcasting and insularity within precincts once belonging to modern Orthodoxy are the following comments coming from a written "*d'var* [words of] *torah*," by Rabbi Herschel Schachter as circulated on an Internet site called Torahweb. Schachter, often described as "the preeminent student" of Rabbi Joseph Soloveitchik, serves at the time of this writing as Rosh Kollel at Yeshiva University, the head of the advanced Talmudic institute where many of the most dedicated Orthodox students prepare themselves and where many of those who will make up the next generation of Orthodox rabbis are being trained. He is thus a key figure in shaping the future and orienting the worldview of the religious leadership of modern Orthodoxy—those who study Torah but do so within a university framework. Here is what Schachter had to say in March 2004:[124]

G-d [sic] describes Himself in His Torah as "a jealous G-d." He forbids us to display any interest in any other religion. We are not permitted to attend a religious service of any other faith, or even watch it on television. We may not study works of or about any other religion, watch films about them, or study any pieces of religious art. A Jew may not enter a house of worship of any other religion even during the hours that services are not being held. We may not even "utter upon our lips" the name of any other god. This jealousness of G-d is not because He feels personally slighted and hurt. The Tehillim [Book of Psalms] described G-d as sitting in heaven and having himself a good chuckle over all idolatrous practices. But the concern is rather that these practices have a negative effect on mankind.

We may not donate any funds towards the furtherance of any other religion, nor advise or help in any other way to maintain any other religion. It is well known that certain religions encourage their clergy to engage in dialogue with the Jewish clergy in order to further conversion. It is obvious that we may not aid the clergy of any other faith in furthering their religion in such a fashion, or in any other fashion. There [sic] mere comparison of the Jewish religion with any other religion already constitutes an affront to the Jewish G-d, as if to imply that there is something substantial shared in common between the two.

Schachter supported these decrees by copious footnotes referring readers to a variety of Talmudic sources and discussions of Rabbi Soloveitchik's thinking as well as that of Samson Raphael Hirsch, the great avatar of German modern Orthodoxy; there was even a reference to an article in the *New York Times*. Clearly this message was directed to an Orthodox audience identified with the putative modernism and culturally integrative values associated with it, a population that reads and is familiar with Torah sources but also reads the newspaper and watches television. This is not a message for Haredim. Yet it is a Haredi message, for it clearly resonates with the religious sectarianism, insularity, and sense of superiority that is taken for granted among the Haredi Orthodox. The reference to the Holocaust, in terms common among the Haredim, is also there when Schachter adds, "The chosenness of our people is everlasting, even during periods of churban and after." On another occasion, the same Rabbi Schachter, speaking at a suburban centrist Orthodox synagogue, asserted in an even more religiously chauvinistic tone, "[W]e believe that the *neshama* [soul] of the Jew and the *neshama* of the non-Jew are made of different material," adding in a kind of pseudoscience that Jews "have it in our genes" that they are the chosen people.[125] Here is outcasting raised to the level of theology.

This assertive exclusivism and sectarianism, so essential to Haredi Orthodoxy, has increasingly made inroads into the rest of Orthodoxy. What were once common aspirations among the modern Orthodox—such as living in areas that were not exclusively populated by Orthodox Jews like themselves, having engaging relationships with non-Jews, passing as non-Orthodox, and even the once high-cultural goal of attending an elite university in order to pursue a professional career not at all tied to Judaism—are no longer expressed without reservation. When the university, American culture, and the non-Orthodox are all outcast as leading to the endangerment of Orthodox survival, it becomes difficult to continue to embrace them enthusiastically. The demand in the late 1990s of five centrist Orthodox Jewish undergraduates at Yale to be exempt from residence in the co-ed college dormitories because they argued that by living there in a pluralist and permissive environment they would be exposed to life-styles and practices that undermined their Jewish commitments exemplifies these reservations.[126] The comments by Rabbi Herschel Schachter that the religious requirement to avoid "idol worship" must be understood as a prohibition by Jews to have supportive interaction with Gentiles or to even learn about Christianity (including even watching a mass on television in the privacy of one's own home) likewise illustrate this turning away from anything that is not exclusively Orthodox Jewish. Indeed, as Schachter continued, the moment the Jews were given "equal rights" with the Gentiles, they took the step away from the sectarianism and exclusivism that alone would save them.[127] Even the democratic principles of Americanism are suspect in the new enclavist Orthodox worldview.

Perhaps one additional and important factor helped support the tilt in favor of a more assertive traditionalism and Haredi Orthodoxy. During the opening years of the current century in America the notion of the superiority of secular society began to come under increasing attack by a rising national appreciation and idealization of religion, a phenomenon that some have dubbed the "Third Great Awakening," a religious revival to rival the so-called Great Awakening of 1735–44 and the Second Great Awakening of 1790–1830.[128] This had been building throughout the last quarter of the preceding century with the rise of the Christian right and its success in infiltrating mainstream American society and culture. During these same years in America, Christian fundamentalism was becoming ever more public in its demands on the culture. In the spring of 1980, for example, a huge prayer vigil was held on the Mall in Washington, D.C. Believers were expressing the desire for their churches to become more assertive in determining the direction and character of American life and to preach about every issue, including politics, social issues, and education. Some saw this as a belated response to the upheavals of the late 1960s and the decade that followed. As enthusiasm built for a nationwide Christian movement, Jerry Falwell and the Moral Majority, a multidenominational political organization, came to prominence. Falwell then undertook an ambitious recruiting campaign, speaking in all fifty state capitals. Other leaders also used the media to spread their message of conservative Christianity. Indeed, already in 1966, the Christian Broadcasting Network began airing Pat Robertson's 700 Club, among the most influential programs in the spread of this sort of message. By the 1980s soon-to-be President Ronald Reagan was endorsing the methods and many of the views of the Moral Majority when he addressed a group of Christian leaders in Denver, and in 1985 on the Robertson program Reagan would assert, "I am convinced this is a nation under God. And as long as we recognize that and believe that, I think He'll help us."[129]

By the year 2000 a November Public Agenda poll, for example, demonstrated that, by overwhelming majorities, "Americans want religion to play a greater role in public life" and that large numbers believed (perhaps with an exaggerated utopianism) that if Americans were more deeply religious they would do more volunteer work, be better at raising their children, engage in far less crime, and even diminish greed and materialism.[130] This was an environment in which being an openly Orthodox Jew for whom religion was very important was acceptable, even admirable, no less than being openly evangelical. In this atmosphere of a newly assertive religion that expressed attachments to fundamentalist-like faith, traditionally Orthodox Jews could easily say they felt no less convinced. Indeed, in these days they may have even have begun to feel more common cause with their Christian counterparts than with their liberal co-religionists.[131] In short, when Christians are more assertively Christian, Orthodox Jews of all stripes can be more assertively Jewish. That is what seems to have happened in recent years.

The journey from post-Holocaust survival to a rightward inclination among American Orthodox Jews is seen in a variety of concrete ways. It displays itself in demographic trends, however subtly. It reveals itself in the way that going by the book has begun to dominate Orthodoxy in America, and in the transformation of Orthodox Jewish education. It even shows itself in the posters the Orthodox put on the walls of their neighborhoods, in their communications among themselves. But this trend does not go on unimpeded. There are points of resistance. For the Haredim resistance comes in the economic realities that this kind of Orthodoxy imposes upon its adherents. For the contrapuntalists, the resistance comes in the lives of some recent college graduates and adolescents. We shall turn to these issues in later chapters.

First, however, let us turn to the numbers. How many Orthodox Jews are there in America? Have these numbers shrunk or expanded? How many of these Jews are what have been called enclavists or Haredi, and how many are contrapuntalists? Finally, what do the numbers tell us? These concerns are next.

CHAPTER 2

The Numbers

"Our survival has never been determined by our number . . . .
On the contrary, in our small numbers lies our strength."

Rabbi Yaakov Haber, "The Strength of the Few"

How Many Orthodox Jews Are There in America?

A number of years ago, the late Daniel Elazar explored the question of Orthodox demography under the provocative title "How Strong Is Orthodox Judaism—Really?"[1] While he looked at Jews the world over, he based his estimates on the 1970 National Jewish Population Survey (NJPS), which found a total of 600,000, constituting 11 percent of American Jewry at the time. This was also, by his calculation, about 11 percent of a worldwide total of 5.5 million who, he stated, identified with Orthodoxy, "whatever their level of personal observance." Realizing that the actual number did not tell the whole story, he added that a significant number (he did not say how many, since the surveys did not provide that information) were "nominal in their commitment" and that those should probably dropped from the count, although he decided not to drop them on the assumption that, if people *choose* to call themselves Orthodox, those who count them need to believe them. Nevertheless, he concluded that while Orthodox numbers had for generations been "declining precipitously," the decline had by the beginning of the 1970s "probably bottomed out." Moreover, with the dropping out of the nominally Orthodox, those remaining were probably harder core and therefore less likely to switch out of the movement.

This last point is important. In Elazar's analysis a hard core was critical for establishing a stable demographic future, and it affected how one understood the numbers. Six hundred thousand people of whom a third are only nominally Orthodox is fundamentally different from an identical number among whom Orthodox commitments are powerful and consuming. Similarly, 600,000 among whom more than a third are insular Haredim is different from the same number among whom only 20 percent are. Numbers alone, then, do not tell the whole story of Orthodoxy in America.

With these caveats in mind, we can look at today's numbers. The proportion of Jews who call themselves Orthodox in today's American Jewish population is smaller than it was in earlier years, when so many of the Jewish immigrants who came to the New World were nominally attached to traditional religious identities and were in retrospect often called Orthodox.[2] Exact or reliable figures are hard to come by for those early years, and even data for the 1940s and 1950s, when the forebears of many if not most of those who fill the ranks of today's Orthodoxy arrived as war refugees or Holocaust survivors, are more a product of estimations and often guesses. In part this is because the best count of Americans, the U.S. Census, has for the most part never asked questions about religious identity.[3] This has left the counting to projective surveys done by the Jews themselves at both the national and local levels. The most recent of these, including most prominently the 2002 NJPS, find the proportion of American Jews who call themselves Orthodox to be somewhere around 10 percent of those who self-identify as Jews. If we enlarge the overall total to include as well all "persons of Jewish birth," even if they do not self-identify as Jews, the proportion of Orthodox falls to 8 percent.[4] That puts the number somewhere around 520,000, which includes 420,000 Orthodox Jews eighteen years old and over. Given that there is strong evidence of an undercount in the 2002 survey, that many of the Haredi Orthodox—most of whom have many children—do not respond to surveys, and that Orthodox Jews are overrepresented in senior citizen facilities that are harder to poll, the figure of American Orthodox Jews is probably closer to the figure of 500,000 above age eighteen.[5] If we add to that the 20 percent that by the NJPS 2002 count constitutes children under the age of eighteen, the number rises to 600,000. But perhaps a figure of 20 percent under age eighteen is low. As we shall see below, in a number of Haredi enclaves those figures approach 50 percent. Thus the overall figure of those under eighteen could rise on average to around 30 percent, raising the overall American Orthodox population to about 650,000.

On its face, this represents only at most an 8 percent increase in the thirty years since 1970. To be sure, this is a growth that exceeds that of the general American Jewish population, which according to the NJPS surveys numbered about 5,400,000 in 1970 and probably about 5,500,000 in 2001. But keeping in mind that the people who today call themselves Orthodox are not like those who so identified themselves in the past, we must see this figure as reflecting an even stronger showing for the move-

ment than the number itself indicates. This latest NJPS estimate is in
marked contrast to the Orthodox figures reported in 1990, when estimates
based on the NJPS put the Orthodox in America at around 7.5 percent of
5,515,000, or somewhere around 414,000. Hence the indication that the
Orthodox in America are back up at least to 1970 figures is quite significant
news. But the numbers may be even higher.

Preliminary data from the 2000 U.S. Census for two almost completely
Haredi Orthodox villages in suburban New York—namely, Kiryas Joel,
home to Satmar Hasidim, with a population of 13,000, and New Square,
a Skvirer Hasidic enclave with a population of 4,600—reveal astonishing population increases of 80 and 67 percent respectively since 1990. The
former has grown by 13.5 percent in the two years following the 2000 census and is expanding beyond its 1.1 square miles, and the latter has grown
by 14.4 percent in the same period.[6] While these figures may come from
in-migration as well as the high birthrate in these places (the median age
in both places is about fourteen years), and while they do not necessarily
reflect the general growth rate in other Orthodox populations, they are
not insignificant. In Kaser, a village north of New York City in which, according to the 2000 census, there are 3,300 people, almost all of whom
are Wiznitzer Hasidim, 46 percent are below the age of fourteen, and by
2002 the median age was just over fifteen.

Lakewood, once a rural village in New Jersey midway between New
York City and Philadelphia, where on the eve of the Second World War
Rabbi Aaron Kotler replanted the famous Beth Midrash Govoha Yeshiva
(with a full-time enrollment of just under 3,000 in 2002), has, as the 2000
U.S. Census reveals, mushroomed into a Haredi Orthodox enclave of approximately 25,000 souls out of a total of 38,000 Orthodox Jews, all living within a mile radius of the school and its associated institutions. These
include at least six more Orthodox schools that in total enroll approximately another 1,000. The Orthodox Jewish population is growing, with
some of the census tracts having average family sizes ranging from 4.9 to
6.2 and over 1,000 households having seven or more persons living in
them.[7]

Moreover, the 2002 New York Jewish Community Study, which surveyed the city's five boroughs as well as Long Island and Westchester
County, found that Jews calling themselves Orthodox were one in every
five they surveyed, or about 19 percent of the respondents (up from 13
percent just ten years earlier).[8] This translates to approximately 110,000
Orthodox households in the survey (assuming at least one Orthodox Jew
per household, the respondent). There were on average 3.4 Jewish per-

sons per household in the entire survey and about 378,000 persons in households where there was an Orthodox respondent. Assuming that in the overwhelming number of households where one member is Orthodox the others are also (there are of course cases where one member is newly Orthodox and the others are not Orthodox at all), we reach a number of Orthodox Jews in the survey area of at least 375,000.[9] Since many of the most Haredi Jews live in Brooklyn (from which nearly 54 percent of the Orthodox respondents came), and since their birthrates have been skyrocketing (indeed, among those who still call themselves Orthodox the birthrate is the highest of all American Jewish denominations), the likelihood that even this figure is an underestimate is great. Hence we may be approaching 400,000 Orthodox Jews in the New York metropolitan areas covered by the 2002 survey.

If we add just the 13,000 of Kiryas Joel and the 3,200 of Kaser from Orange County, along with the 4,600 of New Square from Rockland County in New York, the numbers come to nearly 420,800. This is without counting the city of Monsey in Rockland, where there are at least 20,000 Orthodox (about 6,000 of whom speak only Yiddish, a characteristic common among the Hasidim and older Haredi Jews). This would bring the New York State numbers to about 440,800.

Orthodox Jews of metropolitan Lakewood, New Jersey, add about 38,000. Add to that Orthodox enclaves like those in Greater Baltimore, where there are about 15,500 (17 percent of the nearly 100,000 persons living in Jewish households in 1999);[10] Los Angeles, with about 28,000 as of 1997;[11] the Midwest communities in Greater Cleveland, Columbus, Toledo, Youngstown, Dayton, and Akron, Ohio, St. Louis, Missouri, and vicinity, and Milwaukee, Wisconsin, with about 26,000;[12] southern Florida, with about 45,000;[13] and about 100,000 more from all the states with significant Jewish populations, and adjusting for growth, we get a grand total of around 700,000 in 2001.[14] That would put the Orthodox in America at about 13 percent of the Jewish population in 2002—almost double what the 1990 NJPS claimed. For a group whose experience in the last century was one of ongoing diminution and contraction, this is an extraordinary turnaround.

In 1990, researchers found large proportions of Jews who claimed to have been raised Orthodox but who were when surveyed self-identified as non-Orthodox (on average about 44 percent of Conservative Jews and about 15 percent of Reform). In fact, when we look at all of those who in the 1990 NJPS claimed they were raised Orthodox, only 20 percent of those still claimed to be Orthodox by 1989 when they were polled. These

TABLE 1. Percentages by Denomination for Jewish Adults (Age Eighteen or Above) Who Immigrated to America between 1938 and 1956 and for All American Jewish Adults

Denomination	1970 Immigrants, 1938–56	1970 All American Jewish Adults	1990 Immigrants, 1938–56	1990 All American Jewish Adults	2000 Immigrants, 1938–56	2000 All American Jewish Adults
Orthodox	25.1	10.8	14.8	5.8	16.5	7.9
Conservative	49.9	43.9	47.9	34.0	28.2	24.6
Reform	15.4	32.4	16.9	36.8	22.4	34.6
Others	9.6	12.9	20.4	23.8	32.9	32.9
Total	100	100	100	100	100	100

figures echoed the accepted wisdom that Orthodoxy was still the movement from which large numbers of Jews defected in favor of more liberal denominations.

Yet as the figures offered here indicate, this situation is changing rapidly. Part of the reason must surely be the impact of immigration. Until the Second World War many of the most dedicated Orthodox were reluctant to come to America. They were warned by many of their rabbinic leaders that America was a *trefe medina,* a defiled and defiling state, where Jews might survive physically but Judaism would not. They were urged to stay in the European enclaves where there was a rich Orthodox cultural life, where the synagogues and yeshivas were plentiful and rabbis were abundant. But when the Nazis began their campaign against Jews and Judaism, those who had stayed realized that the advice given by these leaders had been wrong. Indeed, although many of the same leaders who shunned immigration died with their followers, a number of them fled, leaving families and supporters behind. By the late 1930s and then after the war, Orthodox Jews were at last coming in significant numbers to America. These were, moreover, the most dedicated and hard-core of Orthodox Jews, far more loyal and committed to their Orthodoxy than most of their American counterparts. They were, as we saw in the previous chapter, profoundly affected by the Holocaust and the notion of the responsibilities that came with survival. They added a significant demographic to American Orthodoxy. We can see some of this in table 1, which shows the denominational distribution in 1970, 1990, and 2000 of Jews who immigrated to the United States between 1938 (the eve of the closing of the

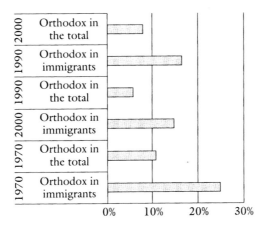

FIGURE 1: Proportion of Orthodox in U.S. population and among postwar immigrants, 1970–2000.

exits for European Jewry) and 1956 (when the last of the Holocaust survivors who came out of Hungary arrived) and for comparison the distribution of all American Jews (numbers are percentages)

This table teaches us several important things. By 1970, the year of the first of the reliable national Jewish population surveys, the proportion of those immigrants who remained Orthodox was over twice as high as those within the population overall. Figure 1 shows even more dramatically and graphically that the Orthodox were a significant proportion of the postwar immigrants.

These observant Jewish immigrants who came to America because of the Holocaust were less likely to abandon their Orthodoxy than others. Moreover, even though the number of the immigrant group who remained Orthodox had dropped twenty years later (perhaps in part because significant numbers of them had died and in part because some had left the movement), the ratio of those who remained Orthodox over time among the immigrants compared to the overall Orthodox population stayed demonstrably higher, by over two to one. Their numbers were augmented by a Haredi ethos that mandated early marriages and large families, considered an imperative of the Torah's commandment to "be fruitful and multiply." There are undoubtedly still defections from Orthodoxy as we enter the twenty-first century, but the decline of such defections is particularly striking among the young, many of them offspring and heirs of Orthodox immigrants and beneficiaries of the institutions they built.

More important than the figures demonstrating that many of today's Jewish non-Orthodox adults over fifty were once Orthodox is the fact that among young adults eighteen to twenty-nine years old who were raised Orthodox and who grew up in a self-assured and institutionally rich observant community bolstered by the post-Holocaust immigrant hard core, almost two-thirds are staying Orthodox—more than twice the retention rate of those aged thirty to forty-four and four times the rate of those aged forty-five to sixty-four.[15] Indeed, there is evidence that this trend is being maintained and perhaps even intensified. In comparison to the 1990 NJPS report that 20 percent of those who had been raised Orthodox were still Orthodox at the time of the survey, the 2002 NJPS gave the figure of 38 percent. That increase in the movement's retention of those it has raised can be explained only by recognizing that adulthood is for these young people no longer defined by religious "moving out." Something is happening in youth that is rooting today's Orthodox more firmly in their movement.

Perhaps nowhere is the tendency of the young to remain Orthodox more clearly seen than in one of the major American Orthodox youth organizations, the National Council of Synagogue Youth (NCSY). Formed in 1959, this synagogue-based association affiliated with the Union of Orthodox Jewish Congregations of America (OU) has grown to serve "tens of thousands" of young people across the United States and beyond.[16] Surveyed in 1999, 92 percent of its members claimed to be affiliated with a synagogue, and 80 percent of the men and nearly 50 percent of the women said they attended at least once a week. Almost half of those surveyed reported that during their years as members they had increased their level of religious observance, and another 16 percent said they had maintained a high level of observance; 58 percent said they were "more religious" at the time of the survey than when they had been raised. After high school, 40 percent continued their Jewish education, and half of all those surveyed attended a yeshiva educational program in Israel.[17] Sixty-five percent told researchers that they spent at least some time studying Jewish texts every week. Nearly all (96 percent) agreed with the dogma that the "Torah was revealed to Moses at Sinai," and a similar percentage agreed that religious faith was "very important" in their lives. Perhaps most significantly, 94 percent of those who said they had been Orthodox while in high school continued to so identify themselves afterwards.[18]

These figures are confirmed by visits to Orthodox synagogues, where young people—those younger than thirty—are ubiquitous, in stark contrast to congregations in non-Orthodox synagogues, which tend increasingly to be peopled by those in their middle and senior years. Moreover, the young are found in attendance not just on Sabbaths and holy days but far more frequently. They are as likely to be there to study Torah or to be engaged in some other activity with their fellow members as to worship, actively expressing their institutional and communal commitments to Orthodoxy. This is surely a reversal of what in the past was typically true for Orthodox synagogues: that they were a collection of old men at worship.

How Many Are Haredim?

One of the most pressing questions in counting Orthodox Jews has been the precise proportion of these Jews who today might be termed Haredim. The very question shows that the label *Orthodox* does not always mean the same thing to all those who identify themselves as such or to others who tag them as such. Moreover, when we talk about Orthodoxy in general and Haredim in particular, we need to recognize that community standards vary somewhat from place to place. Wearing a black hat may cause one to be identified as a Haredi in Baltimore or Los Angeles, but much more may be required in Brooklyn. Moreover, persons may act Haredi when they are in the Orthodox enclave but act in less insular and contra-acculturative ways when they are out and about during the workweek. That is, the choice is not *either* modern *or* Haredi Orthodox; it may also be *both* modern *and* Haredi. As the previous chapter suggested and as the rest of this book will show, the differences between the acculturative contrapuntalists and the contra-acculturative enclavist Haredim are often nuanced, particularly as one reaches the margins of each group. There people may move back and forth between the two, sometimes taking a Haredi, sectarian, enclavist view and other times moving toward a more open, pluralist contrapuntalism. This may be particularly true in times of transition when the norms of Orthodoxy are going through change—as they appear to be at present.

Assuming one can properly make such distinctions in demographic terms, the second and related question is whether this fraction has grown, shrunk, or remained stable. There are difficulties in getting these numbers. While one can define some of the essential ideological and characterological features of Haredim, it is far harder to categorically define particular Orthodox Jews as such and hence to distill them into numbers. Thus even were one able to count each one of these people the decision of which "column" to put them in would be anything but obvious.

Second, unlike the case in Israel, where the number of Haredim can be estimated on the basis of ballots for Haredi political parties, in the United States there are no such elections. To be sure, by no means are all voters who support Haredi parties in Israel necessarily Haredi; the case of the voters for the Haredi Shas party stands out here because most of its electorate is far from Haredi. Moreover, most counts in America are based on projections from surveys. In such surveys, the distinctions between Haredi and Orthodox are not commonly made. The question in the 2002 New York Jewish Community Study that distinguished among the Orthodox between those who thought that giving their children a college education was either somewhat or not very important and those who thought it very important was an effort to draw this distinction by implication, since Haredim view college as at best a religious trial and at worst a moral danger. On the basis of that survey, we might estimate that about 25 percent hold a Haredi attitude. But this number is problematic as well. Some of those who thought that college education was "somewhat important" might have been Haredi or tending in that direction. To be sure, they might be those who acknowledged the need for some instruction beyond the purely Jewish one because they might see a need to learn a skill that would enable them to support themselves financially.[19] Thus, while 25 percent might provide us with a useful minimum proportion of Haredim in this survey area, other calculations could raise the figure. And the figure is only for the counties around metropolitan New York City that were part of this 2002 study. There are other places where the Haredi Orthodox have established communities. How are they to be counted?

I have in fact found some characteristics that can help one get a count of those inhabiting Haredi enclaves. My method was as follows. First, I located Haredi institutions, primarily synagogues and yeshivas that hold prayer services, by consulting a number of institutional lists and a particularly useful Web site, www.godaven.com, which lists the times and locations of daily prayer services throughout the United States. The locations that provide a multiplicity of prayer times are commonly located in communities with large Orthodox populations that can sustain them. In fact, such a plethora of religious services is commonly a feature of Haredi Orthodox communities.

Because of their strict adherence to the prohibition of motorized transportation on Sabbaths and holy days, Orthodox Jews keep their synagogues within walking distance of their congregants' homes. By taking an area included in a mile radius surrounding religious institutions with multiple prayer services, one can use U.S. Census data to locate enclaves in which there are likely to be Haredim or their sympathizers. To do this we look at information the census gathers, including number of children in household, language spoken at home other than English, family income, private education for the children, and the extent of secular education. The census also asks about race. Thus if we locate non-Hispanic whites who may speak Yiddish at home (the language of choice for many Haredim), who have a large number of children at home under the age of eighteen, who have a low family income (common particularly to Haredim with their large families), who have little or no college education, and yet who almost universally provide their offspring with private schooling (i.e., yeshiva or day school education), all of whom live within walking distance of these synagogues, we can get a good idea of the number of Haredim. Adding these figures together, we can then see what proportion of the 650,000 to 700,000 Orthodox Jews might be within the Haredi framework. While this is a far from foolproof method for getting accurate figures, it nonetheless gives us a useful basis for reaching some tentative figures.

Using this methodology, I examined a number of locations in America known for having Haredi institutions and populations. Included here were areas in metropolitan New York and the nearby suburbs (including Kiryas Joel, New Square, and Kesar) that are still the heartland of American Haredi orthodoxy. I looked as well at neighborhoods in Lakewood, New Jersey, and vicinity, Baltimore and vicinity, Cleveland and its outskirts, metropolitan Chicago, and Los Angeles. In some cases I went to the census block level, particularly at a neighborhood's margins. The difficulties here were the speed with which many of these neighborhoods were expanding, a growth sometimes marked by changing maps of *eruvs*, or bounded Orthodox enclaves.[20]

Because Orthodoxy is so large a part of the New York Jewish community, as already indicated, it is appropriate to look more closely at the numbers here. Although a widely distributed Jewish newspaper in 2004 put the number of Orthodox in large families in New York City, the sort of families that characterize Haredim, at 60,000, a closer look will reveal this figure to be a considerable undercount of Haredim.[21] Where might these Jews come from? The 2002 New York Jewish community study helps us locate some of the major Orthodox areas of residence. In New York City proper, these include Kingsbridge/Riverdale in the Bronx, where the Orthodox constitute the largest denomination, 28 percent, or about 6,000.[22] There are Orthodox in other areas of the borough, such as Pelham Parkway and Co-Op City, but they constitute a small and shrinking community, about 12 percent in 2002, significantly below the overall average of 20 percent that the survey found in all of New York. While there are a few Haredi institutions in the Bronx and in Riverdale (the most prominent being a branch of the Telshe Yeshiva), the population here is overwhelmingly affiliated with modern or centrist Orthodoxy. Indeed, some of the best-known modern Orthodox institutions, such as Yeshivat Chovevei Torah, a new rabbinical seminary, originated here.

Manhattan, once an area of significant Orthodox residence, particularly on the Lower East Side, is no longer a place where one will find large numbers. The Lower East Side in 2002, whose number of Jewish households has fallen in the last ten years, counts only about 4 percent Orthodox; much of this neighborhood is today filled largely by Asian minorities. To be sure, an enormous number of the Orthodox residents (81 percent) send or sent their children to day schools or yeshivas. While about 10 percent of the Jews on the Upper East Side are Orthodox, it is not likely that many of these are Haredi, since very few if any Haredi institutions are located there. Much the same could be said about those 14 percent Orthodox who make up the Jewish residents of the Upper West Side.

In Staten Island about 12 percent of the 52,000 residents who live in Jewish households are Orthodox. While a majority of the synagogues in the borough have the characteristics of Haredi or traditionalist institutions, this itself does not mean that a majority of the Orthodox are Haredi. Given that not all synagogues are identical in the size of their membership and that some people hold membership in more than one such institution, it is difficult to be certain how many Haredim there are among the 6,000 Orthodox Jews purely by counting Haredi institutions. Nevertheless, the small overall number of Orthodox in Staten Island suggests that even if a quarter of these, about 1,500, were Haredi, the total would not be a large part of the general Orthodox population of New York.

Brooklyn is another story. Here a significant proportion of Orthodox Jewry is to be found. As the 2002 survey's authors explained, "[I]n contrast to the eight-county region, where the largest proportion of respondents describe themselves as Reform (29 percent) or Conservative (26 percent), in Brooklyn, the largest proportion of those interviewed (37 percent) describe themselves as Orthodox." Moreover, Brooklyn Jewish households are more likely to contain a child aged seventeen or under (30 percent) than the overall eight-county area (23 percent), a characteristic in line with Orthodox behavior in general and Haredi behavior in particular. Forty-three percent of those surveyed in Brooklyn keep kosher, nearly twice as many as in the survey area taken as a whole. Finally, there are twice as many Holocaust survivors in Brooklyn as in the survey area as a whole.[23] Within Brooklyn, several neighborhoods stand out as particular centers of Orthodox concentration. These are Borough Park, where, out of the 160,000 residents counted in the 2000 U.S. Census, 82,600 or 51 percent live in Jewish households and nearly three-quarters identified as Orthodox. A second such neighborhood is Flatbush/ Midwood/Kensington, where about 107,800 live in Jewish households, constituting about 48 percent of the residents, and 52 percent of those in Jewish households call themselves Orthodox. Williamsburg, with 57,600 people in Jewish households, who constitute 38 percent of the whole, is also a heavily Orthodox neighborhood where almost all Orthodox residents are Hasidic. Finally, Crown Heights and Kensington neighborhoods, the former of which is dominated by the 8,700 Lubavitcher Hasidim, has about 21,600 people in Jewish households, making up about 48 percent of the total population. While there are significant numbers of Jews elsewhere in the borough, these four neighborhoods constitute the largest concentrations of the Orthodox. For those who recall the history of Orthodox Brooklyn this may seem like a decline, since formerly Orthodox Jews lived in many other areas there. On the other hand, the extent to which the Orthodox dominate Jewish life in these four neighborhoods today suggests that *vitality* is a more appropriate descriptor than *decline*. Indeed, in these neighborhoods Jewish households have actually increased in the last ten years, bucking the overall trend in New York City. Borough Park has grown from 15,700 to 21,600, Flatbush from 24,700 to 32,500, and Williamsburg from 12,000 to an astounding 57,600. To be sure, this last figure includes non–Orthodox Jewish people who have moved into the lofts and apartments that have recently made parts of this neighborhood an artists' colony and young singles' mecca.

Not surprisingly, given that the Orthodox constitute the poorest of denominations and the Haredim the poorest among the Orthodox, we find that 55 percent of these Brooklyn Jewish households have an income under $35,000 per annum and 52 percent report that they cannot make ends meet or are just managing. Nevertheless, fully 85 percent report past or current day school or yeshiva education for their children.[24] In Borough Park, 63 percent have annual incomes under $35,000, yet 76 percent provide their children with past or current day school or yeshiva education. In Flatbush, where 46 percent of the Jewish households earn less than $35,000 a year, 92 percent now or in the past provided day school or yeshiva education. In Williamsburg, where 92 percent of the respondents identified as Orthodox (and 54 percent in Jewish households are under seventeen years of age), 64 percent have incomes under $35,000, and 98 percent give their children a day school or yeshiva education. Given these numbers it is fair to estimate that about 207,000 Orthodox live in these Brooklyn areas and that about 36 percent or 75,000 of those probably qualify as Haredi by the criteria of large family, private education for their children, and proximity to Haredi institutions.

While the number of Jews in Queens, the last of the five boroughs in New York City, has dropped in the last ten years from 233,000 to just over 185,000, this county, with a 20 percent Orthodox population, has achieved a reputation for a growing and vibrant Orthodox community in several of its neighborhoods. Among the areas commonly thus identified, Kew Gardens Hills/Fresh Meadows/Hillside with 28,200 Jews, Rego Park, and Forest Hills (with just over 39,000) stand out. Commonly, these neighborhoods have been associated with modern or centrist Orthodoxy. While the first of these, Kew Gardens Hills, has actually lost about 9,000 Jews in the last ten years, there has been an influx of Jews from the former Soviet republics in Central Asia, and a number of them have become associated with Orthodox institutions, particularly day schools. Yet this population does not constitute most of the Orthodox in Queens. The Jewish population numbers in Rego Park and Forest Hills have remained more or less stable.

In the Kew Gardens Hills area, the Orthodox, at 51 percent of the population, make up the largest group by far. Ninety-two percent of those here send or sent their children to day schools or yeshivas, even though the same proportion claim to find it hard to make "ends meet or to be just managing" to do so. Exactly what proportion of these Jews is Haredi is difficult to gauge, but about 11 percent have five or more people in the household. If there about 15,000 Orthodox in the area, we might estimate about 1,500 or 10 percent to be Haredi, at least on the basis of household size. In Rego Park and Forest Hills, only about 16 percent, or about 6,700, are Orthodox, and about 6 percent of these, or 400, would qualify by the same logic to be Haredi. Other areas in the borough with Orthodox Jews, including such neighborhoods as Hillcrest, Far Rockaway, and Baychester, add about 16,000 Orthodox, about 10 percent of whom qualify as Haredi in some way. Totaling all these numbers, we come to just under 3,600 Haredi Jews in Queens. Summarizing all this we arrive at the figures given in table 2.

Now let us look at the numbers from areas outside the New York metropolitan region. On the basis of the criteria already mentioned for identifying likely Haredi populations, we have about 16,000 in Los Angeles,

TABLE 2. Estimated Number of Haredim
in Selected Locations

Location	No. of Haredim
Bronx	2,000
Brooklyn	75,000
Queens	3,600
Staten Island	1,500
Manhattan	1,000
Kiryas Joel, New Square, Kesar	20,800
Monsey, NY	11,000
Lakewood, NJ	25,000
New Jersey, except Lakewood	3,000
Total	143,000

12,500 in Baltimore and vicinity, and just over 8,000 in and around Cleveland, bringing us to a total of 179,500. In the rest of the United States, which includes areas like Skokie outside Chicago, Boston and vicinity in Massachusetts, southern Florida, the area in and around Philadelphia, Pittsburgh and Scranton, Pennsylvania, and even suburban Connecticut, there are at least 8,500 and perhaps as many as 28,000, thus bringing the figure of Haredim to an approximate grand total of 188,000 to 207,500.[25]

In his census of Jewish education in the United States as of 2004, Marvin Schick offers figures that largely support this estimate.[26] He finds 48,446 students from four-year-olds through twelfth graders in Hasidic schools. He finds 8,609 in Lubavitcher schools, but because these are commonly outreach schools, only at most half of those might reasonably be expected to be truly Hasidic or about 4,000, which is quite generous. That puts the figure at about 53,000, or about 3,800 per category (fourteen year-categories for four-year-olds through twelfth graders). Now if we add four more categories for the preschoolers under four years old, that adds 15,200. That would put the number of Hasidic children at about 68,000. Assuming that families have about five children on average (maybe an undercount) and commonly two parents, 27,200 parents could be added to the number. The total would then be approximately 95,200 Hasidim in the United States. Now, most observers have argued that Hasidim constitute the majority of Haredim in this country. Others contend that the proportion is closer to half. Assuming the latter (which would be the more demographically generous estimate) would lead to a figure of approxi-

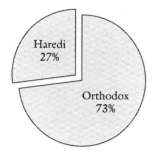
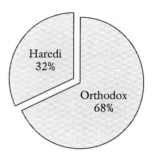

FIGURE 2: Proportion of Haredim among the Orthodox (lower estimate).

FIGURE 3: Proportion of Haredim among the Orthodox (upper estimate).

mately 200,000 Haredi Orthodox Jews in the United States, a figure within the range suggested in the previous paragraph. By all approaches, therefore, one would have to conclude that the Haredim number at least 27 percent of American Orthodox Jews and perhaps as much as 32 percent (figures 2 and 3).

While these are not near-majorities, they do constitute a hard-core and aggressive minority, increasingly certain of themselves and their ability to thrive in America. Moreover, they are being infused by additional young people, in some measure via the higher birthrate among Haredim and in some by virtue of the attraction that Haredi Orthodoxy has nurtured among some modern Orthodox adolescents, as will become clear in the next chapter. Given the high visibility of the Haredi minority and, as subsequent pages will show, their growing role in the rabbinate and other domains of Jewish religious life, these numbers become even more impressive.

Have the Haredim Grown as a Proportion of the Orthodox?

As difficult as the previous question was to answer, this one is even more difficult. People may be counted as Haredi because they are born into Haredi families or because they become transformed into Haredim as a result of changing outlook and conviction. Moreover, transformations are not always categorical or complete; many of the Orthodox begin by shifting back and forth between Haredism, traditionalism, and nuances between the two. Exactly when in their religious journeys they should be counted is difficult to determine. Even those who become, say, Lubavitcher Hasidim do not get a membership card or go through some unequivocal conversion after which they may be counted as insiders. Does one count them when they begin to observe the Sabbath, keep kosher, put on a black hat, begin reading the Lubavitch literature, or simply step into a Chabad house? There are no categorical answers. Much the same could be said about the ideological shift that makes one Haredi.

While I am unprepared to give a definitive answer to these questions in demographic terms and therefore unable to measure change, a look at the two villages of Kiryas Joel and New Square can give a hint of an answer. We have already seen that they had population increases of 80 and 67 percent between 1990 and 2000 and 13.5 and 14.4 percent in the two years following (which translates to about 68 and 72 percent by the time of the 2010 census). While Kiryas Joel and New Square may not be the paradigm for all Haredi Orthodox, this growth is extraordinary and eclipses that of the other Orthodox, which, while higher than that of other American Jews, is nowhere near this rate. By that measure alone, the Haredi population can certainly be assumed to have grown substantially in the last ten years. If the 27 to 32 percent Haredi proportion is the result of that sort of dramatic growth, a near-doubling, the scenario of growth into the future is one of a significant change in the character of American Orthodoxy.

Of course, there is no guarantee that all those born into Haredi families and communities will remain loyal to the enclave or the way of life in which they have been raised. Nor is it clear that these Jews will be able to economically sustain their way of life, dependent as it is on large numbers of males spending extended time engaged in study rather than gainful employment and on women having and rearing many children between the ages of eighteen and forty. But this takes us beyond the numbers and forces us to turn next to the content of Orthodox life.

Perhaps most prominent here has been the matter of Jewish education, which the quantitative data here have shown is considered essential by the Orthodox, for even when they do not seem to have the money for it they have chosen to give their children this sort of schooling. It is therefore to schooling we turn next in our examination of American Orthodoxy.

CHAPTER 3

Jewish Education as a Field
of Conflict within Orthodoxy

> The vitality of religion is shown by the way in which the
> religious spirit has survived the ordeal of religious education.
>
> Alfred North Whitehead, "The Rhythmic
> Claims of Freedom and Discipline"

"And you shall teach them diligently unto your children." This mandate,
repeated twice in the Bible (Deut. 6:7 and Deut. 11:19), is for the Orthodox a solemn responsibility by which they believe they will not only pass
the ancient sacred heritage of Jewish law and lore on to the next generation but thereby ensure Jewish continuity and survival. The only question is *how* best to accomplish this instruction. In the ongoing contest between the contrapuntalist and enclavist views of Orthodoxy, perhaps no
other question has been more debated. Once this teaching was the duty
of the parents, but ultimately the task was handed over to teachers and
institutions who acted in loco parentis. The battle over Jewish education
within Orthodoxy is not simply a struggle over pedagogic methods, curriculum, or other such details. Rather, it is a debate about who best can
carry out the duty of instruction, and it has become part of the ongoing
dispute as to how best remain true to Judaism in modern America. It is
also a struggle within Orthodoxy over which segment of this group has
the authority to determine "correct" Jewish behavior—"correct" here referring to behavior that is in line with Orthodox norms and will best ensure their continuity. In fact, it is part of a conflict that pits an essentially
fundamentalist view against one that sees itself as liberal and progressive,
albeit in a controlled way. It is a fight not only over Orthodox survival
but over which kind of Orthodoxy will survive. A look at the current state
of Orthodox Jewish education, moreover, helps one see which of the two
sides has captured the initiative and taken the lead in this contest.

To see how Jewish education became a primary field of conflict in the struggle between the modernist and Haredi tendencies in American Orthodoxy, therefore, one must first understand the ways Judaism, culture, and education are related to one another. One must then comprehend some basic characteristics of fundamentalism and how they enter into this relationship. Only then can the current state of affairs be properly understood.

Judaism, Culture, and Education

Narrowly defined, education is a process whose aims are to provide skills and information. But it is much more than that; it is also a tool of socialization, a means by which a culture sustains and renews itself. As such, education may be thought of as a form of enculturation, which at one extreme appears simply as instruction but at the other may blur with indoctrination and socialization.[1] When the nature of that culture is the subject of a contest—as, for example, in sectarian conflict—the issues of what should be taught, who should be the instructors, and how the education should proceed often become major battlefields of that conflict. This is because all sides recognize that through the educational process they are able not just to recruit adherents for their point of view but also to infuse them with deeply held convictions that will have long-term effects and consequences. The longer and the more comprehensive the control over education, the more important a tool it becomes in the determination of the outcome of the contest.[2]

Given all this, schools are cultural mirrors of the people who run them and who through them socially construct and transmit meaning. As such they are engaged in a process by which "contents of consciousness are transmitted."[3] The extent to which this is true becomes particularly apparent when the subjects of that education include values, ethos, worldviews, and religion; when the education deals not simply with a presentation of "the way things are" but also with the "shoulds and oughts," the ideas about how things and people are supposed to be.[4] Moreover, when the teachers are viewed not only as "experts" or among the "informed" but also as role models whose task is to transmit, by example as well as by pedagogy, how life ought to be lived, education becomes essentially a process whereby individuals transmit and absorb their group's culture.

This is especially the case when the persons in question—both the instructors and the instructed—understand themselves to be members of an endangered minority whose cultural survival must be ensured in the face of continued threats. One might even suggest that the greater the threat, or even only the perception of it, the more the indoctrinating and enculturating aspects of the education will be stressed. That emphasis will be either implicit or explicit, depending on the surrounding social and political conditions. When educators are feeling empowered and bold or alternatively desperate and critically endangered, they may become explicitly and aggressively indoctrinating. When, however, they sense that a full frontal assault against alternative models of behaving and thinking is culturally dangerous, they may operate in a more implicit, even camouflaged manner. This is particularly true for groups that feel they are engaged in a *Kulturkampf,* as is the case among religiously fundamentalist-like sects in contemporary society.

Finally, in an open and multicultural society, where migration from one to another culture is possible and sometimes even encouraged as part of the national ethos—as is certainly the case in the contemporary United States—an important part of the educational effort among those groups who are trying to hold onto their own becomes focused on persuading and warning their students (and often their families as well) that if they "move out" this will not be to their benefit but will rather lead to assimilation, cultural decline, or some other negative consequences, whereas if they remain inside they will remain protected and superior.[5]

All this is undoubtedly true in the case of the education of the American Orthodox Jews who are the subject of these pages. Acutely aware of being a minority in America—indeed a minority of a minority—whose future existence was for many years in question (and in the minds of some remains in doubt) and of being endowed with what, as I have argued, many have considered a solemn responsibility to survive and feeling anxiety about their strategy for doing so, the Orthodox have built much of their educational system on the premise that its purpose is not only to instruct Jews in the substance of Judaism—"the Torah and mitzvoth," as this substance is referred to in the language of Orthodoxy—but also to create a protective environment in which to carry out "communal efforts to promote Jewish continuity."[6] As such, they aim to make and indoctrinate Orthodox Jews as an essential part of the task of sustaining Orthodox Jewish culture. Some, drawing on the biblical injunction, see this as nothing short of "a religious deed."[7] Indeed, perhaps no other activity carried on by Orthodox Jews throughout their history in America has taken up more of their energy and resources than education. This is true for all Orthodox Jews, and even more so for the Haredi segment, who, in their heightened anxiety about Jewish continuity and integrity, have taken an antagonistic, powerfully contra-acculturative stance toward contemporary society, its values and lifestyle. In this regard, Haredim represent a religiously fundamentalist response to contemporary American life.

Jewish Fundamentalism

Although *religious fundamentalism* is a term historically associated with versions of American Protestantism and more recently has also been used to describe varieties of Islam as well as other non-Christian faiths, it has generic characteristics that seem to capture much that is essential to Haredi Orthodoxy. Commonly, we consider fundamentalist religion assertive and uncompromising in its attachment to what its adherents view as the authentic and hence "fundamental" tenets of the faith, often based on a reading of some authoritative, sacred text or series of texts. Conservative in outlook, such fundamentalisms assert the existence of an immutable and unchanging tradition, whose purity and truth they claim to guard and defend against a variety of contemporary defilements. Seeing the world as drawn sharply between good and evil, truth and lies, they disdain even relatively limited alterations in their historicized tradition, even and perhaps especially when the tenor of the times seems to demand accommodations. In their Manichean view, they assert that they alone comprehend the meaning of history, understand the significance of the present moment, and see how past and future are connected. Some may also believe that there is an end to history and that at the end (which some believe they can hasten) they alone will be among the saved. In all this, they assert that they are being scrupulously true to the tradition. Much if not all of this describes the situation of Haredim.

In that regard, as we shall see in greater detail in the next chapter, they have given enhanced authority to a variety of putatively sacred texts, to which they remain ever more scrupulously attached. This they believe prevents them from deviating from what they assert to be an immutable tradition, even when they are living in an environment like America, where change is endemic. We have seen how Haredim increasingly turned away from the American dream and engaged in what Mary Douglas has called "outcasting" and "downgrading" those outside their enclaves, devaluing the ways of Gentiles that they saw dominating America and all those who acculturated to it. They understand the rewards of the American dream to be transitory, counterfeit, and alien pleasures and therefore inappropriate for true Jews, which they assert themselves to be. In place of these rewards they emphasize the superiority and virtue of their intensely Orthodox and parochial way of life and extend the "power of exclusion" so that anything different is essentially defined as "abhorrent."[8] This includes non-Haredi practices and beliefs. Messianism also plays a role in this worldview—particularly among Lubavitcher Hasidim, as well as among a large number of those supporting expanding settlement in the land of Israel, many of whom live in Orthodox enclaves and have intensified their practice of Judaism because they are convinced that the time of redemption is at hand.[9]

Those alterations that the Orthodox fundamentalists have made in their way of life to adapt to contemporary realities they often explain as either ontologically minor or necessary as part of the effort to fight back against the dangers and threats of modern culture and society, which present them with what they view as a hostile environment for Judaism. To be sure, despite their views about the dangers of the contemporary American cultural environment, many fundamentalisms—and certainly American Haredi Orthodoxy qualifies here—actually thrive in an atmosphere of culture war, which enables these movements to rally their members and keep them from wavering. The capacity to hold onto their own is particularly important in societies that remain pluralist and open, where boundaries among various cultures and groups are easily crossed—as is the case in current American society.

To remain beyond the reach of "sinners" and the precincts of defilement, fundamentalists have often chosen various strategies. Some have embraced the idea of passive resistance. Choosing separation or exclusion, they create powerful boundaries between those who share their outlook and behavior and those who do not. Other fundamentalists have eschewed the quiescent keeping-to-themselves approach and engaged instead in active struggle against those they perceive as opposing (and therefore attacking) their way of life. The latter strategy of *Kulturkampf* is often pursued when fundamentalists feel that they can no longer remain exclusive and separate because the "enemy is at the gates," on the verge of infiltrating their world and defiling it—often by luring away the young (which is why education is such an important matter for them). They will also go on the attack if they are persuaded that their nemesis is weak and on the verge of collapse or if they believe the end of history is near. Should any of these conditions obtain, even the most quiescent fundamentalists may become engaged in active struggle, seizing every opportunity to undo and even obliterate those who oppose them and their way of life.

Haredi Orthodox Jews have acted on both these grounds, particularly in the arena of education. In their chosen insularity, they reject the ideal of the melting pot and mobility, embracing, among other things, the ideal of separate but equal, a standard that has been repudiated in the United States, where integration has been the goal for at least fifty years. At the same time, Haredim have stressed an alternative set of aspirations that increasingly have meant being part of what Menachem Friedman has called "a scholars' society." Full-fledged membership in this society entails engaging in an endless review of Talmud and associated literature, or marrying someone who is so occupied, and viewing this as the supreme and often only valid aspiration in life. It also increasingly requires conformity to ever more conservative behavior—going strictly by the book—allowing almost no room for an acceptance of cultural pluralism, in which other ways of living can be viewed as legitimate or appropriate for Jews. Ironically, this sort of cultural chauvinism is more easily sustained in an atmosphere of American multiculturalism (the melting-pot ideal that preceded it demanded far more in the way of assimilation), which allows for particularism and ethnic pride without sacrificing one's right to American rights and privileges.[10] "We have a *hakaras ha'tov* [recognition of the goodness] of America," as one Haredi put it, "but its culture is not our culture. If in [a multicultural] America we can be a culture apart within a patchwork quilt, that's the best any society could give us Jews."

At first, Haredim did not go much beyond this, satisfied to think and persuade themselves that they were the only authentic Jews and using the public square outside their enclaves as a negative identifier, a place that helped define who they were *not*. Perceiving themselves as still trying to survive the ravages of massive assimilation, which had for generations led to Jews leaving Orthodoxy, as well as the consequences of the Holocaust and its dislocations, they characterized themselves, in the words of one, as "still busy rebuilding, imbuing our children with our ideas and reaching out to people who are leaving."[11] Lately, however, that quiescence and insularity has been turning toward greater activism. This does not consist merely of trying to retrieve the nonobservant in missionizing characteristic of Lubavitchers and others. It also is expressed in an undermining of the confidence of modernists and others who do not accept the Jewish fundamentalist view and cultural insularity by publicly asserting that those who are out of bounds are on the road to oblivion.

In some cases this has occurred because the Haredim find popular American culture encroaching into their domains, already within their gates—often via the modern Orthodox who have repeated contact with them—and feel they have to fight back to push it out. In other cases, it has come about because the Haredi world is convinced that Jewry beyond its domains is on the verge of collapse, ready to be finished off or transformed. Part of this strategy is to mount a continuing and increasingly vociferous discrediting of American values and behaviors as well as those that have been integrated into Judaism. Looking at an America that they, like many in the Christian right, perceive to be falling apart as a result of the radical changes perpetrated by a liberal agenda, they are ready to join with other conservative forces to destabilize and defeat that agenda.

As we have seen, the modern Orthodox did not identify with these efforts. They were ready to take advantage of the liberalism and openness of American life, seeing much of value there. They shunned fundamentalist stances, seeing little or no need to fight back against or insulate themselves from America. Rather, they wanted to carve out a covenant with America that would allow some sort of shared relationship along with a level of separate cultural integrity for their own Jewish way of life: acculturation without assimilation.[12] Only later, as I shall argue below, did they begin to have doubts about their strategies and outlook. These differences between the two trends in Orthodoxy crystallized and can be seen most vividly in the domains of Jewish education.

Jewish Education as the Field of Conflict

In America, two educational institutions evolved as part of these alternative Orthodox cultural stances: the day school and the yeshiva. While some confuse these two types of schools, in part because the word *yeshiva* has often been used in the names of many day schools and because the two types of schools share many characteristics, the two differ in important ways. Moreover, the proponents of each believe that their type of institution is the optimal one for ensuring the continuity of Orthodoxy in America. The differences over which institution better preserves the Orthodox future in a sense parallel the differences that we have already described between modern and Haredi Orthodoxies. The effort to bridge or even blur the difference has become the province of what we have called the "centrist" and "traditionalist" sectors.

THE AMERICAN YESHIVA

In its original incarnation, the old-line American yeshiva (modeled on the European school) was an institution whose principal curriculum was Judaica, and in particular Talmud and the commentaries and codes that emerged from it. In America within the traditionalist Orthodox community and among Haredim, the yeshiva was divided into three institutions: the so-called "yeshiva *ketana*," for primary school youngsters, the *mesivta* at the high school level, and finally the *kollel,* the tertiary-level place of learning for married men. The latter is essentially a yeshiva in which the students receive a stipend of sorts in return for dedicating themselves to Torah study. Normally, the amount of the stipend is insufficient for supporting even the smallest families, let alone the larger ones that are common among the Haredim, leaving wives (or the extended family) with a significant economic burden in addition to childbearing and rearing.

Women had their own versions of the first two, often called "seminaries," which included a separate curriculum. At the tertiary level, although recent developments (mostly in modern Orthodox domains) provide places for Jewish study, Haredi Orthodox women have generally served as so-called *kollel* wives, whose role has been to support and enable their husbands in their learning.

The yeshiva *ketana* was an institution that sought to prepare its students, primarily male, for the *mesivta,* which they would attend after bar mitzvah. It taught subjects other than Talmud, but originally it was meant to enable Talmudic skills. In America, however, where since the nineteenth century compulsory educational standards had been established, these institutions also taught general studies but did so grudgingly, regarding them as secondary and as deserving only minimal attention. Throughout all levels of the yeshiva, the attitude that viewed non-Jewish wisdom *(chochmas ha goyim)* as at best secondary and at worst irrelevant and defiling, and as taking precious time from Jewish learning, dominated the educational atmosphere. It was as if these two types of knowledge were in competition, but in that contest Jewish subjects were *ab initio* considered to be the winners.

Once an institution of the intellectual elite, a place where rabbis and Jewish scholars ruled, in time and in the face of social ferment and cultural change wrought by modernity the yeshiva became predominantly a protective fortress in which those who wished to create a barrier to change and erosion of Jewish identity found sanctuary. This was in contrast to the public school, where all kinds of Americans (and the cultures they carried with them) could be found and where change was the order of the day.

Because of the fears in the Orthodox enclaves about change, an inevitable correlate of the tight embrace of tradition, the American yeshiva mutated from an establishment that was highly selective regarding who could be a student to one that sought to include as many students as possible as part of the battle to save them from the seductions of American culture. Getting students into the yeshiva was perceived to be, as one rabbi put it, "literally the difference between [Jewish] life and death."[13] In these "bastions," rabbis were the heads, but they were not simply teachers; they became role models and defenders of the faith, and of an Orthodox Jewish way of life and values.

As such, yeshivas in America took certain ideological positions that became almost as (some might argue even more) important as their curriculum. These included a denial of the importance of any education that was not Jewish and, as a correlate, a devaluation of, if not an outright opposition to, the American goal of a university education. Not only was the university a place where all ideas were open to exploration and no knowledge was viewed as ontologically superior or sacrosanct (something that a Torah-dominated educational institution like a yeshiva could never tolerate), but also the college campus was more often than not a place where cultures and values became relativized, where "anything goes" attitudes were rampant. This was anathema to genuine yeshivas.[14]

As Orthodox bastions, yeshiva institutions wanted to operate according to their own norms and standards. The teaching of minimal general studies, often in the late afternoon (when attention tended to flag), reinforced the not-so-subtle message that such studies were of secondary importance. Indeed, there was an interest in teaching them minimally, for an ignorance of the secular world would limit the student's ability to exit the Haredi enclave and the yeshiva. Ignorance of the world outside the enclave was thus advantageous, especially when an America university education became available at some level to almost anyone who wanted to attend. With little general knowledge, the Haredim were less likely to leave what was, after all, a voluntary enclave to become citizens of the world. That was why even such subjects as physics, chemistry, geography, economics, and mathematics—which on their face seemed culturally neutral—were not taught in any but the most rudimentary way in the most insular contra-acculturative yeshivas. To be sure, Haredi yeshivas were also uncomfortable with courses of study that called into question the Orthodox belief that the world was just over five thousand seven hundred and sixty-five years old and created by God. On the other hand, some grudgingly granted the need to acquire degrees that would enable their possessors to be employed and hence to support Jewish families as well as Jewish causes and institutions.

The yeshivas also organized their calendar Jewishly, creating a temporal boundary between them and America. Instead of Thanksgiving or Christmas breaks, the schools would follow traditional Jewish calendars, closing during the Jewish holy days and running until the traditional recess of the Hebrew month of Av, falling in early summer. In addition, perhaps most obviously, the yeshiva was not going to be a place where coeducation had any quarter.

Yeshiva study was originally open only to males, on the basis of the "received wisdom" that Jewish law exempted women from the study of Torah, a principle enshrined in Maimonides' codification of the law.[15] Drawing on the Mishnah in Sota 3:4, Maimonides concluded that while women might study Bible, the so-called "written Torah," they were not to concern themselves with the "oral law" as redacted in the Talmud. That point of view pretty much dominated yeshiva education, which was overwhelmingly focused around oral law and Talmudic and rabbinic texts. While it was already recognized in medieval times that women needed to learn how to pray and to know some basic rules of Jewish law, this view did not measurably add to the level of Jewish education that most women received.[16] Much later, around the seventeenth century wealthy German Jews, following their non-Jewish counterparts, began to give their daughters "the rudiments of a general education—especially languages, literature, mathematics, and music."[17] During the Jewish enlightenment, the so-called *haskalah,* the idea of teaching Jewish women matters of Jewish substance grew in popularity, with some schools, like one in Dessau, Germany, teaching Jewish women "fundamentals of religion, Biblical history, Bible reading in German, translation of prayers, and Yiddish writing," and others adding such subjects as Hebrew language and Jewish handicrafts.[18] Among Orthodox Jews, the teaching of women was slower in coming. The German Jews, among whom the *haskalah* was most advanced, founded their first girls' school in 1827 in Halberstadt.[19] The reason governing this move was that women as mothers played a key role in the moral and religious education of their children; they therefore had to be Jewishly informed. But Samson Raphael Hirsch, a German rabbi known for his capacity to broaden the boundaries of what was acceptable within the worldview of Orthodoxy, concluded that at least insofar as the young were concerned there should be no difference in the Jewish education given girls and boys.[20] As his son, Mendel, principal of the Orthodox school in Frankfurt-am-Main, asked rhetorically in accounting for the curriculum in his institution: "Is there any difference between the sexes which would justify a substantive difference in the instruction and education we bestow upon our male and female youth?"[21]

A bit later, in 1917, this idea was also accepted among eastern European Orthodoxy when a Polish seamstress, Sarah Schnirer, returning from Austria, where she had been exposed to these German-Jewish Hirschian ideas, founded a school (sometimes called a "seminary," now the accepted term for girls' yeshivas) for Jewishly observant young women in Krakow, Poland. The seminary's stated, and for the time revolutionary, goal was to provide girls with some basic secular learning (Polish and German), vocational training, and religious Jewish studies.[22] With moral support from the Hasidic Rabbi Abraham Mordechai Alter of Gur and the scholar Rabbi Israel Meir Kagan, known by his nom de plume as the Chofetz Chaim (author of, among other texts, the code book *Mishneh Berurah*), and later gaining the sponsorship of the Agudath Israel movement, this school, named Bais Yaakov (Beth Jacob), would become the model for a whole series of women's seminaries during the 1930s in Poland, Lithuania, Latvia, and even Austria, and later in the century in America and Israel, where they became perhaps the closest thing to a women's yeshiva and *mesivta* in the Orthodox world.[23]

"The Beth Jacob School has as its goal the training of the Jewish woman to fulfill the commandments of the Torah and to educate its daughters in the Torah spirit," as Schnirer put it.[24] In the twenty-first century in America there are now a whole variety of such women's seminaries other than Bais Yaakov and even some tertiary-level institutions for married women.[25]

Other Orthodox groups also set up these women's schools. Today some of them are part of the outreach efforts of the Chabad Lubavitch movement; others are modernist in their orientation.[26] By now Orthodox girls have universally joined the ranks of Jews who are given a solid Jewish education from the primary grades through high school age, but especially in the last twenty years there has been an rapid proliferation of advanced Torah learning institutions and study circles that serve Orthodox women, many of whom now consider such study an obligatory element of their lives. To be sure, some of the women's institutions that developed in the wake of the feminist revolution in America became places where the purpose was not so much to keep the barriers up as to stress feminist-inspired Judaism. These latter sorts of women's institutes, which drew their inspiration from modernist tendencies that were then turned on their heads, sought to create intellectually and spiritually engaging educational schools that would provide women with no less of a religious challenge than men. In other words, these yeshivas were part of a somewhat radical modernist response to Haredi tendencies, even though in time the Haredi world made use of them too.[27]

Haredi resistance to coeducation remained powerful in America, and even after the idea of Jewish education for girls was accepted as a necessity among most Haredim, yeshivas largely refused to let girls learn the same subjects as boys. Even such a putatively lenient interpreter of the law as the late Rabbi Moshe Feinstein, head of the Mesivta Tiferes Yerushalayim Yeshiva in New York, took the view that, as he put it in a responsum written to a Detroit school principal, "according to all authorities, co-education is absolutely forbidden."[28] In addition, his contemporary the late Rabbi Aaron Kotler, head of the yeshiva in Lakewood, New Jersey, asserted that, from the fifth grade on, coeducation was prohibited.[29]

In the early years of the century, prohibitions against coeducation were sometimes disattended in the yeshiva *ketana*. After all, the reasoning went, this was an institution for children below the age of Jewish majority (and by Rabbi Kotler's standards at least below the fifth grade), so the mixing of the sexes would not matter much. Perhaps even more importantly, if these schools were going to attract students away from supplementary and public schools, both of which were coeducational, there was no choice but to follow suit.[30] Indeed, a number of rabbinic authorities asserted that for truly observant Jews public schools were out of bounds, given their imposition of secular culture (and, in the 1950s and early 1960s, also of Christianity, given that the Lord's Prayer and New Testament readings were still commonly recited as part of the day's opening exercises). Thus some sort of Jewish schooling for women was inevitable.

Coeducation has remained an issue that for many has constituted an important dividing line between schools closer in character to the yeshiva and those that embrace the day-school model, about which more below. The former almost never allow for it today, and even institutions that carry the name *yeshiva* and have had coeducation in their past often argue that its acceptance was never meant to be more than a temporary compromise brought on by the dearth of resources or the need to draw students away from the "evils" of public education.[31] While the yeshiva and the day school have differed on important pedagogic characteristics—such as the heavier emphasis of the former upon Talmud and its denial of the ontological or even academic importance of general, non-Judaic studies (except perhaps, as one rabbi put it, as a "handmaiden" to Jewish learning)— as well as attitudes toward college education and even decisions on such matters as whether the winter recess should coincide with the Christmas break at most American schools, coeducation has become one of the most important symbolic distinctions.

As yeshivas increasingly took on the enclavist character of a bastion, a protective fortress against the defiling influences of the outside world, it was obvious that women needed protection too. Accordingly, the women's yeshiva became not simply a place to imbue students with "the Torah spirit" but also a place to keep them from becoming "polluted" by the spirit of the American age and by secular and popular American culture. In this all-female institution, the sexual attractions that were so much a part of American life would not interfere. While the walls separating women from men were crumbling through most of the twentieth century in America, in the yeshiva world these barriers were being kept up.

In the extreme, the Haredi world, drawing on code books for its authority, has increasingly embraced the norm of sexual segregation articulated by the Code of Jewish Law, the *Shulchan Aruch,* compiled by Rabbi Joseph Caro. That norm is, to quote his text, *Tzarich adam l'hisrachek min hanashim m'od m'od* (a man must distance himself from women very much).[32] That standard of separation as an expression of Orthodox identity has insinuated itself into almost every domain of public life, none more so than education, where what is normative is first established.[33]

To a great extent, the issue of coeducation and of the role of women in Orthodox Judaism has remained an important dividing line within most schools, as well as among their clientele. The argument as to what women's role should properly be is often fought in the arena of Jewish education. The modern Orthodox have generally become defined as those who recognize the need to integrate women more fully into the mainstream of Jewish life, beginning in primary school and continuing from there. Thus there has been a high correlation between the support for coeducation and a variety of other elements that allow women equal participation with men. Schools that have embraced coeducation have tended also to emphasize the importance of general studies, college preparatory curricula at the high school level, and a kind of Jewish parallel with what the best of American public education has to offer. In these, women and men can share equally. Those who run and attend such schools have been likely as well to view themselves as part of the American social and cultural mosaic rather than a world apart, as has been the ideal of yeshiva life.

Besides opposing coeducation, contra-acculturative yeshivas often devalued the American vernacular and encouraged insertion of Jewish terms as well as Talmudic inflections and tortured syntax into the English language, cultivating a kind of Jewish-speak ("Yinglish" or "yeshivish") that created a language and hence cultural barrier as a constraint against assimilation. "Although students should know how to refer to these items in English, the norm should be *Motzaei Shabbos*—not Saturday night, *daven*—not pray, *bentsch*—not recite Grace After Meals, *Yom Tov* not holiday," as one Orthodox ideologue put it in an argument that explored techniques to "reclaim" people from the secular education that the state and the language of American life had inserted into yeshivas.[34] If they talked like Orthodox Jews, the reasoning went, they would act like them too.

Yeshivas became increasingly popular because they took children in at a young age and occupied them for long hours—a fact not lost on Haredi families with many offspring who could use the help of the school in caring for them. Moreover, insofar as the yeshiva and the community it served shared values and outlook, the idea of depositing children there seemed a natural expression of belonging in the enclave. Parents depended on it more and more, instrumentally and religiously.

In sum, the yeshiva has become more than an institution belonging to and associated with Haredi Orthodoxy. Indeed in the colloquial parlance of that community, Haredi often refer to themselves as the "yeshivish world."[35] In some neighborhoods, yeshivas, particularly those that cater to adult married males, are not only educating but sustaining whole communities (made up of large families), often at enormous expense.

DAY SCHOOL

Most American Jews did not want this sort of yeshiva education. They wanted to be part of America rather than set apart from it. Accordingly, American Jews who wanted coeducation as well as more emphasis on general education, and who hoped their children would attend college—the great institution of promise in the emerging American meritocracy, were moved to attend public or private but non-Jewish schools. If these Jews still wanted their children to receive some level of Jewish education, they sent them to supplementary schools sponsored largely by synagogues, and, after the primary school years, to Hebrew teachers' colleges and Jewish supplementary high schools, which provided an "after-school" Jewish education.[36] These Jewish schools (commonly called "Talmud Torahs" or "Hebrew" schools) began as six-day-a-week part-time programs and became the mainstay of Jewish community education by the mid–twentieth century, reaching a peak of 3,153 schools in the United States in 1958 (around the same time the day school movement began its acceleration). Today the number of supplementary schools is 40 percent lower, and, instead of offering a five- or six-day week of classes, they provide between one and two, totaling about six or seven hours a week. Most Hebrew teachers' colleges have either closed or evolved into adult Jewish education institutes.

Acutely aware of the seductions and dominance of the general culture as well as the role of education in determining and maintaining Jewish identity, and alert to the shortcomings of supplementary schools, Orthodox Jews who wanted to "make it in America" without abandoning their religious commitments needed an educational institution that would enable this but offer more than Hebrew or Sunday schools. The day school was to be the instrument for this sort of education. Viewed by many of its proponents as the successor institution to both the Old World yeshiva and the once-prevailing supplementary school, it aimed, in the words of one such school, to "give the child not one but two educations" that would offer "the best of both worlds" in a single location.[37] In a sense it reflected the essentially pluralist contrapuntalist ethos at the heart of modern Orthodoxy, and it demonstrated a fuller commitment to Judaism than the one that was satisfied with after-school programs.

Like the yeshiva, the day school was an institution where everyone presumably (although not always in fact) shared a single religio-cultural outlook (so that cultural conflicts would not loom large) and where Jewish studies were viewed as important, valuable, and a source for cultural continuity but not as the only important knowledge to transmit. As in the yeshiva, so in the day school Jewish education was viewed as a way of life, a cultural barrier against assimilation, and a way of construing the world, not simply as a mechanism for acquiring information[38] But in the day school, unlike the yeshiva, the religio-cultural outlook was pluralist rather than monist, acculturative rather than insular. Moreover, the day school was not an academy segregating the sexes or focused on the endless review of Talmud and its associated texts, and commentaries, providing a strong but narrow Jewish education. Rather, it aimed to offer the broadest possible selection of subjects, all given serious attention—even when they appeared contradictory. It was to be part of the liberal arts tradition. Judaism was an important thing, and perhaps first among equals, but not the *only* important thing. Here in principle one did not have to give up anything to become Jewishly educated.

At the outset, the idea that a Jewish day school could compete successfully with the supplementary school was not inconceivable, for it would adopt the serious and enhanced Jewish curriculum of the yeshivas.[39] But to be able to compete with public schools and the best general education that they offered for free was not quite as likely, particularly for the Orthodox, who were among the most economically disadvantaged Jews in America and for whom a free public education was not to be refused lightly.[40] Further, many of the non-Orthodox American Jews who might have been otherwise supportive of the effort to sustain Jewish learning saw the day school—no less than the yeshiva—as an expression not of the liberal arts but rather of ghettoization, no different from the yeshiva or its primary school antecedent, the cheder, which recalled the segregated past that American Jews were fleeing in the era of new beginnings after World War II.

To counter that argument, many of the founders of the day school sought to create schools that were not simply as good as the public schools but even better. General studies would have to be first rate, as measured by graduates' acceptance into the best colleges. To go to these schools would not be a return to the ghetto as much as a way of entering into the mainstream of culture without having to abandon important Jewish commitments and attachments. The idea was, as one such proponent, New York City Orthodox Rabbi Joseph H. Lookstein, saw it on the eve of the Second World War, to create a "school with an integrated program of religious studies combined with general studies—a school in which the culture of America would blend with the heritage of Judaism . . . a yeshivah day school in which a child would not experience an intellectual or emotional clash between being a Jew and an American."[41] In 1937 he opened the Ramaz School, which would be a model for many others like it. All of the eleven members of its first class were admitted to college, including three who went to Ivy League schools, among the best in the nation. By 1942, when enrollment had risen to 120 students, the school received its provisional charter, and in 1950 it received its absolute charter from the Board of Regents of the State of New York. In 1937, Rabbi Joseph Dov Soloveitchik and Dr. Tonya Soloveitchik were embarking on a similar effort in Boston at the Maimonides School.[42] Like Lookstein, the Soloveitchiks believed, as the rabbi later put it, that "the Jewish child is capable of carrying a double load, the universal secular and the specific Judaic . . . to study and comprehend two systems of knowledge and to excel in both." Recognizing that the yeshiva world as well as those who championed public school advocated an alternate view—the former arguing that only Torah could and should be studied and the latter suggesting that secular studies were all consuming—Rabbi Soloveitchik added immediately, "Some people deny it."[43]

The idea caught on. At the start, the distinction between day school and yeshiva seemed insignificant, and in fact the institutions and their founders worked hand in glove with one another. Day schools often called themselves yeshivas, as did both Maimonides and Ramaz. This was in part because the model from which many of the founders were beginning was the yeshiva (to be sure, a yeshiva in which the ideals of the *haskalah* were present). But the day school movement grew and the desires of its users to give up nothing they could get from good public education in America continued to stretch the capacities of this institution.

By June 1944, there were enough day schools that "at a conference of leading religious- and lay-leaders at the Waldorf-Astoria in New York City, Torah Umesorah, the National Society for Hebrew Day Schools, was born."[44] In 1946 there were at least 95 day schools in the United States. Two years later the number had ballooned to 128. By 1962 it had more than doubled to 258, with a total enrollment of around 50,000.[45] By 1975 there were 425 day schools and 138 Jewish high schools with an enrollment of 82,200 in thirty-three states; every city with a Jewish population of at least 7,500 had at least one day school.[46] By one count, the number of students in day schools and yeshivas at the beginning of the 1980s was at about 130,000 and the total of such schools exceeded 300.[47] The Avi Chai Foundation survey carried out by Marvin Schick found that in 1998–99 the number was 185,000 in 670 schools (of which 85 percent or about 570 were affiliated with Orthodoxy), an increase in enrollment of about 40 percent in twenty years and of about 120 percent in institutional growth.[48] Moreover, as the report notes, very few of these schools had trouble filling their seats with students. While many of the students were not Orthodox, the majority (about 80 percent by Schick's count) were in schools under Orthodox auspices.[49] Although at the end of the twentieth century these schools were located in thirty-eight states and the District of Columbia, almost two-thirds of the enrollment continued to be in the New York/ New Jersey area, which has remained the place where most American Orthodox Jews are to be found.

While many who sent their children to these day schools at the outset were ideologically and religiously committed to the ideals of modern Orthodoxy and did so in spite of the relatively heavy cost, enrollment was also helped by events that had more to do with what Jane Jacobs called "the death of American cities."[50] Jews who remained in city neighborhoods during the period of suburban expansion (often working class, petty bourgeois, immigrants, Orthodox, or some combination of these) found themselves in Jewish communities that were losing their diversity and in an inner city from which the white middle class fled—with the result of a sudden deterioration of the public schools. In other cases, it was not the deterioration of the schools but their integration, particularly after the 1954 *Brown v. the Board of Education of Topeka* U.S. Supreme Court decision, that led to white flight from them.

In practical effect, the result was often a boon for day school enrollment. With public education no longer as attractive for many inner-city Jews, the thought of paying some money to put one's child in a small private school made the day school more attractive. Because these day schools still charged less than elite private schools and offered a culturally protective environment, they seemed the poor Jew's panacea and avenue of escape from unappealing urban public schools. Suddenly nominally Orthodox Jews or even those who were marginally observant, people who initially had been satisfied with supplementary school Jewish education and not ready to send their offspring to day schools, were among those most likely to confront the declining fate of public education and therefore to start looking at the day school as a realistic option. Their children helped fill the classrooms just as the day school movement was getting organized in America. Indeed, it was not uncommon in the early days for a majority of the students in a day school class to come from homes where the level of religious observance and Orthodox Jewish commitment was significantly weaker than the ideology of the school and its Jewish studies staff.

Although the committed day school pioneers set the agenda and curriculum, the parents, as always, had a voice in practice. Once having enrolled their children, many of these parents demanded that the day schools become *better* than the public schools. Others (those who were nominally Orthodox or not Orthodox at all) insisted that they would remove their children from the school as soon as possible if "they regarded it as 'too Jewish,' as significantly above the Judaic level of the home."[51] The day schools were thus sometimes caught on the horns of a dilemma. If they aimed too high in terms of Jewish focus, they were likely to discourage families that were marginal in their regard for day schools from sending their children to them. And if they aimed too low, they would fail in their ultimate goal of ensuring the continuity of Orthodox Jewish life and its future. They therefore had to move carefully and patiently until they had a critical mass of committed modern Orthodox families who would make up the bulk of their clientele. That would take time. To the champions of the classic yeshiva, the presence of the non-Orthodox and their influence on the institution were good reasons to spurn the day school. But in many cases, the yeshivas faced similar situations.

As Orthodoxy in America grew, and as it became more affluent, the day schools likewise grew. They moved along with their growing constituency, leaving the inner cities and going to the areas of Orthodox second settlement, streetcar suburbs or outer boroughs. By the end of the twentieth century as many as 200,000 students were enrolled in Jewish day schools "from the four-year-old preschool level through the 12th grade," with an average 89 percent seat occupancy in the schools.[52]

For a time the day schools moved in a contrapuntalist direction, trying to offer a dual curriculum of high order, while the yeshivas continued to try to bolster their Torah studies and insulate their students from life outside the Orthodox enclave. To many American modern Orthodox Jews, the day school represented a cultural ascendance, the institution of the future, a chance to share in the liberal tradition of education, whereas the yeshiva looked like its opposite. To the emerging Haredi Orthodox, however, the yeshiva seemed the symbol of their resistance to assimilation and guarantee of continuity, while the day school was the gateway through which the young would be led astray. Both sides were certain they were right. The question was whether American Orthodoxy could sustain both approaches or whether one would dominate the other. While the early years of the second half of the twentieth century seemed to belong to proponents of the modern Orthodox day school, by the start of the new millennium the pendulum began to swing to those on yeshiva side.

Factors in the Move to the Right

Four factors in combination advanced the swing to the religious right: (1) the perceived decline of American culture, (2) families' complete handover of the responsibility of education to the day schools and yeshivas, (3) the changing nature of the Judaica faculty in the day schools and the related change in the men who were becoming Orthodox rabbis, and (4) the emergence of study in Israeli yeshivas and women's seminaries as an essential experience in Orthodox education.

THE PERCEIVED DECLINE OF AMERICAN CULTURE

As long as American society and culture represented a positive model, the day school ideal of controlled acculturation in a Jewish milieu governed by Orthodoxy and the belief, in opposition to the yeshiva world, that ac-

complishments in the non-Jewish world represented an "improved" station in life could be embraced without danger or hesitation. The student
who did well in a day school and managed thereby to proceed to an elite
university and a professional degree with its attendant social status and
wealth while remaining committed to Orthodox practices and Jewish law
was idealized. He (or she) would "make it" in America, and making it
there was significant for the modern Orthodox, as it had been for so many
other Jews.[53]

However, by the late 1960s and throughout the 1970s the perceived
wholesomeness of America that had seemed so attractive and had promised so much at midcentury was replaced by radicalism, antinomianism,
and the emergence of an often anarchic counterculture. Moreover, the
places of greatest radicalism and chaos were the selfsame elite universities
to which the contrapuntalists had been sending their children. This development aroused sometimes profound reservations among many conservative elements in the population—including many who called themselves Orthodox Jews—about the value of American culture. To many
Orthodox Jews, including the modernists, the liberal tradition suddenly
seemed dangerous, and they recoiled from it, even though they did not
abandon the idea of higher education and professional career.

In subsequent years, the increasing moral relativism and tolerance, particularly on college campuses, of nontraditional lifestyles, from unmarried heterosexuals living together to gays wanting to come out of the
closet and even get married, only increased doubts about American culture among those who remained committed to an Orthodox way of life
and the continuity of Jewish tradition and Halacha (Jewish law). Graham Murdock's comments about so-called progressives at the turn of
the nineteenth century who were beginning to have doubts about the
rise of reason and industrialization, could as easily be applied to modern Orthodox Jews viewing contemporary American society and culture
a hundred years later: looking at the American possibilities they had once
embraced with enthusiasm, they had a "sense of an unlooked-for ending, of values slipping away," and began to feel disappointment bound
up "with an increasing ambivalence" because "their sense of exhilaration
at the opening up of possibilities was increasingly suffused with anxiety" that maybe the choices they had made would not guarantee Orthodox continuity.[54] They therefore sought some way of controlling the
ill effects of American acculturation as the attraction of making it in America began to wear thin. At the same time, the American Orthodox were
becoming more self-confident in their ability to maintain their own stan-

dards of conduct and religious behavior without having to suffer prejudice and discrimination. With "the rise of the unmeltable ethnics" in the late 1970s Orthodox Jews found that their peculiarities and distinctions were more than tolerated.[55]

"For better or worse," as Daniel Bell has suggested, "the very breakup of the cultural hegemony of the WASPs and the growth of ethnicity as a legitimate dimension of American-life . . . 'forced' . . . [Jews] to maintain an identity, and to define themselves in ethnic terms."[56] Whatever it did for the rest of American Jewry, it reinforced the Orthodoxy of the contrapuntalists. Furthermore, the self-confident claims by those Orthodox who had rejected the very notion of stabilized dualism and had argued that such a stand was unstable and would cause Judaism to stumble in America no longer sounded completely unreasonable. The assertion by the emergent Haredim — the most ethnic of the Orthodox Jews — that the modernists had begun to slide down the slippery slope of compromise and defilement was not always falling on deaf ears.

When the 1990 National Jewish Population Survey revealed the high rate of Jewish intermarriage and confirmed the continuing assimilation of American Jewry during the 1980s, demonstrating in particular that younger college graduates were among the most assimilated and prone to intermarriage, Orthodox Jews became even more concerned about the cultural costs of modernity and unintended consequences of a college degree. Perhaps, increasing numbers of the modernists thought, they had made a Faustian bargain in their desire to enter American society. Many Orthodox Jews worried not only about sending their offspring to sites of counterculturalism where the sexual revolution and an attitude of aggressive challenge to authority were rampant but also about the postmodern commitment to diversity and pluralism as campuses became far more ethnically and racially diverse (in fact, the entrance of Jews into campus life turned out to be the first wave of a change that would rapidly move the college population from a whites-only enclave into a far more inclusive environment).

It really did not take too much to get Orthodox Jews culturally anxious. Even the modernists among them were after all fundamentally conservative in their outlook.[57] They understood that campus life beyond the boundaries of the Orthodox community represented a risk to their values of Jewish continuity and the preservation of tradition. It could undermine their commitment to the Jewish family, to a life governed by the Jewish strictures, and to respect for received authority. For day school graduates who for all of their modernism had come out of a relatively sheltered enclave, who had always been governed strictly regarding what they could or could not do, the campus environment, which freed them from the control of both their families and their communities (especially if they went to live in dormitories) sometimes led to a breakdown of all that their Orthodoxy had built into them.

The data suggest that the number of people who called themselves Orthodox declined significantly during this period. Rising rates of inter-dating and intermarriage as well as declining rates of affiliation with Jewish institutions were probably the most dramatic developments, but there were others that made these years seem to some of the Orthodox the worst of times.[58] The risk was not only to those who went to the college campus and gave up their attachments to Orthodoxy on purpose. Even those who went with the best intentions of maintaining their Jewish ways were at risk.

This concern about the unintended and negative consequences for Jewish Orthodoxy of a university education and environment is captured vividly in a recent pamphlet by Gil Perl and Yaakov Weinstein, two graduate students—one from Harvard and the other from M.I.T.—entitled "A Parent's Guide to Orthodox Assimilation on University Campuses."[59] It argues that the campus is a place of "sensual and sexual temptation" where at times "the pressure . . . to be sexually active is so intense that those who defy it run the risk of depression," and that even college courses in Jewish studies that may be taken in the mistaken belief that students will "get credit for learning Torah" may result in situations that will "confuse Orthodox students" and lead to "decidedly unorthodox views" and behaviors because they are not taught from an Orthodox standpoint. Hillel is viewed as a place fraught with danger, for it can and often does lead to "inter-denominational dating" or what is worse, "inter-denominational marriage" (the assumption being that in such a coupling Orthodoxy will be subordinated). Even the argument that campus life offers Orthodox Jews a chance to engage in outreach, or *kiruv*, as it is often called, allowing them to covert non- or marginally observant into observant Jews— the most limited justification for leaving the enclave culture—is attacked. Instead, Perl and Weinstein suggest, in the effort to convince their not-yet-observant counterparts "that Orthodox kids are 'normal' and can have as much fun as everyone else, Orthodox Jews have been known to justify their own bending of *halakhah* in the name of *kiruv*," a condition that leads to their being in places and sharing experiences far from beyond the borders of the permissible. These doubts and anxieties, which reached a peak by the end of the twentieth century, coincided with the modern Orthodox calling themselves centrists. Centrism, unlike contrapuntalism, had associations with conservatism. Unlike modernists, centrists focused not on making it in America but on ensuring that graduates of their schools remained committed to an Orthodox Jewish life, continued Torah study, and maintained high levels of ritual observance and associated commitments—that they stayed away from extremes.

Some went so far as to question the whole modern Orthodox enterprise: "If we are willing to compromise, what makes us different from Reform, Liberal, Reconstructionist, Conservative and Secular Humanist Jews?"[60] While those at the left of center still replied, "If we are not willing to compromise, what makes us different from Haredim?" this response was increasingly found to be flawed by centrists who argued that they were not identical to those on their religious right. Like most American Orthodox Jews, they still embraced the idea of a college degree. But there were growing minorities who began to have second thoughts. The 2002 New York Jewish Community Study found, for example, that about 72 percent of the Orthodox they surveyed believed a college education was "very important." This compared with the more than 90 percent of all other Jews. But more than a quarter of Jews who identified themselves as Orthodox—28 percent to be exact—thought it only somewhat or not important at all.

To be sure, conservative reactions to the radical shifts in American society were not unique to Orthodox Jews. Many conservative Christian communities, as we have noted, reacted in similar ways to what they perceived as the decline of American culture. They argued that more was being lost than gained by embracing the liberal tradition. Their great numbers and influence on American life, moreover, helped lead to a significant shift to the right in 1980s America. Paradoxically, the strengthening of conservative forces allowed those who remained liberal to become even more radical. In this polarized society, moderates found themselves forced to choose between the two extremes. For moderates who were committed to Jewish Orthodoxy, the right, however imperfect a fit, was still a more comfortable home than the left, which was more and more flirting with what Orthodox Judaism defined as heresies but which the left represented as a legitimate form of alternative culture. So when there were initiatives to move the day schools closer to yeshivas in character—whether ending coeducation, increasing the hours devoted to Talmudic studies, replacing instruction in modern Hebrew with Yinglish or yeshivish English, or accepting teachers who came from the Haredi world (about which more below)—many of the centrists acquiesced. All this parents accepted because they believed that the schools would thus better preserve Orthodoxy into the future. To that, above all else, they remained committed.

THE HANDOVER OF EDUCATION
FROM THE FAMILY TO THE SCHOOLS

How did parents allow the schools to make these decisions? Two related causes contributed: modernization and the active engagement of con-trapuntalists in professional careers. A key feature of modernization is the emergence of specialization and professionalization. Max Weber has elo-quently described these as creating an "iron cage" that increasingly has limited the power of individuals to act independently and beyond the boundaries of their expertise.[61] When the Orthodox world created day schools into which they poured financial resources and from which they expected a guarantee of Jewish continuity, they anticipated that the teaching staff (both Judaic and general) would, in the spirit of moder-nity, be professionals and specialists trained to do the job. Just as the par-ents sought to be professionals in their jobs, they assumed the teachers would be as well. Moreover, once the schools were established on a firm base, the parents (although involved in fund-raising and on school boards) effectively abandoned direct personal responsibility for the Jew-ish education of their children. The school would teach their offspring all that was essential.

This process was accelerated by a tendency for more and more mod-ern Orthodox parents to pursue professional careers of their own, which necessitated that they find institutions that could help care for their chil-dren while they were away at work. By the early 1970s, as a new genera-tion of these contrapuntalists was graduating college and entering the workforce and as the dual-career family was becoming the American norm, this dependence on the day school became even more important both in-strumentally and religiously. From the instrumental perspective, a day school, which held children for an entire school day from an early age, was perfect for career-oriented working parents who did not have to feel guilty about depositing their children there while they themselves were otherwise occupied. From the religious perspective, they could feel that they were giving their children a serious, full-time Jewish education in-tegrated with a good general one and thereby ensuring modern Ortho-dox continuity.

As the parents moved further and further afield from the strictly Orthodox enclave culture as a result of their higher education, careers, and interests, they assumed that the schools would serve to anchor their children in Orthodoxy. Thus, if the schools demanded more intensive Jewish behavior than the parents did, they acquiesced, partly in their guilt over their own compromises and deviations from Orthodox norms and partly in the belief that their children would find a golden mean between the sometimes religiously Haredi positions that the Judaica faculty increasingly embraced and the more liberal situation in the modern Orthodox home. When, for example, these schools suggested after-school intensive Torah study programs that emulated the yeshiva model, as many did by the end of the twentieth century, parents welcomed them, for they served a double purpose: increasing the time in rigorous Jewish study, sometimes adding evening study sessions, and freeing the parents from having to spend time with their child in such Torah learning. When the schools required daily prayer in a synagogue (conveniently located in the school), parents gladly packed their children off early in the morning and let them stay late in the afternoon, even though they themselves were often lax about attending services during the week. When Torah teachers spent time with the young in religious exploration, shaping their worldview and instilling "Torah values," the parents accepted this as part of the package they had bought. Inevitably, the school and its professional staff played a greater and greater role in the Jewish life of the community. "Let the school do its job," was the prevalent attitude.

This had several inevitable consequences. First, it gave far-reaching authority to the teacher, a principle in line with the ethos of the yeshiva, which saw the teacher/rabbi often as more important than the parents. Second, it freed the parents from having to grapple with the sometimes complex realities of explaining the philosophy of their contrapuntalism and its sometimes uncomfortable contradictions. Moreover, as they began to worry more about the impact of American culture, they were comforted by the idea that the day school was providing the protective power of Orthodoxy. What was left for them to do was assisting the child with homework and affirming the authority of the school and its teachers, who retained ultimate control of the educational agenda.

In the past, when the primary religious educational institutions were the cheder and later the *bes medrash,* these did not displace the role of the parents because they were essentially supplementary to the family and community. All community members shared a life situation, much as they still did in the Haredi Orthodox enclaves. For such Jews, the family and the instruction of their children were therefore still a major focus of personal concern and satisfaction. Accordingly, the value of a parental role in Jewish education, which remained treasured in Orthodox culture, also remained an active element of their routine. This ideal was very much on the minds of the founders of day schools, who had never meant to free the parents from their teaching responsibilities, even though early on they realized they were doing just that.

"The parent is the teacher," as Joseph Soloveitchik put it. But then in a subtle but important transformation that would capture the transition that was about to occur, he added that the role of "the teacher of the child is [as] his parent." Finally, trying to bridge these two possibilities, he concluded that "the child belongs to both." Indeed, that was what Soloveitchik expected in the Maimonides Day School: "the threefold familial community of father, mother, and child . . . joined by a fourth member, the teacher."[62] In other words, the school had hoped not to replace family and community, but in practice in the modern world it did.

The more the modern world seemed to be pulling away from Orthodox Jewish values, the greater the authority given the teachers of Judaica. It increased exponentially. The teachers into whose hands parents deposited their children were ineluctably given the legitimate authority to supersede and even contradict parents' own view of what was Jewishly right, even if in so doing they were taking a religiously right-wing position. These teachers were after all, persons who devoted themselves to Torah and safeguarding the Jewish future. The teachers thus became key to Jewish transmission, more powerful role models than they had been before, when they shared responsibility for teaching with parents and other laypersons and when a living mimetic tradition was far more visible.[63]

For their part, the educators embraced this role. They too found apt Jewish interpretations to support their new and enhanced position overseeing the education of the young. Indeed, they often accepted the Haredi notion that teachers/rabbis were "the conveyors of Torah" who shared in the honor and authority of God Almighty and "the holy Torah."[64] That is, they tried to embody, at least as far as their students were concerned (and possibly also the parents), the authority of *da'as Torah*, the idea that deep Torah knowledge provides one with the ability to properly advise others in *all* areas of life because one can intuit and extrapolate the intention of the Torah and hence Almighty God. This principle, increasingly enshrined in Haredi Orthodoxy, enhanced the moral and specific authority of the rabbis *at the expense of the values of personal choice and individual moral responsibility that modernism had embraced as normative.*[65]

While once modern Orthodox parents had believed that they could offset the messages of the Haredi teachers with their own religio-cultural input, in practice few had the ability, time, or energy to do so. And as modernism moved toward centrism, these parents had less confidence in their own religious authority.

This division of labor, that rabbis and teachers would take control over Jewish life and learning while the parents pursued other involvements, was not unprecedented in Jewish tradition. Commenting on the verse, "To Zebulun he said: Rejoice, O Zebulun, in your excursions, and Issachar in your tents" (Deut. 33:18), the rabbis of the Talmud had offered a reading that understood the verse to mean "Rejoice, Zebulun, in your excursions for business, because you have thereby enabled Issachar to sit in their tents, where they may delve into the Torah." In the rabbinic calculus, which looked for a way to reward both the scholar and the one who economically frees him to spend his life in Torah, the biblical blessing of the patriarch Jacob to his sons hinted at an agreement that Zebulun and Issachar had made between themselves: Zebulun would go out for business and sustain Issachar, who would study Torah, and the merit of the learning would be thus shared by both. This same reasoning was now justifying or at least resonating in the idea that some of those in the modern Orthodox world would go out into the world to pursue other vocations but that they would nevertheless support the Jewish education of their children carried on by others. As a result, the view of what Judaism demanded was defined not by the home but by the school, and in the school by the teachers of Judaica. This, however, would turn out for the modern Orthodox to be no less of a Faustian bargain than their embrace of America, for the teachers to whom they entrusted their children and the future of Orthodoxy were not exactly what they expected. Issachar in his tent had become quite different from Zebulun in his excursions.

The enthusiasm for day schools and the willingness of parents to deposit their children in them resulted, as we have seen, in a rapid expansion in their number. Filling the seats in the classroom was increasingly not a problem, as the Orthodox abandoned supplementary and public schools. Additionally, with a birthrate of around three children per family (and even higher among the religious right wing) they could not help but boost these schools' student population. Nevertheless, a key question began to emerge in the face of this success: From where were these teachers and rabbis to come?

THE CHANGING NATURE
OF THE FACULTY AND THE RABBINATE

As noted already, the modern Orthodox themselves were not choosing to become Jewish educators or rabbis. While for a time some of the women did choose teaching as a career and played an important part in the development of faculty (in the process implicitly demonstrating how important for the future of Orthodox Judaism in America it was for daughters as well as sons to get a solid Jewish education), in time they too moved to other vocations. Although they have remained an important mainstay of day schools, many of the modern Orthodox women of today are choosing careers other than teaching—including most prominently fields related to the therapeutic professions, in particular occupational and physical therapy, as well as business, law, and social work.

Among men, the numbers who chose Jewish education as a vocation was declining even faster. In this, the Orthodox were not very different from other American Jews. As one report put it, "[R]eligious school leaders in many areas of the country say the expansion of Jewish education is outpacing the training and availability of qualified teachers and . . . causing a shortage of qualified educators." In addition, as the head of the Boston Bureau of Jewish Education head put it, "[P]eople don't need to rely on positions in the Jewish community to make a living."[66]

Modern Orthodox men also spurned opportunities to become practicing rabbis. They instead moved into non-Jewish careers. While the idea of acquiring ordination remained popular in some quarters, a 2002 article in the *Commentator* noted that among those at the Rabbi Isaac Elkhanan Talmudical Seminary (RIETS) at Yeshiva University, long viewed as the premier source for modern Orthodox rabbis, having graduated over 2,600 since its foundation in 1897, commonly these days "students enroll for only one or two years and depart to pursue other careers."[67] That is, they immersed themselves temporarily in rabbinic study, viewing it not as a vocation but rather as a transitory, albeit important, religious experience. Others who wanted rabbinic training and saw it as a vocation went increasingly to yeshivas whose outlook was Haredi. But these were not turning out rabbis whose ideal was modern, contrapuntalist Orthodoxy, at least not after the mid-1970s.

The dearth of modern Orthodox educators and rabbis was particularly ironic. After all, the central organizing principle of the modern Orthodox lifestyle was the ideological conviction that one could remain bound to Jewish traditions, values, and punctilious observance of religious ritual without sacrificing an attachment to the cultural riches and opportunities that America offered. To demonstrate and perpetuate this ideal, most modern Orthodox Jews had chosen to pursue careers far from the exclusively Jewish domain, yet in the day schools they had established for the purpose they had left few teachers who embodied this cultural dualism. Similarly, few of them were attending rabbinical seminaries. Instead, modern Orthodoxy had created a cadre of people who personified these contrapuntalist ideals beyond the boundaries of the day schoolroom and strictly Jewish vocations like the rabbinate. People who had spent so much time in training and initiation in the "best" universities and professional schools were not about to use all that in order to be a day school teacher or a rabbi.

To be sure, nothing inherent to modern Orthodoxy contradicted a life in the rabbinate. Had its adherents been concerned, not just with an instrumental acculturation to America in the professional sphere, the attainment of a middle-class lifestyle, and economic security, but with a thoroughly articulated intellectual acculturation that explored and shared in the full sweep of Western culture to which they had access and to which some of them had been exposed in the elite universities they had attended, they might have seen the rabbinate as a golden opportunity to truly integrate *Torah-im-derech-eretz*. But few modern Orthodox Jews did so.

Finally, for all their emphasis on day school education, the modern Orthodox did not at least at the outset endow their teachers or rabbis with either the economic advantages or the social prestige that tends to draw recruits to a profession. That left the pool significantly depleted.

Moreover, the rabbinic position, perhaps more prestigious because it represented the ultimate Jewish religious authority in the community (for those who took pulpits) or the academy (for those who stayed in the yeshiva), was off limits for Orthodox women, no matter how Jewishly engaged or educated they were. Thus this potential pool of excellence and instruction, which the non-Orthodox movements used to bolster their rabbinic ranks (today more than 50 percent of the rabbinical students in American non-Orthodox schools are women), was simply unavailable. Had it been open to young modern Orthodox feminists, it might have provided an important supply of modern Orthodox teachers and role models who shared the ideas of stabilized dualism.

Given this dearth of contrapuntalist rabbi/teachers, to whom could the modern Orthodox turn next? Even if Jewish educators were available from the larger American Jewish community, most of it was constituted by those who were not committed to the ideals of Orthodoxy—surely not a place from which to draw role models. That left two possible sources: either those who chose teaching because of powerful commitments to Jewish education (people who not only lived *off* Judaism as a vocation but lived *for* it) or people who, because they had come from the traditionalist, insular Haredi Orthodox world, had few marketable skills and, wishing to remain in an explicitly Jewish environment, chose to become day school teachers in order to make a living. They were not only the teachers and rabbis—*they were more and more the only teachers and rabbis.* In either case, these were educators who, by both their example and their pedagogy, would inevitably stress more powerful commitments to a comprehensive and parochial Orthodoxy than many of the modern Orthodox.

There were still a few modern Orthodox teachers. Often they were young, freshly minted rabbis or rabbinical students who were not interested in pulpit work and who had gone into the rabbinate out of a religious revival after or during college. They may have spent a few years at RIETS or another yeshiva, but they still felt called to the day school, at least temporarily. Among them, the religiously revitalized often yearned to return to the yeshiva to renew their own religious enthusiasms as soon as possible and hence did not remain on the day school faculty very long. Others left to make more money. Sometimes faculty came from Israel. These teachers presented their own problems of cultural unfamiliarity with the American scene or, if they were émigrés, presented the negative model of failed Zionism.

So meager was the supply of day school teachers that as the twentieth century ended renewed efforts were made by the modern Orthodox to recruit more into it. Thus Edah set itself the task of providing "major seed money to launch the MeORoT (Modern Orthodox Rabbinic Training) Semikhah student fellowship and its companion program, the Torat Miriam fellowship, a program for women currently in graduate schools of Jewish Studies or already professionally engaged in Jewish education," in hopes of recruiting new Jewish educators using a method modeled on "Teach for America" (the national program that sought to provide teachers in unpopular venues) and strengthening current educators through training by master teachers.[68] In Jerusalem in the late 1990s an independent and privately funded institution calling itself the Academy for Torah Initiatives and Directions (ATID), headed by the American expatriate Orthodox rabbi Chaim Brovender, founder of a yeshiva for the newly observant, organized itself to help create a cadre of " talented young educators and professionals concerned about Modern Orthodox Jewish education to develop the skills and vision needed for the future."[69] There was also the Torah MitZion project, which sent young Israeli rabbi/teachers—generally graduates of the Hesder yeshivas and Israeli army veterans—who shared a modernist, religious Zionist outlook abroad to help foster a non-Haredi orthodoxy.[70] Yeshiva University has likewise tried to add to this pool.[71] Finally, most recently a new modern Orthodox seminary in New York, Yeshivat Chovevei Torah, advertising itself as a place "where open Orthodoxy begins," founded in 1999 and ordaining its first class of nine in June 2004, has been trying to produce a new corps of modern Orthodox rabbis and teachers. All these programs and several more like them, as of this writing, have yielded a relative trickle to the pool of modern Orthodox Jewish educators.

This left the Haredi source. While Haredi Orthodoxy provided a large pool of young men who were engaged full time in Jewish learning (the women soon became mothers, and if they were involved in such education it was always part time), these potential rebbees (as such teachers came to be called in the Yinglish speech of modern Orthodoxy) and rabbis came with certain disqualifications.[72] First were their misgivings about the whole modern Orthodox enterprise of the day school and even the idea of pursuing secular studies, which for them was a prescription for "many of the social ills associated with modern Western society."[73] The Haredi view of one of the most cherished values of modern Orthodoxy was perhaps best articulated in the response of Rabbi Elchanan Wasserman, the head of the yeshiva of Baranowicze, Lithuania, to a question from Rabbi Simon Schwab, who would become famous as the head of the German-Jewish Orthodox congregation in New York's Washington Heights. Schwab had written to a variety of Lithuanian yeshiva heads asking them their opinion about the legitimacy of secular studies. Wasserman's response (shortly before his murder in 1941) was that "Torah studies have to be one's main involvement and that secular studies are the exact opposite of Torah," for Torah was to be studied "as an end unto itself," while secular studies could at best be pursued "only as a means to an end."[74] Just as they ontologically rejected Western society and secular studies that were the pathways into it, so too did Haredi educators deny the need to be part of an institution that facilitated that entry, as day schools so much aimed to do.

If one of the prime concerns of the modern Orthodox was to demonstrate how much they valued "open intellectual inquiry and expression in both secular and religious arenas" (even though in practice they did less and less of it), for the Haredim the key was to remember and stress that "we are different and despite the long *galus* [exile], and the layers of dust that have settled upon us, courtesy of the myriad cultures we have traveled through," and even in a welcoming America, "we still are unique and have a mission of our own." If the modern Orthodox sought "engagement with the social, political and the technological realities of the modern world," the Haredim from whom they were increasingly drawing their teachers wanted "to protect our uniqueness from the onslaught of contemporary Western culture."[75] Hence when they became rabbis they wanted to remain within the confines of a yeshiva where they believed rabbis found their truest calling and not go into a day school or even a pulpit.

Finally, those Haredim who did leave the yeshiva came increasingly with an attachment to the idea of *da'as Torah*. They tried to teach their students or their congregants that when they established a relationship with a rabbi they had to subordinate themselves, accepting the rabbi's opinion as superior and "nullifying" their own opinions before him.[76] Democracy and autonomy, values that modern Orthodoxy at least claimed to hold dear, paled in the face of *da'as Torah*.

Because of the modernists' powerful need to find teachers, and because there were elements of the Haredi worldview and behavior with which they could in some way identify, especially by the mid-1970s — after all they too believed in preserving Jewish uniqueness and fidelity to Jewish law and were now worried about the impact of some aspects of American culture on their children — they began to accept as a given that these Jews from the Haredi enclaves would be the teachers and rabbis serving American Orthodoxy. In the process, both parents and students also absorbed more of the conservatism that they espoused. This was not so unexpected. For all their contrapuntalism, the modern Orthodox revered many of the same texts and authorities as did the Haredim — and, as we shall see in the next chapter, they were gaining access to ever more of them in English translation and learning to accept their authority in all matters religious.

Given their hands-off approach to the actual process of Jewish education, many of the parents were not in a position to offer alternatives. They had long ago ceded control over the Jewish curriculum and largely concerned themselves with the schools' success in gaining admission for their graduates to good colleges (or, in the case of elementary schools, admission to the best high schools). Of course, not everyone used this measure. Some considered the extent and manner in which students and graduates of the day schools publicly demonstrated their commitments to Judaism, but often this too was reduced to shows of symbolic religiosity. Hence the "more religious" modern Orthodox expressed concern with their children's *frumkeit,* and such matters as whether they engaged in prominent public displays of piety or remained in social circles made up of other Orthodox Jews. To be sure, the Haredim often looked for the same things—except that the nature of the displays and the people in the social circle were different.

In many cases, there really was no choice because there were only one or at most two day schools in the community. In such places, parents had to accept whatever the school did because in all Orthodox communities sending a child to a day school or yeshiva had become by the last third of the twentieth century de rigueur. Hence, if the local school did not quite embrace the modern Orthodox lifestyle, then the modern Orthodox did not remove their children to the public school. They just hoped that the projected trajectory of their children's lives—college, maybe a graduate degree and finally a profession, and marriage to another Orthodox Jew of modernist outlook—would in the end offset any Haredi influences in primary and high school. The illogicality of believing that the day school would create a foundation for Orthodoxy but one that could be superseded but not totally obliterated by college and beyond was ignored in this thinking. Either the day school education left an imprint or it did not. In the meantime, the most optimistic among the modern Orthodox parents who accepted the Haredization of the day school believed naively that these rabbis and teachers would by their mere presence in school tacitly be giving a *hechsher,* a religious endorsement for modern Orthodoxy.

What these parents did not count on was that the teachers in their schools and many rabbis did not share their values and remained unprepared to endorse the modern Orthodox life trajectory even tacitly, and that even if they had wanted to certain social factors prevented them from doing so. The teachers often did not share the same neighborhoods and certainly not the same community as the families of the students they taught. They came from places and groups where the prevailing feeling was that America was always eroding Jewish distinctiveness and that the teachers' task was to remind their students that as Jews they were always a world apart, chosen by God, and required to be uncompromising in their Orthodoxy. To accomplish this they had to turn day schools into something much closer to yeshivas, the institutions in which they had been forged. There they had been exposed to Haredi messages. As Rabbi Yitzhak Hutner put it, in a message typical of what these teachers had been exposed to, their job as educators was "to impart and implant in the *talmidim* [students] the knowledge and awareness that *'atta vekhartanu mikal ha'amim'* [thou God has chosen us from among all the nations]."[77] Here was an attitude that directly contradicted the contrapuntalist notion that much of value could be learned from other nations and that it was important to share in their cultures, even while remaining Orthodox.

With their chauvinistic attitude, Haredi teachers gradually sent the message that ideal Judaism was contra-acculturative and exclusive, that the true vocation for an Orthodox man was to study Torah and for an Orthodox woman to marry, support, and build a large observant Jewish family with such a man, and that the place to do this was in a sheltered enclave away from the seductions of all that was non-Jewish. They taught that passing as indistinguishable from Americans—as the modern Orthodox had aspired to do—was wrong. It was not bad to stand out as a Jew, and whatever the tribulations of that distinctiveness, it was infinitely superior to *goyim nachas,* the pleasures of the Gentiles that modern Orthodox Jews vainly pursued. And if one was forced to leave the yeshiva and to find oneself in a place where Gentiles dominated, it was crucial to stress "the importance of remaining a ben [son of the] Torah even after leaving the walls of the yeshiva or kollel."[78]

In effect, the teachers who came from the yeshivas to staff the day schools (no less than the rabbis who came to the synagogues) became agents provocateurs, bringing values and views from one segment of the Orthodox world to influence another. Moreover, the people who made up the leading edge of this Haredi Orthodoxy were not simply old bearded rabbis but young Jews, postadolescent and ready to redefine Orthodoxy in the modern world as uncompromisingly parochial. They were the ones who took over pulpits and classrooms, and theirs was the ideological outlook that increasingly defined what Jewish Orthodoxy should be. By one count, nearly two-thirds of today's Judaica teachers in day schools come from the Haredi world.[79]

Haredi teachers did not always meet success in this contra-acculturative effort. Often they lacked pedagogic sophistication (few if any had any specialized didactic training or advanced degrees). They were not always adept at their job. Sometimes when they transmitted these messages naively they were met with contempt or derision by their students, who were acutely aware of the discontinuity between their lives at home and the views of these teachers. Yet when day school students complained about the teachers' attitude or skills, they encountered resistance from those to whom they addressed these complaints. School administrators who knew how hard it was to find Judaica instructors were loath to terminate one without having a better alternative—which they commonly did not have. Parents, having entrusted the entire project of Jewish education to the school and its teachers, and often feeling like guilty Zebuluns who had promised to support their brother rabbi/teachers, commonly responded that their children needed to respect and revere the teacher. If they did not express such uncritical support, they would be faced with the even greater dilemma of having to supply the Jewish education themselves — and that they no longer felt empowered or able to do.

Encountering this resistance, some students just turned away from Orthodoxy altogether, revolted by the inconsistencies and discontinuities. Sometimes they waited until they were away at college to drop out, a development that raised the anxiety level among many parents and teachers and only led to a greater tolerance of the Haredization of Orthodoxy. Moreover, the abandonment of Orthodoxy by these adolescents (like the desertion of the nominally Orthodox) left those who were more comfortable with or at least tolerated the Haredi message as a larger part of the movement. Those who stayed within Orthodoxy but were *uncomfortable* with all this tried to find other ways to resist without dropping out. We shall see something of their efforts in chapters 7 and 8.

THE ISRAEL EXPERIENCE

By the 1970s the modern Orthodox, increasingly concerned about the religious cost of their encounter with American popular culture (and never fully engaged by its high culture), were at the same time assailed by increasingly insistent warnings of the Haredi world about the folly of their Jewish educational choices. In response, they embraced a strategy that they hoped would inoculate their children with sufficient Jewish attachments and knowledge to confront successfully the ever more anxiety-provoking challenge of the American college campus and the society to which it served as the gateway. This strategy, which they hoped would enable their children to proceed on the path of moderated contrapuntalism toward Orthodox centrism, was to send their day school graduates for a year's study in a yeshiva in Israel.[80] The Israeli yeshivas, which as early as 1957–58 were trying to recruit American Orthodox youth, used education as an ideological tool for fighting back against secular culture.[81] But only a very few Americans joined the programs at the outset. Only in the 1970s did the programs begin to catch on as the contrapuntalists looked desperately for a way of responding to the religious challenges of contemporary America that the day schools and modern Orthodox communities were not able to meet. While the ostensible focus in these study-abroad programs was on Torah study or some sort of Israel experience, they became much more.[82]

In the Israeli yeshiva, which Americans attended after graduation and after they had been admitted to the colleges of their choice (enrollment deferred for a year), there would be none of the seductions of campus life, the toxins of Western culture, or even the pressures of the world outside.[83] There would be no college preparation or secular courses to distract students from Judaic concerns, no grades, and no competition from either other cultures or other students. Here the Orthodox religious attachments that the day schools might have been unsuccessful in implanting could be more successfully grafted. Once attached, they would shield these young Jews against the cultural invasion of defiling American values. The assumption behind these evolving programs was that by immersing themselves in Torah learning and nothing else, and by doing it in the "Holy Land" under the tutelage of distinguished yeshiva heads *(roshey yeshiva)* or other Orthodox role models, American Orthodox students would be reinforced, even reborn, in their Jewish commitments and subsequently unshakable when they went to college—to which the parents remained certain they would still go.

Although at first this kind of trip was considered exotic and specialized, after the Six Day War in Israel, with the sense of security it fostered and the enhanced Zionist feelings it engendered in American Orthodoxy— by the 1970s the new pioneers of settlement, the new Jewish heroes, were the Gush Emunim, the so-called "bloc of the faithful," who were themselves Orthodox Jews—these trips seemed a good way for American Orthodox Jews (who made up 72 percent of the Diaspora participants in the program) to get a kind of double credit.[84] They could at once share in the renewed enthusiasms of religious Zionism and provide their children with the needed "booster shot" of Torah life. For their part, the Israelis were happy to oblige. Not only did the appearance of these Americans fortify their own sense of mission and belief in their role as the religious leadership of world Jewry—that they had the capacity to purify the defiled and that their Zionism would end even the American Diaspora—but the tuitions (between $10,000 and $13,000 per year as of this writing) that the American Orthodox were willing to pay turned out to be a "cash cow" for yeshivas that were always in need and could never collect as much per capita for their Israeli students.[85] The programs became increasingly accepted as part of the modern Orthodox educational career. By 2001–2, 65 percent on average of the New York day school graduates of that year were attending such Israeli institutions, and in some schools over 90 percent of the graduates were going.[86] A whole industry developed around these yeshiva programs, including charter flights and hotel seasons for the annual parental visit, and the number and style of these yeshivas multiplied. Some integrated Americans and Israelis, others offered instruction in English and offered a Zionist experience in translation for Americans who found their Hebrew language skills insufficient or could not match Israeli students' levels of Torah learning and cultural competence; still others, though set in Israel, were essentially American Haredi in character. In a few decades, by the end of the twentieth century, what had once been exotic became almost conventional, with a number of such institutions founded exclusively for American men and women. Even outbreaks of violence and terrorism did not end the programs (though in recent years they have become somewhat curtailed).[87]

By 2001–2 the numbers reportedly had reached somewhere between 1,800 enrollees in the Zionist-oriented institutions and as high as 14,500 in institutions associated with Haredi Orthodoxy. This latter number is likely inflated, given that many Haredi schools get a per capita payment from a variety of sources and therefore have a vested interest in reporting more students than they actually have. Alvin Schiff, whose report on the numbers is widely considered the most accurate, puts the total number of students from the Diaspora enrolled in both Zionist-oriented and Haredi schools during 2001–2 at 3,200 men and 1,400 women in Jerusalem and another 1,000 outside of it.[88]

To be sure, the correlation between day school education and visiting Israel was well documented and established. As the 1990 National Jewish Population Survey demonstrated, among those two million Jews between the ages of twenty-six and forty-six who were part of the generation first exposed to these programs, while 40 percent of day school–educated Jews had been to Israel three or more times in their lives, only between 3 and 5 percent of those who had gone to part-time or Sunday school had been to Israel three or more times (between 76 and 81 percent of the latter had actually *never* visited Israel, while only about a quarter of the day school educated had never made the trip).[89] In contrast, about one-third, 452, of former students of the Har Etzion Yeshiva, one of those with a large overseas contingent, moved permanently to Israel, while a study in 1990 showed that one-third of all Israel study participants in the 1970–71 year had also done so.[90]

The religious impact of these programs exceeded the expectations of even the most optimistic observers. In the only systematic research on these students, Shalom Berger found that the impact of the year in an Israeli yeshiva led alumni to increase their levels of religious ritual practice, commitment to continued Torah study, and Zionism.[91] In fact, in a control group that included high school graduates who did not choose to study in Israel but went directly to college in the United States, no such changes were found.

For the youngsters who were in these yeshivas, the experience was close to idyllic. They were on their own, yet still in a protected setting.[92] The impact of being far from home and family, in an institution insulated against outside influences, and creating new bonds of solidarity with others who share that insider life, has been an important factor of the yeshiva experience since at least the nineteenth century, when schools like the one in Volozhin (Lithuania) were founded that enrolled and housed students from distant communities. Cut off from the familiar, the habits of their home life, and their communities, students depended increasingly on the written codes as found in the texts they studied and the norms of behavior as established in the yeshiva. For the most part, these texts were interpreted as uncompromising in their Jewish demands, while the norms of behavior tended to be *frum*mer than the practices "back home."

Moreover, everyone assured these students that what they were doing and how they were acting was noble and righteous. As a result, when American Orthodox Jews came to these institutions, which far more so than their yeshivas and day schools in America were what Erving Goffman calls "total institutions," places that create "barriers to social intercourse with the outside" and seek not only to insulate but to shield and isolate those inside from dangers outside, *they were more than likely to be changed by the experience.*[93] They moved easily toward the religious right. In the parlance of modern Orthodox, this transformation has come to be called "flipping."[94]

In the first years—before cell phones were the ubiquitous presence they now are for the students—it was complex and difficult for the parents and children to communicate regularly except through letters, which took weeks to make the trip (even when they were sent by "couriers" who traveled between Israel and America). Sometimes the few public telephones in the yeshivas became the only channel to the outside world, and they were hard to use. This added to the feeling that time in the yeshiva in Israel meant dramatic and significant separation from their old world, a feeling that enhanced the students' sensation of being "somewhere else and far away." The flipping thus was imperceptible to their parents and community back home in America until they returned (if they returned at all).[95]

All this was happening while these American adolescents were under-

going the quest for identity typical of their age group combined with the
inevitable struggle to psychologically separate from their parents. As Erik
Erikson reminds us, this is a period when adolescents experience "a revolution within them," when they have to figure out "how to connect the
roles and skills cultivated earlier" to what they will do next in their lives
while they "search for a new sense of continuity and sameness," something they often do by "artificially" appointing "well-meaning people to
play the role of adversaries" and installing "lasting idols and ideals as
guardians of a final identity."[96] In the Israeli yeshivas all this became translated, even more than it had been in the United States, into their seeing
their rabbis and teachers as the ideals and guardians of a Torah identity
that the American expatriate students took on. All the while their parents,
or precisely the culture and society from which their parents came, American modern Orthodoxy and American life, were painted as, if not adversaries, at least antagonists. The *roshey yeshiva* and often the Israeli or
veteran students nurtured this thinking, telling the young Americans that
now that they were here they were the true defenders of the faith and protectors of the Jewish future.

Just when they needed it, these youngsters thus experienced a kind of
triple-barreled liberation: release from the restrictions of living at home
and their communities (some for the first time in their lives), from their
American childhood, and from the demands of grades and the competi-
tive pressures of high school. They were in effect on a threshold, or in what
Victor Turner called a liminal state, a state of being that is all potential.

In this betwixt-and-between state of liminality, what S. N. Eisenstadt
has called the "role moratorium" of youth, the yeshiva experience and Israeli Orthodoxy of the most uncompromising sort became a kind of bea-
con that led them out of the uncertainty of adolescence toward a new identity, new continuities, connections, commitments, and choices.[97] The
teachers in the yeshiva, even compared to the most authoritative rebbees
back home, exuded a confidence and charisma (in part because of the political and social power they held in Israeli religious life and in part because in these total institutions they were royalty) of the sort to which
many of these young Americans had never before been exposed. Here,
then, was an environment that, even more than the college campus, was
truly an ivory tower, where nothing mattered except studying Torah,
where the outside world was almost never allowed to intrude, and where
all that was done not only brought approval from the rabbis and fellow
students but also earned these young people "credit in Heaven."

In the yeshiva, so unlike the day school, the formal classes were distributed throughout the week, but most of the time was spent preparing for the *shiur* or formal lecture presented by teachers. Yet most of the days were filled from early morning to late at night — sometimes well past midnight in the main study hall or *bes medrash* — plumbing the textual sources upon which the teachers expanded, and then in the class's aftermath reviewing those insights. For a year, or maybe more, as they engaged in such review (for the boys this was mostly Talmud, for the girls more often Bible and related Scriptures and commentaries, and for both the codes that outlined proper behavior), commonly in the company of a variety of study partners, *chavruse,* and at their own chosen pace, they found a new sense of belonging and meaning in their lives, and they increasingly felt as if the yeshiva world was their true new home.

But as is the case in all ivory towers, those inside ignore the necessary compromises of the real world. Inside one develops a kind of Jewish practice and belief that are sometimes called "yeshivish," in which one exudes a kind of passion and near obsession with studying Torah, being "holy," and being punctilious in religious observance.[98] Prayers can be and are extended to extraordinary lengths, allowing for a kind of flexing of spiritual muscles. At its pinnacle, *yeshivish* denotes someone so deeply immersed in the yeshiva world and values that he or she is completely unfamiliar with the expectations and social graces of the modern world outside, studiously ignoring them. Perhaps nothing could be more different from the ethos of the day school and its rigorous schedule as well as its attachments to goals in tune with demands in the world beyond the Jewish one.

Even an element of asceticism entered the program at some of these yeshivas. Not only were the dormitories and physical plant of these Israeli institutions frequently austere — often in dramatic contrast to the living conditions in America — but the diet was Spartan. Missing were the rich culinary choices of America, and in the early days (before the junk food wave invaded Israel, putting a pizza parlor within reach of every yeshiva and credit card), it was not unusual for students to return from Israel thinner and with the typical pallor of the yeshiva boy, another external sign of their transformation and their separation from the fleshpots of America and its associated culture.

The yeshivas thus managed a classic transformation, as Eisenstadt has described it, through "transmission of the tribal lore with its instructions about proper behavior, both through formalized teaching and through various ritual activities," and this was combined with "a relaxation of the concrete control of the adults over the erstwhile adolescents and its substitution by self-control and adult responsibility."[99]

By virtue of the fact that the rabbis and teachers did the same things in the same study halls as their students, engaging in study alongside them, they demonstrated that this learning was an adult and lifelong activity. Along the way, they exhorted students to remain with them longer than just a year. They did this either explicitly or tacitly by endorsing repeatedly the value of a life that would remain within the orbit of Torah and the yeshiva—the Haredi ideal of the scholars' society.[100] Some even went as far as suggesting that to leave and choose another life was to sell out or at least not be true to the fundamental demands of Judaism. After all, the teachers displayed this sense of vocation in their own lives. Thus often the best way for young students to demonstrate that they had "learned the lesson," had become transformed, passed out of their American, modern Orthodox childhood, and refused to sell out, was to embrace the idea of *shanah bet,* a second year in the yeshiva, which meant the desire to remain within a more insular Orthodoxy. Increasingly the idea of year two caught on. And the goal of year two was year three, and so on.

Once the students became persuaded that what they were doing was the fulfillment of God's wishes and the Jewish people's hopes, and that they were the Jewish future, they often concluded that leaving all this would be a victory for the perpetrators of the Holocaust—precisely the argument of the Haredim. After all, a world of yeshivas was what post–World War II Haredi Orthodoxy had for years wished to resurrect. After the Americans finally did leave, this life in the yeshiva would be recalled as a kind of safe haven and idyll they would forever after try to replicate.

As part of the process of embracing these alternate yeshivish and Haredi versions of Orthodoxy, the young Jews marked their new identities by external symbols. Among the boys, this might include donning the black hat, white shirt, and dark jacket that had become the uniform of the Haredi yeshiva world or, in the case of the national religious yeshivas, the extralarge knit yarmulke or the overlarge heavily knotted one of the kabbalistic yeshivas (most of which were around the city of Safed). All young men began to publicly expose their tzitzit, ritual fringes which in the past they had kept under their shirts, as if saying they could now "come out" as proudly Orthodox. Among the women, the change in appearance came in wearing long sleeves and extralong skirts that made up so-called modest dress, characteristic of the religious right wing. After marriage, nearly all the women covered their hair, in a fashion that once had been limited to the Haredi sector of Orthodoxy and eschewed by the acculturative contrapuntalists.

In their postures of prayer, these male and female yeshiva products were easy to spot. They displayed their piety in the extralong duration of their prayers, their pious gesticulations during worship, and their continuing dedication to the study of Jewish texts. Moreover, in America this expressive behavior served to draw a clear boundary between them and the rest of modern Orthodoxy. The Israeli sojourners thus returned to America not only with a new set of Orthodox behaviors and values but with a studied alienation from the kind of Judaism that had been normative for them prior to their Israel experience. Sometimes they appeared and sounded as if they had come from an eastern European yeshiva. It may be that among today's Orthodox, the old idea repeated by the historian Marcus Hansen — that what the Jewish immigrant's son wishes to forget, the grandson wishes to remember — has a particular resonance.[101] As Haym Soloveitchik described these returnees: "A new generation has emerged which finds the past ways of its parents and grandparents too unthinking, too ignorant, and yes, if truth be told, simply too lax and accommodative."[102] Often these students actually sought to return to the ghetto, to live entirely with others who had experienced the Israel year or who shared its style of Orthodoxy, peers to whom they felt more attached than to their college cohort.[103] These acquired characteristics and attitudes obviously contradicted the modern Orthodox ideal of living in the creative tension between secular and Jewish culture and society.

These students denied the imperative of getting into the university and then a profession. They suggested that modern Orthodox life lay uneasily on people's shoulders and could be thrown off like a loosely held cloak. This they could do without open objection from the modern but increasingly centrist Orthodox who had been tacitly (and sometimes actively) valorizing the Israel experience to which they had been sending these youngsters in increasing numbers.

Returning at last to college — if they did (and more and more did not) — these young Orthodox Jews found themselves to be older than their classmates, who commonly came straight from high school and living at home. Moreover, they seemed to have solved the problem of their identity, were more at ease being away from home and living with their commitments to Judaism, and were ready to stand apart from the powerful cultural crosscurrents of the freshman or even the sophomore year of college. Gone was the modern Orthodox attitude of the passage into university life as a time for the opening of minds and new possibilities, of transformation. Instead, some of these young Orthodox Jews already transformed tended to look at college as a trial to be passed — after all they had been warned in the yeshiva about how the campus was threatening to

Judaism. Now, as Perl and Weinstein saw it, they would be able to pass the test: "students who spend a pressure free year in Israel growing intellectually, spiritually, and emotionally" and who "spend a year exploring the beauty of Judaism and strengthening their commitment to it" are "less likely" to fall out of Orthodoxy during "their tenure at a secular university campus."[104]

In time many of these young people who did go through the process became reintegrated into the rank and file of American Orthodoxy. Many of the first of them are today in their forties and early fifties, but an even larger group are in their twenties and thirties . They have changed the nature of the Orthodox experience for many in their communities, who are either religiously inspired by them or else forced to display an attitude of inspiration that embraces Haredi pieties.[105] For quite a number of these Jews, hindsight, tinged with a nostalgia for their youth, has associated many of the acquired attitudes about Judaism with which they returned with the best years of their lives. This of course is not unique in the culture of America, in which youth is celebrated and the dominant view is that "adulthood decidedly [is not] the advantageous" or desirable time of life. That is why in America "young adults in their middle twenties may feel old and wish they were back in college."[106] With the Orthodox Jews I have described here, instead of college the time in Israel and the yeshiva (or for the women, the seminary) is the focus of the nostalgia.

Their experience has made these Jews particularly attached to Israel (overall about 20 percent have actually moved there, at least temporarily), but it has also made them feel an additional attachment to yeshivish Orthodoxy in either its Haredi version or an Israeli nationalist one—both of which are to the right of American modern Orthodoxy.[107] They often perceive Orthodoxy and "learning" as more authentic, pure, honest, and satisfying than life in the real world of jobs, family responsibilities, and contemporary society. To connect with that past and feel that they are true to it, the alumni of such programs often become more religiously associated with yeshiva/Haredi (or religious Zionist) values and lifestyles. These involvements in turn have gradually changed the balance in Orthodoxy in America. Where once the modern Orthodox day school was the ideal instrument of continuity for contemporary Orthodox Jews, the yeshiva, particularly the one attended during the year in Israel, has become the leading institution.

The arrival of American modern Orthodox students, even those who have come from yeshivas rather than day schools, has also caused a dilemma for the Haredi community in Israel. On the one hand, the arrival of these students to "lern Toyreh" (study Torah) in the yeshivas of Israel can be and often is seen as evidence of a cultural victory of the Israeli yeshiva world and Haredi Orthodoxy over its American counterpart. After all, the presence of Americans is living evidence of the principle on which the Israeli institutions built their programs for Jews from the Diaspora: "Ki mitzion teitzei Torah—For from Zion the Torah will come forth."[108] Moreover, these days the yeshiva students quickly don the distinctive garb of the Haredi and yeshivish right, and when they leave the study halls they choose to remain within the precincts of Haredi and yeshivish neighborhoods. As these neighborhoods have tried to assimilate the Americans who come to study in their institutions, even in their elite yeshivas, they have also faced the problem of absorbing some of the American culture that these students inevitably bring with them. This, as far as the Haredim are concerned, has added dangers, which at least to the most insular among them are unacceptable. Confronted with the scene of these young Americans meeting one another, sometimes with iPods on which they listen to the latest popular music, and congregating on the streets and in the squares of their protected enclaves, particularly in Jerusalem and vicinity, some of the Haredim and yeshiva authorities have begun to worry that the sights and sounds of these youngsters, particularly when the single men and women stop to exchange conversation (and maybe flirt—an interaction prohibited in most Haredi enclaves in Israel but more common in America), will have a deleterious effect on their own natives. Then there is the question of drugs and alcohol, with which some of the American students are involved. Cases of American yeshiva students who have abused both are notorious.[109] In effect, here are American yeshiva students caught up in (a mitigated form) of sex, drugs, and rock and roll, just what the yeshiva was supposed to save them from falling prey to on the college campus.

For these reasons, Israeli yeshivas increasingly try to isolate the Americans from the Israeli students. Indeed, in an enclave where drugs and alcohol are a deep dark secret and where not only are the schools segregated by gender but repeated efforts are made to separate the sexes in all public places—from buses to pedestrian walkways—the presence of these students, who have not accepted these norms yet (and may never) but who nevertheless perceive themselves to be confirmedly Orthodox and to belong in this enclave, is intolerable. Signs have begun to appear on walls in Shabbos Square in Jerusalem, a major crossroads of Haredi orthodoxy, as well as outside the yeshivas and in other places, beseeching young men and women not to loiter in the streets or to engage in meetings and conversations there. The fact that these signs are often in English, rather than in the more common Hebrew or Yiddish, vividly demonstrates to which Jews they are primarily directed.

Yet for all the efforts to control the impact of the Americans, the world of right-wing religion is not prepared to banish them, hoping instead to continue to transform them and to triumphantly display their success in "capturing" these imports into their brand of religious orthodoxy, of making them *frum*mer. Indeed, these same American yeshiva boys who represent a cultural threat in the Haredi neighborhoods paradoxically represent an opposite cultural threat in their American neighborhoods when they return. There they seem to embody the arrival of Haredi elements that locals fear will transform their communities into Haredi enclaves. Who will change whom, however, cannot be confidently predicted. If the same principles that explain all culture contact obtain, the likelihood is that change will go in both directions. Moreover, the assumption that the few will always be overwhelmed by the many, the visitors changed by those they visit, the natives more powerful culturally than the strangers, has of course been shown to be faulty by everyone from missionaries to field anthropologists. One may assume that anyone who looks carefully at the mutual impact of American Jewish students and the Israeli schools and communities in which they sojourn will also discover the fallacy of this assumption.

To be sure, some argue that neither Israel programs nor Orthodox insularity in the yeshiva world will ensure the continuity of Orthodoxy. Rather, the line of reasoning runs, only an informed, longtime commitment to Orthodox Judaism and its way of life that, long before the college years or campus life begins, has prepared a person to live as an observant Orthodox Jew under any and all circumstances can provide the defense against the ever-present challenges of modernity.

Another argument suggests that those whose Orthodoxy has been protected by their remaining in a sheltered enclave will sooner or later crumble when they find themselves in a free environment. Better, therefore, to prepare them for the challenge in their adolescence, on campus, than to wait for later. Those, this argument runs, who do get through the college years with their faith and Orthodoxy intact—and there are significant numbers who do—will be better suited to sustain and generate an Orthodox Jewish way of life necessary for continuity. But these arguments have for the time being been overwhelmed by the flow of Orthodox high school graduates (and more and more college graduates) to the Israeli yeshiva learning experience and offset by an attitude that suggests one should never leave the Orthodox enclave or its culture.

Is There an Enduring Impact?

All these factors have combined synergistically to make a profound impact not only on Orthodox Jewish education but also on the idea of what
is normative Orthodoxy. To be sure, as already suggested, just as the countercultural trends of the 1960s and early 1970s helped jar the love affair of
some Orthodox with contemporary American culture and its values, despite all that the university offered, and made them worry whether the
tension with America might not be too much for Orthodoxy to bear, so
now the conservative trends of late-twentieth- and early-twenty-first-
century America have helped to create a social environment that has been
hospitable to a more religiously right-wing Orthodoxy. There is no way
to know for certain whether this development will have unintended consequences, whether the expanding numbers of those who wish to remain
caught up in the life of Jewish learning inside the yeshivas will be able to
sustain themselves economically, socially, culturally, and spiritually. After
all, the yeshivas in the past were places where the forces of modernization and Jewish enlightenment and a thirst for critical thinking and individual initiative emerged.

Moreover, the conditions in the United States that today seem to have
allowed for the emergence of this sort of Orthodoxy could change and
once again nurture yet another sort of transformation. Certainly, stability is not assured. Could it happen that the Haredi faculty in the schools
will alienate more students than they inspire—or that the agents provocateurs will themselves be turned into agents of modernity? Might parents take on more of the educational role or new cadres of rabbis emerge
from the new institutions of "open Orthodoxy" and retake the initiative
with a "passionate commitment to Torah and Halakha in theory and practice" as well as a recognition that the Orthodox can be "enriched religiously by the many aspects of the world at large," as the founders of Yeshivat Chovevei Torah claim to want to do?[110] Will the Jewish Orthodox
Feminist Alliance (JOFA) and other similar modern Orthodox women's
groups who have struggled to create space for women in the domains of
Orthodoxy find that they have a role to play in transforming Jewish education in ways that challenge growing Haredi hegemony? Their success
in injecting a new spirit of religious exploration and challenge to Orthodoxy suggests that some may return to Jewish education and expand its
horizons beyond the narrowness of Haredism.

As for the continuing impact of the Israel experience, although yeshivas
have regained some of their enrollment losses that the uncertain security

situation stimulated recently, the vagaries of the situation in Israel continually throw into question the choice of many parents to send their high school graduates for an extended stay there. Perhaps even more importantly, the institutional growth in the numbers of these yeshivas and seminaries, while a measure of their success, has also created a change in their character. It has led, among other things, to the emergence of exclusively American ones that often recreate the American culture in an Israeli setting (complete with American expatriate teachers). Even in the Israeli yeshivas, the practice now has become to segregate the foreign students from the native Israeli ones, creating a separate reality for many of the American students that is culturally closer to home. In some measure, this may dilute the impact of the Israeli components of the experience. When the "away" experience becomes an extension of the "home" setting, the return to home may not be quite as difficult and the time in Israel not quite as transformative.

Along the same lines, the increasingly common routine in many of these yeshivas of allowing and even encouraging their students to return home one or more times during the year—holiday and vacation trips that have become easier and relatively cheaper—also has diminished the totalistic character of the institutions. A year away is now more like a few months away between home visits. Moreover, the near-universal possession of cell phones and e-mail has made it possible and common for the students who are in Israel to maintain their contacts in America and remain in touch with its culture and the values at home. In addition, the relatively large number of American students in Israel at any time as well as their continuing contact with one another (via these same phones and Internet connections as well as face-to-face meetings), to say nothing of the galloping Americanization of Israeli culture, has often made it seem existentially as if the Americans in Israel are still in the United States.[111] When they meet fellow Americans at the local Burger King, talk to and visit home, surf the Internet, or otherwise maintain many of the patterns of their familiar culture, it is far more difficult for the transformations of the Israeli yeshiva experience to take place. The consequences of this for their religious and personal development cannot be gainsaid. The yeshivas understand this, and some have tried to mitigate this reality by, for example, limiting e-mail and Internet access, demanding that cell phones be turned off in the *bes medrash,* and trying to control students' travels outside the yeshiva. No less than the Novominsker Rebbe, spiritual head of Agudath Israel of America, in a speech in 2003 before delegates at the Torah Umesorah Convention, the umbrella organization for Orthodox

Jewish education, asserted that "the Internet, with a flick of a button, invades a Jewish home, a Jewish soul, and makes moral disaster."[112] However, in the face of the political realities and the fact that many of the yeshivas are now in powerful competition for students in a tighter market, these restrictions are difficult to enforce.

In America, the enduring impact of the situation of modernity may also play its part in moderating the impact of this swing to the right. Consider, for example, something called "winter *kollel*." This is a yeshiva session ostensibly designed for high schoolers and some college students who, finding themselves with a long winter break, might normally be expected to take a vacation at some leisure spot. In an effort to prevent the young from "wasting" their time off, some Orthodox institutions have sponsored a session of studying away from home called "winter *kollel*."[113] In places like Israel or in the American Sun Belt, in the words of a typical sponsor, "the Winter Kollel is designed for serious 11th and 12th grade Yeshiva High School boys who desire to learn during their winter vacation while enjoying the beautiful weather of Miami Beach." This program, potential participants are assured, is "endorsed by many Yeshiva University Roshei Yeshiva and NY area Yeshiva High Schools."[114] Now one must wonder whether the culture of leisure and vacation will ultimately overwhelm the one of Torah study and learning or vice versa. After all, though the entire day is spent at study and prayer, the "night activities" include trips to a Miami Heat/Florida Panthers Game, Boomers Amusement Park, and something called "Whirley Ball." While the Web postings of pictures from past seasons show young boys seated at tables and studying Talmud, they also show these same youngsters playing basketball, riding in dodgem-cars, and playing pinball. Who is to say which of these activities will resonate more powerfully in the experience of these participants?

In the final analysis, those considering the long-term consequences of all these trends in Orthodox Jewish education would do well to recall, as Clifford Geertz has argued, both that "thinking is a matter of the intentional manipulation of cultural forms," and that the hallmark of contemporary consciousness is "its enormous multiplicity."[115] Accordingly, anyone trying to manipulate and restrict the religious thinking of young people these days is entering ineluctably into the complexities of cultural contact and culture war. It is increasingly difficult to maintain a narrow and restrictive consciousness for very long these days.[116] Even in what seems to be the most securely insulated enclave, the outside contemporary world and its enormous multiplicity seep inside. Yeshivas and their teachers who try to influence students and their attachments to culture, to regulate behavior, worldview, and values, must prepare for the possibility that they will also be changed in the process. This is a lesson that some of the mullahs in today's Iran, who once thought that with absolute political power they could control change and impose a narrow traditional consciousness on their nation forever, are already starting to discover as many of Iran's youth plot a social revolution.[117] In a sense, what may start out as an effort to inculcate and delimit the "shoulds and oughts" turns out in the situation of modernity and multiplicity to lead to the realization that the escape from freedom and complexity to the haven of tradition and fundamentalism is far from assured. In the end, for those being taught, education often becomes a question of "Will this really work for someone like me?" Or, to put it in terms suggested in the opening epigraph, Will my religious spirit and values survive the religious education I have been given? In the realm of religion and culture, the answers to that question have changed over the generations. Even for Orthodox Jews, that is likely to remain true in the days to come.

CHAPTER 4

Reinventing Tradition
When Going by the Book Replaces Living on the Street

> Custom is potent, but its true power is informal. It derives
> from the ability of habit to neutralize the implications of book
> knowledge. Anything learned from study that conflicts with
> accustomed practice cannot really be right.
>
> Haym Soloveitchik, "Rupture and Reconstruction:
> The Transformation of Contemporary Orthodoxy"

In many ways the increasing influence of the Haredi type of Orthodoxy
has restrained the contrapuntalism of some in the movement. Perhaps one
of the most fascinating has been a process in which the prescriptive takes
precedence over living norms, or, as I shall try to put it in this chapter,
one in which going by the book replaces living on the street. To understand this process, we need to consider briefly some of the developments
of history.

As we have seen in chapter 2, the last two hundred or so years of Jewish
life have been profoundly cataclysmic. This has been a time of dramatic
geographic, intellectual, and social changes. Mass migration, processes
of so-called enlightenment (sometimes called *improvement* or *regeneration*), and the social and political movement of many if not most Jews from
a separate, insulated society and culture into the mainstream of Western
civilization (referred to variously as *emancipation, naturalization,* or finally
the relatively "neutral" *acculturation*). All these fundamentally transformed the condition of Jewry. Moreover, because these changes did not
occur all at once in all places where Jews lived but rather continued for
some Jews through the first half of the twentieth century (particularly
those migrating in the Middle Eastern countries and North Africa), their
impact has not been fully felt until the contemporary era. One of the dramatic consequences of these shifts was that a living Jewish tradition, a
once taken-for-granted lamination to life in a relatively insular Jewish community, no longer dominated life automatically. As the barriers that closed

off the "Jewish street," the circumscribed ghettoized community, from the rest of the cosmopolis were removed, those who had learned the traditions and rules of conduct on that street found themselves changing or losing their bearings more and more. Traditions that had remained relatively stable for generations because the people who carried and passed them on lived a relatively insular life that changed at a glacial pace became increasingly difficult to maintain. After emancipation and enlightenment, the new began always to seem improved. In a world where movement and change were endemic and where other streets were now open for exploration, those who sought to maintain the old ways were confronted by the realization that what was once taken for granted or a matter of fate would increasingly have to become a matter of self-conscious planning and choice.

Those who championed tradition under these conditions—for example, the Jews who called themselves "Orthodox"—had to demonstrate, in an increasingly free marketplace of ideas, that the old was truly better than the new. They also sought ways of keeping Jews from abandoning the traditional Jewish street, a task made even more difficult, as we have seen, in those places where the world outside beckoned and offered intellectual, economic, political, and social opportunities that seemed far more appealing to many Jews than their limited prospects in the ghetto.

Most Jews rejected the arguments in favor of Jewish traditions and the ghetto mentality. Those who remained Jews advocated either easing the transition by holding onto some elements of Jewish character while moving outward or making a swift leap to the new. That is, some selected a kind of cultural pluralism, albeit often only temporarily (for a generation or two), while others embraced undiluted acculturation, where they tried to become something else, though retaining an embedded cultural memory of what they had been as Jews.[1] Indeed, as Ivan Marcus has put it, the latter was a particularly fruitful approach and served, "in large measure, [as] the secret of Jewish creative persistence," since vitality was to be found specifically in such "mechanisms of cultural adaptation," in which Judaism engaged in a kind of open dialogue with other cultures and faiths.[2] In a sense both approaches implied that it was possible to maintain Jewish ties (albeit at varying levels of intensity and involvement) but still go beyond the "narrow spirit" of stultifying traditionalism.

We have seen that the Orthodox rejected both these approaches because they refused to accept the characterization of any part of Jewish tradition as narrow or stultifying. On the contrary, they wanted to stress the rewards and advantages of the tradition in all its glory, even and especially when other Jews were abandoning or moderating their ties to it. This was the heart of the Orthodox "counter-reformation," particularly in Germanic-speaking countries and westward. As part of that effort, some focused much energy fighting religious reform or dissociated themselves politically from the corporate Jewish communities that they saw as moving wholesale into the precincts of non-Jewish culture. This was, in a sense, the beginning of a *Kulturkampf* that the champions of traditionalism and later the Haredim would increasingly wage against the forces allied with modernism and non-Judaic culture. In the most extreme expression of this point of view, they argued, in the words of Rabbi Moses Sofer (d. 1838 in Hungary), that "the new is prohibited by the Torah."[3]

They denied as well that there was any need to leave the protected precincts of the Jewish street, which they saw as the protective enclave of tradition. For some, the way to demonstrate these attitudes was to maintain retrograde dress or refuse to use the vernacular, particularly in matters pertaining to the sacred. While these strategies worked for the most insular among them and for the Hasidim, those traditionalists who over time had been drawn by the vicissitudes of history, the destruction of European Jewry, and the American experience into some engagement with life outside the traditional enclave, often because the Jewish street had been compromised or violated, found they needed something new to maintain their ties to the tradition. That something would become the increasing use of a Judeo-legal literature that spelled out the codes of acceptable and unacceptable Jewish behavior. This is a process akin to what Clifford Geertz called "scripturalism," a practice that gives supreme authority to text rather than to life lived.[4] In a sense, as I shall try to argue here, Orthodox scripturalists turned to this literature of codes because they were no longer certain that they could maintain the integrity of their parochial domains or the allegiance of their members because too much of the constantly changing modern world and civil society was seeping in and undermining the authority of tradition. The literature of the codes thus became at once a bulwark against change and an enclosure that prevented them from adapting to change.

Such a reliance on texts to guide them after national dislocation and exile from a Jewish enclave has a long history among Jews. The rabbinic tradition that begins symbolically in Yavneh after the destruction of the Holy Temple in Jerusalem, and later developments in the Babylonian academies of Nehardea, Sura, and Pumbedita during the early years of the common era, represented a move from the living tradition of a Temple cult organized around sacrifices to the traditions of a "people of the book," in which scholarship and rabbis replaced prophecy and kings.[5] In the aftermath of this latest dislocation, the Jews would once again turn to the books.

The Literature of Code Books

Code books, compendia of Jewish law and custom, were often the key texts to which the Jews turned. As Haym Soloveitchik has noted in his exploration of the role of these volumes and their increasing importance in Orthodox Jewish life, they were actually commentaries and rabbinic elaborations on codes.[6] At first, they (and the extracts from them in prayer books) aimed to disambiguate and order the law for the faithful; they were an accompaniment to life lived, written notes to the music that people knew more or less by heart and that they occasionally improvised. Indeed, they were largely in harmony with a community that understood itself to be anchored to Jewish traditions. They were used with the assistance of rabbi/scholars, who helped the faithful laity to learn and review them and to know when they were to be followed to the letter and when they could simply be viewed as one opinion on how Jewish life was to be lived. Indeed, where life somehow contradicted the letter of the law or the tradition as one of these texts established it, this was perhaps of scholarly or intellectual interest in the academies of higher Jewish learning, but it did not necessarily lead to an abandoning of the living (and fluctuating) popular tradition. In effect, at the outset these texts augmented the popular tradition, even as they sought to protect its integrity. They accepted practice rather than directing it. For example, as Soloveitchik notes in "Religious Law and Change: A Medieval Ashkenazic Example," practices extant within the Jewish community were ratified by some of these texts at least as early as the time of the Tosafists.[7] "We may say, without fear of exaggeration," he argues, "that the Tosafists have overtly fashioned the law so as to align it better with regnant practice and need."[8] Likewise, the code of Moses Isserles, when it came to certain rules for Sabbath observance, found ways of aligning the law with what was possible in Poland.[9]

To be sure, this process whereby the Jewish street could have its practices ratified via reinterpretations of the law was possible, Soloveitchik argues, when and where the community living on that street "was permeated by a profound sense of its own religiosity, of the rightness of its traditions, and could not imagine any sharp difference between its practices and the law which its members studied and observed with . . . devotion."[10] That is, as long as they were sure of themselves as essentially "good Jews" and of their community as a *kehilla kedosha* (holy community), what was customary among the Jews of that community *(minhag ha'makom)* was acceptable. For people of such intense religiosity, custom and these written texts ultimately converged; both were "revelatory of the Divine intent."[11]

The literature that many Jews turned to in the face of the changes that began in the nineteenth and continued into the twentieth century was often that of the code books. These were not the first of the genre. Moses Maimonides' *Mishneh Torah,* written in the twelfth century, the *Arba'ah Turim* (sometimes called the *Tur*), compiled by Jacob Ben Asher in the thirteenth century, and the *Shulchan Aruch,* by Joseph Caro, and *Mappah HaShulchan,* notes and glosses on Caro by Moses Isserles, both prepared in the sixteenth century, all clearly presented laws by which Jews of various traditions should be guided in their behavior. These represented distillations and arrangements of the principles of Talmudic law coupled with custom and usage as well as rabbinic interpretations of them. Over time they in turn became the subjects of many commentaries and emendations that became part of the codes.[12]

In the era that interests us here, the important and most popular books in this literature—those laymen would consult—include *Chaye Odom,* written by Abraham Danzig in 1810; Solomon Ganzfried's tremendously popular *Kitzur Shulchan Aruch,* issued in 1864 and published in fourteen editions during his lifetime; the authoritative *Mishneh Berurah,* authored by Israel Kagan between 1896 and 1907; and finally *Aruch Ha Shulchan,* by Yechiel Michl Epstein, first published between 1903 and 1909. Not all of these books were purely concerned with codes; some, like that of the Hungarian businessman Ganzfried, were also part of an effort to combat Jewish reformers. Ostensibly, compendia aimed at making the complexities of Talmudic and rabbinic Jewish law accessible and clear: these texts sought to help a religiously observant Jewry guide itself according to the Jewish code of conduct. They meant to describe precisely what the Jewish law and tradition called for in the way of intent and behavior. In a sense, these books and the increasing usage of them—principally the *Mishneh Berurah*—can be conceived of as a part of the cultural counter-reaction by those who ideologically attached themselves to the time-honored Jewish ways, the Halacha, and opposed the transformation of the Jewish street. In the face of change, these books could present acceptable variants of a standard tradition and thereby effectively help hold off the change while affirming some consistency in practice.[13] They became tools in the Orthodox struggle to counteract religious reform and change. At times instructions from these code books were also inserted into prayer books, through whose use they became even more influential and widely known.[14]

Increasing Scripturalism

For the Orthodox, as what Peter Berger has called "the situation of modernity"[15] became everyone's situation, the texts—and not just codes but any of the rabbinic responsa that came from the past—became increasingly authoritative, while the workings of what Soloveitchik calls "religious intuition" became increasingly frail. As Soloveitchik puts it: "[O]nly when the naturally imbibed, mimetically acquired *orah hayyim* (way of life) came to an end, did the luminous commentary on the *Sefer Orah Hayyim,* the *Mishneh Berurah,* become religiously commanding."[16] At a time of change, when the continuity of Jewish life seemed uncertain, and particularly when Jews who were increasingly comfortable on the non-Jewish street were using its norms to guide their behavior and beliefs, increasing scripturalism could be used to countermand such non-Jewish behavior and beliefs and show those in a world in transition what the accepted tradition *should* be. The power of legitimacy moved from the street to the book, from practice to code.

The author of the *Mishneh Berurah* had seen this coming (though he might not have guessed its scope). Writing in 1933 to "supporters of Torah in the city of Pristik"—that is, to traditionalists who were trying to shelter themselves from the powerful winds of change—Israel Kagan noted that "in our time . . . parental traditions have become very, very weak, and it is common that one does not at all live in the same place as one's parents."[17] He then explained to his correspondents what the appropriate code of Jewish conduct should be, in effect using the same process as he did in his *Mishneh Berurah.* The book took the place of the community, which had been left behind. It became for many Ashkenazic Jews a set of universal guidelines to take the place of the weakening parental traditions and counteract the uprootedness of migration, what Soloveitchik calls "the portable homeland."[18] However, this homeland had a "one-code-fits-all-observant-Jews" character that sometimes ignored the important distinctions that existed between living communities.

This was particularly true for those who wanted to maintain Orthodoxy but who had *not* remained inside the protective cultural fortress of a yeshiva. For them (many of them yeshiva graduates) the portable book was the anchor they needed to avoid being swept away in the currents of modern secular society. Indeed, the more the increasingly open outside world beckoned and attracted them, the more they used the book and its codes to mediate contact with that world beyond their own. The book was now more than a source of information; it was a cultural counterweight. Continuing to operate according to its demands (which of course required continuing reference to them) prevented one from being swallowed up by this-worldly demands. Studying these books, or at least owning and living by them, became the antidote to standing with one or both feet outside the yeshiva or the Orthodox enclave culture. As the century wore on, using the prevalent as the basis of religious legitimacy could no longer be considered normative because *what was prevalent was a diminishing Jewish practice and religiosity.* When the world that most Jews inhabited was no longer "permeated" by that profound sense of religiosity, when divine intent no longer mattered, the street was totally delegitimated. Scripturalism would now wrest the last fragments of Jewish authority from the Jewish street.[19] Increasingly the code book was seen as "the last word . . . which could replace the mimetic society as the primary educator of . . . daily life."[20]

The past increasingly was not what people did but only the practices these texts validated as legitimate. Put differently, those in the modern world who wanted to "return to the traditions" had to first recreate those traditions. In doing this, those among the Orthodox who were not literally survivors of the world where the Jewish street had existed but were their children found themselves reinventing the past by the book but endowing their reinvention with an enhanced authenticity. This was in fact giving these texts and code books a power beyond anything they had ever had. As most historians agree, "Jews did not do everything that the rabbinic documents [and code books] said they should, and, conversely, they did some things that are not mentioned in rabbinic texts and others that the rabbis explicitly opposed but had no power to stop."[21]

Yet in this environment of post-Holocaust Orthodoxy, as time passed, more and more Orthodox Jews relied on scripturalism—particularly the centrists and the traditionalists among the Orthodox, many of whom found themselves living in American Jewish communities whose standards of behavior were no longer "holy" but instead too inconsistent, compartmentalized, or religiously confused to depend upon. While in the early years contrapuntalists had taken advantage of the decline of tradition and relied other-directedly on local standards, those who were tending toward the religious right looked for a broader standard, which they found by relying only on the books, backing away from a living tradition in favor of a reinvented one.

Part of the reason the American Orthodox were increasingly relying on books was that the "holy community" whose customs and traditions were a source of legitimacy that might even occasionally trump the books was nonexistent in America. This was a place (not unlike the Jewish settlement in Israel in its early days) whose community was made up of (to borrow from a description of Abraham Yishayahu Karelitz) "a people who were not punctilious in . . . their observance of commandments" and was "deprived . . . of people of [Jewish] learning" and hence "could not establish customs that were decisive," certainly none that could counter the texts and their codes, which were now to be interpreted by a new more punctilious cadre of rabbis.[22] In such a community, particularly after the Holocaust, there was no *minhag ha'makom;* traditions were lost, and new standards could be and were established.

By depending on these texts, those who claimed to speak for the tradition but were really innovating were relieved of responsibility of being accurate keepers of the collective memory, so important after the Holocaust. They did not need to trust in memory because they had the "tradition" printed in black and white, endowed with all the authority that Jews had long ago learned to give to books.[23] But by claiming that this was the real way tradition should be, they used the mantle of conservatism to camouflage their radicalism. Thus when the new interpretations in the book seemed to contradict nature or reality—as, for example, in the Judeo-legal measurement standards of what actually constituted the oft-used "size of an olive" minimum or the proper measure of the volume of a Passover kiddush cup, memory was no longer trusted. Instead, the book became the guide. No less an authority than Rabbi Karelitz, the rabbi famous for establishing these measures anew after the Holocaust, contradicted *his own memory* of the size of the cup with which he and the rabbis of Europe had fulfilled the requirement to sanctify the wine on Passover before the Holocaust. Instead, he based his judgments of what should be the proper size on his reading of the texts. As for the size of an olive, even if nature itself contradicted the book, the new Orthodox response was that the "natural realm has changed."[24] Just as the rabbis had been "greater" in the past, so the olives, thumbs, and eggs that were the standards of measure had been greater than now, in line with the code book's standard.[25]

At a time when, as we have seen, the past was lifted to a kind of sacred status, which intensified the natural tendency of traditionalism to always see the earlier as better, these books became singularly authoritative, far beyond anything they had ever been at the time of their composition. This meant that now those who sought to remain true to the tradition and wanted to live Jewishly, as they believed their ancestors had lived, had to do so according to the code book. Even if people remembered practices that their family maintained in the past, in the present the book trumped those memories, and in the present the practices as detailed in the codes became the ultimate authority. After all, in the minds of the traditionalists of the present, their sacred forebears, giants on whose shoulders the diminished dwarfs of the present stood, could not have transgressed the codes.[26]

Scripturalism of this sort experienced great growth in the modern era, when the insecurities of the American Orthodox minority were replaced by a fundamentalist "fighting back" as the supporters of traditional religion sought to re-establish themselves with greater authority in this country. The books were part of this comeback. They were clearly associated with the yeshiva, where they were deconstructed and used to construct new orthodoxies. They became part of the Orthodox offensive against an American Jewry that the Haredim believed was, in the years after 1970, willy-nilly abandoning Judaism and in so doing might also attract the remnants of traditional Jewry. In fact, the text, instead of augmenting street and life, being a model *of* it, became increasingly a model *for* it, a template from which those who knew their way through these books would construct real life, all the while claiming speciously that they had really simply *re*-constructed it. In the effort to make a past as reconstructed from the texts the mold for the present, the current text culture emerged, dominating everything.[27] The prescriptive and the descriptive became intertwined. Hewing more closely to the texts became a symbolic expression of a religiosity that refused to abandon standards (even if those standards were actually new ones).

To be sure, in following this "book tradition" the new Orthodox Haredim were soon becoming other-directed. For no one was willing any longer to trust family traditions, memories of what had been done, or their own instincts of what was correct. Instead they mimicked everyone else and deferred to the codes and books as the increasingly scripturalist and punctilious rabbis read them.

By the last third of the twentieth century, these books, filled with expositions of Jewish law and custom, had almost completely supplanted the authority of established practice, which could "no longer hold its own against the demands of the written word."[28] As Soloveitchik explains, "[S]imple conformity to a habitual pattern could not be adequate, for the problems of life were now new and different."[29] No longer did the Talmudic principle that one could "go see what the people are doing" remain operative.[30] By that principle, life in the community, as practiced on the street, could and should be consulted to augment and fill gaps in the texts. Instead, *da'as Torah* did the job. But this *da'as Torah* grew out of an intimate familiarity with texts. In fact, it sometimes became codified in new texts. The book reigned supreme.

Traditionalist survivors had lost trust in the religious validity of their own lives or experience as a guide for Jewish existence. Even after the Orthodox had succeeded in creating a living culture of Jewish practice in America, the Haredim and the traditionalists did not consider it religiously valid to look around and guide themselves by what everyone did—though in practice they often did so. And even among the modern Orthodox, a growing chorus of voices was urging a return to texts as the ultimate source of authority and what Alfred Schutz calls "recipe knowledge," the taken-for-granted information needed to live everyday life.[31] Even such an "enlightened" modern Orthodox thinker as Charles Liebman was by the late 1960s calling for Jewish texts to be taught to rabbis-in-training in a manner that would highlight their practical application.[32]

New editions, translations, interpretive glosses, and the like were published continuously for an enthusiastic public of traditionalists whose primary goal was to resurrect what they claimed were the "correct" traditions. In such an environment, "religious conduct is less the product of social custom than of conscious, reflective behavior."[33] One could also argue that the move from living Jewish life on the Jewish street to going by the book represents a victory of the academy over the laity, of the rabbis and book religion over the Jewish people and folk religion. It replaces religious vitality born out of the dynamic existence of a living community with the rote standardization that a sacrosanct publication enshrines.

By the 1980s such Jewish publishers as Artscroll, Feldheim, and Ktav as well a series of small presses were producing code books, commentaries, and classic sacred texts in English for an American Orthodox readership who were prepared to guide themselves by these books but could not do it without translation.[34] The English books appeared to provide "the key to Jewish empowerment" for the contrapuntalists who valued autonomy and independence.[35] Literature that in the past had required an erudition and expertise that once might have been beyond their reach was now accessible to anyone who could read English; anyone could now review the books to discover on his or her own what a Jew could and could not do. There were even computer programs that allowed those who understood the technology to gain access to and search Talmud, the commentaries of Maimonides, the Code of Jewish Law, and more, so that nothing was beyond an easy looking up. To be sure, those who had received a day school or yeshiva education knew better how to make sense of what they read, and the English glosses helped fill the gaps in their education. On the other hand, what they learned from these books (often translated and compiled by Haredi Orthodox Jews) paradoxically forced them to moderate or retreat from their contrapuntalism.

As texts became increasingly important and experience counted for less and less, the authority and influence of the people who best understood these texts grew. This enhanced the rise of *da'as Torah*. For all their general education, the contrapuntalists here could not really compete with the people of the yeshiva and the rabbis. These were people who lived *by, off,* and *for* the book. They were its generators, explicators, and defenders.

In the past, yeshiva scholars had been protected by the splendid isolation of the academy and had not been required to deal with the realities of practical life. They could and sometimes did demand that the latter conform to the demands of the book, though often to little avail. But in the modern world they recognized the importance of building support for their book orientation from a committed public. They found that support after the Holocaust among yeshiva graduates and from within the Haredi Orthodox enclaves. To extend it, yeshivas began to send out emissaries to corral more and more lay people from among the modern Orthodox, especially those who were products of yeshivas, into text study groups in which the books would be reviewed and their authority tacitly reaffirmed. Some yeshivas and rabbis even enlisted the Internet as a tool, designing an expanding series of sites that offered the rules and regulations of Jewish religious and ritual life. These Web sites were virtual code books. Community rabbis, who served as local religious leaders and Halachic virtuosi on call, often incorporated the review of books like the *Mishneh Berurah* into the congregational routine—frequently as a daily "class" in the synagogue either at the end or before the beginning of prayers—thereby establishing the books' authority as normative even at the popular lay level. Reflecting this increased utilization, pocket editions of the code books were produced and added to the "worship gear" the devout carried with them as part of their prayer routines, to be read in the interstices of liturgy.

Implications and Consequences

In a sense, the book's enhanced influence today depends on the remaining threads of collective memory of popular practice being broken. For example, in this atmosphere, one can no longer eat a piece of matzah or drink a cup of wine at the Passover seder as has been done throughout the ages, for no one can feel religiously secure about recollections. Instead, one is now urged to eat or drink the precise amounts of each as prescribed by the code books and to swallow both in the book-prescribed time. Anything short of that is considered tantamount to not having properly fulfilled the religious obligation to eat matzah or drink wine. This is a transformation of the past into a Judaism of joyless inflexibility surrounded by legalisms and stringencies that create norms at best difficult if not sometimes impossible to follow.

This sort of aggressive bookishness emerged in the nineteenth century when many of the code books began to proliferate. At that time, they did not stop Jews from culturally and religiously migrating away from all sorts of traditional Jewish life patterns and concerns with what was found in the book or the codes. Indeed, some saw this migration as a rebellion against an overemphasis on the Jewish code book (and the dominance of the world of the yeshiva from which it came). Whether such religious revolt and religious emigration will once again emerge within the reconstituted Orthodox world cannot be predicted. Unlike the bookish generations of the past, who were largely limited to the yeshivas, the current book-oriented generation, inundated by and possessing more and more texts—both virtual and printed—has a far more direct encounter with these books. Surrounded by them in their homes and their synagogues and even on their computers, so proud of their competence in them, which is enhanced by the translations and new access points, this new book-oriented class of Orthodox Jews is not likely to mount a revolt against their own libraries and competence. However, can one say with assurance that subsequent generations will feel the same? Will the emphasis on going by the book continue to fill a need if a generation of American Orthodox Jews rises that is permeated by a profound sense of its own religiosity and gains a confidence that it knows what to do *because* it has absorbed the books' worldview and possesses its attachment and devotion to the letter of the law? Will their new *frumkeit* ultimately depart from the books and create a new set of traditions, or will American Jewry remain a place without a genuine *minhag ha'makom,* where books and their scholar/interpreters remain in charge? Will Jews who grow up in the precincts of tradition, who identify themselves as part of the "yeshiva world" at some point, find the self-assurance that at last allows them to close the book and live the religious life by heart? This would instigate not an escape from the books of the sort that happened in the nineteenth and early twentieth centuries but rather a move in the opposite direction, past the page and into the religious spirit. When people assimilate the book knowledge and endow it with personal style, will it begin to change? When more and more spheres of life become endowed with religious meaning, might the religious imagination once again take flight—not only among those who seek liberty from the law, as is now often the case, but also among those who feel bound to it?

There is of course another possibility. People may discover that while these books may provide understanding of what Jews may and may not do and how to live a Jewish life in the modern world, they may not provide the knowledge necessary for how to make a living in that world. That is, some Jews who are immersed in these books may realize, as Jews did once before, that there is a need for other kinds of wisdom as well. Such a realization may begin to shift some concern among populations who live completely by these books to other concerns. It is to this dimension of contemporary American Orthodoxy that our attention will turn next.

CHAPTER 5

Machon L'Parnasa

The Educational Alternative

> One too deeply involved in business cannot become a Torah scholar.
>
> Mishnah Avot 2:5

> Without sustenance, there is no Torah.
>
> Mishnah Avot 3:17

The previous chapters have shown how modern Orthodoxy has been pulled in a direction quite contrary to its original ideological intentions and toward the religious right by the unintended consequences of its educational system and the changing realities of contemporary America. In fact, much of what has been presented thus far has suggested that all trends point in the direction of Haredization. In this chapter, our attention shifts to the unintended consequences of the Haredi educational system and enclave culture and how it too is being pulled in a direction counter to its ideological intentions. For if the modernists are being undermined in their worldview and ethos by Haredi forces and consequently drawn toward an insular, code book–guided, and enclavist type of Orthodoxy, the Haredim are also being undermined by forces in America that pull them out of the enclave and force them into some degree of improvisation and contrapuntalism. For them the forces have to do with material life. Moreover, just as we saw that the modernists have contributed to the forces pulling them rightward, the Haredim are likewise ineluctably creating social and economic dynamics that will move them more powerfully toward contemporary culture and society. This chapter will show this through the medium of an educational institution called the Machon L'Parnasa.

A Scholars' Society

Before looking at this institution, one must understand something particular to all Haredim: their attachment to what we have already referred to earlier as a "scholars' society." This is the need to remain engaged as long as possible in Torah study (or to support one who is thus occupied) to the exclusion of all else. Israeli Haredim especially reinforce prolonged study because the moment young men come out of the yeshiva or *kollel* they are subject to the army draft. Army service is disapproved of for a variety of reasons, perhaps most prominently because it is seen as a pathway out of the protected environs of Haredi life, giving adolescents a chance to taste dangerous alternatives in behavior, notions of authority, and Jewish meaning. American Haredim have no such looming threats. Like so much else in America, their time in the yeshiva enclave is purely voluntary, and, as we have seen, remaining in it constitutes a choice that distinguishes Haredi from contrapuntalist Orthodox Jews, who choose, like most American Jews, to pursue university studies as well.

Although Americans and certainly most Jews have looked at the university as the apex of the educational pyramid, the place that was once the preserve of the elite and now is open to all those who demonstrate intellectual merit, the institution that promises its students an entrée into the riches of human civilization and its graduates the promise of worldly success, the Haredi population, as we have seen, has perceived and often presented the college campus as the gateway to perdition, drawing Orthodox Jews out of the protective culture of traditional Judaism and away from the enclaves in which they have preserved themselves and their Jewish way of life. Indeed, precisely the promise of a college education to open the eyes of those who receive it, to change their ways of looking at and living in the world and to expand their cultural horizons, is for Haredi Jews the essence of its threat. They do not want to put themselves or their young in an environment that encourages and often succeeds in changing one's perspective. They eschew the curricular and even more the extracurricular experiences of college, recognizing that they operate in tandem and toward the same end.

With its blurring of people's backgrounds and its assimilative tendencies, with what the Haredi community views as its generally permissive and liberal ethos, and with its increasing tendency to bring men and women into equality as well as close contact wherever possible, the American college experience is considered especially threatening. For a Haredi Jew, as we have seen, a permanent attachment to a strictly Orthodox cultural and social background is the essential key to continuity. As for the mixing of men and women so common in college life, the Haredim believe that it jeopardizes the restraint in gender relations that is crucial for maintaining the social and moral order as well as established marital patterns that are fundamental to maintaining the stability of world in which they live.

College education also competes with other priorities in the Haredi Orthodox world. For the men, the pursuit of "secular knowledge" takes time that they might otherwise spend studying Torah in the yeshiva. Indeed, the longer a student remains in the yeshiva, the more difficult it becomes for him to make the transition to a life outside it. For the women, the alternative to college is entering into an early marriage (somewhere between the ages of nineteen and twenty-one—the age has become increasingly younger to short-circuit any temptations or attractions of contemporary permissive society), ideally with a man who embraces Haredi values, and getting a prompt start to having the large family that the Haredim aspire to have. This generally conflicts with getting an advanced education, for, as all the census data indicate, such extended time in education commonly leads to later marriage and fewer children. Thus, while their counterparts are getting advanced degrees, Haredi women are getting husbands and babies, and their spouses are being absorbed in the ethos of Torah study.

Indeed, in the 1990 U.S. Census in Haredi communities of greater New York, where the largest concentration of them live, no more than 13 percent reported being college graduates, and in most cases the proportion was far closer to the 4 percent in Williamsburg, 5 percent in Kiryas Joel, and 8 percent in New Square (this compared with the 33 percent in more modern Orthodox neighborhoods like Kew Gardens Hills, New York).[1] The numbers changed somewhat in the 2000 census, but not by much. While Kiryas Joel reported just fewer than 3 percent college graduates, in New Square the number dropped to 7 percent—all this while elsewhere in the Jewish community college attendance continued to rise.

This opposition to a college education is also part of the culture war with non-Orthodox Jews and with the modern Orthodox in particular, who have claimed that a university education is not necessarily an obstacle to traditional Jewish observance and may even enhance it. In fact, the emphasis of yeshiva learning over the kind of study that goes on in the university may be understood as a manifestation of that culture war.[2] If *they* go to the university, *we* learn Torah, the Haredim seem to say. If they go to get a degree or to achieve some other objective, we spend our time in Jewish study, not as a means toward some end but in purity, as a reflection of our service to the God who commanded us to review his holy Torah "day and night." In other words, Torah study has become for Haredim a weapon in the war against the corrupting influences of life outside the Haredi cultural enclaves.

Insofar as every member of the Haredi enclave is expected to participate either actively or tacitly in this struggle, the pressure to study Torah or to enable the males who are considered its primary students to do so is today nearly universal. This means not only that college is discouraged but also that extended time in a Torah learning institution (a yeshiva or *kollel*), which might seem voluntary, is from the social point of view really mandatory. As a result, large segments of the Haredi male population fail to be engaged in gainful employment while they are studying, and they need others in the community (extended family, free loan societies, philanthropists, and the like) who are supporting them to find ways of enhancing their income. Making money thus becomes paradoxically an endless concern precisely because extended Torah study for its own sake is mandatory.

MATERIAL CONCERNS

This brings us to the second important point: the attitudes American Haredim have toward material well-being are complex and even contradictory. On the one hand, some Haredi values foster low income and dependence. These include interpreting full-time study in a yeshiva by a man who would otherwise be a breadwinner or having a large family despite a low income as evidence of the highly valued *mesirat nefesh,* religious sacrifice and dedication.[3] Max Weber found a similar outlook among Protestant this-worldly ascetics who expressed their religiosity by living in this world without succumbing to its material pleasures, always with an eye on their future salvation. Such people worked hard and had few amusements; in general similar attitudes among the Haredim led to the "hard work" of endless Torah study for its own sake or some other religious activity rather than profane labor or even gainful employment.[4] Thus, Weber's hard workers amassed economic wealth as an unintended consequence of their lifestyle; the haredim instead amass debt. While this Haredi lifestyle is far more prevalent in Israel than in the United States, the attitude behind it is still common in the latter, in part because the Israeli Haredim serve as religious standard setters for the Americans. In both places, the idea of living *for* Torah is idealized, and this-worldly sacrifice and deprivation in its pursuit are seen as ennobling.[5]

While Haredim have been told that "anyone who has knowledge of the Talmud knows everything there is to know" and that other education will move them into secularity, their life experiences driven by the need to sustain themselves materially have begun to raise doubts about the truth of these Haredi assertions.[6] American Haredim do therefore leave the scholars' society of full-time Talmud study and search for some sort of remunerative occupation.

Although the Talmud itself is very clear that there is no conflict between religion and work, there is enough in the text and certainly in the evolving pattern of Haredi life to suggest that seeking a full-time job may in some quarters be seen as evidence that the person has lost faith in God's providence and is hubristically assuming that he can autonomously control his life rather than trusting the God controls everything. The true believer must assume that God's "providence existed in every generation in order to remove his concern to work to earn a living *[parnasa]*."[7] To believe otherwise, the Haredi worldview asserts, is to be like the secular population—the Haredim's cultural nemesis—and hence is proscribed. Moreover, the prestige and esteem that a scholar and those who support him gain in Haredi society also discourage dropping out of full-time study. In America, these attitudes allow men to remain at study even when this places financial strains on their family and restricts their own independence and even though this puts them at odds with the American norm, for married men, of financial and personal self-sufficiency.

These difficulties are, however, experienced most acutely by the women, many of whom not only deal with the responsibilities of childbirth and child rearing (in a culture that encourages early marriage and high fertility) but also often serve as breadwinners and pursue remunerative employment to support their husbands' extended yeshiva study. The women do this out of a sense of religious and Jewish responsibility and in contravention of the American norm in which women who do outside work either have fewer children or give up their employment because of their family responsibilities.[8] Moreover, because men spend long hours studying, they are not expected to share responsibilities for child rearing or duties in the home, both of which are considered of less ontological importance than Torah study. The time the husband and father is at study as well the hours that the woman is either working outside the home or caring for the children limit the amount of time they have for each other to cement a relationship. This may put strains on young families. The "quality time" fathers have with children is also limited, and this may further stress family bonds. Such stress also constitutes part of the sacrifice for Torah's sake that seems to justify a life pattern that is otherwise difficult to understand.

To be sure, the feelings of self-worth and righteousness that redound to those who experience this *mesirat nefesh* provide social and psychological compensation for the hardships. As Durkheim long ago reminded us, the person who has answered what he or she feels is a call from God "feels within him [or her] more force, either to endure the trials of existence, or to conquer them. It is as though he [or she] were raised above the miseries of the world."[9] To study Torah or to support one who does is for these people a vocation whose pursuit raises them above the mundane.

The aversion to orienting one's life around this-worldly success along with the ontological devaluation of this-worldly labor other than Torah study that characterizes the lifestyle and dogma of the black-frocked Haredim and those who live in and around the yeshiva reflects the sort of inner-worldly asceticism that Haredi Jews—no less than the black-frocked Puritans whom Max Weber described—consider important evidence of their grace or worthiness of salvation. Indeed, many Haredi insiders argue that the embourgeoisement of consumer culture that has overtaken those of their Orthodox co-religionists who are well-to-do has led to a decline of solidarity and moral strength as well as an erosion of their religious culture. This is a common critique heard in the less prosperous precincts of Haredi society (particularly in the Israeli view of America) and directed at the relatively more affluent Jews.

Finally, having little money creates not simply a sense of dependence upon the community but also an enhanced solidarity with it (to say nothing of the misery that loves company), something that many in the Haredi world see as an aid to maintaining the boundaries between themselves and the larger society that surrounds them. Given that significant numbers of people in the Haredi community may draw upon the community charity fund (*g'mach*) at one or another occasion in their lives, the stigma of such dependence on assistance is accordingly mitigated.[10] More importantly, to be either a provider or a user of a *g'mach* is to be tightly bound within the Haredi world. Likewise, to be dependent on one's family for financial support reduces the likelihood that one will turn away from them or reject what they consider important. As such, economic dependence fosters a certain level of social stability in Haredi Jewish life.

For some American Orthodox parents who are supporting a son or son-in-law and his family while he studies in a yeshiva or *kollel*, an element in their activity resonates with what Thorstein Veblen once called "conspicuous waste" and "conspicuous leisure."[11] That is, their ability to maintain these dependent children and grandchildren economically is an unmistakable sign of their own financial capacities, which allow them to "waste" the money-making abilities of their adult children and keep them in what might appear to outsiders the relative and conspicuous "leisure" of full-time Torah study. Increasingly, modern Orthodox and Haredi enclaves are connected in that parents who inhabit the former support children who live in the latter. In the Haredi world, the economic ability of parents to support children is a basis of high status.[12] Moreover, where the student in question is a scholar or becomes a respected rabbi or yeshiva head that status is even further enhanced (in much the same way that parents outside the Haredi world who are supporting university students gain esteem). Where maintaining that support is demonstrably difficult for the parents, their doing so enhances their prestige and esteem in the community perhaps even more by showing how much they are willing to sacrifice in order to ensure that the next generation is able to "dedicate itself to the Torah and Judaism"' to the exclusion of all else.

The message of the "scholars' society" thus remains that pursuing yeshiva learning or supporting a son or husband who does so is the highest value. So powerful is the symbolic benefit of sustaining this way of life that a number of communities, and in some cases individual Orthodox philanthropists, have set up and support an entire *kollel*.[13] They thereby demonstrate the Haredi cultural value that Torah study, and its prominent support, provides "enhancement of life and well-being on the whole."[14] What the rest of the world might view as a lifestyle that is conspicuously wasteful of human resources these people, in a conspicuous display of a religious counterculture, consider an indispensable necessity in their community's Jewish life.

Nevertheless, even in America, the economic burden of need has for some individuals and families become too heavy to bear. Heavily committed to the perpetuation of the scholars' society, the Haredi Jews of America have been put into an economic straitjacket. Despite the stipends that many married yeshiva students receive for their full-time study, help from their extended families, the efforts of their wives to balance child care and some employment, and the sense of moral superiority that the community values have attached to these life choices, the costs are simply too high. Parents who have four children, each of whom is married and in the marriage of each of which the breadwinner is studying in a *kollel* and the wife has borne four to seven children, find themselves having to support, partially or entirely, up to thirty-two people in addition to themselves. That is an extraordinary financial burden. The concern for a large income among Haredim comes also from the significant economic needs associated with living in the relatively expensive locations in America where they have commonly situated themselves. Here they must manage to pay for a middle-class lifestyle, even though they have large families and inordinately high Jewish bills. Included in the latter are the high costs of strictly kosher food, private tuition-based education for all their many children, relatively frequent trips to Israel, various Jewish life-cycle celebrations, Jewish organizational dues, ample housing for large families, dowries, and a large number of wedding celebrations. All these financial obligations place many of these people at a level that would require annual incomes among the highest in the Jewish community, something close to $80,000 in the year 2000. Yet in the Haredi neighborhoods of Greater New York the proportion of people living below the level of poverty was according to the 1990 census between 25 percent (in Crown Heights Brooklyn, where Lubavitcher Hasidim have become concentrated) and 63 percent (in the Satmar enclave of Kiryas Joel). Among those who have been attached to a yeshiva or *kollel,* many have now reached a point where the number of children they have exceeds their ability to maintain their living situation. The wife/mother can no longer make enough to support the family while also rearing the children. This reality has placed increasing numbers of Haredi families and breadwinners in an economically untenable position and in desperate need of income. All this tests their dedication to the value of *mesirat nefesh.*

The husband may be forced to find work part time when his studies at the *kollel* allow for it. But because *kollel* study lasts through almost all waking hours, part-time work may not be possible. Moreover, the labors that *kollel* men commonly pursue, such as scribal activity (writing the scrolls for the insides of mezuzahs or Purim Megillahs—Torah scroll writing is commonly a full-time job) or limited teaching, no longer provide sufficient remuneration to support a large family. As they look toward the future, they realize that their material concerns will only grow. Either they will have more children or they will have to help support their married children, who presumably will also be in a *kollel* lifestyle. In addition, as one Haredi explained, "[T]he generation of Holocaust survivors had money, from reparation payments and other sources. My grandfather helped my father and my father helped me. But the money's run out. This third generation can't afford to support its children, marry them off and buy them apartments" or support them in other ways.[15]

American government subsidies for the Haredi way of life are also limited. They come in the form of welfare, certain education grants that have been used for yeshiva study, and aid to families with dependent children—but the restrictions on who qualifies are far greater than in Israel (which offers benefits for "families blessed with many children" and stipends through religious party patronage). Their non-Haredi counterparts in the Jewish community, from whom they often look for assistance, seem to be far better off economically, and indeed they are. At a time of economic prosperity in the surrounding society of America, the perceived burden of poverty is even greater than at other times and is thus yet a further challenge to the nobility of sacrifice. In America, where the boom times have created wealth, and in the vicinity of New York City in particular, where that affluence is visible even inside the Haredi enclaves (particularly among those who have made it in real estate, the financial markets, or retail), or when the reports of it are brought back by those who make the rounds of the Jewish community in search of funds and donations, this feeling of economic deprivation has become particularly acute.

Thus because of both their greater sense of relative deprivation and fewer government funds targeted at their institutions and families, American Haredim experience extraordinary pressures to get more money. They therefore look for a long-term solution. This search directly contradicts the outlook of *mesirat nefesh* and invokes instead the American contemporary ideal of making it on one's own and by personal initiative.[16] "I have been in the yeshiva enough years," Amiram Gonen quotes one such young man who has embraced this ethos telling him. "Now that I already have four children, the time has come to see to the *Parnasa* [livelihood] of the family."[17]

While American Haredim have accepted in principle the value of *mesirat nefesh* and the idea that Heaven will help as an inevitable consequence of their "hard work" in Torah study, they have also, despite themselves, absorbed something of the American desire for material sufficiency and the idea of making it. This subtle difference in attitude means that for many Haredim the idea of getting a good job to improve their lot—rather than depending on God's miracles—is not completely beyond the pale.[18] To be sure, some of the pious may rationalize going to work in the world and making a good income by suggesting that their success is a sign of God's grace, a reward for having studied Torah for its own sake for so long and the Almighty's way of ensuring that they and their offspring will continue to be able to live the Haredi way.

OCCUPATIONAL CHOICES

If one has made the decision to leave the scholars' society and get a job, what sort of work can one pursue? Study in the yeshiva can prepare one for jobs generally subsumed under the term *klay kodesh,* Jewish religious functionaries, a vocation that on average about 45 percent of haredi yeshiva students currently pursue.[19] These include being rabbis, judges in a religious court, ritual slaughterers, *mohels* or circumcisors, and supervisors of kashruth.[20] There are, however, limits on the number of such jobs available and the income they provide. Furthermore, not every Haredi Jew is suitable for this sort of vocation.

Those who have not become such religious functionaries often choose to pursue Jewish education as a vocation, a sort of extension of the life of the scholar. Although the field of Jewish education is experiencing a significant teacher shortage, Haredim, as we have seen, generally do not want to teach in schools of the non-Orthodox or modern Orthodox denominations where the shortage is most acute because they fear that the experience will test or even transgress their religious principles. Moreover, even when they are willing to teach in such places, the schools try to hire those who do not openly spurn the modernist worldview and those who have at least some pedagogic credentials, so that the jobs are limited to a small subgroup of the population. Such teaching jobs may also carry a stigma in the Haredi community. While the Haredim may serve as religious agents provocateurs among the modernists, they appear and are sometimes stigmatized as potential turncoats or cultural risks by people in their own world.

American Haredim who have chosen to pursue work outside the religious or Jewish educational domains often try to penetrate the external job market directly, hoping to acquire on-the-job training that they can parlay into something beyond an entry-level position. In the past, Haredi Jews who have not been employees or salaried workers in occupations that do not require a college degree have chosen to be small businessmen, retailers, owners of real estate, or engaged in the diamond trade. Some of the more successful have become stock market and real estate investors, insurance brokers, currency speculators, and players in other areas of finance. These are occupations that do not require a college degree and can lead to successful on-the-job advancement. Such jobs make use of social networks, which are a significant feature of a highly interconnected Haredi world. They are also cash based, something that many Haredim (who retain an us-versus-them ethos in their financial dealings no less than in all others) prefer because of a desire to conceal their economic resources from outsiders and to shift money easily and with a minimum of monitoring within the community.

While such jobs are still open to them and a considerable number of Haredim continue to pursue them, entrepreneurial success in many of these fields requires significant starting capital or information about the market—something young yeshiva or *kollel* students generally lack. As for Haredim who choose to be small shopkeepers or their employees, most of them tend to be concentrated in Haredi neighborhoods, which have a limit on how much retail economy they can absorb, particularly since certain kinds of businesses are not found in these areas.[21] Moreover, those who want to work in a family retail business often find that the venture cannot necessarily sustain all the members of what are commonly very large families.

In their pursuit of economic stability they have therefore begun to look elsewhere. The occupational niches they seem to prefer are those that do not compete either spiritually or practically with their all-embracing religious lifestyle and attachments. In other words, they want a job and not a career, something to augment their way of life rather than something that will disturb, reshape, or force them to leave it. Two areas that have emerged as potentially suitable are work connected to technology and certain specialized activities in the business sectors.[22]

Haredim have long been aware of technology. At the retail level they have for years been found in the electronics trade, selling computers, telephones, digital cameras, stereo systems, and the like. They even sell and are knowledgeable about televisions, which as a matter of principle most of them do not own because they object to the content of most broadcasts. Indeed, some might argue that these people who claim to be enfolded in tradition have a paradoxical love for the newest in technology. Enthusiastic use of technology also distinguishes Haredim from the Amish, with whom they are often mistakenly associated because of the superficial similarity of their outer appearance. The fact that people firmly bonded to tradition and the customs of the past can also demonstrate an ease with and understanding of modern technologies offers a kind of evidence that being embraced by values associated with eternal yesterday does not preclude an ability to master the instruments of today or tomorrow. This enthusiasm for technology can be a means of demonstrating that although they choose a traditional way of life they do not do so out of ignorance of what the contemporary world can offer. Their familiarity with the newest gadgetry sends the message, "We know what's good in this modern world and can use it better than anyone, but we also know what's bad and we shall stay clear of it." It is an element of triumphalism that the Haredi Jews can brandish in their *Kulturkampf* against a contemporary world that asserts that contemporaneity must be all encompassing.[23]

But technology is not just attractive for this reason. In addition, the explosion of the technology sector has created a new domain of midlevel expertise in which it is still possible to make money. For some Haredim, knowledge about gadgetry can easily become a desire to understand how to manipulate the quintessence of gadgetry: computer and information technology. The ubiquitousness of computers is a fact of life of Haredi culture, as it is in contemporary society in general. Even in Israel, where Haredim tend to be financially less prosperous, one estimate has 39 percent of Haredi households owning one (versus 37 percent of all Israelis) in 1998.[24] Indeed, increasing numbers of Haredi parents have begun to ask that their children be made computer literate.[25]

An understanding of computers is more complex than an understanding of retail electronics. Nevertheless, many Haredim believe they can acquire this skill, which can yield increased rewards, without the cultural encumbrances of attending a college. Often one finds posters in Haredi enclaves that offer brief ad hoc training sessions set up by a local entrepreneur—"learn a new trade in just a few weeks and make big bucks"—to tap this market.

Getting the best of these sorts of jobs, which represent a potential new source of income, requires acquiring specialized and advanced skills, expertise not obtained in the yeshiva or the *kollel*. Yet because these are not necessarily skills that require a liberal arts education, they are appealing. In fact, according to the projections of a 2000 report of the U.S. Bureau of Labor, these occupations are part of the 57 percent of jobs to be created in the next decade that will not require a postsecondary education.[26]

Machon L'Parnasa

All this is the backdrop to understanding the creation in 1998–99 of a school calling itself Machon L'Parnasa, located in the heart of the enclave of Boro Park, Brooklyn, perhaps the single most concentrated area of Orthodox life in America.[27] The name itself is part of the story. The Machon L'Parnasa (whose official English name is the Institute for Professional Studies—both names appear on the red awning over the door) is based on the assumption that the need for *parnasa* (literally, livelihood) is legitimate and pressing. That the institution's name is in Hebrew is also not accidental. Although the school is sponsored by and associated with Touro College, a private institution affiliated with Orthodox Jewry, the only reference to the college on the application is in the logo, a graphic combination of the letters T and C surrounding a flame. Likewise, the signs on the doorway and the overhanging awning do not mention Touro. But with a Hebrew name this institution can present itself as part of the insular Jewish environment, unsullied by the college label. As the Machon's director commented, "The place almost named itself."

To be sure, Touro College is not just an institution formed for the "sake of *parnasa*." Its programs—the Lander College for Men, the Lander College for Women, and the Lander College of Liberal Arts and Studies (divided into separate campuses for men and women)—are situated firmly within the domains of an Orthodoxy that accepts the idea of offering students a secular and Jewish studies curriculum in an environment manifestly dominated by Jewish traditionalist Orthodox values and behavior. This is, as its Web site puts it on the welcome page for the women's school, "an education of the highest quality for Jewish women seeking to achieve their degree goals in an environment which is supportive of their personal perspectives and religious outlook."[28] (For the men, the welcome offers students the chance "to pursue baccalaureate degree studies in a supportive environment while attending yeshiva during the day. Thus, students have the opportunity to prepare for careers and professional advancement without sacrificing their personal perspective and commitments.")[29]

Yet while Touro perceives its natural constituency to be the centrist Orthodox population who, although committed to receiving a college degree, wish to do so in a religiously protective setting, the population that the Machon L'Parnasa seeks to attract will not countenance any institution that is too obviously branded with the "university" or "college" label. In 2000, the Machon was located in two buildings (one for men and the other for women) several blocks apart between 12th and 13th Avenues in the center of the business district of Boro Park. The segregation of studies by gender is one more way the institute demonstrates to its potential clientele that "we share your values and attitudes." To be sure, those who become students at the Machon know full well that they have affiliated themselves with Touro College, and they may even identify themselves as students at that institution in their private conversation (as a number did in face-to-face interviews). Some even describe what they are doing as "getting a college degree," anticipating that they will afterwards be able to lay claim to this credential when seeking a job.[30] No doubt the need to engage in this barely camouflaged subterfuge reveals a weakness in the capacity of the Haredi enclave to supply all its members' needs as well as in its culturally protective capability.

In at most a dozen classrooms, and as of the year 2000 serving approximately 250 students, the institution offers a variety of courses aimed, as its literature affirms, at enabling students to pursue careers in computer programming, network administration, desktop publishing, business management, accounting, marketing, medical coding or billing, and a variety of other administrative office positions. Behind the decision of whether to attend the Machon, an action that will, if all goes according to plan, presumably lead to a job based on and suited to the training received, are some fundamental questions of what part an occupation should play in organizing one's life. Should an occupation be something instrumental, a job that fills a minor place in a person's life and identity, serving simply as a means of sustaining Jewish identity and enabling one to fulfill religious as well as communal responsibilities, as well to provide maximum time for the study of Torah, or should it be a career, even a calling, that has an inherent value of its own? Is the occupation selected one that allows for "role distance," so that it enables those who pursue it to remain essentially who they have been, or is it an occupation that embraces its incumbents and thus may transform them?

ADDRESSING THE SOCIAL RISKS OF SECULAR EDUCATION

Haredim have understood the truth of a principle that the sociologist Everett G. Hughes long ago noted: generally occupations that require a college or advanced degree as well as those that require extensive specialized training carry with them "as a by-product assimilation of the candidate to a set of professional attitudes and controls, a professional conscience and solidarity." In short, "the profession claims and aims to be a moral unit."[31] In general, the longer and more intensive the training— "the more rigorous the period of initiation into an occupation"—the more likely it is to create this tendency and the "more deeply impressed are its attitudes upon the person."[32] For the Haredim this is threatening, since they believe that a profession or any career that represents a calling inherently challenges and therefore undermines the ultimate Jewish vocation and the necessarily totalistic embrace of their Judaism. That is why they are happy with a course of study that is relatively brief and often part time and that they believe will be an adjunct to life rather than making a claim on their identity.

In contrast to such popular careers for American Jews as medicine, law, or other such professions that require advanced training and degrees, the fields for which the Machon offers preparation, while offering the potential for respectable (and in some cases outstanding) remuneration, do not seem to carry with them the same sense of vocation or the cultural weight of a transcendent identity as these other professions. That is, they are considered largely instrumental in character. Hence, while they may draw personnel from the Haredi population, they do not thereby openly challenge the symbolic dominance of Jewish engagement in their lives but rather are presented simply as a mechanism for supporting it. They offer only *parnasa* and not meaning. That in effect is what makes them acceptable.

There is tacit Haredi support for its members to improve the economic conditions of their lives. There remains a kind of undeclared understanding that Machon graduates and those who attend similar institutions who succeed in improving their economic circumstances will constitute a vital donor group and support structure for the community and institutions from which they have been drawn. This has become particularly important as the Haredi population has increasingly defined itself as a culturally and socially separate group, often distinguishing itself by its contempt for Jews who do not conform to what it views as the only legitimate and most authoritative, increasingly stringent Jewish standards. As a result, many of these other Jews return the feelings of scorn, which they often buttress with a refusal to financially support Haredi institutions and needs. Accordingly, generating an internal donor base of people who embrace Haredi values and outlook but have the wherewithal to provide economic resources becomes increasingly crucial. There are as well positive economic consequences of being trained for a well-paying and respectable career, including the power that comes from being self-supporting.

Nevertheless, going to the Machon does require a break from the accepted norms of the Haredi Orthodox world, which is wary of all education that makes the claim to be "professional" and hence personally engaging. What, after all, can legitimately be more engaging than Torah studies? To surmount this resistance, the Machon and places like it must do more than attract a few individuals; they must entice a whole following from within the Haredi community. This is because, as Everett Hughes long ago noted, "*[I]ndividual* deviation may appear as a threat to the whole accepted system; the *organized* deviation, however, may appear as a special adaptation of the system itself, perhaps as a little special example of what humans are capable of."[33] Hughes called such organized deviations that do "not have the support of open legitimacy" and even may "lie outside the realm of respectability" but that nevertheless create a fairly stable form of collective social behavior (and thus operate very much like institutions) "bastard institutions."[34] In a sense, the Machon L'Parnasa is for Haredim a bastard institution, a kind of illegitimate spawn born out of the collective needs of increasing numbers of Haredim for education that will yield a job. The bastard institution can exist only so long as it is ontologically illegitimate and only so long as it claims merely to provide a *parnasa* to support the Haredi way of life. As a bastard rather than a formally approved institution, it does not openly challenge the Haredi outcasting of alternative education and those who get it. Rather, it uses a kind of cultural back channel to provide instrumental skills such as "intensive computer science programs, specializing in networking and desktop publishing, as well as career-oriented programs in such fields as business management, accounting, and medical coding and billing."

To attract many students the Machon's brochure inserts code words (which I have italicized below) that signal that this institution is sensitive to Haredi needs.

"Students can study towards a certificate or associate degree in a *supportive* atmosphere. Staff and faculty are experienced in responding to the *special needs* of this population with warmth and *understanding*."[35] The separation of students by gender and the location of classes in an Orthodox neighborhood signal most vividly that the Orthodox will be at home here.

Just as the name and location of the Machon can suggest to potential clients that they will experience no cultural discontinuity between who they are and who they will become as a result of their enrollment or graduation, so too do many of the key people who make up the visible staff. In the registration office, into which potential students first must come or call, a bureau where women administrators predominate, one finds the modest attire, long dresses, and grooming that Haredi Jews are used to find in their encounters with women. In addition, the gestures, syntax, cadences of speech, and even insertion of Yiddishisms or Hebraicisms into sentences all provide subtle but unmistakable signs to the Orthodox Jewish insider that this is a place and these are people "that speak your language." In the men's annex, the same message is given off. While the instructors are often obvious outsiders, their status as "outside experts and specialists" hired to provide insiders with proficiency in a new skill is not perceived to be a problem.

Haredim are used to the idea that for instrumental help they go to outside experts, doctors being the most prominent examples. It is the administrator, the one who is in charge—the *ba'al habayis* (master of the house), as the Haredi clients sometimes refer to him—who serves as the symbolic link between the community and the Machon. Although armed with university degrees, including a master's in social work, with his beard

and very long earlocks (which he wears tucked under a large black yar-
mulke but which he is forever pushing back up as they slide down into
view), the administrator looks and sounds very much like the many other
Haredi men who walk into the Machon or who fill the streets outside it.
He too presents himself as completely at home in the provinces of Haredi
Jewish life.

Offering his account for the existence of the Machon, the director, who
described his role as "keeping the place safe," meaning he was to keep it
firmly within the enclave culture and hence from threatening or undermining the Haredi Orthodox view of the world, explained the institution as an enterprise that came into being because the Haredi community had succeeded all too well in its growth.[36] This had led to a situation
where the Haredi enclave was at present "bursting at the seams," pres-
sured by a desperate need not only for more housing and schools but—
and this is where the Machon came in—for more jobs that would provide the economic resources to pay for that housing and education.
However, he explained, "the old, traditional jobs," in the retail trade, in
the garment and diamond businesses, or within the community's religious
establishment that were once the primary sources of work for Haredi men,
had "dried up" or could no longer provide the massive income necessary
to sustain the Haredi way of life in twenty-first-century New York. Sys-
tematically he reviewed what had happened.

"In Bombay they can cut diamonds cheaper and as well as in New York;
garments these days are made cheaper in Mexico or Asia, and that has
eaten into the garment trades that many of these people used to ply. On
the other hand, how many *klay kodesh* [Jewish religious or ritual func-
tionaries] does the Jewish community need, and even if they need lots,
how much can a teacher, rabbi or *soifer* [ritual scribe] make? We are in
America," he concluded, "and these people are beginning to expect an
American standard of living," which is high. Indeed, among the students
I interviewed there was a scribe who, as he explained to me, was "looking for a way to make more of a living than I can by being a *soifer.*" He
believed the Machon would offer him a chance to find that way.

Nevertheless, attending a school like the Machon is problematic. How
can the "bastard institution" replace the elite one of the yeshiva? How
can a Haredi who has grown up in the scholars' society be willing to abandon it (even for a limited time) in favor of such a place as the Machon?
Moreover, if yeshiva study leads to more yeshiva study, study in a place
like the Machon leads to increased time away from the world of Torah associated with the yeshiva.

Because of the wariness that the Haredim have acquired about life outside their yeshiva bastions and in particular about college, these bastard institutions must suggest that they are offering a limited rather than a culturally transformative knowledge. The Machon's promise that it takes less than a year of evening courses to get a "Certificate in Programming" (for those who have no English language problems) and two years for one of the advanced "associate degrees" suggests at least on the surface that one can get through without overwhelming burdens or becoming culturally transformed and assimilated into the occupational culture. This is of no small consequence to many of the Machon's students. The location and evening hours also make it possible for students to work part time or to spend the daytime hours in yeshiva studies and still get to courses without traveling far from home (though for quite a few who come from other parts of the metropolitan region the commute to an evening class is more extensive). This also makes the transition and the shift in vocation seem less of an immediate break from what they have been doing and more of a natural evolution in their lives.

Similar programs have been offered, for example, for yeshiva students during the month or so that comes between traditional terms of yeshiva study. Such short courses are not nearly as ontologically threatening. Of course, precisely this inference that the study required is short and simple, a minor instrumentality for acquiring technical expertise on the part of applicants, helps persuade those who are wary of any extended training or college to move into the program.

There are practical reasons for a short course of study as well. "In my age, with a wife and two children at home, I can't now afford to spend four years in college," as one Haredi put it.[37] Indeed, in the Machon's classes, unlike the case at most colleges, those who are married with children generally outnumber singles. Moreover, it is not unusual to see a few students who are well into middle age and looking to improve their economic conditions and life prospects. And their expectations for opportunity are often quite high. "I heard of someone who learned programming and today he makes $64,000 a year and another $10,000 bonus as well as employer life and health insurance," as one such student said.[38] The belief that work in the technology or business sector will provide for this is widely held.

Yet the increasing development of such institutes and programs makes clear that the yeshivas and the skills as well as the stipends they provide are simply not enough to meet the economic needs of the growing Haredi population. That admission ultimately opens the door to possibilities of an escape to freedom. The Machon's provision of workshops for men that include advice even on hygiene issues and how to behave if and when they confront women shows what comes with this freedom.

ADMISSION

The formal requirements for admission seem simple enough, with little that might create an obstacle for those who would attend. Students need at least a GED (general education degree) equivalent of a high school diploma. Some of the students may enter the Machon on the basis of their yeshiva-based high school degrees, which tend to be limited in scope, but in time, as they become more involved in their studies, they come to recognize that while their high school degree may have gotten them into this institution, the limitations of what they learned at their Haredi schools are unmistakable in "the real world," as one student put it. They therefore go on to get a GED degree, which by then they recognize as superior to the degree from their high school. That realization itself—that they need significant general knowledge beyond what the yeshiva can give them—is an element of the transformation or awakening that study at the Machon abets, despite its implied purely instrumental goals. Students may take standardized SAT or ACT intelligence and achievement tests— though these are not required except for the very few who move on to the health science programs that enable them to be technicians in medical work environments. The likelihood of most Haredi Jews having the requisite knowledge to do well in such tests is very low, for they have not been in schools geared to preparing students for them. The application tacitly recognizes this reality and therefore basically asks only for census information, educational background, name of an emergency contact, and "How did you learn about Machon L'Parnasa?" It does not seek to create obstacles to admission.

LEARNING A NEW LANGUAGE

Despite this lowering of barriers, one requirement beyond the high school diploma constitutes for many of the Haredi applicants a significant hurdle. All students are informed that they need to be competent in English, both spoken and written, and to have a working understanding of basic mathematics. While applicants may have their high school equivalency diplomas, a placement test in English and math is required for everyone.

The matter of English competence touches on some fundamental issues. Learning a "foreign" or non-Jewish language has for over two hundred years been a charged matter for the Orthodox.[39] Some have seen it as a vehicle for positive cultural change, while others have perceived it as a corrosive and defiling influence. That legacy is still being felt here.

While a significant minority of the students are immigrants from countries of the former Soviet Union or Israel, many if not most are born and raised in New York. Yet for these natives English is often a foreign language. For them the lingua franca is Yiddish, the linguistic element of the cultural barrier that they have voluntarily constructed to keep the influences of the American culture at a distance. The assumption is that language is not only an expression of but also a tool for extending culture. Yiddish keeps one in the Jewish domain; English allows one to cross into the non-Jewish domain. Indeed, the historical resistance that many quarters of Orthodoxy had to the use of German, Russian, and other indigenous languages in Europe was based on this assumption and stands behind the opposition to using English except when dealing with outsiders.

The very idea that an institute that calls itself Machon L'Parnasa would require them to learn English well is for many of the applicants a surprise and a source of suspicion that what is labeling itself as an inside-the-enclave vehicle for employment opportunity and a better salary may be a Trojan horse bringing in dangerous American influences. Recognizing this concern, the Machon early on its brochure under the heading "Frequently Asked Questions" offers the following explanation for its demand that its students learn English: "Why do I have to take English courses? You must be able to communicate effectively to show how qualified you are. This includes both written and spoken skills."

The message is clear; English is not a value in and of itself. One does not learn it to be a better American, to fit into society, to share in the cultural riches that English offers. Rather, like all else here, it is a means to an end, a tool for *parnasa*. The students appear to understand this well. For example, students enrolled in an English public speaking course displayed a clear sense that they needed to acquire a comfort in English communication skills. Thus, when they would comment on one another's oral presentations, if the comments were made in Yiddish, their "mother tongue" and most natural language of interpersonal communication, other students would quickly admonish them to "say it in English." They embraced the need to immerse themselves in this "new" vernacular. They even seemed to enjoy it, as if they were preparing to travel in a foreign country where they would need this foreign language and in the excitement before the journey were practicing the new lingo. As their teacher saw them, and as direct observation confirmed, these were students who were "highly motivated."

As one will need to learn computer language or the language of accounting or medical coding for the purposes of making money, so one will need to know English. Students understood that learning English includes reading literature, and literature is a vehicle for the transmission of culture, worldview, and ethos. Literature allows the reader to share an understanding of the world, to get inside the mind and heart of characters, to identify with alternative ways of behaving and living that are normally far beyond the bounds of what Haredim are likely to experience. Moreover, those who teach literature, who are sufficiently familiar with it, are also necessarily agents of the transformation that literature abets. In a sense, these teachers act on behalf of the authors, translating their vision into terms that are comprehensible to the Haredi students. For that reason, and because they have been made sensitive to the implicit dangers that the Haredi world perceives in this encounter, they must repeatedly check that both the texts and the messages in them that they intend to teach will not frontally attack the values and beliefs of their students. Consequently, they are often coming to the school's heads to ensure that a reading they have assigned meets the social and cultural criteria of the Haredi community.

"Material that's risqué," the director noted dismissively, "we don't want to deal with that." Of course, the definition of the risqué is by no means universal. While, for example, Lawrence's *Lady Chatterly's Lover,* with its graphic descriptions of sexual intercourse and use of coarse language, would obviously be banned, the choice of a John Updike or John Cheever short story that for most contemporary American readers would be far from prurient would probably raise the hackles of most Haredim simply because it describes as normative American contemporary culture and behavior that Haredim are likely to consider reprehensible. Indeed, when allowed to select their own reading in English Haredim often choose inspirational stories such as tales of Jewish suffering and survival during the Holocaust or tales of the rabbis that come from the growing genre of English-language hagiographies of Haredi leaders, choices that the teachers often encourage in order, as one put it, "to make it more comfortable for them, to make them want to read."

Even when a work of non-Jewish fiction suggested by the non-Haredi faculty is acceptable at first glance, however, the discussion may take on a life of its own that subtly undermines Haredi standards. For example, in one session a class read and discussed the well-known short story "The Lottery," by Shirley Jackson.[40] The story explores issues of community and punishment, focusing on individuals who are annually selected to be stoned to death by an otherwise self-righteous and straitlaced population. Yet the power of an organized community with high moral standards choosing to put to death one of its own who deviates from the norm touches on many underlying values of the Haredi enclave. It resonates with biblical law and sanctions. It puts a mirror to those values of a community conservatively enforcing a single standard and subjects them to discussion and implicit criticism. To some Orthodox Jews such a mirror may be uncomfortable, and the story may resonate with intimations of heresy. The contemporary reader who lives in a world that values individuality may be ready to reassess the value of strict community control that Jackson's story makes possible. But the reader who feels that community control is an essential value and feature of life and who believes in the community's right to control, even arbitrarily, the existence of the individual—as Haredim are wont to do—will have a different take on the story. Although the non-Haredi teacher may see the ensuing discussion as stimulating and valuable for understanding the power of fiction and literature, protectors and defenders of Haredi faith and practice may see it as threatening and undesirable.

For many of the Haredi students who read the Jackson story, the shock that modern readers often encountered when reading that tale was missing. Instead, their consciousness shaped by their traditionalist and communal perspectives, they saw the story as an affirmation of "tradition," a description of "doing something because it was always done," and concluded, as one guardian of the faith put it, that the community members in the story "handled it very well." Thus a story that could have been freighted with all sorts of complex issues about religion, the unbearable weight of custom and ritual, collective versus individual liberties and the like turned into a nice, if somewhat odd, story that demonstrated the ongoing authority of tradition, a lesson not at all at odds with Haredi Orthodox culture. That the story's punch was vitiated was not a problem to the faithful; on the contrary, they were glad that the matter was "handled."

GETTING A PIECE OF THE AMERICAN PIE

All this is secondary to the question that comes at the top of the same page in the Machon's application brochure: "Which program will help me make the most money?" Those who have succeeded in finding a way to wealth—people who have amassed some capital, become landlords, become successful businessmen or entrepreneurs, or gained a share of family affluence—do not make their way to the Machon L'Parnasa. Rather, this is an institution for those who do not have the money necessary to support themselves, their growing families, and their aspirations for a better material life. Utilitarianism and instrumentalism are the operative principles. This is all about *parnasa* and material concerns. These Haredim, most of who come from Hasidic Brooklyn, are not just *in* America; they are native born and therefore lacking the immigrant sensibility or assumptions that they cannot have all that America offers. Even though they have embraced a Haredi cultural insularity, they have absorbed the American attitude that they too deserve a piece of the pie in this land of opportunity. Or to put it differently, they expect to share in American wealth even though they do not want to share in the entire American cultural package. But part of the problem for many of them is that they are trapped in a life pattern and social structure that prevent them from accessing that wealth.

The hunger for wealth, so much a theme in America during the late twentieth and early twenty-first centuries, can be perceived in attitudes expressed by some of the Machon students. "I am a big spender," one explained, "and I want a big house, to eat well, and to be able to go spend the summer in the mountains with my family," referring to the Haredi summer colonies in the Catskills.[41] In other words, they are not just trying to make ends meet; they want more. Accordingly, they are no longer satisfied with "a dead-end job."

Although this sort of openly materialistic attitude is increasingly common in practice, there remains as we have already seen, a powerful counterattitude of *mesirat nefesh*. Somehow these contradictory attitudes must coexist, and they do: the attitude of *mesirat nefesh* remains the ideologically approved one, while the desire to economically improve one's life remains the unspoken one. One might suggest that the approved institutions—yeshiva, *kollel,* and the like—represent the ideologically approved attitude while the bastard institutions—such as the Machon— embody the unspoken ones. But the bastards may be winning. Although there have been "warnings" from the courts of a number of Hasidic rebbes that studies at the Machon are dangerous and should be off limits, their statements off the record may be different. "We have people here," the director of the Machon explained, "who have *rebbeim* [rabbis] who publicly have said 'no' but who privately said, 'go.'"

Further, some of the students, particularly those who come from among Hasidim, have looked on the rabbinical announcements with a jaundiced eye. As one Hasidic student argued: "When a rebbe has a wedding at which twenty to fifty thousand people come, and I know who paid for that, but I can't put an honest piece of bread on my table to feed my children, then forget about it—I don't pay attention to those warnings not to come to the Machon."

The Israeli researcher Amiram Gonen quotes a Haredi student of the Machon who, while visiting in Israel, was asked by a Haredi leader there why he was studying computers at the Machon. The student replied by pulling out a wad of several hundred U.S. dollars and saying: "This is my first check which I received for work that I did with what I have already learned at the Machon. I came home with the check and showed it to my wife. When I saw the pride in her eyes, which seemed to me greater than the pride she displayed when I told her how much I had already managed to learn in the kollel, it became clear to me that I was going on the right path."[42] The comment was apparently enough to silence the questioner.

The school has succeeded in allowing students from all the various sectors of the Haredi world to find a place here. "If nothing else," as the director put it, "getting everybody together in one room, under one roof, coming and working together is no small thing." Trying to frame this in terms that resonate with religious significance and to show that the institution does not counter the Almighty's will, he added, "It's a *z'chus* [blessed privilege]."

A PLACE FOR THOSE "AT RISK"

It would, however, be a mistake to consider an institution like the Machon as serving only those who have decided they want to acquire skills that will enhance their earning power. The school also draws from another clientele and in doing so helps Haredi Orthodoxy deal with an ongoing problem: how to deal with those among its young who have become alienated from its way of life and values or are beguiled and attracted by the surrounding society and culture—or both. While leaders of the Haredi community would like the world to believe that they are extraordinarily successful in holding onto their own, that their young are not seduced by the outside society and that they have successfully passed their values on to the next generation, the fact is that some of their young are "at risk." These are youngsters or young adults who do not find sufficient satisfaction or success in the yeshiva lifestyle (they "flunk out," as the director put it in the language of education) or discover that their spirit is out of sync with the rhythms and activities of the Hasidic court. As Joseph Shilhav has pointed out, "There is tremendous pressure in the haredi public coming from people who are in yeshiva but don't belong there. It's only natural that most people are not capable of learning all day; only the intellectual elite can handle it."[43] Those who are not among the yeshiva elite, who cannot handle the learning, are on the prowl for "other" things to do. *Other* here means "illicit," or at least illicit as the Haredi world defines it. That can mean anything from going to movies, wandering the streets of the city beyond the borders of the Haredi enclaves, reading prohibited material, or surfing the Internet (commonly in a library) to using drugs or frequenting prostitutes. Some in the community have concluded that enrolling those on the prowl who are no longer tightly embraced by life in the enclave culture — those sometimes called the *shababnikes* — in an institution like the Machon provides a way of holding onto at-risk and often intractable members while still offering them a channel for their cultural wanderlust.[44] A wife, explaining why she agreed that her husband should leave the yeshiva, put it this way: "Not all men are by nature made for studies, so if he won't enjoy I'd say he should get work instead." The hope here is that the skills the Machon teaches will focus the energy and attention of these wandering souls (to say nothing of absorbing their free time) and thereby successfully reduce their feelings of alienation or distract their attention from the most seductive aspects of the outside world. At least, the expectation is that they will become "literate and functioning." Thus the Machon, which, in the eyes of Haredi cultural gatekeepers, can defile the "pure," may in some sense also serve to keep wayward members of the community flirting with "impurities" from becoming completely defiled — or at least so the thinking goes. Given that a recent report within the New York Haredi community's educational establishment estimated that approximately three thousand young people were thus "at risk," this represents a significant potential clientele for the Machon or institutions like it.

Within Haredi society, *shababnikes* among Hasidim are slightly less at risk, for the simple reason that wayward Hasidic youths do not immediately break away from the enclave and its life patterns when they find themselves unable or unwilling to remain in the Torah study environment meant to hold onto them. Rather, the community tries in some way to assimilate them and find a framework in which they will feel at home — as long as the wayward youths do not become a "toxic" element in their midst whose waywardness contaminates those around them.[45] But in the non-Hasidic yeshiva world, where the primary relationship to the community is a school connection, when that connection is broken because the one in question cannot or does not want to continue as a student, Haredi Jews have no safety net into which he or those who depend upon him can fall until he finds a way to reconnect. Hence these people are even more at risk. For such individuals places like the Machon may represent a refuge as much as an instrument for retooling themselves. This is valuable because *shababnikes* in the yeshiva world often have no ability to keep their connection to the yeshiva and can be a disruptive presence if they remain enrolled. Indeed, when and if they do turn to the job market, they are often the ones most critical of their rabbis and teachers for insufficiently preparing them for the "real world."[46] A place like the Machon has the potential to mitigate this criticism, especially if the rabbis and yeshiva teachers have directed (however obliquely) the *shababnikes* to it.

Not all those who recognize that full-time study in a yeshiva environment is not for them should necessarily be considered *shababnikes*. Those who, refusing to delude themselves or others about the quality of their Talmud study skills, admit that their aptitudes may be in another direction may also see themselves as better served by a school like the Machon. "When I recognized that I was not going to be the greatest *talmid chochom* [sage]," as one student explained in an interview, "I decided to get a training that would help me get a good job, and not a dead-end job like working in an electronic store." Yeshiva students who do not display the intellectual wherewithal or who express a felt need to support themselves and their families beyond what they can do as full-time Torah learners will find that yeshiva heads and rabbis do not press them to stay in the institutions. Rather, they will discover rabbinic advisors ready even to encourage their quest for another sort of vocational habilitation.[47] "If they can't lern Toyreh," as one such rabbi put it, "let them learn how to make a *parnasa*." Yet what makes sense to the yeshiva rabbi does not necessarily make sense in the world of the institute.

THE IMPORTANCE OF BEING EARNEST

The Machon's course standards, unlike its admission requirements, are relatively rigorous—after all, the school's success in the community is to some extent measured by the ability of its graduates to make a decent living, which in turn depends on their having the requisite skills. Thus students who are not among those "doing well" in the yeshiva and who have "drifted off," as the director explained, are not the ideal Machon students, and those from the yeshiva world who shunt such idlers to these schools simply to keep them "secured" will soon discover that this is not a good strategy. Just because a student does not "keep up" with Talmudic studies does not mean he is able to handle a textbook on information technology that is part of the course work. Only the cultural contempt in which the Haredi yeshiva world holds such "external wisdom" and the world outside the scholars' society could lead them to believe that a student who cannot succeed in the yeshiva might nevertheless do well in studies and skills that a place like the Machon provides.

The students who are more likely to thrive are those who have made an earnest and deliberate decision to try something new. They are better prospects, for they are ready to make a commitment to make their best effort. Among these one finds not the drifters or idlers but some of the brighter yeshiva students. Those who are moved to venture into the world outside the Talmud study hall because of economic considerations or a desire for taking control of their own lives are precisely those with a self-confidence that grows out of their yeshiva experience and success. "If I can understand and explain a complex page of Talmud," as one young man put it, "I'm sure I can handle any of the complexities of the world of business or IT." To be sure, this statement contains an implicit assumption that Talmud is the apex of all intellectual activity and that the abilities it calls for indicate an aptitude that can master all else. This too is a part of the yeshivists' attitude of condescension toward the wisdom beyond the enclave and an expression of the outside world's ontological inferiority. But it also indicates that the Machon and the pathways it opens for its students do represent a rival institution and an ultimate challenge to the hegemony of the Haredi enclave and its culture.

As for the assumption that competence in Talmud is a good starting point for these new pathways, students soon discover that while a positive attitude and a mind disciplined by the complexities of Talmud study may be helpful in mastering the studies at the Machon, these cannot make up for unfamiliarity with English or other insufficiencies in basic secular learning skills as well as cultural incompetence in dealing with the world outside. This does not mean that the mind that masters Talmud is not sharp. As the director put it, "If the concepts and texts were written in *gemara loshn* [the vocabulary and language of Talmudic discourse], they would *chap* [grasp] the ideas right away, but in this fat textbook they find terms and words they never ran into before, and that often makes it hard for them to figure out what's going on." Here is the linguistic expression of the cultural divide that separates Haredi Jews from the contemporary society that surrounds their enclaves. The same barrier that they have carefully constructed to protect their culture from infection also makes it difficult for them to breach that wall when they need to do so.

One serious student, faced with difficulties in understanding all the language in a course he was taking, was assured by an administrator that he need not worry; he "would pass anyway because that teacher gives good grades." The student responded with indignation: "If the stuff is important, I want to know it; and if it's not important, then I don't belong here." In other words, the only legitimate reason he had for defiling himself by going to such an institution and immersing himself in its educational culture was that what he would learn there was important for his advancement, his *parnasa*. His goal was not simply to "get good grades." To one of the teachers, this earnest attitude was explained by values and study habits that the best students had absorbed from their immersion in the scholars' society. Once they had committed themselves to study, the attitude that the subjects to be learned needed to be taken seriously—which had been inherent in their yeshiva experience—was carried over to this new course of study. Explaining why it would take most of the students in his class a relatively long time to complete a brief quiz he had just distributed, he commented, "They're so concerned with getting everything perfect. They are used to that idea, and they think, if we don't get it perfect, we're not good scholars, and it's critical for them to be good students." Indeed, when they failed, they apologized. As someone who was not Jewish and who taught in other non-Haredi venues, he found this earnest attitude remarkable.

An earnest and serious attitude was also important to the school for economic reasons. To get students to marshal the funds for tuition, the school had to persuade them that learning the material was important for their futures. Although by college standards the tuition of $3,000 per semester was low, for many of those enrolled that did not qualify for government or other sources of tuition assistance the cost was considerable. After all, many of them were here precisely because of their desperate financial straits—and for them an investment of several thousands of dollars was a heavy burden. To encourage potential students, as well as to signal to them that the Machon would be able to help them file for tuition assistance, the application information noted that interested applicants should bring "public assistance information (where applicable), welfare benefit information (allotment letter), food stamp card, Medicaid card," and a variety of other documents that those below the poverty line normally possess. The inclusion of such a statement in the application materials made it clear to those who were in such financial straits that their situation was not unknown or even uncommon among those seeking entry to the program. While not all Haredim live in poverty, the poverty that does exist within its enclaves is often quite profound, at times reaching— as we have seen—well over 60 percent. This is something that all those who serve the Haredi community know.

For prospective students who had the money or were reluctant to ask for the aid, administrators also had to justify the expense in their recruitment by arguing that if they were starting a business they would purchase equipment or other necessities and get the best they could, even if they had to borrow money to do so, because that was what was needed for success. In the same way, according to one administrator, they would tell the student who balked at the expense: "You're the most important investment you have; you're the most important machine you've got, and if you realize that and what the payback is on that machine, you'll understand why the tuition is worth it."

BREACHES IN THE ENCLAVE CULTURE

Once students complete their course of study or at any time, they may begin the search for a job. This social encounter also requires some preparation. Graduates want to find a work situation that does not expose them to ideological and cultural risks. That is, they look for a place that will minimize their exposure to what they consider the seductions of sex and seek to avoid environments where contact between men and women is free and easy, particularly where women are "immodestly" dressed. At the same time, they must be prepared for the fact that in the modern marketplace and workplace they are likely to have far more cross-gender contacts than in situations to which they have been accustomed. Whereas in their day-to-day life they would not deign to carry on an extended conversation with a woman other than a close family member, they are advised that this will occur in job situations. The men must be prepared for being interviewed by and even supervised by women or working alongside them, and likewise the women must be prepared for such extended contact with men. Moreover, they must be prepared to experience the social and cultural atmosphere that constitutes the contemporary American workplace, where all sorts of conversations, jokes, and values will be exchanged that are different from what they are used to and where the level of sociability required, though not formally part of the job, may not be what they are expecting. In effect, Haredi students must realize that the very people whom they may have considered the insidious agents of impure American culture will now be their colleagues, partners, superiors, and at times subordinates or assistants. The long-term consequences of this transformation of relationships and perceptions will necessarily lead them to moderate their sense of "us versus them," bring attitudes from the outside into the Haredi enclave, and ultimately change their worldview. Alternatively, they will need to learn the art of compartmentalization, the very skill that the contrapuntalists have been practicing.

In this way, one can say that the imperative of making a living, which the Machon answers, creates a series of ripples that will ultimately disturb the tranquillity of life in the Haredi Orthodox enclave culture. Moreover, to recognize that this is inevitable is also to appreciate that the putatively protected Haredi enclave has a potential and perhaps fatal breach, engendered by the need to work "outside." This, however, is not the only opening in the cultural membrane. The fascination with technology is another.

That fascination is, as already noted, another element that brings Haredim to the Machon. Because so many of its students come from relatively insolvent homes or places where there is little room for them to have privacy, the Machon has become a kind of hangout for those who want to use its computers. For many, the school's machines and its connection to the Internet make it a place to practice their computer skills and do their homework. For others, the school can become a kind of Internet café, a place where in their extra time they can connect themselves via the Web to the world outside without anyone in their home or neighborhood knowing about it—in defiance of the view of many Haredi leaders that such Web surfing leads to "moral disaster" and that the Internet is "a force that contains spiritual and moral poison."[48]

"I wander around," the director explained, "seeing what people are sticking their noses into." Part of his watchdog function and gatekeeper roles requires that he monitor these forays into cyberspace, for if the word gets out that this place is a sanctuary for forbidden behaviors it will swiftly be placed on the list of prohibited institutions by the organized Haredi enforcers of community standards. Yet there are limits to how much the director can monitor. As he admitted, even in his own home he has had limited success in controlling his children's access to the World Wide Web. Though he did not hook his home computer to the Web, they found a way to link up with a free Internet provider and have established connectivity—not just technologically but culturally.

Their father greeted this development with far more bemusement than disquiet. Given his occupation, he perhaps more than most has realized the permeability of the membrane surrounding the Orthodox enclaves, inside one of which he has placed his family. Using the metaphors of computerese, he concluded, regarding his children, that "whatever filters you put on, they're smart enough to go around, and so one tries to create a stable platform upon which they can grow into autonomous *b'nai* [children of the] *Torah,* and that's all one can do." In effect, the director admitted that this order of existence that he tried to establish for his own children was also in some measure the goal of the Machon. Yet it was an order disrupted by the digital superhighway into whose traffic many Haredim were being pulled faster than any controlling authorities could hold onto them.

SYMPATHETIC OTHERS

Beyond serving as a gateway to opportunity and a potential opening to outside influences, the Machon serves to create a circle of sympathetic others, people who share a common situation. In part this is because many of those who have come here feel they have needs that cannot be satisfied within their enclave. To be sure, they are told that this is a "supportive environment," but most know that by going to such a place they are taking a step that may put them in a culturally and even socially precarious position. In that sense, they are moving toward the margins, both of the Haredi world and of the one that surrounds it. This marginality can make individuals feel somewhat vulnerable and alone, even alienated. Seeing others who are in a similar state engenders feelings of sympathy and even empathy that often transcend what might otherwise be lines of cleavage. Thus age differences or Hasidic/Lithuanian divergences or differences between Hasidim of one branch and those with allegiance to another that might ordinarily be barriers to a friendly relationship largely evaporate in the Machon's domains. Moreover, this is one place where none have to explain themselves and what brought them here. This makes the Machon a place where these Haredi Jews may feel at ease and not self-conscious or apologetic, even though they are engaging in activity that might in their home communities be considered somewhat deviant and not particularly Haredi. That feeling of ease will make the transition to doing non-Haredi things without other Haredim around somewhat easier. Put differently, the school is a kind of liminal zone, and time spent there consequently allows for a transition from what is normative to something new. From the norm of sitting and studying Torah together, these students shift to studying other subjects together and preparing themselves for a job and new career trajectory. Over time this leads to the sense of confidence that one senses among the veteran students. "This is something I feel that I can do," as one Hasid said, explaining his feelings about the skills he was learning, and perhaps as well his shift in orientation.

Since an adjustment of identity that might be desirable for a normal college student is not appropriate in the Haredi world, where the message is that what one is one should always be, students at the Machon often attempt to reframe their personal history so as to make their attendance conform to their sense of who they are and who they claim they always were. Thus one Hasidic student denied that coming to school here was a complete break from his family history, pointing out that his father and grandfather had taken courses in their time that were equivalent.

This sort of reframing is not as hard as it might seem. The contemporary Haredi scholars' society is a relatively recent development in Haredi society, fostered by a combination of relative wealth (compared to European life) among American Jews, the desire to emulate the Haredim in Israel, ideological consequences of the Haredi culture war against modernity, Holocaust survivor guilt, and the changing worldview of Haredi society.[49] A look past these relatively recent developments, however, easily locates in many Haredi families a connection to "outside" work and the study of "outside" materials. Indeed, it is reasonable to suggest that at some future time, if enough Haredim begin the process of migration via the quest for a job, the reframing of personal biographies may lead to a society that looks upon a life of Torah study as being only for a specialized few or for a limited period of one's life. Indeed, there is evidence that this is already beginning to happen in America, and not only among the so-called modern Orthodox.

CONFIDENCE IN OBTAINING WORK

The real test of the success of schooling at the Machon is graduates' ability to find the jobs to which they aspire. Their very hopefulness reflects not only their confidence in the Machon and their own abilities but also their confidence in America and their conviction that its increasingly multicultural, tolerant, and meritocratic society will be open to them, regardless of their appearance or their religious principles. "Anyone who is a good programmer and who knows how to work as he should can find work anywhere. No one looks at how he's dressed or whether he has a beard and earlocks. What matters is that he knows how to do the work they assign him," as one student put it.[50]

Yet this confidence is not blind. Prepared for the possibility that potential employers might not be quite as willing to overlook the exotic appearance of particularly the male Haredi applicants and might balk at the idea of hiring one of them, another student, displaying no less confidence in his ability to persuade someone to hire him, argued that he would pitch his case to a potential employer whose primary interest is good workers by pointing out that "Haredi employees are stable. They stay in their communities, don't jump from company to company, city to city, state to state, like others in the computer business." That constancy was, he continued, critically important to an industry that suffered from a high rate of employee turnover, much to the distress of those who invest a lot in training workers, only to have them leave for some other place. "Having haredi workers decreases the damage to employers caused by a high rate of employee turnover."[51] In other words, the prejudice against Haredi workers that any potential employer in the computer field might have would be offset by the business logic that this young man was prepared to explain. The key was acquiring the skills that the business needed; all the rest, he was confident, would fall into place.

The more Haredi Jews succeeded in finding employment, the more they were likely to assist their fellows to do so as well. First, their success on the job would help diminish lingering resistance to their being hired by firms that needed computer expertise. Second, once Haredi Jews were in place, and when they reached positions of responsibility and authority, a Haredi network would begin to operate. Indeed, a number of yeshiva boys and Hasidim already have made use of such networks, not only to persuade one another that there are opportunities for a life outside the Torah study hall or the neighborhood and thus about the advantage of attending schools like the Machon, but also to learn about job openings or internships—a process not unlike the one that has emerged in the modern Orthodox world that helps these Jews find jobs. The same social solidarity that is part of the ethos of their enclave culture turns out to have an instrumental advantage in the marketplace. In a culture that views itself as a world apart and that is as relatively small and geographically concentrated as that of Orthodox Jewry, word of mouth and the web of affiliations work quite well. The sudden and widespread popularity of computers as a field appropriate to the Haredi lifestyle was undoubtedly promoted via just this process. But precisely these confidences and networks may also be working to undo the insularity that is so much valued in the same Orthodox environment.

THE WOMEN

For women, whose prime responsibility within Haredi society remains childbearing and rearing, the jobs for which the Machon offers training are often those that can be done from home. The interest the women have in working with computers is in part also based on their recognition that such skills make it possible for them to work even after they have begun to bear and rear children. These jobs include desktop publishing, Web design, and computer graphics. By and large, the young women who attend programming classes are determined to earn as much money as possible to support their future families and enable their husbands to stay in the yeshiva scholars' society as long as possible. Indeed, in a strange twist of Thorstein Veblen's notion of "conspicuous leisure," the length of a husband's stay in the yeshiva becomes a status symbol and point of pride for Haredi wives.[52] "I want to learn programming and I want to get a job because I want to be able to eventually support my family," as one eighteen-year-old girl put it. "And especially since the rent is very expensive in Williamsburg—'cause there's a great need for the property. I feel I'll have to help my husband and also because we try to encourage our husbands not to start working immediately after they get married but first learn Torah, and to study so I'd like to support myself and my family so I'd like to get a degree in programming and then I'll find a job. And programming is a very well-paid job."[53]

Women also have an incentive to work in their desire to be freed from economic (and symbolic) dependence on their parents for support. One of the female students explained, accounting for her enrollment: "If you make a nice amount of money you won't have to rely on your parents."

This goal of independence of course is especially characteristic of American non-Haredi and non-Jewish youth, who look upon self-sufficiency in general and financial self-reliance in particular as valuable. In contrast, the Haredi world assumes that children will, even after marriage, be dependent on their elders. Yet as the Machon demonstrates, the American desire for autonomy is making inroads among even the most insular Haredim, and particularly among women who remain formally subservient to their husbands. In a sense, when these women gain independence via their work they gain not only freedom from their need for parental economic aid but also a self-reliance that undercuts the formal hierarchy in which the husband is dominant. The working woman who brings in a significant salary is simply in a stronger position vis-à-vis her husband, her in-laws, and parents. He and everyone will have to depend on her.

For women who are interested in getting out of the home and pursuing "office jobs," there are courses that teach "managing an office in the technology fields" and "business management." To prepare women to work in the secular world, the Machon has organized three workshops where students learn how to apply for jobs and how to behave in a job interview. These are lessons that guide women culturally as well as instruct them instrumentally to fill positions as administrators in so-called "professional" offices, especially those of doctors and dentists. The instrumental skills include particular expertise in running a "medical office" as well as "human resources" management. There is even a certificate program in "medical coding and billing." The cultural skills include knowing how to handle a clientele that is not Haredi and how to operate by the conventions and realities of the social order in the world outside, the rules of etiquette. Yet these positions are also desirable because they put Haredi women in a public space where they run few or no risks of finding themselves alone in a room with a man other than their husband—one of the cardinal prohibitions that these Jews tend to stress. Moreover, a medical office is an outside institution with which they are likely to be somewhat familiar. After all, Haredi Jews often make use of doctors and dentists—indeed their places of work are among the most common destinations outside the Haredi enclave to which women travel—and it is therefore comforting and useful for them to have their "own people" out front in such places.

In part because women can "pass" more easily in the world outside the Haredi one—their appearance allows for the camouflaging of their religious identity, since only the Orthodox insider or the informed observer can recognize the wigs, long sleeves, and low hemlines as markers of Haredi identity—they see jobs in the outside world as more conceivable than do the men, who, as we have seen, have had to construct arguments to convince potential employers to get past their appearance. On the other hand, precisely because women can more easily pass in the outside world, they are limited by internal means from wandering beyond the walls of virtue. These limitations include, as we have noted, having many children and the responsibilities that come with them, which at least in principle are expected to be paramount. They include as well an ethos that discourages women from taking jobs outside the boundaries of the enclave.

For example, even Haredi women who live in or near New York City and work outside the home may sometimes (though not always) turn down work in Manhattan. Or those who do work far from the enclave travel to and from work in their own buses, supplied by the Haredi community. In these buses, the gender separation and social order characteristic of the Haredi world predominate, with women sitting in the back of the bus.[54]

In an effort to minimize disruptions to the culture of Haredi Jewish life, some have tried to limit women who work outside the home to jobs geographically within the Haredi enclave, a practice fortified by the need to be home with young children—of whom there are many in the Haredi community. Yet here too, as with the economic realities, certain aspects of the structure of Haredi society also ease women's turn toward a career orientation. The large families make it possible to share child-rearing roles between a mother and her older children who take care of their younger siblings. Schools, with their long day and relatively few days off, provide, as earlier noted, a place for children while their mother is busy at work. Then too, the instrumental tasks that were once part of being a housewife and mother have been lightened somewhat by machines and technologies that make everything from doing the laundry and cleaning to shopping and cooking far more efficient and less time-consuming.

To be sure, women, like men, recognize that at times they will have to leave their Jewish cultural enclaves and go to work, but that is not by any means their dream prospect. Asked how she would like to work outside the Hasidic community, a young Satmar student at the Machon replied, "Probably wouldn't like it so much. Probably wouldn't look for a job that's too much outside. . . . I mean, it depends, I don't know I've thought about it. It's part of my worries to get a job, we'll see, I'm not sure. . . . It's very hard for a Hasidic girl to work in the non-Hasidic, non-Jewish world." As another young woman student, recognizing the risks involved in life outside the precincts of Orthodoxy (which for these people is tantamount to what is genuinely "Jewish"), put it: "Our parents would rather have us working in a Jewish atmosphere than in a non-Jewish atmosphere because we can get influenced by the non-Jewish environment. And after all our years of learning you wouldn't want that to happen."

"I'd love to work in Brooklyn," still another young woman student at the Machon explained, "because that's where I live." Then she added, "but if I find a job I'll probably work in Manhattan because there's more jobs available there." Such moves to the outside world, making it in Manhattan, which might be a goal for many other young women in the metropolitan region, are, however, only a means to an end, that end being a return to the security of the enclave and the family. "Eventually, after a few years," the young woman concluded, "maybe I'll be enough popular or whatever, experienced, so maybe then I'll go on my own, start my own business at home."

Another woman summed it up succinctly: "I'd feel uncomfortable working in a surrounding of people that are completely different from what I am. I really would." That of course is precisely the attitude that Haredi culture wants to predominate

In the face of these limitations, the occupational pattern to which the Machon's curriculum is attuned reflects a change in the role of women within these traditional precincts. While the primary impetus behind the transformation has manifestly been economic, the latent elements of autonomy and the emerging power of women suggest that signs are to be found here of the subtle but undeniable influence of the culture outside the Haredi enclaves. Most obvious is the openness of American society to the idea of women working outside the home that makes such jobs possible. Beyond that is the idea that women can become "professionalized" and take on positions of responsibility that diverge from traditional homebound models. Even housewives and mothers who work from home—a practice by no means uncommon in today's digitized and Internet-connected society—are altering the focus of their activities and edging away from being "family-oriented women," an ideal they still value, toward becoming what Helena Lopata has called "career-oriented" women, who are at least in part "focused upon a role or set of roles outside of the family institution" with their own imperatives and commitments.[55] At times, the sense of accomplishment and professional treatment as well as the clear definitions of success that these women acquire when they concentrate on their careers versus the far more subtle and hard-to-articulate achievements they sense when they act as wives and mothers generates invidious comparisons between the two roles, enhancing identification with the former even as the culture presses for the latter. This is the danger that some Haredim see in the unintended consequences of studying at an institution like the Machon. Yet economic necessity and the tenor of our times increasingly make it more difficult to ignore the appeal of its training for young women.

While many of the women in the Machon go to seminaries (women's yeshivas), they come here afterwards in the afternoons or early evening to augment their education with the marketable skills that this school offers. This clearly requires a contrapuntalism and compartmentalization far more characteristic of modern Orthodoxy than of the Haredi world.

For some, studies at the Machon may be viewed as part of the preparation for marriage in that they give young girls a skill that makes them more able to support their husbands, for whom an extended opportunity to continue in a *kollel* is no small attraction. While college attendance might sully women's reputations in the Haredi marriage market because of the assumption that exposure to campus life will distort their values, the skills learned at the Machon may not carry the same sort of risk (even though they may in time have many of the same consequences as college life, albeit at a more subtle pace). Accordingly, some families may encourage a girl who has not yet married to take the courses here. After marriage, taking the time for courses will be more difficult, particularly if the new couple, as is commonly the case in the Haredi world, has children quickly.

Obviously the path for the woman is difficult. To take the courses, she must either be unmarried, without children, or have the support of a network of people who will care for her children while she studies. To acquire the skills and reputation to work at home, she must have some outside work experience—and that too is difficult with children. Sometimes the work experience cannot but help lead to some limitations in family size, as most career women have discovered. Since the husband/father will be fully engaged in the yeshiva studying Torah and the woman will be making her work reputation outside the home, they will essentially be living the life of a dual-career family, with all its limitations on family growth and strains on the traditional mother and wife roles.

In a letter to the editor of the *Jewish Press*, a New York newspaper largely read by and targeted at the Orthodox, one self-identified modern Orthodox woman, Judy Ostrow, responded angrily to correspondence in the paper suggesting that the problems of women with professional careers whose children suffered from lack of mothering were particular to and a failing of modern Orthodoxy and something that the Haredi community did not experience. Rather, she argued, "perhaps those who feel that way have not heard about the countless kollel wives who have been forced to work—and at run-of-the mill jobs, at that. Is the effect on their children any different?"[56]

Recognizing this danger, and also acknowledging the priority of the wife and mother role, one of the young women at the Machon, like many others there, claimed that she would "eventually stop working." Then, thinking about all she now hoped to learn, she retracted: "Well, maybe I'll be able to work from home if I can adjust my schedule, this is what I hope to do." Yet she knew that "after I'll have my own children either I'll look for a part-time job once or twice a week in a local place, a business shop or something that, you know, you don't need to be there every day, or I'll work on my own, I'll adjust my hours."

The truth is, however, probably closer to what the woman admitted at the end: "I didn't do any plans for so long ahead. First I'm doing this. I'm trying to take it day by day. And after I get married, even if I start getting children, I can go on working maybe until I get four or five children, then I'll probably have to stop. Maybe I'll get a very rich father-in-law that will be able to support us, well, I have no idea what's going to happen in the future." But of course time will tell.

The decision these men and women have made to gain marketable skills via the Machon and similar educational institutions in effect forces them to face the question of how they will orient their lives. For some it represents an abandonment of a way of life that they once believed was ordained by their religion and blessed by God, a recognition that devotion to Torah alone will not provide for their economic needs and that their Haredi enclave cannot be their entire world. For others, it may signify an incipient realization that the assurances of the Haredi community that the values and restrictions it demanded would not place undue burdens upon them were at least mistaken and, in the minds of some, downright injurious. Thus the move to such schools—while perhaps driven simply by instrumental needs—may result in far more consequential reevaluations and attitudes toward some of the central tenets and norms of Haredi Orthodoxy, making it and its adherents far more like their contrapuntalist modernist counterparts. These consequences are precisely what some of the community leaders and ideologists of the Haredi world fear, and are among the reasons that they have been ambivalent at best and hostile at worst to such institutions. Nevertheless, if they are unable to provide alternative means for supporting the large Haredi families and the lifestyle that they have encouraged, and if they want an infusion of funds to help support the community, they will in the end have to look away when increasing numbers of their population turn toward these schools and institutions.

Some argue that American Haredi orthodoxy has already made this turn, which is why it is as a whole far less insular and restrictive than its Israeli counterpart. Berel Wein says as much when he writes that "the yeshiva and Hassidic societies in North America have successfully co-opted much of modern Orthodoxy's agenda and promised achievements."[57] While Wein argues that in all this the Haredim have, nevertheless, done so "without risking undue exposure to the undermining lifestyle and value system" of contemporary America, his assertions are more matters of hope than statements supported by fact. He and others who have claimed that one can remain anchored in the Haredi enclave while wandering out of it freely fail to understand that such a strategy was and remains the essence of contrapuntalism. When Haredim begin to act like the modern Orthodox, how likely are they to remain truly Haredi? Indeed, from the perspective of their Israeli counterparts, those who see themselves as the true defenders of the faith, the "Americans," as they often call them, are already beyond the pale.

We have seen how the economic realities of Haredi culture may have precipitated a countertendency in the trends that otherwise seem to have been moving American Orthodoxy in the direction of insularity and against contrapuntalism. Another area in which we can see signs of such countermovement and even resistance to the Haredi ways is among some of the younger products of modern and centrist Orthodoxy who have not been lured by their education toward the right. It is to them that we now turn.

CHAPTER 6

Much Truth Said in Jest

Humor, Role Distance, and Young Orthodox Jews

> [T]he jest made in humor is not the essential; it is only the
> value of a demonstration. The principal thing is the intention
> which humor fulfils, whether it concerns the subject's self or
> other people.
>
> Sigmund Freud, "Humor"

Those who analyze humor have long ago recognized the principle that
much truth is said in jest. Freud convincingly informed us all that, as he
put it, "humor has in it a *liberating* element."[1] It allows what might otherwise be kept hidden and troubling to escape and thereby frees us from
the need to keep it repressed. (It also provides the observer a chance to
glimpse what might otherwise remain concealed.) Humor accomplishes
all this in a way that allows us to defend ourselves from the damaging
character of what we reveal by allowing us to laugh off what would otherwise be hurtful. We often joke about what would otherwise cause us anxiety, and we often joke about things that if we said them outright might
causes irrevocable breaches in the life to which we are committed. Accordingly, humor by Orthodox Jews about their attitudes, behavior patterns,
dogmas, concerns, and common life experiences tends to reflect the underlying effort to speak the truth while also liberating those who share in
the humor from the apparent limitations, tight controls, and consequent
challenges that an Orthodox Jewish way of life imposes upon them.

Perhaps no group of the Orthodox is more in need of these truth-telling
and liberating rewards of humor than young, *modern* American Orthodox Jews. These people are living within and even committed to the closed
domain of Orthodox Jewish interpretations of law, custom, and practice
as well as the community that enforces them (increasingly with a Haredi
imperative) but at the same time are trying to experience the liberation
and breaking of taboos that are so much a part of contemporary American adolescence. Simply put, they want to be both Orthodox Jewish and

modern American. They are also adolescents and postadolescents who are, in Erik Erikson's formulation, dealing with the issues of "identity and fidelity," trying to decide—for perhaps the first time in their lives—who they are, where they come from, and whether they wish to remain attached to the way of life they have led until now or whether this is a time for them to separate from their past, move on to somewhere else, and become someone different.[2] Many of them are trying to deal with often ambivalent feelings about all this.

Unlike their American forebears a century earlier, for whom the escape from an Orthodox community and way of life could not come swiftly enough, and for whom separation from their pasts often meant a complete break, the future for these young people is not necessarily outside Orthodoxy. They have learned, like many of their parents, to be anchored in Orthodox communities and to guide themselves by community norms and established patterns of behavior. To be sure, as already noted, there continue to be young people who do abandon Orthodoxy, who find its demands excessive, meaningless, hypocritical, and the rest, or who simply drift away from its orbit because they have been attracted by other involvements. However, while the number of Jews calling themselves Orthodox has continued to decline in every survey in the twentieth century, the tide seems now to have turned and the losses seem to have stopped. As we have seen earlier, the numbers may actually have begun to rebound. No longer can we assume that the Orthodox passage always leads to an exit. For many American young people who have grown up in it, Orthodoxy remains a culture in which they have felt at home, and the Jewish behavior it mandates defines a role they cannot conceive of leaving. Today the assumption within the Orthodox world is that a decline in numbers is no longer inevitable and that a significant number of those raised in the faith will voluntarily remain within the orbit of Orthodoxy, with some even changing the valence of their interests so that they turn increasingly inward and become embraced by an enclavist and intensely parochial Orthodoxy.

In a study of modern Orthodox Jewry, Steven M. Cohen and I discovered that by the late 1980s those thirty-four years old and younger were about 34 percent more ritually observant than those between thirty-five and fifty-four, and were about 69 percent more observant than those fifty-five and older. Their religious beliefs showed a similar intensification as one moved from older to younger.[3] That trend continues. Indeed, we have seen that particularly in their Jewish educational experiences these young people often turn in the direction of more intensive Orthodoxy and greater insularity at the very time that they are on the quest for a distinct identity.

The quest for intimacy, which Erikson tells us follows fast on the heels of the quest for identity, may sometimes make the young ready to follow leaders, charismatic or otherwise, and to join groups. For many young Orthodox Jews the groups and leaders to which they are drawn are insular and enclavist, more Haredi and uncompromising in their Orthodoxy than those that characterized the world in which they grew up.[4] These young people we have already discussed.

At the same time, however, there is continuing evidence that even as a powerful Haredi tendency is influencing many of these young Jews, others are seeking some way of loosening the ever-tightening Orthodox and particularly Haredi grip to allow for a more flexible identity, one that will allow them to swing easily from one side of their Jewish world to the other American one, from the parochial to the cosmopolitan. But theirs is a tethered swing. To accomplish it they invoke what Erving Goffman called "role distance," a way of separating some of themselves, elements of their character, from the Orthodox Jewish role that they nevertheless do not (and do not want to) deny they continue to inhabit. Likewise, sometimes they seek distance from their American role as well.[5] Where do these Jews come from and what do they teach us? These questions drive this chapter.

Banging out Modern Orthodox Jews

Contemporary American Orthodoxy has spent much of its "social capital" on producing—we might say "banging out"—a next generation that would not feel alienated from the Orthodox version of Jewish tradition, lifestyle, or values even as they found their places in contemporary society.[6] This has been a goal underlying much of the Orthodox day school movement, postsecondary school education, summer camping, a variety of Orthodox youth movements (from high school through college), and often an Israel experience that includes Jewish study in a yeshiva-like or other Orthodox environment. In principle these institutions, as we have seen, were designed to show the young that they could be both modern and Orthodox, attached to tradition but in and part of contemporary culture, successfully connected to a Jewish yesterday without sacrificing an American today or tomorrow. How exactly to negotiate that double identity, however, was not always clearly spelled out, and finding the ways to do so therefore represents, as we have seen earlier, one of the thorny

difficulties the younger generation of post-Holocaust American Orthodoxy has had to resolve. Part of a tightly knit community of shared values and common biography, products of this largely successful socialization process, today's modern Orthodox youth, born in this country and
at home in it, have by and large made autonomous decisions (like their
American peers), directing their "loyalties and energies to the conserva-
tion of that which feels true to them."[7] But because they live in at least
two cultures that feel true to them and that may not always be in harmony, this has required a contrapuntalist set of decisions.

On the one hand there are the Orthodox decisions, whose ways of life
offer many benefits, particularly in the transitional period of identity resolution and the search for intimacy that is so much a part of adolescence.
These are patterns of acting that young modern Orthodox Jews share with
others like them, patterns that serve to "counteract a threatening sense of
alienation with positive ritual and affirmative dogma," as well as giving
insiders a sense of "we are all in this together."[8] This creates a culture of
familiarity that allows them to go to all sorts of places and find kindred
spirits and familiar ways of life within the boundaries of Orthodox Jewish communities.

Yet these are also young people who have been "out in the world"
during their college years, in their work experiences, while traveling
(which they do as much as if not more than many of their contemporaries), via electronic media, or simply by virtue of living in urban, cosmopolitan environments like Manhattan (particularly its Upper West
Side), where so many of them have gravitated for the last twenty years.
In this world, where although there are people like them the *dominant*
others are not Orthodox Jews, they also feel somewhat at home and have
a sense of belonging. Not surprisingly, for many of these young modern Orthodox Jews the two senses of belonging chafe against each other.
To handle this antagonism, which, if left untreated, might threaten to
undermine the choices they have made and unravel the lives they have
spun, making them suffer the consequences, some have turned to humor, which in its core is, as Freud has shown us, a "repudiation of the
possibility of suffering."[9] To be able to make fun of and laugh at who
they are, the way they live, the constraints that both protect and limit
them, the often contradictory choices they make that are often so at odds
with the hip culture that is just outside the borders of the permissible
but to which they feel attached, provides them with a way to "ward off
possible suffering,"[10] a way of treating themselves like the parochial and
limited Orthodox Jews that they are while at the same time playing the

part of the superior cosmopolitan and hip outsider—the American urban "twenty-something." Humor offers a means of expressing role distance, of conveying a detachment from the Orthodoxy (and the prohibited elements of the contemporary world) to which they nonetheless remain publicly identified. As such it makes the restrictions of the Orthodox Jewish role (and the "sins" of being somewhat of an outsider) weigh lightly on their shoulders as well as making the attractions of the world beyond less compelling.

An analysis of the subjects that make up this humor, moreover, not only demonstrates this effort in process but also helps highlight exactly what issues could arouse feelings of suffering, where the friction between being loyal to Orthodoxy and being part of young America is felt, and where the weight of the role is heaviest. The jokes tell us about those who make and enjoy them—the thoughts on their minds, what is troubling them, what they want to laugh at so that they will not cry.

Collecting examples of such humor among the young modern Orthodox might seem at first a daunting task—particularly for one who is not an insider by virtue of either age or circumstances. However, in the age of the Internet, one can gain access to domains far afield from one's own. Moreover, for the Orthodox and young, the virtual community of the Internet has offered a way of expanding the network of relations and web of affiliations that is essential for those who wish at once to be tied to parochial values and communities but move about more like the rest of a highly mobile young America. The Internet, accessible from cell phones, palm devices, and of course computers that they all have, also allows one to eavesdrop on the interchanges across this network. To be sure, the insiders' terms and concerns might frequently restrict the ability of outsiders to tap into the electronic enclave. Thus outsiders may not always "get" what a particular Web site is all about or may comprehend only part of the message that various degrees of insiders will understand more fully. Within the domains of virtual territory no less than in real territory, sometimes a guide is necessary for a proper tour. (In a message on the Web site serving the young Orthodox New York scene, which is the focus of this analysis, surfers are informed that one of the "top ten ways you know it's time for a vacation from the Upper West Side" is that "you find yourself actually getting the jokes" on that site.)[11] Yet beyond these not insignificant limitations, the realm of cyberspace is a wonderful place to find this humor, or at least parts of it.

While by no means the only such domain, a site called bangitout.com, identified as a place "where Jews can laugh . . . at themselves" (ellipses in original), run and edited by a group of young modern Orthodox Jews from New York, offers a window into the world I have been describing.[12] There are other such cybersites (many of which are linked to this page and most of which come and go without much warning). One of the more recent is an interactive cybersite called www.jewlicious.com that describes itself as "100% Kosher." But for sheer span and constant updating of subject matter, the bangitout.com Web page offers the most. In addition to humor, which is its general subject matter and is modeled on similar humor magazines like the *Onion,* originally distributed in print and also available online, the site serves as a kind of bulletin board for the young and Orthodox.[13] Thus in June 2002 its cover page headlines "the daily bang," containing "your daily dose of kosher comedy," as well as lists of what is a regular feature: "the kosher top 10," a takeoff on a popular routine on the late-night David Letterman program on television (a reference that in itself communicates that the readers and writers are familiar with this feature of popular culture). But there are as well listings for "apartments that bang" (notices of housing available in areas where the young modern Orthodox live, making connections among those seeking Jewishly observant apartment mates, and the most frequented part of the site for visitors), "jobs that bang," (employment opportunities requiring some Jewish competence that the Orthodox commonly have or that are appropriate for those who want work that will allow them to maintain their religious observant lifestyle), "movies that bang," "event guide" (often gatherings where they can meet other like-minded Jews),"torah that bangs" (humorous interpretations of Jewish texts), and "buzz links" (connections to sites that may be of interest to readers, such as a humorous site that tongue-in-cheek suggests the paving over of France as a response to recent outbreaks of anti-Semitism there).

Clearly, not all of these sites are concerned with humor as much as with providing information of relevance and need to the community that the editors see as their audience. Some of this information seems to have little if anything to do with their Orthodoxy and more to do simply with their being part of the youth culture (such as reviews of recent music recordings or cinema). Indeed, this is a reflection of the site's owners, who wish to stress thereby that one can be Orthodox but still be "with it," and interested in and able to talk about the same sorts of things as one's non-Orthodox peers.[14] In addition, one headline that resonates with the ongoing concern of finding a mate (about which more below) mixes humor with information: "Before the West Side Was Won—Places you'll never meet your Shidduch [mate]." There is also a feature called "Life's Little

Jewish Instruction Book," which provides instructions for those who are new either to Orthodoxy or to the freedom of life outside it.

Were this all there were, one might argue that the site would be little more than a reflection of its editors and primary authors, two young brothers, Seth and Isaac Galena, in their twenties who grew up in a modern Orthodox community outside Philadelphia and a friend, Aryeh Dworken, who grew up in a similar community in suburban northern New Jersey, all of whom met at Yeshiva College and now live on Manhattan's Upper West Side, a mecca for others like them. In fact, the Web site began as something the Galena brothers would just "bang out" on their keyboards for fun, but by the spring of 2002 it was getting a quarter of a million hits—cybervisits—a month, among which, according to their accurate user statistics, were approximately thirteen thousand "unique users," first-time visitors. The rest were Web surfers who obviously returned again and again to the site.[15] Clearly, the site had an audience, and one that visited repeatedly. It was thus a virtual community and perhaps represented a real one as well.

Recognizing the interactive and communal nature of those whom they addressed—"we all feel as if we know one another," as Dworken put it—they naturally provided an option that would allow readers to add their own responses and variations on the material as well as an invitation and incentives for them to submit articles. The readers responded. On a part of the site called "feedback that bangs," one discovers comments like "Just thought you might like to know that all of Brovenders [an Israel-based yeshiva for American Orthodox women] is currently obsessed with your website. Thanks for keeping us laughing during a somewhat tense year." Another reader, for whom "all Jews" are some sort of Orthodox, writes: "Your site is a wonderful source of entertainment for all Jews, from Orthodox to Modern Orthodox."[16] Thus the jokes ("bangs" in the terminology of the site) become not only a mirror of what is on the minds of the writers and readers but also an opportunity to see how the ideas and underlying concerns are developed and articulated in a reactive way.[17] Indeed so powerfully reactive did the site become that a local New York rabbi (with a large congregation of twenty-something Orthodox singles) sermonized about it and then in a submission to the feedback page noted that "some things on the site do cross the line and should be removed" in order, as he explained, "to raise everyone's attention and awareness of the issue of what's right to write and read."[18] Jokes, the rabbi seemed to imply, have a tendency to come uncomfortably close to the truth, to go past the boundaries of the acceptable. But of course, *it is precisely the way that humor teeters on the line between propriety and impropriety and allows one to touch on what otherwise seems untouchable that is often so appealing about it.* This is certainly the case for these modern Orthodox Jews who are trying to stretch the boundaries of what is appropriate and also get some things off their chests.

As the editors of the site explained, they (and presumably their readers and writers) are at once poking fun at and expressing an allegiance to their Orthodox way of life. At one level, the writers want to show themselves and anyone who gets to their site that, as one of them put it, "Wow, we are really interesting people," not just an insular, marginal, and parochial Orthodox minority. That is, they want to prove to themselves how "hip" they are. But at the same time they are ready to "focus on the hypocrisies" and the "ridiculous" elements in their way of life, demonstrating its very "un-hipness."[19] Trying to lift up the example of Orthodoxy while also putting it down is of course a reflection of ambivalence, a mixed feeling about what they revere and what they feel limited by in their way of life. And that double, sometimes oxymoronic, feeling is what marks the site. Or, as Dworken put it in an interview: "We want to be funny and irreverent and at the same time completely reverent and respectful." What could be more contrapuntalist? Finding that balance, knowing where to draw the line between these plural life-worlds and loyalties, is of course not just a matter of taste for these young people. At some level it also gets at the question, "How hip can an Orthodox Jewish young person be?" Or, as an earlier generation might have phrased the question, How modern and Orthodox can a contemporary Jew be?

While my purpose here is not to provide an exhaustive survey of all the jokes, I want to use the site as a way of exploring some themes embedded within and revealed through them regarding what is on the minds of young modern Orthodox Jews in twenty-first-century America– or at least in a few compartments of it. To understand its audience, however, we need to explore something about the nature of their experience and concerns as well as how these relate to identity

IDENTITY

Frum and Frummer.   In his now classic analysis of ego development and a person's integration into society, Erik Erikson articulated eight ages.[20] In each of these turning points or developmental stages, he argued, the person inaugurates and completes a new sense of self and thereby confronts the possibility of successfully articulating who he or she is and in-

tegrating that newly formed self into society. That is, we must all repeatedly discover, rediscover, and present our changing and developing selves
to others.[21] The successful resolution of the challenge of one age not only
helps us find out who we are and what the group in which we locate ourselves expects of us at a particular age but also enables us to deal with the
next age in the series. Success leads to further development and new challenges, while failure leaves the ego fixated at the point of difficulty, trying to find a way out of a position of arrested development. These turning points, Erikson believed, are more frequent in childhood because of
the growing child's greater number of changes—from infant through tod-
dler to prepubescent youngster. Beginning in adolescence, following pu-
berty, the transformations are fewer but in many ways far more challenging: little children, little problems; big children, big problems. The
challenge of youth, Erikson argued, focuses on the often rocky and fitful
transition into adulthood, when life seems to begin again but when, unlike early childhood, everything seems to be "for keeps." The essential issues here are three. First are questions of identity: Will the world accept
me as I am now, or must I revert to being the child I have been all my
life? Next comes intimacy: If I am no longer a child, can I find others who
will love me, want to be with me, share my life with me as I now am? Finally comes generativity: Given who I have become and the people I am
with, can I make a contribution, add to and leave something of myself in
that part of the world that matters to me? This last age, Erikson argued,
one arrives at later in life, and it constitutes the bulk of adulthood. For
young adolescents emerging into young adulthood—in our times the
twenty-somethings or, given the median age of American Jewish marriage
at twenty-eight, even some early thirty-somethings—establishing a clear
identity and "the search for something and somebody to be true to," are
the essential and core concerns.[22] Erikson summarized this in his declaration that contemporary youth experience "a bewildering combination
of shifting devotion" but ultimately are "seeking after some durability in
change" and a "reliability of commitments."[23] Because of these common
needs, youth are often desperate to learn how their counterparts are doing, hoping to glean thereby some hint as to how to proceed. Navigating a time when they are, in Kaspar Naegele's vivid terminology, "sus-
pended between a 'no longer' and a 'not yet,' youth is forced to balance
continuity and discontinuity."[24] Youth are hence tremendously concerned with finding and gauging themselves against their peers because
finding a group of persons in similar circumstances could make this passage in life easier to negotiate. The fidelity of others to a way of life, val-

ues, and group could help the individual find what he or she should choose as a focus of loyalty.

For modern American Orthodox youth this passage contains an additional complication. They must as we have said, integrate themselves into and create loyalties to more than one culture, and—to make life even more difficult—the cultures in question are in some senses diametrically opposed, or at least putatively cognitively dissonant. On one side is the culture of Orthodox tradition, custom, and constraint that limits individual autonomy and emphasizes continuity with a sacred past and community; on the other side is American youth culture, characterized by revolution, discontinuity, changing trends or fads, and personal, sometimes radical, freedom that assumes that "life is open" and that "the future will improve on the past."[25] To be sure, the extent of the revolution and radicalism of American youth has varied widely during the last fifty years—from the relatively wild 1960s and 1970s to the more staid 1980s and 1990s and into the different adaptations of the early twenty-first century. Yet the American infatuation with openness and change has always been a pole apart from what a conservative Orthodox Jewish culture considered ideal, or at least this has been the message of the Orthodox defenders of the faith.[26] In all events, the young modern Orthodox Jewish adolescent or newly emergent adult has to find a way of being properly part of these dueling cultures at precisely a time of life where group loyalties and cultural fidelity are paramount concerns.

All this is complicated even more by the fact that both these cultures are undergoing change. For American popular culture, change is endemic, indeed anticipated. Ours remains a society that expects that "all new generations must accommodate themselves" to such change, in large part because as Americans we believe that "one of youth's historic roles has been to provide the enthusiasm—if not the leadership—for still further changes."[27] Although wedded to tradition, Orthodox Judaism has from its earliest beginnings in nineteenth-century Europe been at its root a reactive and oppositional movement, shaped by what it fights against. Thus it has been constituted by selective retrievals from that tradition, elements that emphasize and reinterpret whatever is needed to meet the challenges of the day and place in which its adherents find themselves.[28] Anyone who has lived an Orthodox Jewish life is aware of these changes in the effective demands of the tradition, often presented as reinterpretations or "clarifications" of what are the true claims that Orthodoxy can make on life and belief. For example, the continuing announcement by Orthodox rabbinic authorities of new stringencies in the interpretation of the demands of Jewish law, the initiation of so-called *chumra,* is a part of this process, one that modern Orthodox Jews often chafe at but that their Haredi counterparts champion.[29] The *chumra* often seeks to challenge practices that allow integration into modernity and contemporary culture. The June 2004 announcement by some Orthodox rabbis that New York City tap water might not be kosher is an example.[30] If even drinking a glass of water risks transgressing the rules of kashruth, the Orthodox, in their strict adherence to these dietary laws, will have a far harder time moving about the world outside their enclaves. For modern Orthodox youth, who have tried to buck these trends, this makes fitting in harder.

Hence one of the primary concerns among youth, for whom the question of identity is close to an obsession, is precisely where and among whom they fit in, what it means to be Orthodox under the present circumstances. For young modernists—the bulk of those who make up the writers and audience for this Web site—there is also a felt need to make certain that they manage to stake out space for an identity that keeps its distance from the growing influences of the Haredi tendencies that have gradually overtaken many of their peers. Accordingly, much of the humor that focuses around identity matters addresses these distinctions within Orthodoxy as well as the question of how one knows who's who and what's what. What is Orthodox, and who qualifies for inclusion and how? How does one know where to fit in and what is required to fit in?

Addressing this double-edged question, Michael Winner, in an article (accompanied by responses from other readers) entitled "60 Ways to Appear Frum and Intellectual," tries to use humor to demonstrate the constancy of this concern for him and his peers.[31] But understanding these sixty jokes requires a bit of preliminary cultural competence: the meaning of *frum,* which, as already noted, remains one of the most common insider terms for identifying the Orthodox.

What is *frum* is by no means always and everywhere the same, and in the struggle for the hearts and minds of Orthodoxy, the Haredi and modern Orthodox are in a contest to see whose definitions of *frum* and *frumkeit* will be definitive. Consequently, one of the concerns of Orthodox Jews seeking to resolve the issue of who they are and with whom do they fit in may focus around the question, How should I be *frum*? or "How *frum* should I be? Should I identify with the Haredi or with the more liberal versions of *frumkeit*? Is it enough to appear *frum,* or must I truly believe in and embrace what I am doing?

Implicit in the Winner headline is another related issue: *frumkeit* and intellectualism are potentially rivalrous positions, so one who wants an identity affiliated with both—the Orthodox university student or graduate, for example—would appear to be in a dilemma. The assumption here is that *frum* is unthinking acceptance of normative Orthodox life patterns, while intellectualism involves freely deciding what makes sense. But, the headline implies, there is a way to minimize the contradiction between the two. The suggestions for how to do so, if they were completely serious, would constitute recipe knowledge for how to be successfully contrapuntalist and precisely what the young modern Orthodox Jew might want. However, in this case the suggestions turn out to offer a burlesque of such recipe knowledge, hinting that there is *really no way to be both*, since thinking and being *frum* are in essence antithetical to each other.

Hence, the solutions to the dualism that Winner offers conclude, as an analysis of his jokes makes clear, that one need not give up being intellectual, apparently the dominant of the two identities from his point of view; one needs simply to learn how to manage the impression of being *frum*.[32] His advice in a sense draws distinctions between inner and outer identity, between what one really is and how one may appear.[33] Winner's list echoes with the experiences of someone who has tried to manage this impression or observed others trying to do so. There is humor here, but also an oblique sort of guidance for others who have been caught in the same Orthodox identity dilemma. Thus he offers, at item 12, "Put Hebrew dates on everything, and stop using civil dates altogether." This is a reference to the increasing insularity of an enclavist Orthodoxy that has ideologically spurned the Gregorian (i.e., Gentile) calendar and the culture attached to it. At item 9, he suggests, "When davening [praying] with a minyan [quorum], remember it's very important to say the first three (some hold four) words out loud, and then mumble the rest quietly." This satirical reference to displays of piety in prayer also adds a subtle dig at the enclavists. To insiders, the syntax and language of this item mimic the way the demands of Jewish law are presented ("some hold") among the Orthodox, offering a crafty jibe at the Yinglish or yeshivish syntax of Haredi orthodoxy that marks it as "foreign" to American spoken English. This is even more explicit in his item 16: "Must speak in that annoying Brooklyn accent."

In item 30, he adds the use of props as a way of appearing *frum*: "When learning [studying Talmud], make sure to have as many Sfarim [holy books] open as possible. Many poskim [rabbinical authorities] hold you should have out: 2 Mesechtas [tractates] of Gemara [Talmud], a chumash [Bible], a chelek [volume] of Shulchan Oruch [Code of Jewish Law], a

Ritva [an acronym for a particular rabbinic commentary], and a sefer [volume] written by an achron [rabbi of the late period] that nobody knows."[34] The code switching here, so characteristic of yeshivish culture, and the use of acronyms and phrases that only Orthodox insiders understand resonate with a send-up of the sectarian nature of the *frum*.

The list goes on. One reader, caught up in the exercise, submits, for example, "A fake Galician [Jewish] accent is extremely frum (i.e. boorich instead of baruch, oomayin instead of amein, etc.)," a reference to the style of pronunciation popular among the Haredi Orthodox, whose Hebrew echoes European Jewry of the pre-Holocaust period rather than the pronunciation associated with American Jewish life. The former accent has been taken on by those who wish to suggest the authenticity of that European past and its "superiority" over American or even Israeli Hebrew, as a way of asserting that the past is better than the present version of Orthodoxy—another characteristic of contemporary Haredi Orthodoxy. This accent and the worldview it represents are often imitated by young Orthodox who grew up with the American or modern Israeli pronunciation but wish to display that they have been "transformed" following an extended stay in a Haredi yeshiva. Embedded in Winner's humor and the responses to it is the message that Haredi Orthodox Jewish identity is subject to easy manipulation and faking and that one can negotiate its difficulties without getting caught up in the struggle of what should be one's "true" identity. There is also a suggestion here that some modernists do not believe in the authenticity of the transformation that these put-on pronunciations seek to signify.

All these list items contain unmistakable jabs at the Haredi version of Orthodoxy. They suggest that manipulated displays of piety or *frumkeit* are all it takes to be Haredi. To the informed, however, Winner's and his contributing readers' recommendations are not only caricatures of a Haredi-style identity in Orthodoxy but also a critique of the modern Orthodox who seek invidiously to emulate those to their religious right. At the same time, this list suggests that Haredi-style identity can really be turned into nothing more than a performance or managed impression rather than something deeply rooted in conviction and sense of self. The jokes are an attack that pokes fun not only at the performances but also at those who perform them but do not truly believe in them.

Of course, by keeping the attack in the form of a joke, these modernists have tempered it. Were the humor and satire to be removed from it, it would be a far more divisive assault, a criticism that could lead in its most extreme in schism, something the small and relatively fragile (at least in its own perception) post-Holocaust American Orthodoxy could not abide. Yet it remains important enough for Winner and others like him to ensure that everyone recognizes that not all Orthodox are alike and not all are Haredi.

Insularity, Enclavism, and Alternative Realities.   Insularity, a common accusation against Orthodoxy and increasingly a tendency in the growing enclavism of the movement, also comes in for ridicule from these jokesters who chafe under the sectarianism of Orthodox identity. This can be seen, for example, in the humor of Sarah Galena's "Top 10 Ways You Know You're an Observant Jew Attending a Secular College."[35] For many American modern Orthodox adolescents who have lived mostly within the parochial environment of their Jewish world—school, synagogue, community, Israeli yeshiva—college (particular one that is residential) is the first place they truly have to deal with close contact with Gentiles and those outside their familiar milieu. Now they must decide how much to recoil from contemporary campus culture and how much to accommodate themselves to it. Galena's jokes focus on the tensions inherent in their situation. One way of dealing with the unfamiliar campus culture, she reports, is to minimize its differences from their own, so that "the Friday night kegger is conveniently renamed 'an *Oneg.*'" A "kegger," of course, is a free-for-all beer party, but an *oneg* is what the Jews call a Sabbath get-together. These are quite different sorts of gatherings, one celebrating the sacred and the other the profane. The joke here is that, in Galena's locution, it is possible to turn them into equivalents with a simple semantic trick, to fool oneself and others that although one is at a kegger it is really just a kind of *oneg.* The joke is an expression of the difficulty of contrapuntalism. But it also makes fun of the absurdity of some efforts to minimize the differences between the two cultures. A Friday night kegger cannot really be called an *oneg,* except by those who have disattended or ignored the essential characteristics of each. Yet these young people persist in trying to bring together the seemingly irreconcilable.

"Instead of frat parties, there are Shabbos onegs [festivities] with divrei torahs [Torah talks] and peach schnapps." Here the reverse is tried, treating a truly Jewish event as something profane.

The joke in both these examples is that the only way to bring these opposites together is to stretch the meaning of what is Jewish beyond recognition. In other words, contrapuntalism is presented in such a burlesqued fashion that one is forced to admit implicitly that the Haredi critique of modern Orthodox duplicity and hypocrisy is correct. After all, can one really claim these equivalencies?

Another item on Galena's list contains a self-deprecating reference to observant Jews' propensity to cultivate cliques. Cliques are communities, movable enclaves. They are a key reference group for the Orthodox on the move and in some ways a protection against the assimilative tendencies that this group so fears. The desire both to be identified with this clique and to distance themselves from it and establish a more cosmopolitan identity, a hallmark of the modern Orthodox on campus, is articulated in the self-referentially ridiculing statement that "you think you are 'open-minded' because you have one friend who is African-American." The humor here is that the Orthodox claim to be open-minded is largely symbolic and shallow.

Then there is the reference to an ongoing dilemma for anyone who wishes to be true to Orthodox Jewish religious demands as exercised inside the enclave and still be very much a part of the university: the need to withdraw from worldly pursuits (including classes) on Jewish holy days without being penalized in any way for that withdrawal. The requirement to "take off" holy days, which the rest of America knows little if anything about, tugs against the modernist desire to join in American life and its rhythms. This sometimes incompatible goal is articulated in the one-liner that "your professors begin studying Jewish laws in order to verify that the holidays you tell [them] you observe actually exist."

The idea that as an Orthodox Jew one lives in a different temporal realm or carries an alternate (sometimes secret) identity that constitutes another layer beneath the level of perception of outsiders or nonmembers—namely the American social world—is touched upon here by implication. Some of the readers who responded to Sarah Galena's list with their own entries articulate this even more explicitly. For example, one submits a one-liner that reminds readers of how the Orthodox exist in a kind of alternative universe that is out of rhythm with the modern environment—in this case campus life: she explains that you know you are an Orthodox Jew attending a secular college when "campus is dead when you walk to shul [synagogue services] Shabbos [Sabbath] morning. It awakens three hours later as you prepare for your Shabbos shluff [nap]." The joke is that Orthodox Jews operate not only in a different cultural landscape but also in a different timescape. They are out of sync with the campus world (or America) of which they seek so much to be a part.

This alternate universe with which the modern Orthodox college students identify, albeit uncomfortably, as this particular list demonstrates, is also associated with an alternate sets of values that Orthodox Jews have but that they must somehow keep camouflaged if they are simultaneously to be part of the secular college culture too. Thus a reader reports that one hidden identity is connected to the "guys who spend their free time in Beis Midrash [the Talmud study hall]." These are fellows who "are secretly praised by all the girls as being masmidim [diligent Jewish scholars] of the campus." Here again, the joke refers to a double life that the Orthodox Jew who tries to live on the American campus must carry on. The very identity that would garner praise in the Orthodox world (and certainly in its Haredi enclaves)—to be diligent Talmud scholars—remains a secret on campus except for those among the initiated, yet it still garners some status. The Orthodox seem to constitute a secret society because on campus the diligent yeshiva *bochur* does not draw praise, except from the women who, like him, truly identify with Orthodox values of the yeshiva enclavist culture. Similarly, the secret Haredi identity is reflected in the joke that you know you are Jewish on a secular campus when "you become known as a skirtwearer.'" Unwilling to wear pants or shorts or minis—as other college coeds do—the young Orthodox girl on campus hews to the "modest" norms of the religious right wing. What is clear here as well is that the nature of the Orthodox observance to which reference is made is much stricter, *frum*mer, than was once normative on American campuses.

Modern Orthodox Jewish adolescents are torn. On one side, they are ready to be with it, even antinomian, and to bend the rules of Judaism almost beyond recognition. "Your idea of intense chavrusa [Torah study dialogue] is debating whether you should make a bracha [benediction] on pot [marijuana]-brownies." Or they are ready to present themselves in a way that seems quite distant from what is Orthodox: for example, one submission to Kenneth Rosen's "Top 10 Indications That You Were a 90's Yeshiva High School Punk" is "Although you could easily converse in Yeshivishah shpruch [the lingo of the yeshiva associated with Haredi Orthodoxy), you prefer to greet everyone with 'Waaass Up?'" a phrase associated with the street culture of black American adolescence and its imitators.[36]

On the other side, however, is the choice to remain bound by the strictest rules of Orthodox behavior, like being a "skirt wearer" who dresses in ways that conform to religious conservative norms or rushing to spend hours reviewing Talmud in the study hall. Which of these choices is the right one? That is the question that confronts these young people, who try to be both but laugh at themselves for the effort and at the absurdity of trying to diminish the distance between contrapuntal identities.

So troubling is the question of identity that even being from some-where does not help one know exactly "where one is." That is to say, whereas parents and elders may just need to locate themselves somewhere specific, to become anchored in a community, in order to know what to do and who they are, their children need more. Orientation is an abid-ing concern. How do I know where I am, and therefore how do I know how to behave or, perhaps more generally, how to *locate* myself? In a telling question in a piece called "The Official Modern Orthodox Quiz," Aviva Leibtag captures all this when she asks the question that in a sense is be-hind all this quest for identity: "How do you really know if you're mod-ern Orthodox? These days you can't just go by what your parents do."[37]

Such puzzlement over who one is and where to locate oneself is not unique to these Jews; it is an essential feature of adolescence. Yet how much more complicated it seems to be for these youngsters who are try-ing to balance themselves in several contradictory worlds at once. Thus bangitout.com is filled with lists whose aim, albeit humorous, is to en-able them to figure *who* they are by knowing precisely *where* they are and then being given guidance for how to act there. The lists include the "top ten signs you are in Flatbush," the "top 10 signs you are from Jewish Chicago," the "top signs you are from Jewish Minnesota," "ways you know you're from Jewish Baltimore," the "top 30 signs you are from Jew-ish Elizabeth, N.J.," the "top ten ways you know you're in Teaneck for Shabbos [Sabbath]," or the "top ten ways you know you're in Staten Is-land for Shabbos." Or, with a slight shift from geographic locations that help determine who one is, the humor focuses on figuring out identity on the basis of activity. Thus there are the "top 10 ways you know you work at a Jewish organization."[38]

Appearances and Displays. Inherent in all these somewhat cynical con-ceptions of a manipulated Orthodox Jewish identity is an acknowledg-ment of how much of Orthodoxy is a matter of appearances and displays. This too highlights the degree of other-directedness inherent in much of Orthodox behavior, of the felt need to gauge one's behavior and attitudes by what others in one's surroundings are doing or at least what they dis-play. The focus on display reveals an exquisite sensitiveness to identity, performance, self-presentation, and being observed that these young Jews have, a skill that undoubtedly has been sharpened by their need to inhabit often-conflicting domains of belonging, playing on multiple stages at once. These are people who are carefully (perhaps even frantically) try-ing to calibrate who they are and where they belong and then trying to decide before whom they are presenting themselves. Because they know they march to different sets of drummers and in more than one parade at a time and know too that this takes a lot of manipulation and perfectly timed and articulated performances, they have become acutely aware that they constitute a separate and somewhat alien group trying to find a place for themselves on the margins of each culture. That is why role distance is so much a part of their identity repertoire. Desperately, laughably, they endeavor to fit into secular campus life and by transitivity American society and culture, but always they do so knowing that this requires some sort of masquerade.

In the absence of religious authorities ready to guide them through the multiple realities they seek to inhabit, finding a community of like others and using conformity with them as a means for guidance becomes crucial for them, as it does for their modern Orthodox parents. Consequently they are even more dependent on their peers than most people their age. The jokes and the Web site on which they appear (as well as other such virtual sites) help them create that community even when their actual circumstances make it difficult. To be sure, the joking references are meant to be funny. But there are truths in these jests, and they offer, if not perfect guidance and community, then at least a sense that one is not alone. Reflecting this truth is a comment posted by one young woman: "I thought I was the only one who had to deal with this!" In that exclamation point, one can almost hear the relief of discovering she was not alone.

In the humor, all this is not just highlighted but criticized for what sometimes might be viewed as manipulative insincerity. In some cases, the young take a step back and in addition to making fun of themselves and their predicament censure themselves and the world that elicits particular performances from them for its spiritual emptiness and questionable theological assumptions. How funny that this is all just a masquerade. Thus item 34 on Winner's list refers to the need for *kavanah* [devotion] in prayer and jokes about the dubiousness of the capacity for such devotion: "Who needs kavanah when davening? Just scrunch up your face, purse your lips, shut your eyes tight, bang one fist into your palm, whisper the words loud enough to disturb your neighbor, let your spit be liberated from the confines of your lips, and get that really, really constipated look on your face. Only then will the Big Guy hear your supplications." For a population that spends so much of its time at prayer as these young people do and often does display piety, this item suggests lingering doubts about the way of effecting that worship as well as the identity implicit in the effort. In the same vein, item 42 is an injunction to "make sure to always look miserable, because G-d [*sic*] forbid, people might think that you are taking some form of pleasure in this world." And item 17 offers the insight that if you wish to appear *frum*, "meditation is completely assur [prohibited]. (G-d forbid you should spiritually become closer to G-d)." The use of the "G-d" word, an effort to not write out the full name of God, is itself a sign of a certain level of piety and reverence, as is the sarcastic reference to the lack of genuine spirituality among the *frum* and the *frum*mer. Yet the impiety of the comments contradicts the orthography, or at least again reflects ambivalence.

In these jokes, the writers do not make fun of the effort to deny the differences between the Orthodox and the modern, as we saw above. Here instead they attack with humor the sincerity and genuineness of the Haredi expression of Orthodoxy, suggesting it is more show than passion. Here are young Orthodox Jews, on the cusp of committing themselves to an Orthodox way of life, tossing barbs at the duplicity of much of what passes as *frum*: not only the dominance of appearance over genuine religion in the emphasis on certain practices but also the frequent covering of transgressions by pretense and posing. There is at the same time a tacit admission that in some respect being Orthodox, even Haredi, is simply a pose — the critique that many of the Haredim have made vis-à-vis the modern Orthodox.

The jokes take aim as well at a variety of modern Orthodox norms that are associated not so much with matters of identity linked to religious ideology as with bourgeois values and culture that are only masquerading as displays of Orthodoxy. Some of these jokes also poke fun at Haredi Orthodoxy, or at least at its tendencies that have made inroads into the changing norms of contemporary American Orthodoxy. Thus one finds at item 26 on the Winner list the expectation that the bride or groom will "videotape your wedding even though nobody on either side of the family owns a television," a common tendency among Haredim, who view television as a window through which the most defiling aspects of popular culture can enter their enclave and desecrate its integrity. The desire for the videotape is not only a fascination with technology but also an expression of materialist excess that clashes with the purism that not having a television monitor symbolizes. Again, according to item 28 part of the *frum* display requires that you "go to the Hilton or any other expensive-type hotel on your first date." These gags are elaborated upon in a reader's addendum: "Buy a Lincoln town car or a long station wagon." For those familiar with the divisions within Orthodoxy, these jokes not only poke

fun at Orthodox conspicuous consumption but also carry another message. They hint at the animosity of the modern Orthodox toward the
Haredim as hypocrites who are no less duplicitous than they accuse the
modern Orthodox of being. These are the Orthodox who do not own
televisions because of their opposition to all the destructive culture that
it depicts, yet insist on videotaping their lavish weddings. They look for
a "date" in a public place like a hotel so that they will not transgress the
Haredi Orthodox prohibition against unwed males and females being
alone together in a room, yet go to places that are meant arouse envy. And,
for their large families born as a result of the emphasis on childbearing
and opposition to birth control, they buy large cars.

These jokes in a sense suggest that each side is more concerned with
display than with genuineness. The jokes here say, a pox on both your
houses. Neither of you is beyond ridicule. Though both groups claim to
be the real thing, we can show that each has its problems.

INTIMACY

Important and continuing as they are, concerns over identity—which have
been part of these people's developing self-consciousness for most of their
teen years and beyond—are greatly overshadowed by a new and increasingly compelling matter on their minds: the question of intimacy. Whom
should I be with (and therefore like)? That question is, in Erikson's words,
the passion of "the young adult, emerging from the search for and the in-
sistence on identity," who now "is eager and willing to fuse his [or her]
identity with that of others," who is "ready for intimacy" and ready to
commit "to concrete affiliations and partnerships" as an adult.[39] Knowing who one is and with which community one wishes to be affiliated
plays a part in enabling one to deal with matters of intimacy, and often
the two issues become conflated. Knowing who one is must surely be the
first step, followed by knowing whom one should seek to be with and
how that relationship may be expressed.

Behind all this normal concern of the age with issues of intimacy is the
additional factor of the high valuation on marriage and family in Orthodox Jewish society, which cannot be gainsaid. This is a post-Holocaust
culture that, as we have seen, suffered significant population decline and
today has become nearly obsessed with its waning in numbers over the
last several generations; thus it is seeking to ensure its continuity by bol-
stering those numbers through marriage, fertility, and fidelity. Though
it tolerates dating and premarital heterosexual relationships (with vary-

ing degrees of social control), it sees them as at best a means of promoting marriage and fecundity. (The nature of these relationships as well as what should be the standards of intimacy—is touching permitted, is spending the night together acceptable, or should powerful restrictions on these relationships be practiced—are all part of the debate and the jokes—about which more below.)[40]

Among Orthodox young people, the "pressure to get married," as Galena and Dworken put it, is immense and unending—both from parents and as an acquired value shared among peers. To some extent, this pressure has been paradoxically enhanced because, with Orthodoxy's gradual move to the religious right over the last quarter-century and its recent demographic rebound, these young people have found themselves increasingly in institutions (schools, summer camps, youth movements) that segregate them by gender, so that it is difficult for relationships between males and females to develop in an informal, extracurricular fashion. More and more, meeting members of the opposite sex becomes a challenge while they are in school. When they are out of school, moreover, those who are not in the Haredi world suddenly are forced to find their own ways of meeting that will lead to matrimony.

In the Haredi Orthodox model, which these young people mock, some of the same pressures exist. Indeed, the need to marry and have children by their early twenties, generally earlier than the modern Orthodox, most of whom are still in college at that age, is acutely felt in Haredi circles. However, among Haredi young people, adults largely arrange the marriages, thereby mitigating the pressure by shifting the search for marriage partners to others in the community or family.[41] The young people may have a right of refusal, but the institution of matchmaking is still very much in force in the Haredi enclaves. Matchmakers pair those with common religious values, behavior, and orientation as well as those with social and educational similarities. Love will have to come after marriage.

However much the young modern Orthodox make fun of this Haredi practice that appears so to restrict free choice and stifle the pursuit of romance, they realize that they, no less than their Haredi counterparts, are committed ideologically to demographic growth and the ideal of life within a traditional family, and they too seek partners who share their religious outlook and behavior. There is thus something appealing about a system that takes care of finding young singles a mate, taking much of the pressure of the search off them. This is especially because the question of what constitutes an appropriate mate is complicated for modernists who are also highly traditional in their religious affiliations. Perhaps as a result, a modified version of the *shidduch*—the arranged marriage—has gradually made its way into the modern Orthodox world as well. Here however, the matchmakers are not parents or professionals from within the community, as they are in the Haredi variant. Instead, the persons who work on matches are commonly peers and self-appointed volunteers. In a way this modified practice tries to bring together two apparently contradictory models of intimacy: choice by the individual and matchmaking by the community. In adopting the help of the community, it challenges the American cultural romantic model, in which a young single autonomously seeks a mate on the basis of personal preference. But in making the matchmaking community the peer group, it is an attempt to wrest control from the adults who represent more conservative tendencies and in this respect is like the actions of American adolescents of all backgrounds (although the latter may be less interested in marriage and more just in finding intimate partners).[42]

The powerful social pressure to marry thus creates conditions in which community norms, expectations, and dependencies run up against the countervailing American value of the autonomous, independent single on the make. This tension shows itself repeatedly in a variety of bangitout-.com riffs on dating and *shidduch*. It is there as well at a site linked to bangitout.com and called www.frumster.com that describes itself as "the first online dating site designed exclusively for Orthodox Jewish singles worldwide. Whether you are very modern, or a real frummie, this is the place to find your match."

Many of the jokes on bangitout.com and the existence of sites like frumster.com point to the tremendous difficulty young modern Orthodox Jews have solving the problem of intimacy on their own. The effort is generally described as difficult to impossible. Hence the many gags that offer advice about Orthodox Jewish "pickup" lines—including a list of the "top 40 synagogue" pickup lines as well as a selection of lines for all Jewish holiday occasions, such as "If I could rewrite the word Purim [a Jewish holiday], I would put U and I together."[43] On Purim, when people are likely to be in masquerade, one might pick up someone with the line: "Excuse me, ma'am, is that costume felt? Would you like it to be?"

The coarse nature of these lines resonates with the crude locker room humor of the frat boy, that all-American youth in the fantasy projection of the Orthodox young man, but also with a kind of insider humor related to Judaism, which insiders alone fully comprehend, that tries to be hip. It betrays a hunger for intimacy in its most basic sexual form but also reveals the pathetic futility of trying to obtain it on one's own.

These jokes and others like them focus on the search not just for intimacy but for the right words to say in the right way that might be the key to the complex mechanism that locks all these young people in their desperate dialectic. The "Dating Dictionary," by Ahava Leibtag, is a half-humorous key that offers a code for understanding the difference between what is said and what is meant. In her "Choose Your Own Dating Adventure," a takeoff on a series of children's books with which many of these 'Generation-X-ers" grew up, Leibtag offers readers a dating course that can take either the "yeshivish" (i.e., Haredi affiliated with yeshiva study) or the "modern Orthodox route," depending on the critical choices they make in the dating quest.[44] Their choices mirror the Manichean alternatives that face them as they seek ways to navigate between contrapuntalist modern Orthodoxy and an increasingly insistent Haredi enclavism.

Found here are tacit admissions of the frustrations of and impediments in looking for a mate on one's own. The dreams are futile, cues are missed, choices are critical, and pickup lines are endlessly improved upon, but in the humor of the Web site all of these efforts are never quite good enough. Even with the help of peers who try to set one up with a match that is "perfect for you," the difficulties are immense. Item 5 on the list about when you know it's time for a vacation from the modern Orthodox singles scene of the Upper West Side of Manhattan is: "You've rejected numerous setup-date proposals with 'no, I know her/him already' line." What can more simply encapsulate and express the disappointment, exasperation, and desperation of the young modern Orthodox quest for intimacy?[45]

Perhaps the most fully elaborated of the gags articulating these concerns, however, is a contribution by Eli Goldman (who presents herself by the decidedly non-Orthodox Jewish nom de plume of "Justin Timberlake," the current heart-throb of young America) entitled "J-Escorts."[46]

After taking two subways and a long fragrant ride on the "Chus-Bus" to Monsey,[47] you are dreading going to this Le'chaim [toast to the newly affianced] (your 3rd this week). Walking into the shul [synagogue] gym, disguised only by fake flowers and a cheesy keyboardist in a tux, all your fears have been realized. Everyone at this so-called "simcha" [joyous affair] is either married, engaged or seriously dating. Like those commercials for Paxil, you feel the piercing stares of Mrs. Rosenstein, Rabbi Kotter, and Mr. Shoenberg (names may vary slightly). They stare at you in pity from the dessert table across the room. Mentions of "Mazel tov" and "Im Yirtzah Hashem [God willing] By You" fill the air. . . . Faige Hershenfeld has only been on one date with Shimmy, but he's there as well. They are going ring shopping afterwards. Figures. As Surah's newborn spits up all over your Prada bag, you think to yourself, there must be a solution . . . and as you leave you promise yourself that you will never walk into a Vort [engagement party] alone again!!! Finally an answer . . . J-Escorts!

Here is an elaborated expression of all the pressure to find a mate: the commonness of the engagement parties and their routinization, the expectation, the hope, that you will be next—and, if you are not, the sense of opprobrium and shame you must feel, and finally the idea that it is at least important to manage an impression that you are dating and will soon be engaged yourself (particularly important for women, as the author implies). J-Escorts provide the solution. This is not really a joyous affair; it is a trial for the solitary.

Into this difficult situation Goldman inserts her imaginary service that will provide help in the form of "quality frum individuals, servicing all your social appearances." The need for this sort of help is not limited to engagement parties. It includes assistance for when one encounters "parents pressuring you about getting married." On this day, the young single Orthodox Jewish woman will get an obviously Orthodox young man, "Shmulie," who "will accompany you home for Shabbos Nachamu! [the Sabbath in the summer that inaugurates a popular Orthodox marriage season]." Or, if you "[d]on't feel like being the only single person at your table . . . Chani will go to that wedding in Staten Island with you!" The names of the escorts are all recognizably *frum,* although, as the fine print explains, "frum is a subjective term. Escorts may not be technically Jewish through all 'halacha' standards. Escorts may not be objectively good looking either. J-Escort Inc is not liable for anything escorts do (get drunk at a livaya [funeral]) or say (talks about Off Track Betting with your Rabbi's Wife)." In a disclaimer that might best describe the whole purpose of the site, Goldman adds, "This service is for entertainment purposes only." As the humor makes clear, even J-Escort (which takes its name from a popular and far more serious venture in cyber-matchmaking called J-Date), cannot completely help avoid the awkward situation that the lifestyle these young people have chosen is bound to create. In other words, even fantasy solutions cannot be guaranteed to solve these problems.

The piece concludes with a list "of the types of escorts we offer," an array of types within the subculture that its readers know all too well. These include, at the right end of the spectrum, "Black Hat . . . Shomer Negiah . . . Learns (NCSY Kollel on resume)," a young man who not only appears to be Haredi or yeshivish but is scrupulous about not touching a woman before marriage and spends time studying Talmud as a vocation.

Included too are "Black Hat . . . Fools Around . . . Machmir on Ge-bruktz," the young Haredi male who, although wearing the identifiable black hat, is nevertheless ready to break the sexual taboos connected with dating, though he still distinguishes himself by keeping some (minor and obscure) stringencies in ritual norms connected with Passover dietary laws; "Shabbos Black Hat . . . Sees Movies . . . 4 years in Hatzalah (Walkie Talkie Included!)," the young man who appears to be Haredi on Sabbaths but is ready to step out and go to the movies, a practice associated with the more "with-it" yeshiva crowd, and who serves as a paramedic in the Jewish Hatzalah ambulance corps, something he chooses prominently to display by carrying a radio device all the time; the "Srugi Kippah . . . Knows Tanach By Heart . . . Doesn't believe in G-d [sic]," the young man with the knit yarmulke, symbol of the modern Orthodox world, who, though he knows Bible and Scriptures so well that he has them all memorized, has lost his faith in God;[48] "wears skirts . . . Davens 45 minute Shmoneh-Esray . . . (HASC Sweatshirt is optional)," a woman who is unwilling to wear pants (which according to a Haredi prohibition contravene the biblical injunc-tion against wearing the clothes of the opposite sex), who in a show of piety takes an inordinately long time to recite the prayers, and who also at least *displays* a dedication to doing good works, such as working at the He-brew Academy for Special Children (HASC), a school for severely disabled Orthodox Jewish young; the "Carlebach Girl or Guy . . . Long Hair, Dirty Feet and acoustic guitar included!", an Orthodox hippie follower of the late singing Rabbi Shlomo Carlebach; "wears skirts. . . . Davens . . . Goes to R rated Movies . . . YUSSR 2 years in a row!", the young woman who, although appearing quite pious and having served on a mission to Jews in the former Soviet Union, a popular program for many young Orthodox looking for extracurricular activity, nevertheless is ready to watch risqué movies; and "wears pants . . . Goes to Clubs . . . Doesn't Believe in Shab-bos . . . But Knows Gematria!!!", the woman who has largely abandoned her Orthodox affiliations or comes from a non-Orthodox background and does not even believe in Sabbath observance but who has embraced the new Kabbalah fad and knows its mystical numerology as well as the sin-gles club scene and perhaps has been so transformed that she now calls herself "religious" without ever feeling the need to take another step in that direction.[49]

These identity categories, although colored with absurdity, describe a spectrum of variations not all that different from the one that frumster.com and other Orthodox Jewish matchmaking services treat seriously.[50] They reveal the exquisite sensitivity that these young Orthodox Jews must have to the nuances of Jewish identity within their world and among their peers (while making fun of it) and resonate with the tremendous pressure among these young people to find just the right mate within their nuanced but narrow universe. What the fantasy J-Escort service purports to provide is a staged exhibition of what both writer and readers understand they really need. It is the jest just beside the truth.

The effort to make these subtle but real distinctions is a kind of protest against the Manichean choice, a desire to suggest that there are important differences within the Orthodox world and that perhaps there are more than two kinds of Orthodoxy left from which to choose. Yet the subtle combinations presented also are laughable. Their comic aspect is that these efforts at nuance in the end lead to fantastic, in the sense of unrealistic, expectations. Thus the fantasy mate many of these youngsters on the search for intimacy are really looking for probably does not exist—or at least that is the indirect message of the humor. This is a person who is, in one version, "a combination of Julia Child, Christie Brinkley, Dr. Ruth, and Rebbetzin Jungreis."[51] The mate who can cook, look like the American definition of beauty, offer psychological insights without seeming to deny Jewish values, and arouse one's religious sensibilities is an impossible dream. If the quest for intimacy is to some extent an extension of the goal of identity formation, "to provide a sense of inner self-sameness and continuity, to bind together the past, the present and the future into a coherent whole," then the search for the impossible dream escort or mate reflects the impossibility of a perfect resolution of this quest or chance of reaching the goal.[52]

So important is the quest for another person who seems in tune with oneself that these young contrapuntalist modern Orthodox Jews persist in it despite discouragements, in hopes of achieving some coherence in their lives, creating a synthesis, or at least establishing a moratorium between the apparently contradictory elements of their multicultural existence. But all too often the effort to find the right match fails, as the "top 40 thoughts on a bad date" demonstrates, including the conclusion that "if your shadchan [matchmaker] deserves a gift for finding your perfect companion, he/she deserves the bill for setting you up with the exact opposite."[53]

Farce as a Form of Fighting Back

As a way of easing pain, the satire on sites like bangitout.com not only expresses intimacy and identity concerns but is directed toward things that

Orthodoxy normally treats with utter seriousness. Prominent here is the Talmud, the increasingly intensive study of which has become a hallmark of the scholars' society. These young people try to lighten the load of Talmudism by in a sense turning its code on its head, perverting it by interpreting the prohibited as its opposite and vice versa. This is done with ribaldry, profanation of the sacred, and offbeat interpretations of classic Talmudic terms. For example, Seth Galena takes the classic warning by which the Talmud tried to keep men and women apart, *Al tarbeh sicha im ha isha* (Do not converse too much with a woman), advice the rabbis meant as a warning that talk with a woman might lead to licentiousness at worst and indolence at best, and satirically interprets it as its opposite, a "solid excuse for fooling around"—that is, advice that men skip the small talk with women and instead get right to the action. In other words, Galena implies, the very idea of using the Talmud as a means of helping one on a date is a laugh. Indeed, it is such a laugh that several readers submit their own reinterpreted versions of Talmudic dicta with an application to dating, as if liberating themselves and this text to explore the prohibited.

The humor here comes from taking a stance outside the Orthodox boundary and laughing not at the things these young Jews are prevented from doing out of restrictive religious conviction but at the restrictions they have simply slipped away from and the religious dilemmas they have solved by opting "out," or acting in a relatively liberal fashion. In these cases the jokes play a parallel and opposite role to the ones that reflect the acceptance of the restrictions and constraints. Here they reassure the jokers (and those who laugh with them) that in their various decisions to step outside the boundaries of the straight-and-narrow, or at the very least to stretch those boundaries, they are not alone. More importantly, of course, it lets them continue to identify as Orthodox despite (and through) it all by their inverted use of and familiarity with Talmudic terminology.

Then there are those who want to stretch the limits of the acceptable without seeming to do so. Making fun of this effort (but also demonstrating that it exists as an option), Winner's list entitled "60 Ways to Appear Frum and Intellectual" portrays the incongruent motivations of young Orthodox Jews on the make in the youth culture of America: "Go to bars dressed in your hats and jackets, drink, stare at teenage girls, and claim to be doing kiruv [outreach]." According to Haredi views, going to bars is a profane and defiling practice associated with the worst in American youth culture; only those who are lax or at the very least extremely flexible in their understanding of the behavioral demands of Orthodoxy would engage in it. On the other hand, someone who appears in the bar in a hat and jacket is presenting himself in an outfit that has become de rigueur for the yeshiva student. To stare at teenage girls while drinking seems quintessentially non-*frum* (perhaps the image that a yeshiva student has of what his opposite number might be doing). In Winner's joke, the way to harmonize these antithetical behaviors is for the barhopper (farcically) to claim to be trying to do Jewish Orthodox outreach *(kiruv)*. There is a kind of self-deprecating absurdist humor here (as well as a barely veiled reference to a recent incident in which a rabbinic yeshiva head was discovered in a bar and claimed in his defense to be there on an outreach mission—a claim that was met with derision in many quarters of modern Orthodoxy and beyond). The absurdism expresses the paradoxical difficulty of conforming simultaneously to the norms of traditionalist Orthodoxy and to the antinomian and in many ways radically dissimilar lifestyle of contemporary American youth, a difficulty that in truth is no joke for those who try to do so in their endless search for the right mate.

Activity and Ideology

The search for the proper ways to act in order to be in line with a specific identity—a search that is at the heart of this last joke (and the others on Winner's list)—recalls as well what Erikson describes as "another of the chief tasks of identity formation," namely "the development of an 'ideology,' that is, of a philosophy of life, a basic outlook on the world which can orient one's actions in adult life."[54] In the search for the proper way to act, many of these young people find themselves having tacitly to evolve an ideology that combines their own emergent and often paradoxical outlook on life with one that comes out of the social and cultural conditions of their modern Jewish Orthodoxy. For this reason, they must not only articulate what to be and whom to be with or like but also find activities that they may legitimately pursue that will enable them to remain in the space they have made for themselves on the margins of the several cultures they inhabit. Should I act in a purely Orthodox Jewish fashion or like a modern American my age? Can I find a way of avoiding an either/or choice and acting like both at the same time? While the latter option may seem the obvious choice, will that not put me in odd—indeed, absurd— situations, like the ones on Winner's list? Is it all right or even possible to try to stretch the limits of the permissible, or should I retreat to the shelter of Orthodox institutions? In short, what should I do (activity), and what should I believe (ideology)?

In attempting to answer these questions, Orthodox young people devise new solutions to the contradictions of their existence. Ironically, however, many of their new or provisional solutions inaugurate new dilemmas for them. For example, going to a bar in a yeshivish suit and black hat (or, in real life, more likely wearing a yarmulke in the bar), an activity that seems to reflect a contrapuntal effort to inhabit contradictory lifestyles at one and the same time, raises the question of whether in doing this one has not in fact stretched the limits of the possible beyond ideological reason. Choosing such new paths of behavior, young people must and often do in the end ask themselves: Does all this make sense for someone like me?

These are not insignificant questions for young people who, as Americans, are trying "choose between competing versions of past and future"[55] and, as modern Orthodox Jews, are trying to find the line between acting independently on the basis of personal passions and acting in accordance with the strict dictates of Orthodox interpretations of Jewish law. For some the answer becomes: no, this is impossible. Those who reach this conclusion may abandon one or the other side of their contradictory identity. For some this means giving up being Orthodox, or at least giving it up in everything but name. For others it means turning one of the identities into a charade, a performance that for a time covers up their alienation from the role or identity connected with this behavior, but this option is usually temporary, since such alienation is hard to sustain.[56] Finally, for still others, it may result in turning away from American youth culture and toward an intensified embrace of Haredi Orthodoxy. In short, it may lead to what insiders call "flipping," the move from one ideology (and associated behavior) to another.[57] In either case the center is abandoned in favor of a move toward the extremes.

Expressing this implicit concern with ideology in a most explicit and transparent way is the already cited "Official Modern Orthodox Quiz" by Ahava Leibtag. Because of the changes in the contemporary conditions of Orthodoxy, and because for American young people, in the words of Kenneth Keniston, "the world is seen as fluid and chaotic," readers are told they must invent new solutions, as yesterday's are no longer useful.[58] They will need to know what choices to make. What Leibtag and others who take her quiz are providing is a chance " to see if you really know how to pick and choose." To help in this task, they look to their peers, hoping to be able to emulate their activities and beliefs and hence follow their path to resolution. Under the guise of humor, Leibtag is allowing her readers to discover how they compare to peers who also want to know if the choices they make qualify them as "modern Orthodox."

Depending on how many "right answers" one has picked, the identities offered are either "Hey you're uneducated and frum. Enjoy life — you have it easy," or "You do the best you can to be halachic [in line with Jewish law]. You're doomed to a life of struggle" or, finally, "You could care less about Halacha! How'd you get so lucky?" In other words, you have selected the straight-and-narrow path where all your choices are already made by the tradition which you embrace, you are trying to navigate between two extremes and struggling to find a way, or you have abandoned being Orthodox and are liberated from its constraints. There is clearly an irony in this last possibility, as the question "How'd you get so lucky?" suggests. Is it really considered lucky to have turned one's back on Jewish law and the "path" of the Halacha? In fact, activity, ideology, and the identity they create are really not a matter of luck at all; they are matters of choice — and in the choices Leibtag sets out, the middle way, the contrapuntalist, is the most difficult

Other-Directedness

As I have suggested, the choices, when "these days you can't just go by what your parents do," turn out to be made by establishing intimate bonds and finding a community of like-minded others with and among whom one can work out a modus vivendi. Here young people will evolve common life experiences, acceptable behavior patterns, attitudes toward Orthodox dogma and ritual, and understandings about how they can adapt to the sometimes conflicting demands of the various aspects of their lives. Bangitout.com and the Upper West Side of Manhattan are places, virtual and real, where this happens. In practice, as these jokes allow us to infer, this will often result in variations and displays that are very much a consequence of "other-directedness," an attitude in which people take their standards from the groups in which they aspire to live and realize themselves as they identify with what they deem respectable, acceptable, and enviable in the social world that surrounds them.[59] In so doing, these young people defy expectations, for as Orthodox Jews we might have reasonably expected them to be either what Riesman called "tradition-directed," people who rigorously obey ancient rules, or at least, given their intensive and parochial Jewish education, "inner-directed," people whose values and purposes are implanted within themselves and who live largely as they were taught in childhood, regardless of where they find themselves. Yet while these young people do retain some of the qualities of both tradition- and inner-directedness in the practices they maintain and even in the guilt they feel when they violate implanted ideals, they seem, if the humor on these Web pages accurately reflects where they are today, overwhelmingly and powerfully driven by the desire for intimacy and community, to be "loved rather than esteemed," that key feature of other-directedness, and therefore to be properly attuned (socially, behaviorally, and emotionally) to the situations in which they find themselves. As such, they are in the end not so different from their parents. In truth, one should not altogether be surprised. A group that has taken personal choice, democracy, and acculturation as a basis of its character—as modern Orthodoxy has—inevitably produces other-directedness in adults—whether younger or older.

To some extent the other-directedness of these young Orthodox Jews is, like that of their parents, exacerbated by their inhabiting enclaves in which they are surrounded by people with whom they have so much in common. They have gravitated to these places where life for them is easier because they can draw heavily on the "social capital" of modern Orthodoxy, the networks, norms, and social trust that facilitate the desire to cooperate for mutual benefit and allow dilemmas to be resolved. In effect, these enclaves of the young Orthodox are a bit like support groups.[60] To be sure, the felt need to live in such enclaves (a practice that, at least according to Robert Putnum, runs counter to contemporary American trends during the 1980s and 1990s, in which "aloneness" seemed to be on the upswing) is a direct consequence of these young people's commitments to live in accordance with Orthodox Jewish norms and communal standards—a sentiment that may be the result of inner- or tradition-directedness.[61] If they have always lived in the sheltered enclave of Orthodoxy, then the boundaries between tradition-, inner-, and other-directedness may not be all that clear or even significant in practice. However, when and if they find themselves either cut off from the Orthodox milieu or in a position to break from it, they may for the first time in their lives discover the strength of their orientation. And even under these conditions, they find themselves, as Ahava Liebtag in her quiz put it, "doomed to a life of struggle." In the humor of bangitout.com, we can watch how they grin and bear it.

CHAPTER 7

Orthodox Jewish
Calls from the Walls

Posters and What They Teach Us

> Certainly beliefs, concerns, feelings, attitudes, are "expressed";
> "inner states" are documented.
>
> Erving Goffman, *Frame Analysis:*
> *An Essay on the Organization of Experience*

Adopting a practice popular in certain Haredi precincts of Israel and in some of the ethnic neighborhoods of New York, American Orthodox Jews—particularly in the Brooklyn enclaves of Crown Heights, Williamsburg, and Boro Park as well as in Kew Gardens Hills in the borough of Queens—have increasingly affixed posters or broadsides to the walls in public thoroughfares. The ostensible purpose of these placards is to advertise or publicize information to the people who populate these streets. In fact, however, as Menachem Friedman in his pathbreaking study and analysis of such broadsides in Israel has demonstrated, much more is going on.[1] In effect, they express beliefs, concerns, feelings, and attitudes while they document inner states. As such, they are what I have termed "calls from the walls."

In their content, language, and placement, these calls from the walls show something else as well: that within contemporary Orthodoxy, at least as exhibited in these places, a contest is going on and that there are increasingly clear signs of an assertive Haredi version of the faith taking over the public space—the walls that everyone passes. That takeover is stronger in some of these neighborhoods than in others. But in general, the voice that is most distinct in these signs is one that expresses the proud parochialism of those Orthodox that I have called enclavist in these pages. Less prominent and often displaced or covered over are the signs of a contrapuntalist Orthodoxy that seeks to live and express Jewish *and* non-Jewish interests, parochial *and* cosmopolitan concerns, or desires to integrate into American culture and not just to keep that culture at bay. My purpose here is to show more about the character of those Orthodox communities through this medium and to show how the Haredi trend has put modernists on the defensive, how Orthodoxy in these places is *frum* and getting *frum*mer.

In his study of advertisements, Erving Goffman repeats a principle that he found to be true in all his analyses of human behavior. "Displays," he argues, "provide evidence of the actor's *alignment* in a gathering, the position he seems prepared to take in what is about to happen in a social situation."[2] Building on that definition, one may suggest that *displays organized by a group in a public space may provide evidence of the social alignment of those who organize those displays well as those who consider the displays appropriate and interesting.* Borrowing again from Goffman, we may insert "the group" wherever he writes about "the individual." Accordingly, with Goffman's help we arrive at the following conclusion: all of a group's behavior and appearance informs and at least minimally reveals something about its social identity, mood, intent, and expectations. Moreover, "displays very often have a dialogic character of a statement-reply kind, with an expression on the part of one . . . calling forth an expression on the part of another."[3] Broadsides, posters, flyers, handbills, and the like are such displays. They make clear what is virtuous or acceptable behavior and what is not. They serve as expressive media that show what those who prepare and post as well as those who allow the poster to be displayed (the latter by attending to its meaning and not removing or covering it) consider to be acceptable or worthy of notice. When a person is attentive to a poster or leaflet, that person in a sense *animates* the message and intentions of the person or group who prepared and/or posted that sign.[4] The informed observer can thus use such signs as a window through which to glimpse what is appropriate behavior as well as what is on the mind of the community, its interests and concerns. Like the look at the Orthodox Web site, this look at the calls from the walls will reveal the inner states and conflicts of today's American Orthodoxy.

To be sure, one could argue that by looking at these New York City enclaves we are getting a very particular view of Orthodoxy. That is true. Yet as we have seen, a significant proportion of American Orthodoxy lives in these neighborhoods. Recall that Brooklyn holds a large fraction of Orthodox Jewry in America, somewhere around a quarter. Moreover, both politically and ideologically, New York Orthodoxy has managed to speak for the rest of its American co-believers. Finally, the fact that many of the Orthodox elsewhere in the country have often had extended residence in the New York area, either during their school years or at some important point during their lives, makes this Jewish population loom large in the American scene. Anecdotal evidence suggests that contrapuntalists in particular are often more plentiful in places where the Orthodox are both less numerous and more integrated into the surrounding cultural environment. But that does not mean that they have commensurate influence. New York Orthodoxy still sets the tone and the informal standards of the movement. Moreover, in New York neighborhoods, posters are more plentiful—and, as any good anthropologist must admit, one has to follow the signs.

How Posters Communicate

In a sense both the poster and reader are part of an interpretive process that reflects cultural judgments implicitly or explicitly understood by insiders. Beliefs and worldviews are the lens through which people see the meaning of the posters. The settings in which these posters appear are not simply geographic locations but cultural enclaves, places in which time, space, activity, values, and ethos are structured in a way that enables the individuals living there to learn and transmit the normative patterns of culture inside the area.[5] As is the case in other cultural enclaves, in these four districts inhabitants share cultural ideas and recipes for behavior, most of them having to do with the basic outlook and life patterns particular to an Orthodox observance of Jewish tradition. Responses to what they see on the walls in turn add to or affirm those outlooks, norms, beliefs, and values, thickening the texture of life in the enclave and ultimately setting the stage for other posters and their messages, and so on endlessly.

Posters communicate their messages in a variety of ways. Most obvious is the actual message printed on them, in words, pictures or both. Second, the placement of the poster matters. One placed at a location that many people might be expected to pass and notice or one affixed to many walls may be considered a louder and more general call than one positioned in a more obscure spot that only a limited and particular audience will attend to. Furthermore, a notice affixed next to a poster that has a related message may under certain conditions be understood as a gloss on or response to the other. Thus if one broadside advertises a circus and another next to it announces a rabbinic decision that prohibits attendance at such venues or offers an alternate involvement at the same time, the posters may be understood as carrying on or reflecting a debate within the community about the appropriateness of circus attendance or how people should properly spend their leisure time. This may be a debate not just about what to do but about what is the Orthodox Jewish way to act.

Third, as Peter Berger has noted, because "language is both the foundation and instrumentality of the social construction of reality," the choices a group makes in the language in which it posts a message also say something about how they construct their reality, who they are, and whom they address.[6] Hence the language of the poster is another part of its expressive equipment. Given that matters of language in particular are culturally significant for these Jews, the use of English, Hebrew, or Yiddish says something about their sociocultural orientation and ideology, especially an ability, willingness, or refusal to be fully part of the surrounding American society. Furthermore, where a placard's language is not the lingua franca of the national locale but rather another one, the clear message is that this is addressed only to a select group of insiders, those who understand that other language, and that it is being kept from the scrutiny of outsiders. Thus, in the New York neighborhoods in question, any posters in languages other than English communicate thereby that they are part of an insiders' dialogue and not for the general public in New York. Moreover, where the public is multilingual (as is the case in the enclaves in question), the language selected for communication inevitably provides an expressive lamination and adds cultural overtones to the poster. When the poster switches codes from one language to another or uses Hebrew or Yiddish for certain subjects and English for others, this is not arbitrary; rather, it is often freighted with meaning.[7] Among the Orthodox, language choice tells us much about affiliation and attitude. Yiddish remains the language of choice among the most insular of Orthodox enclaves, indicative of an attempt to maintain distinctiveness from the surrounding society.[8] To post something, for example, in Yiddish is to say that the only people who matter to the author(s) and posters of the notice are those who understand Yiddish. English is the choice for those whose attachments to American society and culture are the most direct, a sign of contrapuntalism, albeit sometimes in a very limited sense. As for Hebrew and Russian, they may be used respectively for immigrants or expatriates from Israel and the countries of the former Soviet Union, people who are *in* but not yet fully part *of* American culture. Hebrew, however, can also be used as *loshn koydesh,* the holy tongue associated with religious matters, or as an Israeli vernacular—and in each case the audience addressed is different. To be sure, the subject of a poster matters too. To know whether the Hebrew represents a use of *loshn koydesh* and the religious implications associated with it or simply an accommodation to Israeli expatriates one must also look at what the poster is about. If a poster advertises a cheap phone card in Hebrew, this does not mean that the phone card is seen as an object with religious significance. Similarly, some matters could not possibly be addressed in any language other than English. In sum, as the sociolinguist Joshua Fishman has pointed out, "[S]ome topics are somehow handled better in one language than in another in particular multilingual contexts."[9] What the community considers those to be can be discovered in the language of the posters. Poster language, then, is most expressive, and studying it is clearly part of what Dell Hymes has called "the ethnography of communication."[10]

Fourth, in the expressive language of a poster, images are important too. The choice of human figures who appear to be Haredi—males with skullcaps, earlocks, and beards, and perhaps wearing traditional black garb, for example—makes it immediately apparent, even if the language is English, that the audience addressed by and reflected in the poster is of a particular sort, one that by its appearance has set itself apart from contemporary America. Thus a placard for a blood drive that shows as the poster child a young boy with earlocks tells all who see it that Haredi Orthodox Jews are being called upon to donate blood for the Haredi community (figure 4). It also implies that among those who post and look at this poster this illustration is iconic. The assumption is that the Orthodox look like this.[11]

As this case makes clear, posters require observers to look not only for the information *given* but also for the information *given off*, and the latter may be understood as telling us as much, if not more, about the essential nature of those who prepared or put up the poster and those who may be expected to respond to it. As Goffman notes, it is "hardly possible to imagine a society whose members do not routinely read from what is available to the senses to something larger, distal or hidden." Objects "cast a shadow, heat up the surround, strew indications, leave an imprint," and in often unattended ways inform "whomsoever is properly placed, trained and inclined" to get the message.[12] With posters, all this is writ large upon the walls.

Notices and placards are most frequently posted by members of the community (women no less than men) in places that they assume will have high insider traffic—either in Jewish shopping districts or near entrances of major

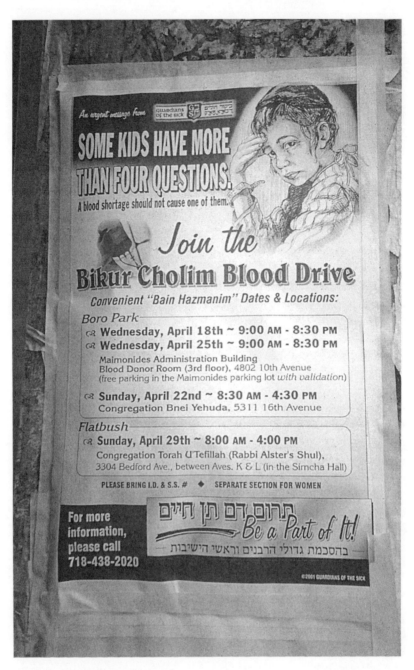

FIGURE 4: Blood drive poster.

FIGURE 5: Posting a broadside in Boro Park; note that the reader arrives even before the poster is completely positioned.

community institutions such as synagogues, yeshivas, or schools. Obviously the notion of a target audience plays a part in placement. This practice demonstrates that cultural enclaves are not undifferentiated territories and that the power of the poster is not everywhere and always the same even within a single enclave culture. Posting implicitly recognizes certain zones as defining the public square, as figure 5's image of a woman posting a notice on a street corner illustrates.

Characteristically, in the shopping districts, as soon as—sometimes even while—a poster is affixed to the wall, people will gather about it to read it. Commonly, other broadsides or handbills will be posted nearby (figures 6a–d).[13] At doors of yeshivas or synagogues, as in the view, shown in figure 6a, from in front of the Satmar Bes Medresh in Williamsburg, posters accumulate. The number of signs posted varies, but in general signs are put up until they can no longer physically compete for the space and attention. In time, frequently after holiday seasons, posters will be torn down in a general cleanup, and then the whole process will begin again. In short, posters are part of a dynamic and changing cultural life.

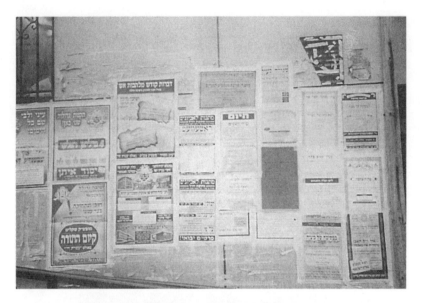

FIGURE 6a: Poster wall in Hebrew and Yiddish: Williamsburg

FIGURE 6c: Poster wall in English: Kew Gardens Hills

FIGURE 6b: Poster wall in English, Russian, and Hebrew: Crown Heights

FIGURE 6d: Posters on a lamppost: Boro Park

Williamsburg, Boro Park, Crown Heights, and Kew Gardens Hills: Four Orthodox Enclaves

Cultural enclaves, particularly those situated in open and multicultural societies like those of urban New York, are often concerned with boundary issues. They seek ways of informing their members what is inside and what outside the boundaries of the acceptable and the community, while simultaneously keeping members connected to one another and the enclave by a powerful sense of social solidarity. This is particularly true when the inhabitants consider themselves an endangered minority whose survival is of cosmic or religious importance. Moreover, if insiders deem the surrounding environment a cultural threat, a source of invidious comparison or social pollution, and especially when that contamination may be particularly seductive to the unprotected and uninformed, the concerns over maintaining boundaries will be particularly powerful. In a sense, the four Orthodox neighborhoods considered here, though different in significant ways, fit these criteria.

At the same time, they represent points on a spectrum. In general, we may say that the enclavist Jews of Williamsburg are among those most acutely aware of, one might even say obsessed about, the dangers to their minority culture of defilement from the world outside and that they seek to remain maximally insulated from them. The Jews of Boro Park share much of this perspective but, as part of a more diverse and larger Jewish district, have allowed for a more permeable wall between themselves and the domains outside their enclave. Jewish Crown Heights, surrounded by African and Caribbean Americans, is today a relatively small and essentially Lubavitcher Hasidic enclave whose members are caught up in a cult of personality and messianic fixation on their late rabbi, Menachem Mendel Schneerson. Even the New York Metropolitan Transit Authority bus shelters here have posters that indicate the Lubavitch presence, as seen in one in which the Seventh Rebbe's image in prayer shawl figures prominently.

While ideologically committed to worldwide Jewish outreach and therefore used to moving in environments where they are surrounded by and must engage outsiders and experience culture contact with contemporary society, the Crown Heights Lubavitchers remain within their home territory largely a sectarian and insular Haredi community who swing between increasingly agitated messianism and obsessions about their "rebbe" on the one hand and their parochial and local interests on the other. Nevertheless, their outreach has resulted in a continuing flow of outsiders and neophytes into their enclave. Finally, in Kew Gardens Hills, the Jewish neighborhood, on the edge of a major City University of New York campus, is more heavily populated by centrist or modern Orthodox Jews and even by significant numbers of Israeli, Russian, and Bukharan Jews whose connection to religious observance and Orthodox lifestyle is attenuated; here the boundaries are far more open and Jewish concerns contrapuntally mixed with contemporary American.

FINDING BOUNDARIES AND MARKERS

Because no formal borders mark these enclaves, finding their boundaries requires a certain cultural competence. Among the most obvious signs that one is inside the enclave is the presence of visibly Orthodox Jews, identifiable by their distinctive dress, particularly their head covering including yarmulkes (skullcaps) or hats for the men (black fedoras and round *biberhat*s on the Haredim, and during Sabbaths or holy days *shtreimel*s on the married Hasidim among them) and kerchiefs, snoods, hats, turbans, or wigs on the married women, as well as skirts with low hemlines.[14] The ubiquitous presence of young mothers pushing baby carriages (often with multiple children) in a population that encourages a high birthrate and that accords high social status to the young woman with many children is another sign. Beyond that one looks for a mezuzah on the door, often a particularly large one in Haredi neighborhoods (this is particularly important in Crown Heights, where the Lubavitchers have given the mezuzah an intense communal and theological significance).[15] Even more easily identified as a sign of Orthodox Jewish residence is the presence of porches so arranged as to have an unobstructed line of sight to the sky, a requirement for the building of a sukkah during the seven-day holiday of the same name.[16] These verandas, a particular architectural feature of apartment buildings and other multifamily dwellings in the urban Orthodox neighborhood and few others in the New York area, disappear as soon as one has moved beyond its boundaries. The presence of shops and businesses that cater to Orthodox Jewish needs (as well as the absence of those that do not) helps one find not only boundaries but also important commercial arteries of the enclave. Finally, and as these pages shall show, the presence of certain sorts of signs and posters on the walls and on lampposts in these districts also lets one know one is inside the enclave. In a sense, they, better than many of these other markers, also tell one what sort of an enclave it is.

While this is not the place to provide a comprehensive history or thick description of these Jewish enclaves, a few words about each are useful before moving on to look at the posters within them and exploring what they tell us about the populations there. Since three of the four neighborhoods to be considered are in Brooklyn, a description of this borough of New York City is in order first. According to the UJA Federation–sponsored 2002 New York Jewish Community Study of New York, 37 percent of the Orthodox in their sample reside in Brooklyn (20 percent live in Queens).[17] Indeed, if Brooklyn were a separate city (as it once was), we could say that, after Los Angeles, there would be no city with more Orthodox Jews living in it. While in the not too distant past many neighborhoods in Brooklyn contained large numbers of traditional Jews, at the beginning of the twenty-first century the Orthodox have largely concentrated in Boro Park, Flatbush, Williamsburg, and Crown Heights. Williamsburg is probably the most insular of these.

Just across the East River from Manhattan, Williamsburg was first settled in the 1660s by the Dutch and was laid out as a town in 1810 by a Colonel Williams, who lent his name to the area. Ferry services to Manhattan were instituted in the first half of the nineteenth century to develop the area as a residence for the Manhattan workforce. Williamsburg became an independent city in 1827. By 1852, the population had reached 31,000, and in 1855 it was consolidated with the city of Brooklyn. The opening of the Williamsburg Bridge in 1903 made the area more suitable for industry and swelled the working-class population employed in the factories to 260,000 by 1920. The old factory buildings have now been turned into artists' spaces. Like the subway line, this development has made Williamsburg more connected to the cultural and social life of Manhattan than it has been for a long time. In fact, Williamsburg has over the years been culturally and socially distant from what is often called "the City" and its fast pace and cosmopolitan character. By the 1950s the neighborhood became home to what we today call "white ethnics," predominantly Irish and Italians as well as some Jews. In 1954, in a move that many have argued led to a decline of the area, the urban planner Robert Moses ran the Brooklyn-Queens Expressway (BQE) right through the center of the community. Afterwards Williamsburg steadily lost most of the Irish and Italians as well as many of the Jews who had called it home. Now it became the residence of the economically less well off, predominantly Puerto Ricans, while among the remaining Jews the majority became Hasidic and concentrated in the southwest corner. Those Italians who remained were concentrated in the west, and Poles settled in the north near the district called Greenpoint.[18] Prominent among the Hasidim were those who followed the customs of Satmar, a group from Hungary whose Judaism tends to be highly insular and contra-acculturationist, fighting back against the norms and values of contemporary American culture, and who still constitute the largest group in the enclave. In addition there are today a variety of other Hasidim, including Spinka, Pupa (both also of Hungarian origins, the dominant European root culture here), Nitra (Czech in origin), and Vizhnitz (Ukrainian in origins). In general, their attitude toward contemporary American society tends to mirror that of Satmar.

While today's Jewish enclave is bisected by the BQE running north to south across it, the community has found it possible to bridge the divide. This is because the highway is for the most part below ground level in much of the neighborhood. Lee Street (the main shopping thoroughfare) and several of the other major arteries of the quarter cross over it and have therefore enabled the community to ignore the traffic artery and expand on both sides of it.

For all of its insularity, Jewish Williamsburg contains some prominent non-Jewish sites within or adjacent to it, such as the Transfiguration Roman Catholic Church, the Spanish Gospel Assembly, and St. Paul's Lutheran Church. Near each of these, however, are Orthodox Jewish institutions that in effect geographically engulf and cancel the churches' capacity to dominate the neighborhood. They are, respectively, the Satmar *bes medrash* (study and assembly hall), perhaps the premier religious institution in the enclave, the *mikveh* or ritual bath of the Pupa Hasidim, and the Congregation Beth Jacob Ohev Shalom and Yatev Lev synagogues. In part this is because those who utilize the Jewish institutions, which serve to anchor the community around them, all live within walking distance of them and make use of them daily. On the other hand, while the worshippers who attend the churches may live nearby, on most days of the week one is hard pressed to find them as one walks the streets of the Jewish enclave, which appears to be overwhelmingly peopled by the Haredim.

The elevated J and M rapid transit lines run north and east along Broadway and serve as another dividing artery that helps concentrate the Haredi residents within their enclave. In the shopping district beneath the elevated rails, which is distinct from the Jewish one, an observer comes upon all those others who may worship in the churches but are certainly not Haredi Jews. At the perimeter on the south along Flushing Avenue is an industrial zone (which has recently become an area rezoned for housing), and some housing projects nearby on Nostrand Avenue likewise corral the Jews within their enclave to the north.

FIGURE 7: Typical scene in Williamsburg, a plethora of strollers, babies, and mothers: evidence of the population growth.

Demographically, the relatively compact Orthodox Jewish enclave of Williamsburg is a community that in 1990, according to the U.S. Census, contained about 25,000 people, of whom about 40 percent were thirteen years old or younger and an additional 15 percent were between the ages of fourteen and twenty-one.[19] While the numbers for the year 2000 remained about the same, the proportion of those less than thirteen years of age grew to near 50 percent. Although the average family size in the 1990 census was about 4.7, the mean in suburban Kiryas Joel, where many sons and daughters of the Williamsburg Satmar Hasidim now live, was about 6.6, suggesting that among the Satmars of Williamsburg the number of children might actually be quite a bit above the 4.7 average.[20] In line with the large families common among Haredim, about 20 percent of the people were living in households with seven or more persons in them (the highest category in the census)—more than ten times the proportion for New York City (figure 7). Even more dramatic is table 3, which shows that the household size of Kiryas Joel was more than twice as large as those for both New York City and New York State in both the 1990 and 2000 censuses.[21]

Among the Jews of Williamsburg, the overwhelming majority (slightly less than 85 percent) of those age three and older were in private

TABLE 3. Persons per Household in Kiryas Joel versus New York City
and New York State, 1990 and 2000

	Persons per Household		
	Kiryas Joel	*New York City*	*New York State*
1990	6.27	2.54	2.61
2000	5.75	2.61	2.63

SOURCE: U.S. Bureau of the Census, "Census 1990" and "Census 2000," retrieved
October 30, 2005, from www.census.gov.

schools, most likely yeshivas and women's seminaries. Only about 3 percent
had a college education, since these enclavist Jews eschew such higher
learning. With a median annual household income at around $13,000
(compared to about $30,000 for New York City as a whole), about 55 per-
cent were living below the government-established poverty line, although
one imagines that given the high expense of maintaining a large family
and an Orthodox Jewish lifestyle they were finding financial support
through a variety of communal loan societies and government assistance
programs—as well as perhaps an illicit or hidden cash economy.[22]

To walk the approximately one-square-mile neighborhood of Jewish
Williamsburg is to step into a world that seems overwhelmingly defined
by Judaism. Not only are the people on the street dressed in ways that
identify them as part of the Haredi world, and in particular its Hasidic
variant, but nearly all the conversation is in Yiddish. In the 1990 U.S. Census, 52 percent here reported that Yiddish was the language spoken at
home, but one suspects from what one hears on the streets of the neighborhood that this number would be even higher if respondents were asked
their preferred language. While most of the store signs are in English, significant numbers of them are in Yiddish, which figures more prominently
than the English. This is particularly the case when the products sold in
them are only or primarily of interest to the locals. Thus while the Satmar Meat and Poultry Market is so identified in an English sign, far more
prominent is a sign that provides identification in Yiddish and that indicates that the meat's kashruth is certified by the Satmar community. Similarly, a hat shop whose specialty is the distinctive *biberhat* that marks Hasidic weekday wear or the black homburg that the non-Hasidic Haredim
prefer has its name, Feltly Hats, displayed in English; but its far more in-
formative message that it stocks and sells "the best and nicest" high, fe-
dora, and biberhats as well as those of "highest quality" is in Yiddish

FIGURE 8: Yiddish/English hat sign in the Williamsburg neighborhood.

(figure 8). Moreover, for its "models" of satisfied customers it uses rec-
ognizable and stereotypic images of Haredi Jews whose visages announce, no less than the many Yiddish words and phrases on the sign,
that this is a shop for Jews of a particular orientation. In other words,
even a cursory look at the neighborhood makes clear that this is a place
serving particular Yiddish-speaking Jews for whom American culture is
at best distant background.

Indeed, while there are many signs that American culture passes
through the enclave, from city buses to delivery trucks, postal workers,
and a host of non-Jewish laborers whose presence here is undeniable, they
are perceived by locals as *in* but not really *of* this place—"background
noise," as one insider characterized them. Thus, if the outsiders passing
through the enclave want something to eat, they will often have to con-
sume kosher edibles that make up the overwhelming majority of food
available here. And if they want a drink at a bar, they will have to go elsewhere, for there are no pubs in the enclave. Even if they want to take a
look at what is on television, they will have to find somewhere outside
the neighborhood to do their watching. If they want to know what is going on locally, what news everyone is talking about, they will have to find
someone to translate it for them, as the media that locals use for finding
out what is going on are commonly in Yiddish.

On the other hand, for the locals, most of what they need is here, though some go out of the area for their jobs or for medical care. Yet while the big city is just a short subway ride away, it does not successfully beckon them as it may so many others; or if it does, it holds an attraction of which they must remain wary and whose appeal to them they must hide, sometimes even from themselves and surely from others in their community.[23] Interestingly, as this is being written Williamsburg is, as earlier noted, also experiencing gentrification by a young bohemian and artist population attracted by the loft space in old factory buildings, the relatively low rent, and the proximity to Manhattan. This is similar to what happened to the SoHo section just across the Manhattan Bridge in the preceding decades. It is a result of decisions made in the 1980s when the first Manhattan-refugee artists colonized Williamsburg. They came after 1985, when the Board of Estimate authorized residential use of commercial loft space. Between 1990 and 2000 the median monthly rent in the area increased by 67 percent, more than anywhere else in New York City.[24] Williamsburg is reputed to be home to the highest density of artists in the world. Dominicans, Ecuadorians, new Poles, Mexicans, and Chinese have joined the mix. At the same time, the Haredi Jews of Orthodox Williamsburg are expanding into new housing as they continue to grow in numbers. This means that populations with very different outlooks on life will soon be or are already rubbing shoulders with each other in sometimes uncomfortable ways. For the Orthodox, this means that their efforts to remain comfortable behind the barriers of their cultural enclaves in their home community may become increasingly difficult. One can therefore expect to find more evidence in their posters (as well as in their behavior) of the effort to fence out the prohibited and to anchor members of the community even more firmly to their Haredi ways of life.

Boro Park, settled in 1645 on a tract of land on the bay of the North River between Coney Island and Gowanus, was purchased from its native inhabitants for the Dutch West India Company and was originally called New Utrecht.[25] During its early years it was a sparsely settled agricultural area that became increasingly residential. With the extension of the subway lines from New York City during a real estate boom of the 1920s, the district took on a suburban character as rows of single- and multifamily homes were built facing one another on tree-lined streets and avenues that had formerly been farmland. Already Jews had begun moving to the area (although not necessarily to its extremities), and by 1930 over 50 percent of the neighborhood, or around 60,000 people in Boro Park, were Jewish.[26] These Jews were not new immigrants but rather those who had already begun the climb up the social and economic ladder and chose the larger houses of Boro Park for their homes. But toward the end of the 1950s, many of these Jews began to leave the neighborhood for greener suburbs further from the city center, and their Orthodox counterparts, who had always been slower to leave the inner city than other Jews, began to take their places, a trend that increased during the ensuing years. For many of the Orthodox, the move to Boro Park represented a suburbanization, an embrace of the American dream. The larger homes of the neighborhood offered an alternative to the tenements from which they had come; moving here was tantamount to moving up and sharing in American opportunity but without giving up Jewish loyalties. This was because Boro Park still provided for their Jewish needs and a geography that would enable relatively large numbers of Jews to live within walking distance of a synagogue. It was a modern Orthodox American dream: a combination of the enclave and a taste of life beyond it.

In time, the suburban elements of the neighborhood declined while the Jews who made their homes here diminished in their variety, a trend intensified by the increasing influx of Orthodox Jews and their institutions. Over the last thirty years, Boro Park became more and more the exclusively Orthodox and increasingly insular enclave that it is today. The late Egon Mayer, whose 1979 book *From Suburb to Shtetl: The Jews of Boro Park* documented the start of this process and remains the single most comprehensive study of the area, reports that the New Utrecht neighborhood came to be known by its current name around 1891 when that farmland was first subdivided for residential housing and some real estate speculators began to refer to it thus. In fact, even today, while the name is universally recognized, there are no formal boundaries that either the state or the city of New York recognizes as "Boro Park."[27] This of course has made it difficult to definitively demarcate the district's boundaries. Nevertheless, the lines surrounding the Orthodox Jewish enclave are fairly clear today.

A walk along its outer perimeter as determined by shops, institutions, the architectural features already cited, and the population that fills its streets suggests a nearly two-square-mile area in which Orthodox Jews constitute, if not always a majority, certainly a plurality of those who live and work there. While it is not always easy to determine precise boundaries, certain elements help define the perimeter. Looking to the northwest, past 9th Avenue, one finds an Asian enclave, made up largely of Chinese. To the southwest, below 60th Street, are housing projects and an industrial area. To the southeast, below 18th Avenue, there are few if any Orthodox Jews. Finally, if one heads toward the northeast one is going toward the Orthodox neighborhoods of Flatbush. However, Flatbush, which lies about a half-mile away from the northeastern edge of Boro Park, although growing increasingly Orthodox, is separated from it by such powerful boundaries as the multilane Ocean Parkway, the non-Jewish shopping district along Church Street, a cemetery, and a wedge of blocks filled with other working-class ethnics (including a large Arab and Muslim enclave).

Demographically, in terms of both numbers and variety, the Orthodox community of Boro Park is more diverse than the one in Williamsburg. In part this is because few if any urban developments have undermined the community here either geographically or socially. In fact most of those who have left have been drawn by the lure of the suburbs or larger houses rather than repelled by Boro Park.[28] Today, the overall ambience and clear majority in the enclave remains Orthodox. In fact, a number of Orthodox Jews and their institutions that were once located in other Brooklyn neighborhoods steadily migrated here as these other areas went through economic decline and population change during the 1960s and 1970s. In line with the tendencies already described in this book, as Orthodoxy has been pulled further to the religious right, so too have the Orthodox Jews in Boro Park. The Haredi mix, moreover, includes a variety of Hasidim and Jews attached to the yeshiva world.

Until the 1960s Boro Park also was home to the nominally Orthodox and some religiously right-wing Conservative Jews. As the twentieth century drew to a close, however, these two groups waned and are now a tiny fraction; even the modernists have either moved elsewhere or begun to change their own religious and cultural orientations to be more in tune with the Haredi inclinations of the growing majority.[29] On the other hand, some Jews from the former Soviet Union and some Israeli expatriates, neither of who are particularly pious, have lately moved into the neighborhood.

Because of its geographic ambiguity, determining the population numbers in Boro Park is difficult, even using the same sorts of census cues that were used for estimating the demographics for Williamsburg. Still, using many of the same census tracts that Mayer used in his 1979 study, one is able to arrive at fairly reliable figures. Drawing on the 1970 census data, Mayer estimated a population of about 46,000 Jews.[30] The proportion of Orthodox Jews in that figure may have grown in the ensuing twenty years, and so too the percentage of Haredim among them, even though the overall number of Jews at the beginning of the twenty-first century remains almost the same.

These days one may find all these Jews bumping up against one another on the street and in synagogues, stores, and a variety of institutions. While the overwhelming impression one gets while walking through the main shopping districts or along the streets of the neighborhood is of an attachment to the traditions of Judaism, one is more likely here to hear English or even Hebrew or Russian spoken than the Yiddish so common in Williamsburg. And while the black hats and coats, earlocks and beards, or wigs and long skirts that are endemic in Williamsburg are visible here in abundance, they are more than offset by more colorful, contemporary clothes. In some cases, the only sign that a young man is Orthodox may be his yarmulke, and the longer skirts of many of the women do not immediately mark them as Orthodox except to the culturally informed. Furthermore, even among the Haredi Orthodox of Boro Park the intersection between the two extremes of Orthodoxy is visible, as when one witnesses a woman who appears quite "up-to-date" and American walking with her husband who appears to be from another far more insular world. This type of couple walking side by side is far less likely to be seen in Williamsburg, where the women are less attracted to contemporary American stylishness and often walk separately from their husbands.

In addition, as can be seen by their dress and appearance, quite a number of people who are not at all Orthodox or even Jewish pass through here. These people are not just part of the background but make their presence felt. Indeed, several important non-Jewish institutions within the enclave bring them in. These include the Post Office at 12th Avenue and 51st Street, Public Schools 164 and 180, and the large telephone company offices a block away, as well as the Maimonides Hospital along Fort Hamilton Parkway (10th Avenue) and the Brooklyn Public Library at 60th and 17th.

Nevertheless, both the plethora of Jewish institutions, from bookstores to synagogues to shops that cater to Jewish needs, and the many signs that speak to Orthodox Jewish interests reveal the essential character of this urban enclave. Thus a camera store will fill its windows not with nondescript images of generic Americans, as might commonly be the case elsewhere, but with framed portraits of the Grand Rabbi of the Bobov dynasty, whose Hasidic headquarters and largest number of followers are in the neighborhood. Similarly, a newsstand will offer, in addition to the New York area newspapers that would be found throughout the city, an assortment of publications in Yiddish and Hebrew as well as English whose concerns are exclusively Jewish and particularly Orthodox, while the local pharmacy will adorn the wall outside its shop with a huge billboard advertising vitamins and makeup whose special appeal is that they are "strictly kosher."

The neighborhood of Crown Heights lies on both sides of the ridge that is Eastern Parkway. Known as Crow Hill until 1916, when Crown Street was cut through it, in time it developed into a posh residential neighborhood, a "bedroom" community for Manhattan's growing middle class. Along its streets one still finds large, imposing private houses with sizable and lush front lawns that date from that era, as well as the low-rise apartments that later followed. In 1950, there were 75,000 Jews here, most of them middle class and only some Orthodox. As the neighborhood began to age and change both ethnically and racially, classic patterns of urban white flight began, slowly at first and more rapidly in later years. Concurrently, private home property values started to fall, accelerating the neighborhood's change, as both white and nonwhite middle-class families felt compelled to move out before their investments decreased even more in worth. Apartment vacancies increased and pressures mounted on property owners to rent to those with lower incomes. Among these new residents were eastern European refugees and later African American, Hispanic, and particularly Caribbean minorities. The early 1960s was a time of turbulence in race relations, as riots and violence plagued New York and other American cities. A number of Jews in Crown Heights were victims of knifings, beatings, and muggings, leading to the departure of most of their fellow religionists who had remained in the neighborhood. During the Johnson administration, Crown Heights was declared a primary poverty area due to high unemployment, high juvenile and adult crime rates, poor nutrition, low family income, a relative absence of job skills and readiness to work, and a relatively high concentration of elderly residents.

At this time, the Lubavitcher Rebbe, Rabbi Menachem M. Schneerson, seventh in the line of Hasidic leaders who traced their origins to Ukraine and Lithuania, urged his followers who had concentrated in the vicinity of Eastern Parkway not to leave the neighborhood. He argued that flight would not improve their Jewish lives, for while suburbia and other neighborhoods in the city to which Jews from Crown Heights were moving might be good for their physical safety, these same neighborhoods would be dangerous for the integrity of their Judaism because of assimilative pressures. For all of its risks, Crown Heights, he argued, would not be a place where Jews would be swallowed up socially and culturally by their neighbors and would be a location where their Orthodoxy and Hasidic customs would therefore thrive. Moreover, he argued,

Lubavitcher Hasidim had fled too many places throughout the preceding fifty years, and the time to run was now over until the day the Messiah would return to lead them to redemption and the ancient Jewish homeland. He assured them that staying put until then would be the best option, and, like the dedicated disciples they were, they complied. In this argument to stay put until the end, he echoed one of his predecessors who had made similar arguments to his followers when they wanted to flee the Czarist regime for America.[31]

While significant numbers of the Lubavitchers—so called *shluchim* or emissaries—leave the enclave on outreach "missions" to Jews the world over, in line with the Chabad-Lubavitch ideology, which sees Lubavitchers as hastening the coming of the Messiah via their religious outreach work among an unobservant Jewry, a core population has remained in Crown Heights and made 770 Eastern Parkway, the main Lubavitch synagogue and *bes medrash* (study hall), its "world headquarters."[32] In time, the Lubavitchers set up a variety of neighborhood watch organizations, housing associations, and other social service projects. Ultimately, all these came under the direction of a single umbrella organization: the (Lubavitch-dominated) Crown Heights Jewish Community Council. While other Jews fled the area, Rabbi Schneerson's people did not. Today the only Orthodox Jews—perhaps the only Jews of any orientation—left living in Crown Heights are Lubavitcher Hasidim, for whom this has become an important, if not the most important, enclave.

In a sense, then, this is a Brooklyn Orthodox enclave that is a culturally and religiously monochromatic society of Lubavitchers. Distinctions here are those that exist *within* this Hasidic group: differences between those new to the way of life (the products of outreach efforts) and those who were raised as Lubavitchers. There are also differences between Lubavitchers from abroad and native American Hasidim. Finally there are those who have been swept up by recent active messianic enthusiasms and those for whom messianism is but a part of their overall religious outlook.

Although today Lubavitchers claim to have members living along Eastern Parkway as far west as Nostrand Avenue, as far east as Utica Avenue, and as far south as Lefferts Avenue, a closer examination of the area finds few at the edges and most living within five blocks south and three blocks east and west of the building best known as "770," although called today by many Bes Moshiach" (House of the Messiah), in reference to a widespread conviction among many local followers that their Seventh Rebbe, now deceased, is the Jewish Messiah and will return to lead them all to redemption. Indeed, the matter of the rebbe's messianic qualities has become a preoccupation among many if not most of his followers, and concern with the subject now permeates much of the life of the Lubavitch enclave in Crown Heights. Lacking a single agreed-upon charismatic leader in the rebbe's absence, they make much of his "presence" in their hopes and expectations of an imminent redemption. Toward this end, they plumb his writings, letters, and even videos of his appearances for messages and inspiration while they await his revelation and return. Much of this they sell in Jewish bookshops along the main shopping district and in a place they call the International Moshiach Center. In the meantime, they prepare for his coming and "welcome him with ubiquitous signs throughout the enclave referring to the rebbe as Messiah, yellow-framed pictures of the rebbe, and a slogan in Hebrew that says: "Welcome, the King Messiah." The messianism drives the outreach efforts, which in turn force Lubavitchers to become less enclavist and insular.

For all of the Lubavitchers' assertions of their influence, which is magnified by their extensive missionizing among Jews and their many outposts throughout the world, they remain a relative few in Crown Heights, numbering only about 8,800 persons as of the 1990 census and a nearly identical number in the 2000 census. Just over a third of them (about 3,300) were listed as thirteen years old or younger and approximately another 1,500 between fourteen and twenty-one years old in 1990 and nearly the same in 2000. About 7 percent were in households of seven or more according to both the 1990 and 2000 figures. This last figure, about twice the rate for New York City, is comparatively small for a Haredi neighborhood and may be a reflection of the fact that the median age of the locals has remained about twenty-eight and that many have sent their children to boarding yeshivas that Lubavitch has in a variety of other locations.[33] Perhaps because many Lubavitchers are newly Orthodox, Jewish "souls" imported via successful outreach in, among other places, Chabad Houses on college campuses, the number of college graduates in the enclave in 2000 was at about 25 percent, considerably higher than one finds in either Williamsburg or Boro Park, although not as high as in Kew Gardens Hills.[34] With a median family annual income around $25,000, about 25 percent at the time were living below the poverty line, although given the large number of foreign nationals (mostly Israeli Lubavitchers who have come for extended stays) these numbers might actually be higher. Yet a look at the Crown Heights enclave suggests that they number far fewer than is asserted in the extravagant claims made in the media and by these Hasidim themselves.

Finding Lubavitch residences is not difficult, since theirs are the only ones in Crown Heights with mezuzahs on the door. For Lubavitchers, the mezuzah has become an even more important symbol than for many other Jews because their leaders have convinced them that a proper mezuzah, one whose scribal contents have been recently checked for accuracy and completeness, will ensure good fortune for the house's inhabitants and hasten the day of redemption. Accordingly, these Hasidim have large, prominent, and easily accessible mezuzahs on their doorposts. In addition, as in the other Orthodox neighborhoods considered here, the presence of sukkah-ready porches on apartments is easily observed.

The appearance of Lubavitchers is also quite distinctive, particularly that of adult males. Although the women dress in a traditionally modest way, the married among them covering their hair and all wearing long skirts and long-sleeved blouses, the men, who wear beards like most Hasidim, wear fedoras rather than the rounded hats of other Hasidim and do not wear the fur-trimmed hats or *shtreimels* common as Sabbath and holiday wear among other Hasidic groups. Moreover, these Hasidim, who have so much interaction with modern life as part of their efforts to missionize among Jews, take on some of the trappings of the community they seek to attract; hence it is not unusual or impossible to see one of them wearing a hat like a Yankees baseball cap. The messianists among them (particularly young boys) can be found wearing skullcaps with a verse running along their edge extolling the rebbe as Messiah. Although the shops along the central shopping artery, Kingston Avenue, overwhelmingly cater to the Orthodox Jews of Lubavitch, the district is relatively small and runs only a few blocks. In addition, many elements of the enclave indicate its porousness, including the presence of a large number of churches in the neighborhood such as St. Mark's (at the intersection of Brooklyn and Union and a block away from "770"), St. Michaels, Mount State Zion, and the Apostolic Church of Christ, as well as at least thirteen others just north of the enclave and Holy Cross Cemetery just to the south. Unlike almost all the other enclaves considered here, this one thus seems to contain many outsiders whose presence is felt in their ubiquitousness on the streets. To be sure, to many Lubavitcher insiders these outsiders are socially invisible and culturally irrelevant and are not integrated into their neighborhood.

Tucked into Flushing's southwest corner, on the east side of Flushing Meadows-Corona Park, is the compact community of Kew Gardens Hills.[35] This neighborhood in the borough of Queens is the fourth of the communities to be considered here. While, as earlier noted, the number of Jews in Queens, the last of the five boroughs in New York City, has dropped during the last ten years from 233,000 to just over 185,000, this county, with a 20 percent Orthodox population, has achieved a reputation for a growing and vibrant Orthodox community in several of its neighborhoods. Among the areas commonly thus identified are the adjoining localities of Kew Gardens Hills, Fresh Meadows, and Hillcrest, with a total of 28,200 Jews, as well as the nearby Rego Park and Forest Hills, with just over 39,000.

Kew Gardens Hills has had several name changes: it was previously known as Head of Vleigh, East Forest Hills, and Queens Valley. By the 1920s it had changed a great deal from the swamps, marshes, and meadows the Dutch had found when they sailed into Flushing Bay in 1628. Developers were hoping to draw New York's prosperous and affluent residents to the area, and several golf clubs soon opened in the region. A number of cemeteries were also in the area; one, called Cedar Grove, was soon surrounded by a larger Jewish one called Mount Hebron. At its inception, this cemetery was considered far beyond the city limits, but today it is walking distance from where many Jews live, marking the northern border of Kew Gardens Hills.

With the success of the neighboring developments and the opening of the IND subway service in 1936, it was not long before the area became especially attractive to developers. Abraham Wolosoff designed a community of small homes and apartments, which he named Kew Gardens Hills. Twenty minutes' traveling time to Manhattan via the subway, coupled with the completion of the Grand Central Parkway for automobiles, attracted hundreds of new residents to "the hills," and by the time the World's Fair opened in 1939 not far away, more than 1,200 homes had been built, with plans for hundreds more. In 1950, the Flushing Post Office, responding to the population surge, opened to handle the mail.

In the 1960s, Orthodox Jews from Brooklyn and the Bronx, many of whose neighborhoods were undergoing ethnic and economic changes, were attracted to this area in part because the district, like Boro Park before it, had some of the qualities of suburbia, the sort of place that was drawing so many Americans away from the inner cities, while still having the Jewish population and infrastructure that made Orthodox Jewish life possible.[36] Here was an area of single- or two-family homes with gardens, many synagogues, kosher food establishments, and shops that catered to diverse Jewish needs and whose number had grown significantly during the last thirty years. Throughout the closing years of the twentieth century increasing numbers of Orthodox Jews moved here, particularly young couples with a baby or two looking for affordable housing that was family friendly and a place where they could live a Jewishly observant lifestyle. Some wags have even gone so far as to nickname the neighborhood "Jews' Gardens Hills." To be sure, there is evidence that the population of young Orthodox couples who move into rental units or starter houses here will, as their families grow, relocate elsewhere. Recently Bukharan Jewish immigrants from the former Soviet Union as well as some Israelis have moved in. Today, the Orthodox Jewish enclave in Kew Gardens Hills, located between the parkways, the expressways, a cemetery, and a City University of New York (Queens) college campus, and extending as far south as 78th Street, is a tightly packed neighborhood of garden apartments, co-ops, both new and conversions, and private homes.

There is mounting evidence that Haredi elements are moving into Kew Gardens, in terms of both the population and some of the institutions that are making their appearance here. The overwhelming majority of those who live here as these words are written remain what is commonly called centrist or modern Orthodox.[37] Even so, this is an Orthodoxy far more assertive and public than it was in earlier years, when the stance of the Orthodox in the United States was often driven by a desire to try to fit into American society rather than to stand out or apart from it. This latter stance is what has come to be associated with a more Haredi style of Orthodoxy.

A walk through the enclave will allow the informed observer to perceive these transitions. The appearance of the people is one sign; the explosion of the number of synagogues, including a large number of small one-room *shtibblach* (chapels) as well as yeshivas and other Orthodox Jewish institutions, is another. All this gives one a sense of an enclave in transition, shifting toward a more visible and demanding religious observance and belonging that mirrors the changes that American Orthodoxy is itself undergoing. Perhaps nothing more vividly symbolizes this new attitude than the architectural decisions the community has made in building synagogues and yeshivas over the years. Thus the Ohr HaChayim Yeshiva and Hall, built during the late 1990s, is an imposing and striking, massive block-long structure, clearly standing out from its surrounding buildings of brick-and-mortar, and constructed of a white hewn limestone that many Jews have come to call "Jerusalem stone." It echoes in a sense the Haredi attitude of a willingness to make one's religious identity visible in the public square, an attitude that seems to say, "We are here but not made of the same stuff that everything else here is made." In contrast, the Jewish Center of Kew Gardens Hills synagogue-school across the street, built closer to midcentury, when Orthodoxy was far less sure of itself in America and aimed at acculturating itself to this country, is a brick flat structure that blends in with its surroundings and looks not too different from the bank beside it and other structures in the surrounding neighborhood.[38] Like the Orthodox Jews who built it, it architecturally echoes their attitude. "We are here," it seems to say, "and at least on the surface look like everything else here; the difference between us and the other buildings is what goes on inside, hidden from public view."

Built between these two extremes in both time and character is the Yeshivat Ohel Simcha, a building that is both school and synagogue and that reflects the changing nature of Orthodoxy that in the late 1970s and early 1980s was beginning to be ready to stand apart but only slightly from surrounding society. Still made of brick, its bricks are simply blond instead of the standard-issue red. These variations in the character of Kew Gardens Hills Orthodoxy, as will later be seen, are also reflected in the posters and handbills visible in the public spaces of the neighborhood.

No less than in the other enclaves, however, the dominant tone here is Orthodox Jewish, and even stores that were there before the influx of the Orthodox have for the most part taken on that character. Thus a liquor store once selling a variety of wines now offers almost exclusively kosher ones and advertises these in its windows, and pharmacies now offer kosher vitamins just as the ones in Boro Park do. Nevertheless, some elements of this enclave reveal that in comparison with the other two discussed here it is far more subject to outside influences. Even as yarmulkes on the men and wigs or kerchiefs on the married women are much in evidence, the varied colors and styles of clothing and the general atmosphere reflect an openness to America and its lifestyle.

As in Boro Park and Williamsburg, the newsstands here offer Jewish publications, but missing so far are the particularly Haredi ones found in Brooklyn, although at least one of the bookstores is owned and run by Brooklyn Haredim. Moreover, passersby will find mass circulation newspapers and magazines the likes of which will not be found in Williamsburg, Boro Park, or Lubavitcher Crown Heights.

Beyond the televisions and computers hooked to the Internet that abound in residences and are available in several eateries, among the specific sources for the outside influences is a major interurban bus route along Jewel Avenue, a major east-west artery that bisects the neighborhood and brings in a continuing flow of outsiders, including many

FIGURE 9: A bearded Haredi young man, in emblematic black coat and white shirt with his ritual fringes prominently displayed, walks along Main Street in Kew Gardens Hills. Note as well in the background an Orthodox woman, her hair covered in a fashion associated with rigorous Orthodoxy, pushing a stroller.

shoppers coming from downtown Flushing to the north and heading toward points west and east, as well as students from Queens College, the Townsend Harris (public) High School for the Gifted, and City University Law School who traverse the neighborhood on their way to and from their schools located on its perimeter. These outsiders, while largely just passing through, also sometimes stay awhile and are served by a number of stores, including a nonkosher fast-food place and a barber shop as well as a convenience store, that remain in the enclave. Nevertheless, the sight of an obviously Haredi Jew, whose dress and demeanor reflect an unabashed and public identification with the rigorous Judaism that is emblematic of this Orthodoxy, is not at all unusual now on Main Street (figure 9). Not only do the various schools make their presence felt (and even enroll some of the residents of the community), but the Mount Hebron Cemetery serves all sorts of Jews, not just the Orthodox. The Flushing Post Office, located at the southern edge, likewise brings non-Orthodox and non-Jewish people through and into Kew Gardens Hills, as do banks and a movie theater (now a five-plex) that screens the latest films. The latter attraction, patronized by locals as well as people in neighborhoods around the Kew Gardens Hills perimeter, is missing in Williamsburg, Boro Park, and Crown Heights, where the idea of going to a first-run contemporary movie is either unthinkable or at the edge of the permissible and certainly not to be done inside the enclave. The movie multiplex serves as another clearly visible and highly symbolic element that illustrates the rather more culturally open character of this enclave when compared to the others.

Some geographic boundaries to the area are not likely to be changed in the foreseeable future. These include several highways, including Grand Central Parkway to the south, the Van Wyck Expressway to the west, and the Long Island Expressway, as well as the Mount Hebron Cemetery to the north and Queens College and the Pomonok housing projects to the east.[39] And to the south, beyond 78th Street, one finds some housing projects and the Queen of Peace Church and Day School. There are also other non-Jewish ethnic populations on the perimeter who have created their own well-established ethnic enclaves that have been expanding up to the borders of the Jewish area. They include African Americans, Koreans, Chinese, Indians, and other South Asians. These populations, which continue to expand, do not commonly mix with Orthodox Jews. But insofar as their children attend Queens College, one of the most attractive units of the City University of New York, which sits at the intersection of these various ethnic enclaves, they may encounter one another on campus and through the medium of their common educational aspirations.[40]

According to the 1990 census, the total population of the area was about 15,000, of whom about two-thirds were likely Orthodox Jews. By 2000, the proportion of Jews (and indeed of whites) in the area had decreased by about 14 percent.[41] About 18 percent are thirteen years old or less and another 8 percent are 14 to 21 years of age. Moreover, in contrast to the three other neighborhoods, only about 1½ per cent of families have seven or people in a household. Indeed, the average family size is just over three people per household, far more in line with the rest of contemporary white New York and significantly lower than the 4.7 of Williamsburg, the nearly 3.8 of Boro Park, and the 3.7 of Crown Heights. Over 55 percent speak only English at home—in sharp contrast to the 10 percent of Williamsburg residents.

With a median household income of over $40,000 in 1990 and only about 6 percent of the people living below the poverty level, the inhabitants of this enclave are clearly in a higher economic bracket than their

counterparts in the other enclaves. In part this is due to their higher educational attainments. Over 55 percent have been to college, and about 33
percent have a degree, a proportion that puts them above the general population of New York City as well as Long Island's Nassau County. In
short, the people of Kew Gardens Hills may live in an Orthodox Jewish
enclave, but they are clearly taking advantage of much that America has
to offer and share in it more fully than their Haredi counterparts.

THE CALLS FROM THE WALLS

While there are a variety of ways in which cultural enclaves can erect an
invisible wall of virtue that keeps the cultural hazards from the outside at
bay, enhances their sense of social solidarity, and helps define for insiders the domain of their common values, concerns, and interests, posters
or handbills—what I am calling here "the calls from the walls"—are, as I
have suggested, one of the simplest, most transparent, and most commonly used in these Orthodox Jewish neighborhoods.[42] These posters
do a great deal. To recap briefly: they inform insiders (and knowledgeable outsiders) about what is of interest to, appropriate for, and expected
within the enclave. They help local residents understand which activities
and products they should properly pursue as well those they would do
well to avoid. They enable people to get at what sociologists have called
"the definition of the situation"—that is, "to assess correctly what the situation ought to be for them and act accordingly"—while providing a
reflection of common worldviews and beliefs.[43] By their placement, they
help define a territory of concern and public attention. Finally, they serve
as a mechanism that sustains and enhances these definitions of "the way
"things are supposed to be and people are supposed to act."

Because, as has been emphasized, the boundaries of these contemporary Jewish ghettos are largely voluntary and self-imposed, the elements
in the calls from the walls that enhance solidarity and communicate a sense
of community take on greater cultural and social importance than might
otherwise be the case. Accordingly, communications that are significant
or comprehensible only to insiders, or messages that remind readers how
much they have in common with or are dependent upon one another,
take on greater meaning in such circumstances. I want to argue here that
this is what gives special sociological meaning and importance to the
posters that insiders affix in public places and address to other insiders and
allows them to serve as an important medium of research for the student
of society and culture.

Not all posters aim at the same target population. Insofar as Ortho-dox Jews make up a *single* community of interest, distinct from other Jew-ish movements and from non-Jews, some posters are of general interest and will be found in all the enclaves (although not outside them). Some address the entire Orthodox community: for example, posters that announce the program of a concert, a talk by a distinguished and widely known rabbi, an upcoming religious conference or convention to be held outside the locality, or a special trip or a pilgrimage whose primary con-sumers are Orthodox, or that call for help (fund-raising, blood drives) where it is crucial that the largest audience of the interested be addressed. While manifestly aimed to inform and arouse the appropriate responses, these interenclave posters latently serve to remind readers that they do share a community of concern and to recall what those concerns are.

Other posters target particular segments of the Orthodox community. Some have profit-making motives, while others have explicitly social or religious aims. These include signs for products or services (everything from kosher foodstuffs to clothes, new books that speak to general Or-thodox interests, or cheap telephone service—particularly to Israel). At times the distinctions blur, as when a sale is announced of a volume con-taining prayers or religious lessons that everyone might use.

Sometimes, however, although the products, services, or programs may seem generically equivalent, certain particularities make them relevant to only to a specific subcommunity within the Orthodox world. When this is the case, the poster will be tailored to demonstrate that particular-ity and posted where it is most likely to find its proper audience. Some posters are parochial in the extreme. In general, the more insular the en-clave the more frequently will highly parochial posters be displayed there. What makes a poster highly parochial is not only that it is primarily of in-terest to specific insiders but also that its meaning can be deciphered fully only by insiders. It may be in a code that only insiders understand (e.g., Yiddish), or its significance may be apparent only to them, so that even if one understood the language one would need to be a true insider to catch the full implications of what was being announced.[44] Let us con-sider some examples of each of these cases and use them to understand something about the enclave and community in which they were found—and in turn about contemporary American Orthodox Judaism.

Perhaps the most ubiquitous sort of poster found across all commu-nities is the one that seeks to raise money, usually for an Orthodox Jew-ish cause. That this should be the case is not surprising when one recalls that of all Jewish groups in America the Orthodox are the ones with the lowest economic position and the highest Jewish bill.[45] With a plethora of institutions to support (from schools and yeshivas to synagogues and *mikvehs*) and larger families than all other Jewish groups, they are increasingly on a quest for funds. Moreover, given that the growing Haredi segment of Orthodoxy has made a virtue of having a large proportion of their able-bodied young withdrawn from the workplace—whether because they are males studying full time in a yeshiva or because they are females occupied with childbearing and rearing—their economic need is becoming even greater. Finally, Orthodox Jews spend a great deal for some basic needs—food, housing, and education—because of their religious commitments.[46] Reflecting all this are many appeals for cash.

Yet the differences within each enclave are also obvious. Where the percentage of people not gainfully employed is highest, posters appealing for funds are found in greater number. In our sample the enclave with the largest proportion of people below the poverty line, Williamsburg, displayed the most posters whose aim was to raise funds. If one counts notices for raffles, fund-raisers for prospective brides or building campaigns, and festive fund-raising dinners, as well as requests for money to support the poor, about 40 percent of the posters I collected within a six-month period were directly or indirectly related to this matter. Although such pleas were posted in the other neighborhoods, none came close to this figure but rather hovered around 7 to 10 percent. Moreover, the nature of the pitch for funds differed. In Williamsburg, the following posters were typical.

With a picture of a van (the preferred car for the large families of Williamsburg) and the promise of $20,000, $10,000, and $5,000 prizes, the Nitra Hasidim of Williamsburg announce (in Yiddish and English, the latter because this quest for funds necessitated posting outside the neighborhood as well as in it) a raffle to raise funds for the "spread of Torah" (figure 10). This appeal to support their own institutions and community is but one of many such pleas for assistance. Similar appeals include one showing hands exchanging a wad of dollars, surrounded by Yiddish (the only relevant language for those addressed) assurances that by participating in this raffle one not only has a chance to win $10,000 but can "share in the effort to strengthen Torah," while receiving in return (if not the winning raffle) "good health, a livelihood, pleasure and the fulfillment of all their heart's desire for good." If that is not enough, the readers are informed that "according to the rabbis, this [raffle] can be purchased with tithe money" *(ma'aser gelt)* funds set aside by Jewish law for charity. In other words, this raffle (one of a series of recurring such lotteries that have

FIGURE 10: Poster advertising a Williamsburg raffle for a van and a variety of cash prizes.

been turned into a channel of badly needed funds) is a religiously worthy cause—even if it is a game of chance. A similar message is communicated in another poster that calls upon donors to "participate" in the study
activities of a Torah *kollel* in Jerusalem by virtue of a $120 donation; the
implicit message is that in return for this participation, which is implied
to be tantamount to Torah study itself, one will live to the magical Jewish age of 120.

Preceded several weeks before its posting by a broadside that primed
readers with the scriptural (Lev. 19:16) caution, "Do not stand idly by in
the face of your brother's blood," and concluded boldly, "Details will follow," an all-Yiddish poster pleads for funds under the framing phrases
"gifts to the poor," "the cry of the poor," and "For the scrupulously religious, in accordance with the instructions of the sage rabbis, may they
live long and good lives," with the screaming headline that calls out:
"RESCUE a family from going under!" (figure 11). As the notice continues, in a line from the midrash, "The waters have literally risen to where
we breathe." This major appeal has been organized because the family in
question is one of a putative *talmid chacham,* a Torah scholar," as the tag
line on the broadside's bottom makes clear. With facsimiles of letters of
support from a wide array of rabbis, typical of what local mendicants often

FIGURE 11: Poster calling for "rescue" from financial ruin for the family of a scholar, including reproductions of letters from prominent rabbis endorsing the call for financial help.

carry around in their solicitations for funds, the poster concludes that in return for supporting the scholar (who perhaps because, in accordance with Haredi fashion, he is engaged in Torah study and is not gainfully employed, and is unable to financially support himself and his family), donors will be rewarded: "In the merit of sustaining a *talmid chacham,* you will be blessed from the haven of blessings."[47] This appeal shows that the scholars' society is insecure. Its call for help resonates far more powerfully among those who believe in the particular merit of supporting Torah scholars and among those who care about the opinions of rabbis. But in this Haredi enclave there is a surfeit of "scholars" who have no other gainful employment, in great measure because they most certainly *do* care about the opinions of rabbis—even excessively so. The poster shows us where this has gotten them, on the verge of "going under."

The predominant Yiddish in all these signs testifies to the insularity of the enclave; these appeals are addressed to Yiddish-reading insiders. For these insiders the promises that they will gain blessings or live to a ripe old age or the assertions that one needs to find a target for tithing matter. This is language and these are values particular to the Haredi world of Williamsburg, where blessings, tithing, and divine intervention on behalf of the insiders are commonly held concepts, and where religious sanction for an activity is essential. But they also show us a community in financial crisis.

To be sure, concern with the poor is not only for those residing in Williamburg. Funds are also solicited for those Orthodox poor who share the outlook of those in Williamsburg but are found elsewhere. Hence another poster promises a distribution on Passover of funds for "thousands of the poor in our holy land," which would be a show of concern to *yungerleit b'nai Torah in Eretz Yisrael,* the young men and boys who study the sacred texts in the yeshivas in *Eretz Yisrael* (the Land of Israel) (figure 12). This historic "Holy Land" is in contradistinction to the "state of Israel," the secular nation from which and for which the Williamsburg Haredim expect no support.

In contrast to these appeals in Williamsburg, consider the following fund-raising poster in Crown Heights. First of all, the poster is predominantly in English, a reflection of the fact that many of the readers in this neighborhood speak and read English, in contrast to the more insular Williamsburg Yiddish population. Crown Heights has many newly Orthodox (the bounty of the Lubavitcher outreach program) who may have disposable income. Moreover, the messianic focus of Lubavitch activity and the cult of personality there have led to a steady influx of outside

FIGURE 12: A Williamsburg poster in Yiddish calling for aid for the poor "b'nai Torah" in "the Holy Land of Israel" and another poster in English for the same charity. Yiddish version promises distribution of "over $3 million," while English version promises "over $1,360,000."

visitors, whose support is an important resource for locals. An appeal for funds, no less critical here, must be addressed in a way that they can understand. Indeed, the tag line at the poster's bottom—"May our master, teacher, rabbi, the King Messiah, live forever and ever"—that has become the ubiquitous prayer among the Crown Heights messianists and insiders, signals that this project is somehow connected with a belief in and fulfillment of Lubavitch messianic aspirations, which have a missionary element. Accordingly, the idiom of this poster (a Sunday "phone-a-thon," with tickets sold in multiples of $25 rather than in some number with a Jewish subtext)[48] is almost completely contemporary American, attesting to that outreach as well as acculturative elements infecting the Lubavitch Orthodox community. To be sure, there are Jewish elements in the text and in its objective. This is an appeal for a Lubavitch yeshiva, a target of interest primarily to supporters of the Lubavitch educational mission. The poster notes the Hebrew calendar date of the phone-a-thon, although here too it adds the general calendar date, presumably for those unable to calculate the secular equivalence for the Jewish date. Perhaps more significantly, one of the prizes offered is a $3,000 "shopping spree" at a well-known Brooklyn Jewish bookstore, something of value to only Jewish insiders and perhaps especially to those newly Orthodox who have not yet acquired the Judaica library that is today a sine qua non of contemporary observant Judaism. Yet here too, alternative and not particularly Jewish prizes are offered: a shopping spree in a Jewish-owned electronics chain or $2,500 cash. The picture of a menorah and silver prayer book has its counterpart in a picture of a phone and stereo system on the poster, as if to suggest that in life these are somehow equivalencies for what one might wish to possess. All this reflects something of the porousness and more diverse culture of the Crown Heights enclave.

An English-language posted appeal for money found in both the Boro Park and Kew Gardens Hills enclaves announces a "Chinese auction," a fund-raiser in which sponsors list prizes or items up for bid and bidders drop tickets or entries for the items they want; later someone picks out a ticket and whoever has the matching stub wins the item. An increasingly popular benefit among American religious and voluntary organizations, from churches to Elk lodges, the one publicized seems at first glance not particularly different. Indeed, there is even an Internet address listed, indicating that at least some in the target audience may openly be expected to use it. For the informed observer there are, however, some signs, both obvious and subtle, that the sponsoring organization is Jewish and Orthodox. The insertion of a Hebrew date next to the English one is an un-mistakable signal. Equally noticeable is the box devoted to the art exhi-bition that will accompany the auction and in which are displayed iconic Jewish symbols like a mezuzah and a yarmulke-wearing youngster por-ing over an open Torah scroll. More subtle but in some ways more re-vealing is the notification that the affair is open to "women only," an in-dicator for the informed that this is an event for religiously scrupulous Orthodox Jews who discourage the mixing of men and women in pub-lic gatherings.

Though the content of the event is Jewish, the venue, the Brooklyn Museum of Art, although partially taken over for the occasion, is certainly neither exclusively nor particularly associated with Jews. Nevertheless, as the poster reflects, this event, like the communities of Boro Park and Kew Gardens Hills to whom it appeals, mixes the Jewish with the gen-eral, the parochial, and the cosmopolitan. Similarly, among the goods and services on which participants bid are a majority of such generically American items as a ladies' watch with diamonds, a notebook computer, an easy-fold treadmill, and a "luxury getaway spree." Yet there are as well distinctively Jewish items such as the Art Scroll Publications Talmud, a month's stay at Camp Bnos Yehuda (a religiously sectarian) summer camp, and membership for two at the "kosher gym," an institution on Flatbush's Coney Island Avenue in Jewish Brooklyn offering "a perfectly *tz'niyus* [modest] environment: Separate hours, frosted front windows, front desk separated from training area," features important to the Orthodox clien-tele who keep American contemporary culture and values at arm's length. There are a number of designer wigs, for Orthodox married women who, even as they seek to observe norms of religious "modesty," also want the chance to "flatter your features," as one prize description puts it.[49] These are surely items of value only to the Orthodox.

While it is useful to compare a single kind of poster and its variations across these enclaves, as in the case of the omnipresent appeals for funds that indicate the economic fragility of Orthodoxy, an even more reveal-ing analytic strategy is to explore the particular concerns of each enclave as reflected in the overall nature of the subjects of these broadsides. A list, given in the Appendix, of descriptions of posters found in each commu-nity (identified and referred to below by community abbreviation, W = Williamsburg, BP = Boro Park, CH = Crown Heights, KGH = Kew Gar-dens Hills, and by number) is helpful in this regard.[50] Looking at its con-tents both as a whole and in its parts tells us a great deal about each en-clave. That is what concerns us next.

WILLIAMSBURG POSTERS

Nearly all the posters from Williamsburg are written in Yiddish. This should not be a surprise. According to the 1990 U.S. Census, over 50 percent of those five years and older in the Jewish areas of Williamsburg listed Yiddish as the language spoken at home (and if we look at the community of Kiryas Joel, the Satmar Hasidic suburban enclave where many relatives of those living in Williamsburg have moved, the proportion rises to 93 percent, an indicator of the true presence of Yiddish as the everyday language of the population to whom most of these posters are addressed). Yiddish in the posters vividly signifies the cultural insularity of the enclave and how language helps ensure this—particularly in a crowded urban environment where outsiders are geographically close and coming closer. Language difference acts as a distancing mechanism to keep outsiders at bay and as a bonding device to keep insiders close—and the Yiddish posters both affirm and abet this process. They are part of the cultural "wall" that encloses this enclave.

The exceptions are those that, while found in Williamsburg, appear in other neighborhoods as well. Thus an announcement of genetic testing also posted in Boro Park as well as in suburban Monsey is in both Yiddish and English, in a nod to residents of other enclaves for whom Yiddish is not the lingua franca.[51] The texts of the two posters also betray important differences. For example, the English version uses both the Jewish and the Gregorian dates, while the Yiddish one references only the Jewish date, stressing that for these readers that is sufficient and the other irrelevant. Moreover, the Yiddish version, addressing an insular group perhaps not as versed in the science of these tests, warns readers "not to wait till the last minute," when the test may come too late. As insiders will immediately understand, "too late" refers to the time when a child is already conceived and when, according to Jewish law as observed in the Orthodox precincts of this neighborhood, terminating a pregnancy is out of the question, even if the fetus is diagnosed with a serious or fatal genetic disease.

Some English does appear. In a handbill advertising the sale of Deco sneakers, although the name of the company is in English, the framing information about them, the sales pitch ("lightweight and strong, comfortable and very good for sweaty feet; we're open straight from 3 to 7:30 P.M.") is all in Yiddish, a clear indicator that the person behind the poster knows the audience. Indeed, the use of the English for the actual product is probably more iconographic, like a trademark enabling the locals to recognize the product in question when they see the sneakers in the store.

Beyond the matter of language are the particular interests and subjects of the Williamsburg posters. Noticeable, as we have already seen, are the many fund-raising campaigns, a clear signal that marshalling funds for this community, its institutions, and its members is an endless concern. This should come as no surprise when one recalls that the annual per capita income here is about $5,000, the lowest by far of all these enclaves, and that over 56 percent of these people were listed in the census as living below the level of poverty, a number rising in the 2000 U.S. Census to around 70 percent among those with children under five years of age.[52] The locals' need to sustain themselves financially is a powerful one. Moreover, given their insularity (and hostility to non-Orthodox Jews) and the diminished relations with others that this engenders, the likelihood that they will find sympathetic outsiders from whom they may solicit economic support is likewise reduced. They certainly do not expect that very many such outsiders—if they *do* exist—will be wandering the streets of their enclave where they might view the posters, nor that they are likely to understand the Yiddish. As a result these Jews must continually find ways to pry loose money from their own.

So desperate is this quest that insiders have found a way to turn celebrations for prospective brides or ice cream parties, ostensibly social occasions, into fund-raisers. In the enclave, engagements and weddings are an almost daily affair, constituting the nearly universal rite of passage for people between the ages of eighteen and twenty-three. Williamsburg women are encouraged to marry and to remain in the bosom of the family, where they are to be concerned with childbirth and child rearing (reflected in the posters that offer genetic testing for the pregnant). This is the ideal pattern, as the ubiquitousness of these posters demonstrates.

The wedding and everything connected to it before and after thus plays a large role in the community. Not only is the population concerned about marrying off the young, ensuring continuity, but also they use weddings and their associated activities as an important and legitimate source of entertainment and socializing, albeit segregated by gender. Moreover, the funds a couple gets at the wedding are the indispensable stake they need to establish a Jewish home and family. With large families, parents alone cannot do the job. So raising money for a young couple is at once critical for continuity and the impetus for a social event, a "party." In one poster, we find that Goldie Greenbaum and Zussy Witrial, prospective brides, are being thrown an "ice cream party" in the Lanzter community *bes medresh* on a Sunday morning. In another we find an "open house party" scheduled at the same time in the hall of the Spinka Hasidim for other brides-to-be. These multiple occasions compete for crowds and for financial support for the dowries for these various couples. The initiatives, taken by eight "hostesses," listed on the poster, are sustained by reference to the holy dictum (Prov. 21:21) that those who pursue charity and loving-kindness will be granted longevity, the blessings of charity, and honor. In other words, what appears merely as an entertainment and social competition is in fact a fulfillment of scriptural advice. Give and you shall receive: ice cream and exciting raffles now and the blessings of heaven later, to say nothing of helping ensure Orthodox Jewish continuity of "our crowd." Above all are clear signs that without funds continuity here is in question.

We Have Our Own Activities and Values.   In the Manichean worldview of the Orthodox Jews of Williamsburg, as already noted, the world and culture outside (and increasingly approaching) their enclave is an "ever-lurking risk" that also seductively beckons them.[53] To keep their surrounding wall of virtue intact, they must see to it that their population remains Jewishly virtuous. Toward that end they generate a variety of activities and cautions to help in the process; their posters act often as both an instrument and a reflection of these efforts. Accordingly, the posters reveal what sorts of activities are considered appropriate and what not. In Williamsburg what *is* encouraged, virtuous, as indicated in the posters, includes going to and buying raffles when the cause is Jewishly support-ive, attending a sermon of a Hasidic rabbi (W 7), participating in a Torah study program with one's children (W 8), taking part in a community day of prayer (W 19), attending a commemoration of the *yarzheit* (death anniversary) of legendary Rabbi Shimon Bar Yochai (W 30), and of course helping the poor (W 16, 22).

Included as well are abiding bans on places that *should not* be visited or things that should not be utilized. Sometimes, the bans are most aggressive against places or activities that might otherwise *appear* to be acceptable. Hence the ban on a particular restaurant that claims to be kosher is an example. The Yiddish poster warns: "Jews!!! Do Not Let Yourselves Be Fooled" and proceeds to describe the "Kosher Garden" as an establishment (with shops in Williamsburg, Boro Park, and other Orthodox enclaves) that, while calling itself "Kosher," is "run by an 'Arab' and an 'enemy of Israel'" whose stores the rabbis have proscribed. After detail-ing the full extent of the ban, the broadside concludes with the call: "Remember! Buy only from Jews and may your 'brother live with you.'"[54] This last line is key. It is the chauvinistic argument that Jews (particularly religiously observant ones) are superior and alone deserving of community support. In a sense, this xenophobic response to threats to cultural integrity of the enclave culture is communicated and reaffirmed via the poster. It is the basis of legitimation for the attack and ban.

This unsigned broadside's claims were subject later to litigation, the shopkeepers of the Kosher Garden claiming the accusations to be libelous and hugely damaging to their business. Leaving aside the truth of the accusation, which was never resolved as the store closed in the face of the ban, the suit and shop closure demonstrate at least that such flyers, though small and having no aesthetic attraction, are read and do exert influence.

Leisure activity is a product of American affluence and an important element of contemporary culture. But for a community committed to living within the straight and narrow of strict Orthodoxy, and which is bound by strictures that prevent corruption and defilement by the surrounding society and its debased values, leisure activity represents a significant challenge. Indeed, the very idea of leisure and fun is something for which Jewish tradition offers little if any guidance. Consequently, the Jews in this neighborhood need guidance as to what are virtuous activities. Weddings, fund-raising parties, and pilgrimages—as we have seen—are approved. But what else is permitted? This is relevant particularly on school holidays. What can one do with the children? One possibility is to take them to the circus, the zoo, or other such "fun" activities. These would seem innocuous enough.

But posters in the Williamsburg enclave make clear that choosing to go to such venues during the intermediate days of Sukkot or Passover, the traditional holiday vacations within the Orthodox calendar that governs life here, may be prohibited. In fact, when a traveling circus was set up in the parking lot of one of the local yeshivas, drawing parents and children during the interim days of the holiday, people of Williamsburg were faced with a placard importing (by reprinting and posting) a prohibition from Israeli Haredi rabbis on attendance at just such "extravaganzas," warning that those who "guard their souls should distance themselves" from these assemblies and not "send their children" to these places and activities because to do so would be to follow in the pathways of the "goyim."

Drawing on the time-honored Jewish tradition of the need to distinguish all things Jewish from all things Gentile, a Manichean dualism that is de rigueur among Haredi Jews, the rabbis concluded, and those who put up this poster concurred, that the circus and petting zoo were too much like American (read: Gentile) pleasures and hence to be avoided. Moreover, as the poster suggests, this was an inappropriate activity because of the risks of mingling with people of the opposite sex and seeing animals engaging in coupling, actions that might lead to licentiousness in thought or in deed — or at least to having to explain to children about sexuality at "too early an age." To be sure, the fact that the poster was affixed to the wall also suggests that in spite of its warnings at least some of the locals *were* visiting zoos.

Still there was the question of how properly to fill leisure time. Another poster offered an alternative. Children and adults could go see an inspirational play ("under the supervision of the Council of Rabbis of the United States and Canada") called *City of Fear,* a story of the cultural and religious dangers facing the faithful beyond the invisible walls of virtue that enclose the enclave of Jewish Williamsburg. This was obviously permissible, as no counterposters were visible prohibiting it.

Other posters offer other, virtue-enhancing activities for one's free time. These are broadsides that alert insiders to opportunities to enlarge and augment their religious activities. Thus one finds among the Williamsburg announcements a public notice of a grand rabbi's visit or a sermon, a proclamation of an extraordinary communal "day of prayer," a notice of a talk about the norm of female modesty (to which all women are encouraged to "bring a friend," for this is a community-wide concern and the more women are exposed and "fortified" to this moral teaching the better), a message of moral teaching (sometimes an epistle from the rabbis) transformed into a poster, placards providing a listing of classes and Torah study, and, perhaps most explicitly, the announcement of a program that encourages parents and children to study Torah together "one hour a day," particularly during the intermediate days of the holidays, and not to miss the opportunity, "for those who come all four days will get gifts," and there "will be raffles each day." All this is the reward for those who avoid the "ways of the goyim."

To ensure that insiders will not stray from the path socially constructed for them, the community tries repeatedly to fortify the faithful so that they will not be enticed by the deceptively charming wolf-in-sheep's-clothing of contemporary American culture and instead will remain within their own *orach chayim* (way of life). Thus the vacation trip that Americans might wish for is to be replaced by a pilgrimage to a place of Jewish religious significance. The posters tell of such travel opportunities. For example, one reports the "joyful news" from the "committee for

travel to the graves of the righteous in the U.S. and Canada" of a forthcoming "trip to Chelsea [Massachusetts]" to visit the tomb of the late Grand
Rabbi Menachem Nahum Twersky. Along with the details is the boxed
rabbinic note that "it is good to go and pray at the graves of the righteous,"
especially when such graves are "not among the well-known," perhaps a
reference to the fact that Chelsea, Massachusetts, is not among the prominent Jewish pilgrimage sites in the world or even in America.

If such trips and gatherings are insufficient to keep the allure of the
outside at bay, then there are books to be read. First are the holy and inspirational books. But should one be helplessly drawn to the books of the
outside world, these too can be "translated and improved." Their troublesome references to forbidden pleasures can be removed and cleansed;
even their non-Jewish provenance can be hidden and the message they
send can be directed to local concerns. Thus *Around the World in Eighty
Days,* the classic tale of adventure and boundary breaking, recently was
put up for sale in the bookshops of Orthodox Williamsburg in a new Yiddish translation (where it sold out quickly). Gone is the Gentile Jules Verne
who originally authored the book; he has been replaced on the book's
cover (and the posters advertising its sale) by the far more acceptable and
apparently Jewish "Yoel Behrman" (figure 13). As for the lesson of Jewish consequence, the following "epilogue," printed on the last page of the
book, suggests what it might be:

In the contemporary world, in which the nations of the world carry on with their
depravity and wantonness and there reigns no humanity *(menshlichkeit)* and man-
ners, where one does not know how to honor one's elders or consider another's
feelings, it is highly interesting to read an account of a goy [i.e., non-Jew] of 130
years ago.

And one may from this learn that if even a goy was able to tear himself away from
his times and was prepared to lose his entire fortune in order to rescue a person,
for thus was he brought up, it is certain that a Jew who is completely obligated
to serve the Almighty, "with all your might,"[55] must be prepared to give of his
time and money to help another in his time of trouble, and assist in the [fulfill-
ment of] Torah and mitzvoth [its commandments].[56]

Having seen what even a Gentile can do, one who reads this book will
perhaps be better prepared to respond to the calls from the needy Jews,
to lend a helping hand, to rescue the poor scholar, and hence to be true to
the demands of Judaism—a quality certainly in demand in the precincts
of Williamsburg's Orthodoxy Jewry.

FIGURE 13: *Around the World in 80 Days* in Yiddish, by Joel Behrman.

Keeping Outsiders and Their Ways Outside. Avoiding the ways of the goyim and keeping the enclave protected from their influence has, as earlier noted, become increasingly difficult because of the changing nature of Williamsburg. The rising rents and the appeal of the area to artists, bohemians, and young New Yorkers have placed the insular Jews here in a dilemma. Some who own property have been tempted to take advantage of the rising value of this real estate and the rental market. For these Jews the very high need for added income and the possibility of making it by renting space to upscale artists are hard to ignore. At the same time, to bring in these artists and what the Haredi Orthodoxy of Williamsburg Jewry views as the culture of defilement that they carry is to undermine the protective wall of virtue. This dilemma is seen in the following Hebrew prayer posted in January 2004 under the headline "Plague of Artists."

Master of the Universe, have mercy upon us and upon the borders of our village and do not allow the persecution to come inside our home; please remove from upon us the plague of the artists, so that we shall not drown in evil waters, and so that they shall not come to our residence to ruin it.

Please place in the hearts of the homeowners that they should not build, God forbid, for these people, and strengthen their hearts so that they can withstand this difficult test and so that they will not sell for the lure of money.

Please, our Father God of Mercy, have mercy upon our generation that is weak, and remove this difficult test from these people, these immoral antagonists that by their doing will multiply, God forbid, the excruciating tests and the sight of the impurity and immorality that is growing in the world.

And here we live in fear that owing to the encroachment of these individuals upon our community we will not be able to teach our sons and daughters according to the methods of Israel.

Please, our Father of Mercy, for the sake of our fathers and our sages who gave their lives to allow religion to remain upon the lowly American soil, and for the sake of their merit, preserve the residence, do so for your love of those who came from the dust. Please, our Father of Mercy, do not give the aggressor the portion that you have acquired and that you have freed from slavery with your great strength.

And we know also, we know that we have no strength other than our mouths, and if we have brought on a decree from you, please repeal this harsh decree, because we lack strength and may not be able to withstand this difficult test, God forbid.[57]

Of course, the fact that this prayer needs to be recited suggests that the temptations and seductions, both economic and cultural, have already penetrated the "village" and that the "ways of the goyim" now confront "the methods of Israel." It also reminds us how the need for money to keep the outside world at bay is the element that brings it in. Echoed here too is the post-Holocaust need to survive as Orthodox Jews.

Indeed, a plethora of other posters echoing these same anxieties have of late begun to appear in the enclave. Some show the neighborhood in flames beneath the banner, "Williamsburg under Fire." Others list the names of individuals who are offering apartments to "outsiders" under the headline, "An abomination has occurred among Israel: residents of Williamsburg, we are in danger." The broadside concludes with the cry: "Wake up and do not allow such lowlifes [i.e., those named in the posters] to do what their heart desires." Following one's heart rather than the dictates of the group and its values is the great risk, the "sickness" that has taken over contemporary America.

The risk is not just that outsiders will come in but also that the cost of housing will rise as the rent people can and will pay goes up. That will force young Orthodox couples to move elsewhere and also endanger the continuity of the monoculture of the enclave. As we have seen, the economic pressures on Haredi Orthodoxy are what threaten its integrity. They lead some to places like the Machon LeParnassa and jobs that will breach the cultural barriers that the enclave has erected, and here they are leading to factors that will open the neighborhood to the cultural penetration of outsiders.

Another effort to maintain the wall of virtue and cultural barriers protecting those inside the enclave from falling prey to what is outside it is the increasingly ubiquitous prohibition on the computer, an instrument that many of the most conservative insiders have recognized as a double-edged sword. While an important source of livelihood and a piece of technology that seems indispensable in the modern world (as we have seen in the Machon L'Parnasa, where its use is a central subject of instruction), it is also a threat that can tear the fabric of their insularity. It may do so via its capacity to connect them to the Internet, a gateway into the global community through which all sorts of corrosive influences may enter their homes and hearts. The gatekeepers of Haredi orthodoxy know full well that the most common use of the Internet is for pornography. But they know too that it allows one to go virtually anywhere, far beyond the limitations of Haredi culture, without ever leaving the physical confines of the enclave and with no one besides the Web surfer knowing, a dangerous possibility for a society that seeks solidarity and insularity. Hence one is not surprised to find a poster announcing an "urgent call for saving a generation" to "not keep a computer in one's home" because to do so is "to undermine one's own soul and the souls of others, one's own blood and the blood of all those dependent upon him." That the computer is already making significant inroads into this community is to be recognized not just by the *urgency* of the call (as its wording makes clear) but by the statement that it comes "from the great [rabbis] of the U.S. and Canada" suggesting that this is a matter of concern to *all* the Orthodox guardians of religious virtue.

Internal Squabbling.   For a group that considers itself an endangered minority, internal conflict is a significant threat. Nevertheless, quarrels have become a part of Satmar Hasidic life, the dominant Orthodox community in Williamsburg, at least since the ascension to power of the current rebbe, a selection that was not universally welcomed within the group's ranks. As the current rebbe's sons and their supporters jockey for position as the next head of the dynasty, in view of their father's physical infirmities, continuing clashes and controversies that serve as proxies for this conflict break out. But these disputes are troublesome to many who support one side or the other, as well as to those who recognize the fragility of life in an enclave surrounded by what insiders view as a hostile and dangerous culture. Accordingly, there are often community calls to diminish these internal tensions and hence bring tranquility back to the virtuous. These calls are often oblique, trying to deny the quarrels and hide them from public view even as they call for peace. This development too is revealed in the Williamsburg posters, many of which call for unity. One, for example, tells an audience characterized as "dear Jews, our brothers, the children of Israel" to prepare for a party whose theme is "Who Is Like unto You Our Nation Israel," while another advertises the availability of a new volume filled with adages and readings to "arouse the heart as to the seriousness of dissension and the high value of peace." These concerns suggest how much the enclave must work at minimizing discord.

BORO PARK POSTERS

When we look at the posters in Boro Park, a different, though not completely dissimilar, picture emerges. This enclave, with about twice as many Orthodox Jews as Williamsburg, is more diverse and, as already pointed out, not nearly as insular, although the signs are that Haredi tendencies are ascendant. Although there are non-Orthodox and even non-Jewish

FIGURE 14a&b: Felder for City Council

elements nearby and indications that a cosmopolitan population not altogether unlike the one now invading Williamsburg may increase its presence here, for the time being a broad range of Orthodox Jews pretty much run things.[58] We see this in *political* matters, as displayed in posters plastered all over the enclave by supporters of a candidate named Felder who was running for a seat on the New York City Council. In one poster (figure 14b), the candidate's first name, Simcha, the Hebrew word for "joy" and a name foreign to the American street, is prominently repeated, reminding voters that he is someone whose identity as a Jew can never be erased. In another (figure 14a), his picture, showing a bearded face, a yarmulke atop his head, a neat necktie, and a white shirt, demonstrates a generic Orthodox identity sufficiently ambiguous to be both highly parochial and also somewhat American (though to a yeshiva insider it has a familiar look). Subtly suggesting the American theme are the poster's colors: red, white, and blue. But the candidate's slogan is perhaps the key. It suggests that while others seeking this office may not be the genuine article representing who and what Boro Park is, Felder is "the real thing." Felder won.[59] In Boro Park, the real thing seems to be Orthodox. But exactly what kind of Orthodox is the real thing? That requires a closer look.

What Is Orthodox Here?.   In Boro Park Haredi concerns to keep out dangerous elements of American contemporary culture are sometimes set off by efforts on the part of centrist observant Jews in the enclave who do not want to be as isolated from the world around them or the larger host society as their Williamsburg counterparts and seek rather to forge a more complex contemporary culture of Orthodoxy that is at home in, without being swallowed up by, America. As they have increasingly done in the last number of years throughout the denomination, these two sides of Orthodoxy inevitably contend for the hearts and minds of the local population, a competition reflected in the posters that appear throughout the enclave. In a sense that contest is one of the primary themes that emerges from a reading of the walls here (figure 15). The broadsides and flyers that come from and speak to the Haredi residents seek to increase the rigor of ritual practice and the distance from secular American culture. These include advertisements of opportunities and venues for Torah study (BP 3, 8, 13, 18); posters concerned with enhancing the practice of Jewish ritual (BP 6, 7, 25); broadsides drumming up support for a Haredi worldview (BP 2, 17); announcements of pilgrimages to holy places (BP 16), and ads for buying religious gear, including items that are particular to Hasidim, like a *shtreimel*

FIGURE 15: Boro Park dueling posters on how to spend one's time on Passover's intermediate days or after (clockwise from top left): taking classes with rabbinic scholars, testing and balancing the body, taking a trip to the grave of the late Hasidic Rebbe of Sanz, or listening to seventy-five minutes of music.

(Hasidic fur hat) or other Haredi garb—clothes sold in Williamsburg *and* Boro Park, evidence of an element common to both these enclaves.

Not only does the effort to market Hasidic clothing in this neighborhood indicate a growing population whose fashion needs are far from modernist, but also a sign warning men about the prohibition of "cutting the beard" ("published with the endorsement of leading halachic authorities," as the fine print on the bottom asserts) shows religious trends in the area (figure 16). The flyer, provided in both its original Hebrew and an attached English version, is a sure sign that many men are indeed still cutting their beards in Boro Park—were this not the case there would be no need for the poster. But here is an effort to change their habits, to make public the venerated "halachic [Judeo-legal] ruling" of the late Rogatchover Gaon, Rabbi Yosef Rosen, that cutting the beard is an "absolute prohibition."

No such posters are found in Williamsburg or Crown Heights, where beards on men are nearly universal and reminders of the "law" on

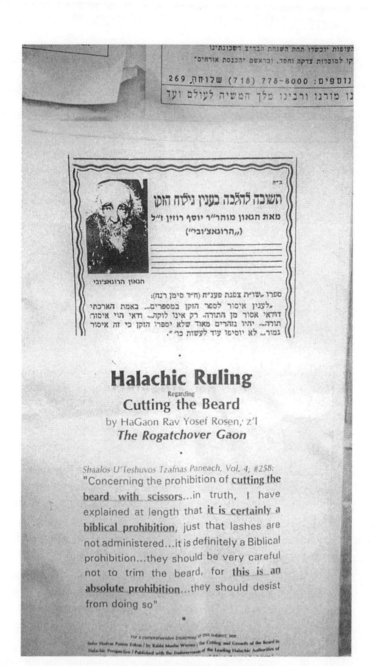

FIGURE 16: Prohibition on cutting the beard.

shaving are unnecessary. In Boro Park, where a more modern Orthodox population has been living, the forces that seek to turn the community toward the religious right, as symbolized by the presence of beards on the men, are contesting for the hearts and minds of Orthodoxy. To be sure, the poster suggests an effort to persuade not only clean-shaven modern Jews who claim to be attached to Halacha (Jewish law) that Jewish men need beards but also Haredi Orthodox men who might be tempted to be clean-shaven that they should not give way to this modernist temptation. Based on the timeworn Haredi assumption that for many men such a trim is the first step on the slippery slope of assimilation and religious decline, this proscription is promoted to remind those in Boro Park who are ready to take what they might view as a small step toward Americanization that the simple clipping of the beard (not even its complete shaving) is a transgression of the highest order, a "biblical prohibition." That the notice is in English as well as its original Hebrew, as it appears in a book of response, moreover, makes clear that the effort is double: to prevent the Haredim from moving to the left and perhaps also to bring those on the other side, for whom English is far more familiar, around to a more Haredi orientation.

Fortification. In the contest for Orthodoxy, Boro Park is apparently a front line. A poster announcing a gathering, sponsored by Agudath Israel of America, whose purpose is to offer *chizuk,* spiritual fortification for the confrontation with the corrupting values and life patterns of contemporary America, reflects this (BP 2).

Although commonly expected to remain close to home and hence within the protected cultural confines of the Orthodox world, women are not immune from corrupting dangers and need fortification as much as men. Accordingly, one finds the announcement (BP 9) in English of part two of a lecture series for Jewish married women about marriage, home, and family issues. This is a direct attempt to fortify Orthodox Jewish family values, clearly under attack in America, where according to the 2000 National Jewish Population Survey nearly three-quarters of the Jewish households have no children living in them.[60] Moreover, as the placard makes clear, this is a series that will inspire, as it already has inspired "over 2000 Jewish married women." That the point of view of these lectures is to counteract the tendency of modern Jewish women to seek career alternatives to being exclusively wives, mothers, and homemakers with the Haredi ethos that encourages just these roles is confirmed by the advertisement of the inauguration of this series in both Boro

Park and Williamsburg. There is within these precincts a powerful effort to draw the Jews of Boro Park toward the sort of Orthodoxy that is at home in Williamsburg.

But there are also notices that the forces pulling the other way are at work, even though they remain firmly grounded within Orthodoxy. These include broadsides concerned with Jewish dating, a matter that we have already seen is very much on the minds of the Orthodox, for whom continuity and marriage are prime concerns. Dating is a way of finding a spouse that exhibits far more autonomy than the matchmaking that is normative in Williamsburg. There we find fund-raisers for couples; here we find vehicles that aid couples in finding each other. Hence we see a notice of a "meet your match Jewish singles every Saturday night at the Diamante Café." Here are posters advertising the use of the Internet, television, or videos, most of which are far more highly regulated by the powers that be or missing completely in Williamsburg and certainly are not subject to promotion. Here there is even a posted notice for a course that prepares people for the Regents chemistry examination, a requisite for a pattern of life and study that is not normative in the insular Haredi environment, where the idea of needing to pass the New York State examinations for college admission is unlikely to draw much interest. All these posters point to matters that the modern Orthodox *do* care about and for which an audience is still likely to be found on these streets. Such posters fortify those who want to know that these are still the concerns of the people here.

Dueling Posters.   A particularly interesting display of the contest between centrist and Haredi Orthodoxy as revealed in the Boro Park calls from the walls can be found in the juxtaposition of two posters. Found on the streets around Passover time, a period sometimes called *ben ha zmanim,* or "between-times," when the yeshivas are closed and the students (i.e., men — women are commonly on another schedule) have free time, they deal with how to fill that time in an appropriate way, and they seem to be engaged in a duel. Representing the religiously insular perspective, one poster lists a schedule of public Torah study opportunities specially designed for the period and targeted for the Orthodox communities of Boro Park, Flatbush, Williamsburg, and upstate Monsey, locations where the Orthodox population is relatively abundant. However, adjacent to this poster of public Torah talks, and wherever it is to be found in the neighborhood, is another one competing for the same free time: under the headline "rides, rides, rides, rides," it promotes a "Pesach [Passover] Spectacular," in the heart of Boro Park with many "amusements" including a

FIGURE 17: A "Pesach Spectacular" advertising "rides, rides, rides" above a poster that warns in Hebrew, "A Great Danger to the Continuity of Generations."

FIGURE 18: The rabbis' forum versus the circus and Uncle Moishy, as presented by dueling posters in Boro Park during Passover.

"military marching band," the quintessential American mark of celebration. This is the very sort of "extravaganza' that the placard posted during a similar holiday period on Sukkot in Williamsburg warned people not to attend (figure 17).

To be sure, one might argue that the one poster advertising Torah talks offers something appropriate to men while the other presents options for women and little children. If so, we can see these posters as subtly reinforcing the Haredi idea of a hierarchy of interests and concerns that separates men from women and children. Yet even if we accept this interpretation of the underlying message implicit in the juxtaposition of the posters, we find yet a third placard adjacent to these that adds to the message. As if to combat the dangers of taking the young to lighthearted entertainments, someone has placed beneath that announcement another one that, while asking for funds for a Jerusalem institution, offers a massive headline that could just as easily be referring to the entertainment hyped above. It reads, "Great Danger for the Continuity of Generations," as if to say that the public must decide, in light of this danger, how best to fill their spare time and spend their money.

Was the adjacency incidental or does it reflect an ongoing debate about appropriate activity in the Orthodox community? While there is

FIGURE 19: A choice between listening to the CD *I Believe* versus *Dance with the Stars:* dueling posters in Boro Park.

no unequivocal answer, such dueling posters appear frequently in the enclave, particularly during holiday periods when people are neither at work nor at school. Another example is in these two posters that side by side offer alternatives for the locals: one advertises "3 fascinating forums" from the Organization of Torah Classes: what is kosher, what is a *bracha* (blessing), and what is Halacha (Jewish law). The other offers "full 5 hours of world class entertainment" that includes a trip to the circus and "Uncle Moishy" and the Yeshiva Boys Choir. Which way will the truly Orthodox spend their time during the Passover break: with the rabbis at the fascinating forum or with Uncle Moishy at the circus? The message that there is a choice is either explicitly or subliminally unmistakable (figure 18).

Perhaps the most visually dramatic example of dueling posters found on the walls of Boro Park, however, involves two giant placards that are actually produced as a single advertisement, as if to affirm that the two tendencies in the Boro Park Orthodox community are institutionalized. One of these seeks to remain tightly embraced by the parochial demands of Jewish tradition, Yiddish, insular, and vividly Haredi, whereas the other tries, albeit in a limited fashion, to find a way to be worldly and American, or at least American-like, while still firmly attached to Jewish Orthodox parochialisms. Both are ads for competing discs (figure 19). One is all in Yiddish, entitled *I Believe* and showing the image of a bearded Hasid elder addressing a young Hasidic boy and sharing with him stories and parables that will instill faith; the other, in English and phrases adopted from American popular music, offers thirty-two of the "greatest dance hits of 1990 to 2004" and is called *Dance with the Stars*. To be sure, the dance hits and stars are all Orthodox groups, and they may instill faith too. But the contrast is unmistakable. This pairing sends dueling messages whose ubiquitousness is like an echo of the debate between conservatives and liberals within Boro Park's version of Orthodoxy. Buyers will have to choose between instilling a clearly Haredi faith in their children and dancing with the stars.

Leisure and Disposable Income.   We have already seen how the issue of how to spend leisure time is troublesome for Haredi Jews. It is an oxymoron for those who see the need to serve God via Torah study and prayer as constant. The American weekend—and particularly Sunday—hence is the temporal arena where the battle over leisure is fought most consistently. Thus, while some in Orthodox Boro Park are urged to "watch Judaism the series on Glatt Kosher Cable TV" every Sunday at 7:30 PM (a program, we are informed, that is endorsed by a rabbinic organization), others are offered a weekly class of the Drobritziner Rebbe in the laws of Sabbath as well as those dealing with female ritual impurity (BP 18). Now, none of these alternatives is truly redolent of American leisure—this is Boro Park, an Orthodox enclave where even the centrists tend toward Haredi practices. Yet for insiders the difference between spending the weekend before the TV or in a Torah class is significant.

The people here have a bit more money than those in Williamsburg. But how should they spend their disposable income? Other than charity, what do they do with their money? Here again the competing trends within Orthodoxy display themselves. Thus for the more religiously right-wing Hasidic subcommunity, ads (in Yiddish) urge that the money be spent at a *shtreimel* sale in Boro Park's shopping district or for a Megillah (figures 20 and 21). For those who want a more adventurous way to spend their money, there is an expensive pilgrimage to the grave of Rabbi Elimelech of Lizensk (BP 16) in eastern Europe on the anniversary of the passing of this pioneer of Hasidism. But this is no simple international journey. It is a trip toward tradition. Hence the poster shows a modern jet airplane whose logo reads *Darchei Avot* (the Ways of the Fathers).

FIGURE 20: Yiddish poster advertising "special sale" of *shtreimels* (Hasidic fur hats) in Boro Park: "The best quality, the cheapest prices—we have experienced young people who guarantee full service."

FIGURE 21: Yiddish and English poster advertising a Megillah (handwritten scroll) sale in Boro Park. "All Megillahs are 'computer checked'" for accuracy, and there are "100 to choose from."

The Haredi Trend. To discover the increasing inroads of the Haredi trend one may look at the many announcements of services providing for religious or ritual needs that implicitly mark this enclave as one friendly to the needs of a particularly scrupulous Orthodoxy, or at least one moving (or being encouraged) in that direction. These posters give a clear sense of the rituals that are considered part of the local public agenda. Thus one finds at Passover time (a period when there are many religious and ritual needs to be attended to) broadsides announcing the availability of "Pesach food for seniors," *hagalat keylim* (the painstaking process whereby utensils are immersed in vats of boiling water and thereby made kosher for Passover use), or the mystical meal for the Messiah held by some Hasidim at the holy days' end. Similarly, around the Jewish High Holy Days of Rosh Hashanah and Yom Kippur one finds notices of a *kaporos* schedule for the fulfillment of the religious redemption ceremony done by enthusiastic traditionalists with slaughtered chickens at this season.[61] And in preparation for the holiday of Shavuot, when the Jewish people's receipt of the Torah is commemorated and the Ten Commandments are read aloud in the synagogue, one finds a notice urging parents to bring their tots to synagogue to hear this recitation and join in the celebration. These all point to a more scrupulous level of observance than one might find in other Orthodox neighborhoods.

At one level, one might simply suggest that these posters reflect the scrupulosity of the Haredi Orthodox who are part of the enclave. But the fact that many of these posters are in English indicates that they are targeted to an audience for whom this is the language of religious instruction, a more acculturated audience than we found in Yiddish Williamsburg. Moreover, they suggest that this is an enclave that publicly concerns itself with its ritual observances and is trying thereby to enhance and intensify the level of community practice. For an American Orthodoxy that half a century earlier was largely invisible and followed the American dictum to keep its religion in the private domain, this is a remarkable turnaround.

KEW GARDENS HILLS POSTERS

If Williamsburg is predominantly insular and Boro Park a place where the insular and the contrapuntalist though decidedly traditionalist-leaning Orthodox contend with each other (albeit with little open rancor), and—if the numbers of posters reflecting the contra-acculturative tendency are any indication—Haredi-like Orthodoxy appears in both enclaves to be setting the trend, on the evidence of posters Kew Gardens Hills seems to

be a place where modernist tendencies and an openness to American culture and all its promises are more prominent. To be sure, even here one
can see how Orthodoxy is being pulled in Haredi directions so that what
passes as modernism and acculturation would to the non-Orthodox appear hopelessly parochial. Nevertheless, modern Orthodox Jews who are
simply contenders among the Jews of Boro Park and practically nonexistent among those in Williamsburg here have a pride of place. Thus a
"Beat Goes On" advertisement for a new record of Jewish-oriented rock
music (BP 32) that was nowhere to be seen in Williamsburg but that everywhere met its match in Boro Park, where a poster offering a schedule of
Torah study was appended to it, was posted throughout the Kew Gardens Hills shopping district during that same June. Here, however, no
contending announcements placed were nearby that tacitly and effectively
offered a more traditionally Jewish alternative of Torah study. Instead,
there were additional posters advertising other modern music for those
who wanted it. In fact, far more than in any of the other neighborhoods,
the signs in Kew Gardens Hills pointed to a Jewish community ready to
enter the garden of delights that they found in contemporary America,
yet still within a situation and setting that were clearly Orthodox.

Even here, however, and for all the apparent modernity of the Kew
Gardens Hills Orthodox population, there is ample evidence of a growing religious observance and a desire to break free from conformity to the
rest of America. We have already seen it in the architecture of synagogues
that changed from the red bricks of the early buildings that are like the
surrounding structures to the aggressively different Jerusalem stone of
today's Ohr Ha Chayim Yeshiva/Synagogue. We see it too in posters advertising everything from Dr. Ben's Kosher Vitamins to wigs for covering
married women's heads. These are signs that are common in the Haredi
sector but now have their place here. To be sure, vitamins and the wig
sale are in Boro Park, and Dr. Ben looks like a modern physician (albeit
with a beard) while the wigs are described as "stylish and glamorous," an
effort to satisfy both those who want to separate from the rest of America (wear a wig) and those who want to be like it (stylish and glamorous).

These increasingly *frum* tendencies are seen too in posters' calls to organize new synagogues on every block or even new congregations in already established synagogues, a process called by some the "shtibbliza-
tion of Orthodoxy." *Shtibbles,* or one-room chapels, are, after all, most
common in the most intensive Orthodox enclaves. They concentrate worshippers in small, intimate spaces rather than cavernous cathedral-like synagogues. Another poster concerns itself with the disposal of sacred frag-

ments of holy texts, which according to religious law must be buried along with the dead. The poster announces that for those who care about this requirement there are "pickups available."[62] These and other signs reveal an Orthodox enclave humming with intensified Jewish ritual activity, much of which is publicly proclaimed from the walls on Main Street. But the intensification of Kew Gardens Hills Orthodoxy, the process by which locals are getting *frum*mer, is not simple. Rather, it presents itself at some level as continuous with the more contrapuntalist Orthodoxy that was at one point far more dominant here.

Modern Orthodoxy in a Haredi Key.   If in Williamsburg efforts to collect money were heavily represented in the sample of posters collected in Kew Gardens Hills a cursory glance suggests that the posters' predominant concern is to promote entertainment, an indication of a community with more income and one that places a premium on leisure activities, personal pleasure, amusements, and distractions. Fund-raising is only the nominal excuse for all this; it offers moral license for the fun. The entertainments include parties and dinners, musical performances and recordings, radio station promotions, circuses and video sales. There is even a flyer offering voice lessons, something of an indulgence or extravagance. A closer look at all these, however, reveals that they are not quite what they seem and that Kew Gardens Hills is increasingly stressing its Orthodoxy in the public calls from the walls. Thus each of these entertainments is at its heart an expression of insular and parochial interests. Accordingly, one of the parties is an after-Sabbath *melave malke* (the ceremony by which the Sabbath "queen," the holy spirit of the day, is ushered out) with talks by rabbis and sponsored by two yeshivas; another is held to observe Hanukkah and another for the Jewish holiday of Purim, to be celebrated with Jewish music and more rabbinic talks. The dinners are actually a combination of fund-raisers for such causes as the Skulener Rebbe's Hasidic institutions and the support of Yeshiva Torah Vodaath, while the mixers for singles are ones meant to lead to matrimony among the Orthodox, such as the one at Midrash Ben Ish Hai for Jewish singles that offers eight-minute dates ("Date in 8") for those who are unwilling to "waste time" on dates they believe provide no chance of matrimony and who think they can quickly assess who might be suitable. The videos for those who seek home entertainments are not simply from today's films; they include one retelling the Jewish experience during the Spanish Inquisition. The circus is actually the "Amazing Fun Park" in Jacob Riis Park or "the Pesach Circus with Uncle Moishy and the Mitzvah Men who will appear in

Crown Heights." The concerts are by such entertainers as Rabbi Abraham Fried and his "Pesach-in-the-Park" musical (Jacob Riis Park in Queens, not to be confused with the Paul Simon Concert-in-the-Park in Central Park—or maybe actually to be confused with it) as well as a Jewish concert extravaganza with "13 performers in one night." And the big concert of the year with Orthodox superstars Abraham Fried and Mordecai Ben David, held in Manhattan's Metropolitan Opera House, is actually a fund-raiser for the Hebrew Academy for Special Children, an institution for disabled Orthodox Jewish children. Finally, the voice lessons are not simply for singers and speakers who want to "increase voice range, breathing and projection" or "develop a clear voice and eliminate hoarseness"; they are also for would-be cantors whose goal is to lead prayers. So what looks at first glance like a contrapuntalist Orthodoxy invited to have fun turns out on a second look to be a series of activities with more parochial and religious aims.

Even the placards advertising musical recordings for sale are presented as having a Jewish aspect. They are disks on which all the songs are either liturgical or in some way associated with Jewish themes but are set to a rock beat, and the advertised recording entitled "Trax to Relax" presents itself as the *Jewish* musical antidote to frustration, while another claims to bring "Jewish music to a new level." There are also posters extolling recordings like the album of *West Side Z'Mirot,* Sabbath songs in six-part harmony for those who, though living in provincial Queens, want to share in the more sophisticated and "in-crowd" tastes of Manhattan's Upper West Side, the current residence of choice for a hip Orthodox Jewish singles scene (of which many of the newly married of Queens may have recently been a part). There is even a CD that styles itself as appropriate for the S'fira seven-week period between the holy days of Passover and Shavuot, a time of Jewish national mourning when some traditionalists and certainly many religiously punctilious Orthodox believe the joy of music should be tempered if not completely forbidden. But in this enclave such an a cappella *kumzits* (folk gathering) recording is characterized as "100% pure" and "the perfect album for S'fira and all year round."

In short, while the language and the idiom in all these posters are overwhelmingly American and the primary frame of reference is unmistakably contemporary popular culture, the *key* of this Orthodoxy is far more parochial. Erving Goffman defines the concept of "key" as a mechanism by which something already meaningful in one way is transformed into another, patterned on the original activity but "seen by the participants to be something quite else." This process, which Goffman termed "key-ing," has the power not only to alter but also even to "inhibit original meanings."[63] That is precisely what is happening here. What might be too American, at least when looked at from the perspectives of the more insular and Haredi Orthodox, is in fact an inhibited Americanism, a parochialized cosmopolitanism. What was perhaps once viewed as a modern Orthodox neighborhood is now replaying itself in quite another key, as we learn from the posters. The inhibitions, though less powerful than those in Williamsburg and Boro Park, show an increasing influence of Haredi Orthodoxy, its norms and ethos. The posters are one of the tools of this process—both an expression *of* the change and a vehicle *for* advancing it. The shifts in key are subtle, but over time the melody of Orthodoxy will be quite different from what it once was.

Kew Gardens Hills, once a place where modern Orthodoxy was at home, is a fertile ground for those with Haredi or at least traditionalist tendencies to find an audience for their moral guidance that will keep people from being seduced by the base popular culture of America. Its change in a sense reflects the changes in modern Orthodoxy, where the constraints of what was once considered appropriate for American Orthodoxy have multiplied and become more powerful. Thus on a cold night in February a local synagogue invites in Rebbetzin Esther Jungreis, a preacher famous for her inspirational Orthodox pep talks to the religiously lax, to provide a message on "Finding Commitment in Today's Society," a lecture that will demonstrate and reaffirm the efficacy of more powerful Orthodox Jewish commitments. Similarly, another congregation announces the commemoration of the *yahrzeit* (death anniversary) of Rabbi Aryeh Kaplan (1934–83), an Orthodox moral leader renowned for his success in launching a Jewish return-to-faith movement, to be commemorated by an inspirational talk by a Rabbi Buxbaum, who will share his knowledge of the "mystical power of Jewish storytelling," a power that seeks to capture the hearts of even the most wayward Jews. Likewise there is the announcement of a series of talks by Rabbi Leib Tropper, who, aiming to prevent moral slippage among modern Orthodox Jews, will address the subjects of "Honest Truth and Real Truth," "Does Judaism Need to Be Fun?" and "A Message on Jews Uniting." One suspects his message will be that the real truth is Orthodox Judaism of an uncompromising sort that eschews the base definition of what is "fun" in favor of a deeper joy around which all Jews should unite: a message with which Haredi and traditionalist Orthodoxy would be quite at home.

Attending to these same matters, but stressing the risks that come from contact with the outside non-Orthodox environment, the dangers that lie at the bottom of the slippery slope of engagement with the modern world beyond the enclave, is a handbill informing parents that if they attend a brunch at the local Young Israel synagogue they will get a "wake-up call" from "Rabbi Shaya Cohen," described as "founder and dean" of a program dealing with "youth at risk," a euphemism for those involved in drugs but clearly carrying a far more wide-ranging meaning of risk in the context of Orthodoxy. The rabbi, local readers are told, will address the topic of "our children out of control." The concept of "control" here has a nuanced meaning, for it refers not simply to parental control but also implicitly to the control that the values, traditions, and ethos of Jewish Orthodoxy should in this enclave normally hold over its youth but that those "at risk" no longer experience.

Here in Kew Gardens Hills, where the protective barriers against acculturation are more porous than in Williamsburg or even Boro Park, there is apparently a sufficient audience for such a wake-up call. Readers are informed that this is not simply an entertainment; it has healing value, it is "better than therapy." That pitch, resonating with popular American attitudes of the "triumph of the therapeutic," would have little appeal in Williamsburg, where therapy, if pursued, is done in secret lest the stigma attached to such treatment redound to the Haredi family's disadvantage in the conservative atmosphere of the enclave.[64] In the more cosmopolitan districts of Kew Gardens Hills, however, where therapy is not nearly as stigmatizing and may even have a cachet, as it does in "sophisticated" suburbia or Manhattan, this promotion of a talk from a rabbi as "therapeutic" makes more sense. But the "therapy" is meant to make the *frum frum*mer.

These talks so frequently announced are generally discourses both for the already religious (who, judging by these posters, apparently need confirmation of their way of life before they slide down to America's lower cultural level, with its false values, continual demands for fun, and Jewishly destructive pluralist relativism) and for those with the potential to experience Jewish renewal. The latter are a common target audience for such speakers and are found among the increasing numbers of Russian or Bukharan Jewish immigrants in the area, as well as Israeli expatriates who are residents here or in nearby Forest Hills and Rego Park, have businesses in the neighborhood, or come to patronize the businesses in the area (often food establishments or minimarkets that offer Israeli-style food). The appeal may even be to the students attending nearby Queens College, where all manner of heresies may be taught. Indeed, the presence of a potential population for religious renewal and awakening in this enclave is demonstrated by the presence of one of the Chabad/Lubavitch mitzvah tanks (about which more below), parked on Main Street and advertising its capacity to ready the locals for the messianic age of salvation and religious revival. Chabad moves its "tanks" where it believes the frontlines in the culture war of Jewish Orthodoxy against secular society are to be found and where Jews can be retrieved for Orthodoxy.

Just as the "therapy" in Kew Gardens Hills turns out to be a way of becoming *frum*mer, so we discover that what appears at first glance to be a poster advertising an opportunity to experience "the *mitzvah* of nurturing yourself," a self-indulgent "evening just for women," where one can purchase cosmetics and other beauty products, turns out to be a means of drawing those who are attracted by such pleasures to a Judaism more concerned with enhancing and fortifying the Orthodoxy of the women. The event, it turns out, is to be held at a synagogue and, as the fine print on the placard makes clear, is not at all self-indulgent (as it might be in the countersociety of self-oriented American modernity). Instead, it offers as part of this "self-indulgence of self-nurturing" fund-raising for Orthodox causes and even more importantly "women to women inspiration," a kind of religious support group, lessons in braiding challah (the twisted loaf a traditional Jewish woman is expected to bake for each Sabbath), and an inspirational talk from a Rebbetzin Tehila Jaeger. To be sure, a *rebbetzin* is a rabbi's wife—no Orthodox women serve as rabbis yet—but her presence suggests an implied seal of approval from her husband. Moreover, the careful reader discovers that even the advertised "miniboutique" is also part of the fund-raising for an Orthodox Jewish organization (indeed, there is a Hebrew reference to chapter 10 of Proverbs, in which the assertion of the benefits of charity is powerfully made) and as such serves to offset even that small portion of the evening that might otherwise be viewed as an exercise in feminine vanity. Hence we can say that this is self-indulgence in a new key. Clothed, at least superficially, in the language and imagery of modern American femininity and concern for self, the evening is really just another effort to make the people in this place *frum*mer. In a sense, the poster, using the language of modern America but for a purpose that is all about Orthodox fortification, graphically and symbolically captures the nature of the Kew Gardens Hills enclave: on the surface modernist but on the road to a more energized parochialism. Contemporary American culture is simply the patina, while the content is anchored more powerfully in the substance of Orthodox values, institutions, and norms.

This is not to say that the traditionalists and Haredim have completed their conquest of the local streets. On the contrary, there are still signs of

FIGURE 22: Poster announcing "Wake-up Call" talk for parents on "our children—out of control" placed over poster advertising "Learn to Fly, better than therapy" in Kew Gardens Hills.

life in modern Orthodoxy, whose adherents have other matters on their minds. The careful observer will therefore have noticed that behind the previously discussed "wake-up-call" poster are the partially visible remains of another in which locals were offered a chance to "learn to fly" (figure 22). Those remnants of the earlier flyer are also a reminder that in this neighborhood there are dramatically different alternatives to Orthodox Jewish pursuits and the scholars' society. The observer seeking signs of alternative interests will notice a placard promoting "reflexology," which promises to teach techniques to "balance all body systems and glands." But like the partially hidden flyer, it has been concealed by the notices that assert new concerns, activities, and notices far more relevant to the people here now than the chance to learn to fly or learn reflexology.[65]

CROWN HEIGHTS POSTERS

Perhaps more than any of the other enclaves considered here, Crown Heights at once represents a far more homogeneous Orthodox Jewish community and defines a neighborhood whose boundaries are more porous. Its homogeneity comes from the fact that nearly all of the Jews who live here are either adherents of Chabad Hasidism, followers of the Lubavitcher Grand Rabbis or Rebbes, or people seeking intensified exposure to it. On the other hand, because many of the residents are also either engaged (or planning to become involved) in outreach activities to Jews, a pursuit essential to their particular philosophy, which seeks to increase the level of Orthodox religious observance in general and to draw people closer to Chabad Hasidism in particular, or the products of such efforts, a large number of those who live here are people who carry with them the cultural memory (and baggage) of another sort of life. While Chabad "converts" may want to leave behind those other lives when they complete their transformations, they cannot always do so successfully. Moreover, the outreach workers may be more open to learning about the outside world in order to better "retrieve" souls from it. Finally, not every visitor to the enclave is necessarily among the converted; many come just for a trial stay or even a first look.

In addition, the relatively small numbers of Lubavitchers in the neighborhood amplify the porous character of the enclave. These people live in an area that contains more than three times as many residents who are neither Hasidim nor Jews, and many of these neighbors have an antipathy to them.[66] The 1991 Crown Heights riots, an outbreak of violence in which one Lubavitcher (actually a visitor from Australia) was murdered and the entire community was attacked by its African and Caribbean American neighbors (who outnumber the Hasidim), was in part at least an explosion of that antipathy coupled with resentment over what many view as New York City's indulgence of the Lubavitchers as well as what some consider Jewish standoffishness and contempt toward them.[67] There have been some notable successes in diminishing these resentments, but the Crown Heights Lubavitchers are fundamentally determined to maintain a wall of virtue between their lives and the culture and society that surrounds them — not so much because of its race as because of its Americanness, perceived Gentile values, and engagement with what is viewed as among the more defiling elements of popular culture. After all, as already noted, the ability to remain apart from their neighbors is at the heart of why Lubavitchers have remained residents in Crown Heights, hoping that here their Jewish way of life will not be undermined by the importation of other lifestyles or the establishment of non-Jewish and non-Orthodox associations. In that sense, Lubavitchers here are essentially Haredi Orthodox, seeking to keep the surrounding world at bay much as the Jews of Williamsburg are. As for those who either seek to missionize or have arrived as a result of it, one must realize that the very idea of saving Jews from the surrounding contemporary culture implies an underlying suspicion of and essential contempt toward it. Moreover, most of the emissaries, or *shluchim*, as they are called in the language of Chabad, are out on their missions and no longer living in the enclave.

Posters and Solidarity. To ensure that Lubavitchers remain powerfully bonded to one another, their community, and its lifestyle and values, insiders have, like other Orthodox Jews, created multiple supportive mechanisms. These include frequent and regular assemblies for prayer and study—"770" remains open and full at all hours of the day and night for seven days a week. They include as well a plethora of uniquely Lubavitcher customs along with a calendar of communal commemorations (a previous rebbe's liberation from prison in Russia, the occasion of another rebbe's ascension to the throne of leadership, anniversaries of deaths of Chabad leaders or important figures, and so on). There are also the distinctive hats and appearance of Lubavitchers, earlier described. Finally, there is Orthodox Judaism itself, so different from the religions of the other people who call this area home (including not only Christianity but beliefs in what Lubavitcher Jews consider paganism). All this, as well as the matter of race, helps the Lubavitchers remain separate from the others in the neighborhood.

The posters found here play a role in maintaining or at least documenting this distinctiveness. Being interested in or able to read them is a way insiders can mark themselves and newcomers can indicate their integration into Lubavitcher life. The placement of most posters on the corner of 770 Eastern Parkway and the main shopping district on Kingston Avenue nearby serves to mark this space as a community bulletin board (figure 23).

Although many outsiders pass by these placards, only insiders will read them and find them significant. Overwhelmingly the notices have some Lubavitch connection, including commonly some reference to the late Seventh Rebbe, Menachem Mendel Schneerson (usually a photo or two), whose likeness dominates the area and serves as an icon that identifies the Lubavitchers. This image and often references to his messianism, so much a part of Schneerson's legacy, reflect the monothematic nature of local Orthodox Jewry. Occasionally, however, where there is some matter of general Orthodox or Jewish significance or of commercial concern not only will non-Lubavitcher signs be posted in Crown Heights but also posters

FIGURE 23: Reading the posters in Crown Heights at the corner of 770 Eastern Parkway, Lubavitch World Headquarters. Note the dominance of the image of the Seventh Rebbe and reference to his messianism, mostly in Hebrew, and when in English using the Hebrew word *Moshiach* rather than *Messiah*.

originating here will be placed in one of the other enclaves (though given the historical enmity between Lubavitch and Satmar Hasidim these are less likely to appear in Williamsburg).[68]

Thus, in the category of general Orthodox concern, we discover a poster announcing the "Bikur Cholim blood drive." While the collection points are in Boro Park and Flatbush, the poster was put up in Crown Heights too because the need for "Jewish blood" transcends geographic boundaries. Similarly, a poster describing the "Pesach experience" featuring "Uncle Moishy and the Mitzvah Men," was found hanging in Queens even though the event took place in Crown Heights and was sponsored by the Lubavitch youth organization Tzivos Hashem (the Army of God). This poster, part of an outreach effort, was hanging in Crown Heights as well at Passover time.

The presence of posters in Crown Heights that can also be found in other Orthodox neighborhoods is not only evidence of the interlinkage of the neighborhoods that make up the network of Orthodox culture. A case in point is a notice found in both Kew Gardens and Crown Heights announcing a "Chanukah Xtravaganza and Grand Menorah Lighting," a happening that has become a signature event for Chabad. Knowing of the wide popularity of this holiday among American Jews, Lubavitchers have long used Hanukkah celebrations as a means of bringing Jews closer to their traditions. Indeed, the poster emphasizes just that, announcing (in English—no Hebrew here, since the outreach targets may not be able to read it) that this will be "good old holiday fun for everyone." This phrase echoes those used by others to describe Christmas celebrations taking place around the same season, another hint not only of outreach strategies but also of the infiltration of contemporary culture into the Orthodoxy of Chabad missionizing. The Lubavitcher show comes with all the bells and whistles: "a laser light show," "live-music and dancing," "sizzling potato latkes," and "edible Chanukah gelt," reference to chocolate in the shape of money often distributed on this occasion. "Local rabbis and dignitaries" will come. The venue—not in an Orthodox enclave and hence a giveaway to the informed that this is an outreach effort—will be a shopping center on Bell Boulevard, a thoroughfare in Queens. But if this is to be for outsiders, why is the poster hung in Crown Heights?

For one thing, the event will undoubtedly be attractive to Lubavitchers, particularly those relatively new to the community for whom such outreach extravaganzas are still an inspiring come-on. They need to be told about its existence. For another, seeing that the outreach machinery is still at work and accomplishing "extravaganzas" encourages and even motivates many of the locals, for whom the knowledge that efforts at outreach and returning Jews to the traditions go on, even after the death of their leader and in the absence of a living successor for him, confirms that they are still fulfilling the essential mission of Chabad on which the rabbi sent them and for some is even evidence of the rebbe's spiritual presence among them.

One Mitzvah above All Others.   This assurance is of no small consequence. Perhaps more than anything else, since the death of their seventh and last Grand Rabbi, the community has been caught up in the dilemma of leadership. Having invested so much in their belief in his messianism and their conviction that these are the days preceding the great Jewish redemption, Lubavitchers are since his death living in what might seem to some to be the days when prophecy failed. The dissonance between their beliefs and the reality before their eyes—which is something short of redemptive—has forced many of the most ardent believers, of which Crown Heights seems these days to have many, to look for some way to resolve the apparent contradiction. In their classic study of "unfulfilled prophecies and disappointed messiahs," Festinger, Riecken, and Schachter note that the common reaction to evidence that contradicts belief is "increased fervor," in which believers often "emerge, not only unshaken, but even more convinced of the truth" of their beliefs "than ever before."[69] To be sure, they must work hard to keep themselves persuaded. Posters such as these help or at least demonstrate this preoccupation. They suggest that Orthodoxy of the Lubavitch persuasion is still, perhaps more than ever, triumphant and attractive.

The signs in Crown Heights reflect some of this increased fervor and effort. Not only do they show that the work that the rebbe encouraged—the outreach and the celebration of rituals like public Hanukkah candle lighting that he thought essential to hastening the Messiah—goes on unabated. They also provide ways for getting continuing messages from the physically absent rebbe. Thus one poster hawks some volumes of the late Rabbi Schneerson's writings, the so-called *Torat Menachem,* twenty-seven volumes that may still be used to receive instruction from him. Obviously addressed primarily to insiders who more than anyone else miss the man who was like a father to them and the focus of what can perhaps best be called a cult of personality, the poster is headlined in red in a Yiddish phrase that means something like "Grab 'em while they're hot" and then explains in Hebrew that for "only $400" a follower can own the complete set and remain informed. Some Lubavitchers also believe they can obtain hidden messages from their absent leader by opening his books at random and looking on the page for relevance to their concerns and petitions.

For those unable to understand this poster, there is one in English informing all that the printed talks of their late leader, "obligatory for every home," are now available. These are "words written in the name of the king and sealed by the king's signet-ring," a reference to the Purim Megillah but adapted here to imply that these too are words of a king, for they are "holy talks" by the King Messiah.

Deciphering the hidden messages in the rebbe's epistles requires knowledge of the Hebrew and Yiddish as well a series of abbreviations and rabbinic idioms that typically mark the text. What is there for Lubavitcher neophytes? How are they to be inspired by their late rebbe? Happily for them, Crown Heights passersby will find a poster announcing the "new release" of yet another book entitled *Secrets of the Rebbe,* a narrative and hagiography purporting to tell how the actions of their revered leaders, the two most recent rebbes, actually "led to the fall of the Soviet Union," an event of major importance not only in world history but also and particularly for the Chabad messianists. The Soviet regime and before that the Czarist one carried on a prolonged war against Lubavitch, imprisoning many of its leaders and followers. Now both these regimes have fallen (and the Lubavitch movement is alive in Russia, where the new chief rabbi and friend of President Vladimir Putin is actually the Chabad emissary in Moscow).[70] Lubavitchers would like to believe these events to be anything but random but rather the outcome of efforts by their all-powerful leaders, whom the faithful deem responsible for the demise of that "empire of evil." This secret power of their rebbe will, the poster and book promise, become manifest to believers when they read the details. The poster also hints at and serves as a marker of another concern of many of the Jews in Crown Heights: the imminence of end times and the miraculous power of their rebbes to bring it about.

As messianic expectations have swept Crown Heights, almost to the exclusion of all else, they have also taken over the calls from the walls. Thus in preparation for Lag B'Omer, a holiday in late spring, someone from the Committee to Hasten the Coming of the Moshiach (Messiah) posted a flyer urging locals (once again) to prepare for the joy of the Savior's imminent arrival. On this happy occasion the poster declaims, "The entire community, our people, the unblemished[71] and the children, are invited to participate." The people are to bring their "Messiah flags" and the women are particularly called upon to bring the "timbrels of redemption," which they will be expected to play as the congregation prepares to welcome the Messiah at 10 P.M. at 770, a building that now serves as the center of all these messianic activities.

The intensification of Orthodox Jewish life, more multifaceted in the other neighborhoods, has here become conflated with messianism and the cult of personality above all else. Thus even the most holy day of the Jewish calendar, Yom Kippur, has become associated with this activity and its concerns. Hence a poster informs believers that on the day after this day of atonement they are to start the new year with a daily schedule of "poems, songs and dances of joy in honor receiving the Messiah," which, the broadside adds, "is worthy of being made known everywhere," for these activities will ensure that all Jews in the future will "dwell in your land safely" (Lev. 26:5–13).

Signs of the near-obsession with messianism are everywhere. Not only are signs greeting the King Messiah with images of the late Seventh rebbe prominently displayed on people's houses and walls, there is also a store—the Moshiach [Messiah] Center—on the main shopping street marked with a prominent sign declaring "Welcome Moshiach." Parked nearby is one of a fleet of large caravans or "mitzvah tanks," as the Lubavitchers call

FIGURE 24a: Lubavitcher mitzvah tank, "Moshiach Is Coming Now."

FIGURE 24b: Lubavitcher mitzvah tank, "Moshiach Is on His Way."

FIGURE 25: Signs at the edge of the Lubavitcher Crown Heights promote the Rebbe and Messiah completely in English, while their non-Lubavitch neighbors promote an All-Star Mother's Day Caribbean Festival at Brooklyn College.

them, painted in blue and white and labeled with "Moshiach is coming now," Rabbi Schneerson's picture, and the Hebrew slogan "May our master, teacher and rabbi, the King Messiah, live forever" (figure 24a). Ready to go into action, the tanks' other side screams out that "Moshiach is on his way," adding that one should "do a mitzvah," for that will hasten his arrival (figure 24b). There seems to be only one "mitzvah": the commandment to prepare for and hasten the Messiah. Even the effort to spread Orthodoxy one ritual act at a time is for the Lubavitchers the means to move Heaven toward hastening redemption. Indeed, while their neighbors advertise their Mother's Day All-Star Afro-Caribbean Soul Festival at Brooklyn College, the Lubavitchers promote their late rebbe and the Messiah (figure 25). But generating and maintaining this belief require ongoing efforts, particularly among the generation who do not remember the rebbe as a living person or were born after his demise. To fire up the children with this fervor, a notice from the Tzivos Hashem Lubavitch youth organization promotes the sale of a magazine taken up with the subject and announces (in English, apparently for those to whom this language speaks most clearly), "Kids can't resist the Moshiach Times." There is of course a wish implicit in this phrase with its double meanings. Are these truly the "Moshiach times?" Can they not be resisted? Indeed, this recognition that there is an ongoing need to instill in the children a sense of connection to a rebbe whom they have never seen in the flesh yet whom they must treat as immanent in their lives is reflected in a poster and the book it promotes: *The Rebbe Speaks to Children*. The flyer informs us that this collection of talks was originally given to the Tzivos Hashem (Army of God) youth groups and is "organized according to the holidays and special seasons of the calendar." Thus it can serve as a way of inserting the rebbe into the ongoing lives of children who never knew him.

Haredi Orthodoxy in a Modern Key.   Beyond the manifest concern with messianism and the rebbe cult, there are signs in this handbill that the Haredi community often speaks in a modern key. In a magazine aiming to fire up the fervor of the young, we can hear the language of contemporary America and the infiltration of its cultural influences that have made Lubavitchers, of all the Haredi Orthodox, most at home in the idioms of modernity, people whose contact with the world beyond its enclave has clearly had an impact upon them. They have learned to speak in its terms, for how else can they bring back those who have strayed?[72]

The notice is addressed clearly to those who are attached to the norm of middle-class contemporary American culture that seeks to provide children with a stimulating and challenging learning environment. Hence potential subscribers are promised more than messianic messages. They will get "20 pages of child-tested fun" as well as "science" and "reports from around the world, nature, history"—in short, "hours of fun in every issue" that will "introduce your child to his or her Jewish heritage" even while also instilling in them the idea of the Messiah and his immanence in their lives.

Because Lubavitcher neophytes are such an important element of the Jewish life here, the Haredi ways and messianic beliefs that they are encouraged to absorb must be presented in terms they can understand and accept. But that language and worldview have undoubtedly had an impact on the natives too. Accordingly both natives and neophytes need fortification. Thus one finds a Hebrew sign (most likely targeted to the Israeli newcomers) that announces "the happy news" that a weekly class in Hasidism, to be led by the *mashpia* (spiritual guide) and rabbi Yekutiel Feldman, will be held at 667 Eastern Parkway (in the shadow of Bes Moshiach) on Sabbath mornings from 8:00 to 9:30 AM, presumably as a prologue to the Sabbath prayers. But natives need this class as well. In the same vein—this time for the English speakers—one discovers a flyer announcing a "Torah studies lecture" for "women and girls" offered by Rabbi Leibel Groner (assistant to the late Grand Rabbi during his last years and therefore sharing a bit in his lingering charisma). Finally, for those whose language and Chabad skills are undetermined or of all sorts, we discover a flyer that offers the late rebbe on video rerun, the viewing of which in a group constitutes an educational social, religious, and perhaps even ritual exercise.[73]

Mezuzah Campaign: Operation Security.   As part of his worldwide campaign of outreach missions, Rabbi Menachem Mendel highlighted a number of ritual practices. These included most prominently the study of Torah (and particularly Chabad) texts, lighting Sabbath candles (for women and girls) as well as those on Hanukkah, and affixing a kosher mezuzah to the doorposts of one house.[74] For many Lubavitchers, the mezuzah, whose placement on doorposts is a general Jewish requirement widely practiced, has, as already noted, become a matter of special concern. To indicate this, they, in line with the Haredi practice of going very public about one's Jewish identity, put up large mezuzahs. Moreover, they repeatedly check to make certain that no words or even letters on the parchment inside become illegible, an eventuality that would render the mezuzah invalid. As time wore on during the rebbe's outreach campaign, this ritual became endowed with additional elements of messianism—if all Jews had a proper mezuzah on their doors this would hasten the day of redemption and at the very least protect the Jews until that day, the belief went. This conviction became so powerful that even after the rebbe's death the lamination of additional beliefs to the mezuzah became a Chabad practice. This is seen in a poster that appeared during the early days of the latest Palestinian uprising in Israel.

Written mostly in English but with obligatory Hebrew references to Scripture, the flyer informs the faithful that when "Israel is under attack" a properly affixed mezuzah, checked by a special committee of the devout in Israel, will provide protection and security, guaranteeing that "in the merit of this mitzvah no enemy will be able to enter into the gates of Yerushalayim [Jerusalem]." Believers who "really want to do something for our brethren in the Holy Land," will spend the approximately $40 (Visa card accepted) on this item, which "possesses the same power of protection as did the blood that the Jews put on their doorpost in Mizrayim [Egypt]." It prevents, as the Hebrew line asserts, "the destroyer from infecting your home."

Without a doubt, this sort of message that portrays the mezuzah as a defense weapon that protects the virtuous would be considered preposterous by anyone other than believers, and particularly the Haredi among them. Its prominent placement in this enclave is possible only because here this sort of message makes sense in the framework of local belief, which the poster enables us at least partially to decipher. What we see here is how these ritual commandments are charged with a kind of folk belief and Hasidic spiritualism. A ritual object meant to serve as an identifier of a Jewish home has in Lubavitch Haredi iconography become a protective amulet, a barrier against contamination and misfortune.

The Movable Enclave.   For Haredi Orthodoxy, there is danger in leaving the enclave. This is a risk that Lubavitchers take on as part of their outreach efforts. However, as Haredim they prefer not to be alone out there. We learn this from a poster advertising what seems at first glance a chance for a vacation in the country but upon closer analysis is really an expression of enclavist solidarity. The ad announces the existence of a Crown Heights Bungalow Colony in White Lake, New York. Here is a chance to leave Crown Heights for the mountains without ever having to leave the protective and insular environment of Orthodox, Lubavitcher Crown Heights. Thus we are told that a hundred miles from Brooklyn is a place that offers the amenities all summer vacationers might want, including a "full size heated swimming pool" and even a "day camp" but also a "*cheder* [Jewish study hall] for boys" and "*shiurim* [Torah-study sessions] for women," an available "professional tutor" for those who need help with the sacred texts and traditions, an "air-conditioned shul [synagogue]," and kitchens that are "kosher."

But this is not just any Orthodox colony; it is one particularly tailored to the needs of the Lubavitcher Hasidim. Indeed, the copy adds that it is "great for shluchim," the emissaries who are most of their lives alone out there among the "outsiders" whom they have devoted themselves to transform. They have migrated from Crown Heights to their "foreign" postings, where they are often the only Lubavitchers around, and are trying to develop the religious life there. As such, for most of the year they do not live in a community of other like-minded Hasidim. But at times they need and want what insiders call *chizuk,* spiritual reinforcement, which they believe they can get from the presence of other Lubavitchers (or could get from an encounter with their rebbe back when he was alive).[75] For some, this means periodic returns to Crown Heights (where their return is trumpeted to everyone, even in the public bus shelters); for others it means gathering with other Lubavitchers elsewhere—for example, on holiday at a colony like the one advertised here. The poster recognizes and speaks to this need. Although Lubavitchers spend their time trying to convert Jews who are part of American culture, on holiday they want to relax in a colony devoid of most of the character of America; they want a Haredi enclave with a Lubavitch face.

Carlebachianism.   Many of those who have come to Crown Heights have done so out of their desire to affiliate themselves with the Lubavitch version of Orthodoxy. They hope that by moving here they will mark their abandonment of other ways of being Jewish and be sustained spiritually as they make the enclave their home. Some of them have made this journey from an assimilated American Jewish society, arriving with the bare minimum of Jewish background. Others, however, come at the end of a religious passage that has taken them through other Jewish renewal movements.

As long as there was a living rebbe here, newcomers and natives could be sustained by the power of his charismatic personality and the activity generated by and around him. But in his absence, they need to be sustained purely by place and community. For some the key to such sustenance is the group's messianic enthusiasms. For others, however, collective expressions of religious ecstasies and Jewish piety must suffice.

Increasingly popular as a vehicle for these is a style of prayer that has also become fashionable within the precincts of modern Orthodoxy and around its margins as part of the quest for enhanced religious spirituality. This is the so-called Carlebach minyan, a style of prayer service that uses many of the tunes and enthusiasms associated with the eponymous "singing rabbi" who died in 1994.

Shlomo Carlebach, who first reached the limelight in the 1960s, was himself a product of a synergy between Hasidic, Israeli, and American trends. Though descending from a line of distinguished German Jewish rabbis and scholars, he attached himself to Hasidic prayer styles and was for a time affiliated with Lubavitch, from which he took the idea of expressive enthusiasms in prayer and absorbed an attachment to the idea of displaying devotional ecstasy as part of Jewish outreach.[76] From American new folk idioms emerging at the time, he took the guitar, rhythms, the practice of sing-alongs, the "talking blues," concertizing, and the idea of making recordings. From Israeli culture he borrowed the idea of *shirah b'tzibbur* (choral singing as a tool of social solidarity). All these he mixed syncretistically to develop his particular style. Although at his death in 1994 Carlebach's popularity was in decline, the contemporary Carlebach minyanim have elevated him and his approach to a kind of mythic status. "Reb Shlomo," as devotees refer to him these days, is the modern Jew's counterpart to the Hasidic rebbes and other immortals that the Haredi world has enshrined. Like these rebbes, he is frequently resurrected in stories, songs, aphorisms, and teachings that are meant to shape the attitudes and religious character of those who invoke his memory.[77]

Yet these services are more than homage to the late Jewish rabbi/folksinger or songfests. More importantly, they seek to engender extravagant and presumably infectious displays of enthusiasm, devotion, exuberance, and fervor that will galvanize all those who share in the service. While once this happened in the context of a Carlebach concert, now it happens in the context of prayer. Bringing his tunes from the performance stage to the synagogue is viewed by many who do so as spiritually transformative, as a means of infusing themselves with his devotion or at the very least enhancing their own. As such, these Carlebach minyanim exchange the humdrum for the far more engagingly spiritual—a particular concern for the moderns, who have been accused and have often accepted as true that their Judaic actions lack the intensity of those who are more Haredi.[78] For them, the appeal of the Carlebach minyan is its capacity to inject a new life into a quotidian religious worship that for many has become too routinized. For the neophyte Lubavitcher Hasidim this is no less and maybe even more of a concern. They, after all, have chosen to be not simply modern Orthodox Jews but modern Hasidim, a category supposedly at a higher level of religiosity and spirituality. For the Lubavitchers, Carlebachianism can provide a kind of vitality and spiritual regeneration they associate with the popular image of Hasidism as a singing and dancing sect of zealous pietists.

The Carlebachian style has surpassed Carlebach, for it uses not only his compositions but all sorts of other tunes as well; the key is to create a kind of seamless choral singing that blurs the boundary between worship and song as well as between individual and group—what in the popular genre of modern Israeli life is called *shirah b'tzibbur*. Carlebachianism absorbs this Israeli experience but puts it into a religious key.

Yet it also mimics what goes on in American, predominantly Protestant evangelical churches, and especially African American, Caribbean, and Hispanic evangelical churches—the very ones that are in and around Crown Heights—where popular music, clapping, singing, ecstatic outbursts, and rhythm are part of the revivalist spirituality that has injected life into the Christian prayer service. Indeed, churches embracing this style of prayer frequently are filled to overflowing, while the local cathedral or parish church with its classic service style often stands almost empty. The worshippers at these evangelical services tend to be religiously conservative and often describe themselves as "born again." Their spirited worship, echoing with pop music rhythms and melodies, has been one of the most American of experiences.

Jews have watched all this without being able to share in it—and perhaps no Jews did so more than the neophyte Lubavitchers who were also concerned with religious revival. Because of their pre-Hasidic lives, many of them were not as insular as their Haredi counterparts might have been or oblivious to the popularity of evangelical styles and sing-alongs in the world beyond the Jewish precincts of traditionalism from which many had emigrated to the Crown Heights enclave. Yet while they knew what was happening among and galvanizing revivalists, they could not easily find a way to adapt this style into their own prayers. To be sure, Hasidism was always associated with singing in the popular imagination, and Chabad did have a rich musical tradition. But the idea of singing an entire service—as Christian revivalists often did—was not part of it.

Some Jews of course had already tried this. The American Reform movement was perhaps first to bring in the guitar and the keyboard and clapping to the Jewish service. The early Chavurah movement in the 1970s, emerging out of non-Orthodox (not Jewishly Orthodox) and un-

Orthodox (radical and countercultural) roots (and actually led by, among others, Zalman Schachter, Shlomo Carlebach's early singing partner), also appropriated some of this style. More recently, the notion of singing the entire Friday evening service has made the Conservative movement–affiliated B'nai Jeschurun Synagogue in Manhattan a destination for the many unaffiliated Jewish seekers who yearn for a spiritual high and a Jewish experience.

To be sure, in the Haredi world and particularly among Hasidim but also more and more in the yeshivas, the idea of *niggunim* (tunes) at prayer time was well established. Many of those who were modern Orthodox, who attended yeshivas or moved into and out of Hasidic courtyards (or those who bought the ubiquitous recordings of these tunes), carried the melodies with them and sought to recreate the style and intensity of such services wherever they gathered. Carlebachianism could bring all these musical and spiritual experiences together.

As a strategy for enhancing religious devotions, Carlebachianism suited modern Orthodoxy quite well because it was generally reserved for Sabbaths—the day in the week that became the spiritual high point for a population still living in the back-and-forth rhythms of a compartmentalized existence that rushed them into other shifting streams of involvements during the workweek.[79] But it suited nouveau Hasidim, who had few musical traditions of their own, even more. These are the sorts of Hasidim who have come into Chabad/Lubavitch. Its resonances of Israeli choral singing were also familiar to Lubavitcher newcomers, many of whom came from secular Israeli backgrounds to the new spiritual home in Crown Heights.

For many of these people the Carlebach experience, which they encountered on their way into Hasidism, is not rejected but treated as an appropriate segue to a higher level of Jewish engagement. As a result, there are those within Crown Heights who seek to enlarge or at least elaborate the relationship between their Hasidism and their Carlebachianism. Reflecting precisely this is a poster that announces a celebration of this conjunction. A closer look at the poster reveals the complex nature of this union. Although positioned on a wall in Crown Heights, the placard is addressed to "Carlebach Chassidim." Now in fact there are no "Carlebach Hasidim." Although he had his followers, Rabbi Shlomo Carlebach was not the progenitor of a Hasidic dynasty. Moreover, the only Hasidim to be found in Crown Heights are Lubavitcher or fellow travelers. This call, then, is a reaching out to those who somehow view themselves as part of this hybrid Jewish construct or who are candidates for it. That Carlebachianism is not totally at home in Crown Heights and may be a route for those who want to widen their spiritual quest beyond the boundaries of Chabad is further suggested by the fact that the celebration is to be held on a Thursday night to mark the holiday of Lag B'Omer. Moreover, the gathering is in Midwood, another Brooklyn neighborhood, and at the modern Orthodox Young Israel synagogue there, an institution not at all associated with either Crown Heights or the life of Chabad Hasidism in its enclave. Hence this poster can be seen as part of the effort of modern Orthodox Jews of Brooklyn to try to attract those who might otherwise find their way into Lubavitch. In that sense, we may understand it as a sign of part of the contest between the two streams of Orthodoxy. Carlebachianism is thus to be understood as an expression and instrument of the modern Orthodox effort at revival.

But the connection to Lubavitch is not irrelevant. A careful and informed reader of the poster discovers that the main speaker at this event will not be a Carlebach devotee at all but rather Rabbi Simon Jacobson, a Lubavitcher Hasid who is editor-in-chief of Vaad Hanochos Hatimimim, a publishing house dedicated to perpetuating the late Rabbi Schneerson's wisdom to the *timimim,* the unblemished (commonly a euphemism for the young) and author of an English-language book that according to its flyleaf sought to present "the Rebbe's teachings in profound, clear language, guiding each of us toward a meaningful life."[80] Consequently, one may safely assume that while there will be the music and spirit of Carlebach at this occasion, there will also be Lubavitcher Chabad teachings; hence the posting of the notice in Crown Heights. Does the poster aim to lead the Lubavitchers to the Young Israel or to inform them that the outreach work of Chabad goes on in Midwood, using the tools of Carlebachianism? What the poster indicates is an association between these two domains of Orthodoxy that otherwise would remain invisible to the casual observer of life in the enclave. Whether this connection suggests the blurring of the boundaries between Lubavitcher and Carlebachian enthusiasms, efforts at outreach, or the emergence of a new variant of Hasidic spirituality, time will tell; but that the Carlebach spirit is now moving into the Haredi enclaves suggests that the pathways between modern and Haredi Orthodoxy—at least in this landscape—are by no means only one-way.

The picture of these four enclaves as it emerges from even this relatively cursory survey of posters and flyers, most of which hung in public during approximately six months of the winter 2000–2001, is necessarily provisional. It is at best a snapshot of life among the Orthodox Jews in these New York neighborhoods at a particular time. In this picture, the presence of a powerful parochialism seems to be dominant.

The fact that posters from one community sometimes are situated in another, allowing various calls to go beyond the walls of a single neighborhood, suggests that these enclaves are not completely self-contained but rather constitute stations on a route traveled by many Orthodox; the influences and concerns of one neighborhood often insinuate themselves into another. And more often it is the Haredi concerns that make their way across the geographic lines rather than the contrapuntalist ones. Indeed, the posters may play a role in bringing the parochialist Orthodox *orach chayim* or way of life into the precincts of the modernist acculturative Orthodox. To be sure, one might argue that Haredim prefer the poster medium while other Orthodox use other media to communicate their views and activities. Accordingly, one might expect any review of wall posters to discover a predominance of Haredi influence. By itself, therefore, such an analysis is insufficient to prove trends.

But life does not stand still, nor does the nature of what is appropriate and expected in the enclave. "A culture is in process of constant negotiation, *within* its membership and *between* its members and the outside," as historian Emmanuel Sivan reminds us.[81] The posters that have taken our attention here and others like them will in time disappear from the walls, and the calls will change. But they will remain useful texts for those who want a window into the life to which they point and from which they come.

CHAPTER 8

Toward a Postmodern American Orthodoxy

Reality strives for diversification.

Fyodor Dostoyevsky,
The House of the Dead

At the outset of this book, the question was asked: "What exactly is American Orthodoxy?" In the language of insiders, that question becomes: "What is *frum*?" By now, the reader has seen that the answers to both these questions are contested and that today there are essentially two rival definitions reflecting two kinds of American Orthodox Jews and Judaism. What both groups seem to agree on is that the Orthodox must forever remain aware of boundaries between themselves and the proverbial other. However, one group of them—the contrapuntalists, as I have called them—believe that those boundaries can be crossed and that Orthodox Jews can become part of the world around them without losing their Jewish commitments and loyalties. In contrast, the Haredi group is certain that to be Orthodox means recognizing that one remains always the stranger, always holding onto a sense of being in exile, and that lines remain that can never be crossed. While the former have tried to be both *in* and *of* America, the latter believe there will always be elements of the way they observe their Judaism that are difficult, if not impossible, to square with American life and values.

These two points of view and the Jews who hold them have, however, begun to blur during this generation as American and Orthodox Jewish cultures have both reinvented themselves in the light of changing conditions. During that time, the Jews who were once sure about their ability to be contrapuntally American and Orthodox Jewish have expressed doubts about both the possibility and the desirability of that goal. Some of them have begun to absorb the beliefs of their erstwhile rivals and now believe that for Orthodoxy to survive they may have to give up trying to cross some of the boundaries and instead remain at a distance from elements of American life. Some have called this "the Haredization of modern Orthodoxy." Many of those who take this point of view are among the Orthodox who have come of age in the final quarter of the twentieth century and are the products of a changing Orthodox Jewish education and religious leadership. They have pulled the Orthodox communities from which they come toward the religious right and often have led their parents with them. This was possible because the contrapuntalist modern Orthodoxy from which they came never fully rooted itself in America: it was largely a product of the early enthusiasms of an immigrant generation and its children who saw in the moderately liberal America of the immediate post-Holocaust period a chance for a new sort of survival. But as liberal America became more radical, the love affair of modern Orthodoxy with it, the desire to stand with one foot in contemporary American culture and the other in Orthodox Jewish culture, gradually waned. Many of these Jews stepped back across the line, even though to take that step they had to move back further than from where they had first come.

At the same time, those who were once certain they could never be at home in America, the Haredi Jews, have found this country surprisingly able to provide them with a most hospitable environment to build their insular enclaves and develop their Orthodox culture. As the conservative side of America reasserted itself, allowing and even encouraging the public expression of religion, and as ethnic churches and identity become a larger part of the American scene, Jews who were very public about their religious practices and beliefs found they fit in more easily in such an America. A multicultural and ethnic America defines even the Haredi holdout as an insider, regardless of his or her assumptions. A Hasid in New York or Washington or L.A. is no longer a total outsider.

There are signs of a growing enchantment with Israel among some contrapuntalists, who were once ready to make their cultural home in America, believing they could have a complete civic and religious life here, but who now believe they can feel completely "at home," be full-fledged citizens and also live a religiously complete and culturally harmonious life, only in a modern Jewish state (albeit one that, in the opinion of many of them, is not yet sufficiently guided by Judaism).[1] Fourteen percent were ready to move to Israel in the 1980s, and that number is undoubtedly higher today.[2] This attitude reflects their newfound doubts about living long term in America and their sense of exile here. That at least some of these Orthodox Jews now look longingly toward Israel is also to some degree a residual effect of the enchanting time many of them spent there in the years after high school. Additionally, the turn against Israel among those who make up liberal America, particularly on university campuses, where the contrapuntalists once felt they belonged, has helped reinforce a sense of doubt about their acceptance in, and a sense of alienation from, American culture. All this has led some of them to fantasize that life in Israel could somehow bring an end their sense of exile, literally and spiritually.

On the other hand, the Haredi Orthodox, although attracted by many of the religious institutions in Israel and the growing political influence of their point of view there, still harbor doubts about the Zionist enterprise and its radical challenge to Jewish identity and belonging. They argue that one can remain in a kind of religious or spiritual exile even among Jews, particularly if those Jews have established alternative Jewish identities to those governed by Orthodoxy, as is the case in Israel. Accordingly, for many of them, while Israel is important, America—as long as it allows them freedom within their enclaves—remains an even a better place for their Judaism to survive. Here, they argue, alternative identities (which are largely Gentile) are less likely to seduce one than the alternative Jewish identities in a Jewish state. Some therefore advocate the idea that one actually can be a *better* Orthodox Jew in a land where Jews remain a tolerated minority. To be sure, in making this case for staying in the Diaspora, they fail to notice that they echo attitudes that European Orthodoxy expressed before the Holocaust.

Yet as a whole, Orthodox Jews of all persuasions still are very much a part of America. Although increasingly recognizing that there are aspects of America that could "lead them astray," they know that no state institutions or policies here specifically attempt to draw them away from even the most parochial of their concerns or behaviors. They now believe that they are more likely to do well in the current ethnic and multicultural America that accepts an Orthodox Judaism and allows those who practice it to be more *frum* in public. If the recent experiences of Orthodox Jews in America demonstrate anything, it is that even those Jews who are prepared to act as if they are totally foreign to American culture can count on the protections of the law and in some cases the political support of public officials for their right to believe what they do and live as they choose to live. Indeed, they have become more attached to American conservativism, which sees their religion as a sign that they no longer share the Jewish affinity for liberalism, and are therefore at odds with most other American Jews, who still embrace liberalism. Not surprisingly, while 75 percent of American Jews voted for the relatively more liberal Democrat

John Kerry in the 2004 presidential election and 25 percent for the conservative Republican George W. Bush, among Orthodox Jews, the numbers were almost reversed: 70 percent for Bush and 30 percent for Kerry.

One is not surprised that in 2004 access to the Oval Office is possible for the most religiously uncompromising Orthodox Jews. Those who came to the White House to light the menorah at Hanukkah this year proudly donned black hats and wore their tzitzit fringes prominently; the women they brought along wore the most modest of clothing, and the president had been warned not to try to shake hands with them, in deference to the Haredi norm.[3]

All this is not to say that this public American Orthodoxy does not experience tensions in places. Thus, while Orthodox Jews have found it possible to shape their neighborhoods—whether in city or suburb—to their particular needs, this has not always come without resistance from those who share these places with them. Sometimes the opposition has come from other Jews, who have sought assimilation and who look upon the Orthodox as unwelcome reminders of unmeltable ethnics; other times it has come from non-Jews who see the Orthodox as clannish and demanding usurpers. Yet the Orthodox have learned how to work the system, politically, economically, and socially. They are no longer willing to withdraw in the case of attack. Indeed, in their demands to live their lives as they choose, to share in the promise of America, they test this nation's commitment to diversity and the full extent of its freedom of religion. Moreover, it is not only the Haredi Orthodox who have done this.

In his very public campaign to become first vice-president and then president, Senator Joseph Isadore Lieberman provided a dramatic illustration of this Orthodox Jewish challenge to America. Lieberman, married to the former Haddasah Freilich, immigrant daughter of Holocaust survivors, is by his own description "an observant Jew" who takes those Jewish commitments seriously, in sharp contrast to most other American Jews, for whom Jewish observances have devolved to a relative few and whose Jewish commitments have limited content. Unlike most American Jews, the senator strictly observes the Sabbath and the dietary laws of kashruth, regularly attends the synagogue, prays each day often in *talit* and tefillin (items that many if not most Americans might find exotic or frighteningly unfamiliar), and has seen to it that his children receive a serious Jewish education (often in parochial schools). In both beliefs and practices he is part of a minority among American Jews, and his selection on a national ticket and serious pursuit of the White House implies that these beliefs and practices—which many American Jews have considered an obstacle to their full-fledged engagement in American life and society—do not disqualify one from being fully *in* and *of* America.

To be sure, as a conservative force within the Democratic Party, he represents a new kind of Jewish candidate. But in his aspirations and national position, his ability to stand with one foot in America and one in the Orthodox community, he helps rescue religion from what has been the exclusive, even jealous, grasp of the extreme right wing. As such, he shows America that one can embrace faith without having to choose policies that scorn or spurn values like tolerance, pluralism, and democracy. Among *frum* Jews he represents the dream of contrapuntalism, embodying the possibility of stabilized cultural dualism.

However, while he shows the world at large that one can be part of America and still Orthodox Jew, he also challenges the Haredization of American Orthodoxy, for he is suggesting by his example that there is no ineluctable contradiction between the values of faith or religious commitment and those of a liberal democracy or contemporary America. As such, he runs head on into the truisms that have in these last years become current in the Jewishly observant community. One is the scholars' society ideal that genuine Jewish commitment requires nothing less than a full-time engagement in Judaic activity. For many who espouse this point of view the goal of Jewish learning and observance has become tantamount to more Jewish learning and more punctilious observance at the expense of everything else. So powerful has this trend become that the old maxim of *tovah Torah im derech eretz,* which means that Jewish learning and observance should be integrated with a positive attitude toward and activity in the world that we inhabit, has become increasingly ignored. In its place, the maxim of *vehagita bo yomam va leila,* one should meditate on and be engaged by the Torah night and day, has taken over and become interpreted as the dominant recipe for ideal Jewish observance and life. We have seen in these pages how this has led many young observant Jews and their mentors to advocate an active ("heroic," as one rabbi called it) retreat from American (read: goyish, Gentile) public life, a stance of being *in* contemporary society but not a part *of* it. Not only has this attitude transformed the yeshivas and Jewish study halls into fortresses and many Jewish neighborhoods into virtual ghettos, but more insidiously it has given birth to a posture of disdain toward any Jews who do not share in this radical parochialism. The assumption here is that true Jewish commitments and sincere observance cannot allow room for anything else. *Frum* must become *frum*mer.

This *frum*mer tendency to dwell in America but not truly share in its culture or life has often, at its most extreme, evolved into a devaluation of American society and culture (a message heard in Yiddish sermons in the fundamentalist havens of Haredi society) or to view it at best as, in the words of one prominent *rosh yeshiva,* a "handmaiden" to Jewish life.[4] Nothing perhaps symbolized this attitude better than the case of the Yale students who, coming out of contrapuntalist Orthodoxy but having been Haredized, were prepared in 1997 to get a Yale degree but wanted little to do with Yale culture and life as found in its dormitories.[5] Of course, to many among the increasingly Haredi Orthodox, the very decision to go to a place like Yale, which represents to some the apex of what American culture has to offer, was wrongheaded. Better to stay in a Jewish environment and go to a yeshiva. Indeed, many of their *frum*mer counterparts have more and more chosen to do just that.

In contrast, Senator Lieberman's embrace of American public life, his active engagement in politics, his attachment to his alma mater, Yale University, his concern for minorities other than his own—as illustrated in his activities in the black civil rights movement as well as his voting record—and his engagement in American culture and social life, even while maintaining his high level of Jewish engagement and identity, shows his fellow observant Jews that there is room in the life of the committed Jew for activities that are not parochial. Even as he defers some of his pursuits in the American public square in favor of the primacy of his Jewish commitments and observances, he reminds his fellow observant Jews, many if not most of whom consider themselves "Orthodox," by his example that there are times when even an ardent Jew has other legitimate concerns—that indeed *tovah Torah im derech eretz.* Observance and Jewish responsibility, he suggests by example, do not ineluctably demand parochialism, a sense of exile, and a retreat from this-worldly activities or full-fledged engagement with America.

The Lieberman example seems to say, in the most public way possible, that the genuine test of Jewish faith and a commitment is the extent to which observant Jews find ways to maintain their religious obligations in this world rather than hiding within the four cubits of the Halacha or the citadels of Jewish learning. It is no trick to remain observant and Jewishly committed inside the walls of the yeshiva or the boundaries of the Orthodox enclave; everyone there does so. Actually, there deviating from the *frum* norm is more difficult than abiding by it. The true test, the Lieberman case seems to suggest, comes for those who understand other explanations for life and experience the tug of other engagements but are still able to hold fast to their Jewish faith and commitment.

This is something that contrapuntalist modern Orthodoxy long ago realized, and it is the premise of the way of life its followers champion. That is why Joseph Lieberman and people like him find a modern Orthodox synagogue to be the Jewish institution in which they feel most at home. And that is why the senator's new prominence energized many of his modern Orthodox counterparts, who see in him a projection of much that they hold dear. Yet even though Lieberman's candidacy did not succeed, his continued national prominence once again reminds those within the orbit of Orthodox Judaism that the trajectory of their lives need not always veer toward the religious right. Even more than a rabbi, who is after all primarily attached to the Jewish domain and concerns and therefore cannot serve as a role model of how to inhabit two universes, someone like Mr. Lieberman can demonstrate the capacity of Jews to be both observant and integrated in American life. As such, he stands as a constant reminder that America is not *trefe* and that Orthodoxy need not be ultimately parochial. *Frum* need not always lead to *frum*mer.

However, because many in the movement no longer consider walking down the middle of the road with a foot on each side of the cultural divide, as Lieberman and those like him have tried to do, as the safest path to ensure Jewish continuity and Orthodox survival, many Orthodox Jews have looked for signs that the senator was not actually *frum*. His discomfort with the label *Orthodox* encouraged them. Indeed, a rabbinical court in Brooklyn in 2000 excommunicated Lieberman for "claiming to be an observant Jew" and "misrepresenting and falsifying to the American people the teachings of the Torah against partial birth infanticide, against special privileges and preferential treatment for flaunting homosexuals, and against religious intermarriage of Jews."[6] While this was extreme, many Orthodox disputed Lieberman's Orthodox credentials by pointing to his infractions of Jewish law and custom in favor of the imperatives of Americanism. His Judaism was, as one commentator put it, "'a-la-carte' Judaism. He takes whatever he likes and rejects the rest."[7] Such autonomy was of course an element of contrapuntalist Orthodoxy that the Haredi version rejected. The concern among these Jews was that Lieberman could come to represent what Orthodoxy truly was and that this would signify a victory for a version of Orthodoxy that the Haredi Jews believed they had already conquered.[8]

In the end, this is a story about survival and continuity. Orthodox Jews are in one way or another still in a kind of internal dialogue and contest about how their commitments to Halacha ought to be expressed in the contemporary culture of America. What they agree upon is the need to survive: what they continue to debate is how best to do that. What complicates the debate is whether the choices they have made represent continuity or change. Those who argue that survival demands change, adaptation to new circumstances, and an ability to live contrapuntally in a variety of social and cultural contexts seemed for the early years of the post-Holocaust period to carry the day. This was helped by an initial silence among those who were doubtful about that strategy of engagement. That silence, however, was not maintained for long. Soon some Orthodox Jews, as we have seen, became outspoken in asserting an uncompromising alternative strategy of disengagement from American culture. They drew their outlook from the world of the yeshiva, which was insular, elitist, and focused on using texts as the basis of behavior. They wanted the kind of Judaism that they had fashioned in their total institutions—a scholars' society—to become normative for American Orthodoxy. That alone, they argued, would ensure Orthodox continuity. In a post-Holocaust America where Orthodoxy was reinventing itself, these two options began a contest to determine what would be normative here. And that contest, as we have seen, continues today.

To be sure, although claiming to be closer to tradition, the desire to create a yeshivist kind of Orthodoxy in America was in fact no less governed by change than was the approach of the contrapuntalists. Both were attempting something new at a time when Judaism was torn from its traditional roots in the Old World and trying to reroot itself in the New. Both types of Orthodoxy understood that "America is different." The difference between them was that the changes that would become the hallmarks of the Haredi enclave were ones that led to a sense of alienation from contemporary American society and culture, while those of the contrapuntalists led to embracing the world beyond the boundaries of Orthodoxy. The former used stringency in interpreting the demands of Jewish law—going by the book—while the latter gave freer reign to autonomy and personal choice. Increasingly, the former had the rabbis and teachers on their side (for they had trained most of them), while the latter drew their strength from the world of college graduates and those who had gone into the professions. But, as we have seen, the latter, insofar as they sought to maintain their Orthodoxy, turned their young over to the former and gave the religious leadership of their Jewish institutions over to them as well. They even sent their young out of America and placed them in the religiously polarized and more assertively Haredi environment of the Israeli yeshiva, all as they experienced growing anxiety about the American society and culture they had embraced. The passing of time also played a role, and a new generation that did not know the America with which the contrapuntalists chose to engage and who saw the Orthodoxy in the Haredi enclaves as triumphant and strong came to the fore. They moved Orthodoxy in America to a new key. In this new key, they would be *frum*mer. Yet, ironically, a *frum*mer Orthodoxy became more at home by the start of the new century with an America that included them.

But can an Orthodoxy that stresses the sense of exile and the protective virtues of life inside an enclave, that wants its adherents to remember always that Jews are strangers and outsiders, and that aspire to make the culture of the yeshiva the dominant model carry the day? One might surely wonder how long any host culture, however multicultural and religiously conservative, can tolerate the presence of a people who emphasize that they are not at home in it. Can a sense of exile be a lasting attribute rather than a temporary condition? In the face of the growing political influence of the Orthodox in America, will an Orthodoxy that advocates withdrawal from American culture truly be able to remain in a life apart from that culture?

Prognostications reflect a temptation among analysts to assume that the future can be predicted on the basis of the present trends. In fact, reality is "infinitely various when compared to the deductions of abstract thought," and groups are, as long as they continue to exist, continually reinventing themselves.[9] Although Orthodox Jewish trends today appear to incline in the Haredi direction, the Lieberman interlude shows us how the direction can shift suddenly, particularly among groups like the Orthodox, all trends of which are so much governed by other-directedness. They are after all tremendously conformist and acutely concerned with what other Orthodox Jews are doing. Moreover, the dynamics of change and reconstitution that are part of contemporary existence make any long-term predictions vulnerable.

Finally, much of the contest between the two trends in American Orthodoxy becomes muted in the atmosphere of postmodernism that has marked Western civilization since the 1980s. In the postmodern world that some have suggested we now inhabit, dichotomies are dialectically redefined. In this world, one often can avoid the either/or option of fragmentation and choose the both/and one of provisionality. In this framework one need not be either contrapuntalist or insular, modern or Haredi; one can actually be both—in a role and distant from it at once. That is why managing impressions, poses, and the ability to play many roles at once is so much part of today's world and today's American Orthodoxy. In time, might what appear to be two options in American Orthodoxy collapse into one? Could it be that sometimes one may be both less and more *frum* depending on where one is—as we have seen in the case of the American yeshiva students flirting on the streets in Israel who are considered insufficiently *frum* there but who, once returned to America, seem in that context much *frum*mer? Could it happen that people who appear Haredi will, in other contexts of their lives, also take on some characteristics of contrapuntalism, as we have seen happening in the Machon L'Parnasa and in the life to which it leads, or that the modern Orthodox will take on elements of Haredi Orthodoxy without necessarily abandoning the alternative engagements and autonomous choices, as we have seen among the young people communicating on bangitout.com? Might the lines among these communities become intertwined, as we have discovered in the posters in New York, as Williamsburg becomes more like Kew Gardens Hills, as the "artists" move in, while Kew Gardens Hills becomes like Boro Park? And what of the intramarital patterns of Orthodoxy—when someone from a contrapuntalist family marries someone from a Haredi family, do both sides bring about changes in the other? Or do people shift according to where they happen to find themselves and which Orthodox Jews they find themselves among? The life of the Lubavitcher emissary who is at once personally Haredi and publicly liberal as he or she tries to reach the Jews outside the Orthodox orbit may turn out to be the postmodern Orthodox Jew. Or, as some suggest, Lubavitch with its messianism may define a wholly new reality, not even Jewish.[10]

William James once noted that "when we conceptualize we cut and fix, and exclude anything but what we have fixed, whereas in the real concrete sensible flux of life experiences compenetrate each other." That is, reality, as the epigraph to this chapter notes, strives for diversification. The postmodern view is "suspicious of authoritative definitions and singular narratives of any trajectory of events."[11] It recognizes that America is a country that invents itself again and again, with each new wave of immigration, with each new generation. American Jews have reinvented themselves, particularly as they have become overwhelmingly native-born to this country.[12] There is reason to suppose that Orthodox Jews in America will also reinvent themselves and their movement again and again, generation after generation. A postmodern Orthodoxy may be contingent and temporary and may refuse to make claims to any single truth or grand scheme for living as an Orthodox Jew. Today, *frum* leads to *frum*mer, but tomorrow—who knows?

APPENDIX:

Representative Posters in Four Jewish Neighborhoods, 2000–2001

Note: This list is a representative collection made over the course of approximately eight months in 2000–2001. Items that appeared in more than one enclave give other enclaves in brackets (W = Williamsburg, BP = Boro Park, CH = Crown Heights, KHG = Kew Hills Gardens).

Williamsburg

1. Announcing a fund-raising dinner for a local yeshiva (Yiddish)
2. Announcing a fund-raising dinner for another local yeshiva (Yiddish)
3. *Dor Yeshurim* organization announcement for genetic testing [BP]
4. Announcing a fund-raising dinner for still another local yeshiva (Yiddish)
5. Rabbinic prohibition against attending circus (Hebrew)
6. Rabbinic prohibition against use of computer (Hebrew and Yiddish)
7. Skvirer Rebbe sermon (Hebrew and Yiddish)
8. Advocating a program of *lernen Toyreh* (Torah study) with your child
9. Siyum (celebration of learning) 7th day Passover
10. Nitra community raffle (Yiddish)
11. Another rabbinic prohibition against use of computer and Internet
12. Ad for a Yiddish version of *Around the World in 80 Days*
13. Announcing the Satmar yeshiva dinner (Yiddish)
14. Public letter from Satmar Rebbe (Yiddish)

15. Building campaign for the Satmar yeshiva (Yiddish)
16. A call to save a poor family (Yiddish)
17. Notice of a pilgrimage to the grave of a rabbi (Hebrew and Yiddish)
18. The (Satmar) Rebbe says: "I want institutions in Monsey" (Yiddish)
19. Announcing the Koshoy community day of prayer (Yiddish)
20. Torah learning for the London/Satmar
21. Prayer against "Plague of Artists" (seen in 2004)
22. "A cry for the poor" (Yiddish)
23. Announcing a $10K raffle [BP]
24. Unity rally for Jewish brotherhood (Yiddish)
25. Selling Catskills development
26. Notice of a pilgrimage to Talner Rebbe's grave in Chelsea, Mass.
27. Ad for Feltly Hats (Yiddish)
28. Announcing a party for a prospective bride
29. Ban and notice of nonkosher restaurant
30. Announcing a Rabbi Shimon Ben Yochai *hilula* (memorial) celebration
31. Sale of new book on intracommunal peace (Yiddish)
32. Sale of phone card [BP]
33. Raffles (three different posters and raffles)
34. Announcement of Megillah sales
35. Sneaker sale
36. A talk on *tzinus* (modesty) (Yiddish)
37. Ulpana (study hall for women) talk
38. Open house party
39. A call for an end to internal quarrels among Satmar (Hebrew and Yiddish)
40. Celebrating fifty years of a school dinner
41. Announcing the play *Stadt fun Shrek* (City of Fear) (Yiddish)
42. Satmar yeshiva dinner on Shabbat Shkalim (a Sabbath preceding Passover)

Boro Park

1. Abraham Fried concert [KGH]
2. Megillah sale and *chizuk* (religious enrichment) talk
3. Seder *ben ha zmanim* (vacation) schedule of Torah study [W] (Hebrew)
4. Pesach Spectacular
5. Pesach food for senior citizens
6. Announcing Seudat ha Moshiach (messianic symbolic meal) on Pesach
7. *Hagalat keylim* (Passover ritual immersion of utensils) announcement
8. Seder *ben ha zmanim* (vacation) Torah learning schedule
9. Convention of "Jewish married women"
10. An ad for *Rebbe Hill* book series [W]
11. "Watch kosher cable TV"
12. "Meet your match" Jewish singles
13. Torah convention schedule (Hebrew)
14. Ad for Jewishly appropriate videos
15. Ad for study aids for chemistry (NY) Regents exam

16. Announcing a pilgrimage to Lizensk (a Hasidic site in eastern Europe) (Hebrew)
17. A call to protest the Tal Commission's finding in favor of a Haredi draft (Yiddish)
18. Announcing Torah classes of the Dobritziner Rabbi (Hebrew)
19. Megillah for sale
20. Announcing "Kahane was Right" dinner
21. Men's clothes sale [W]
22. Lecture on the Jewish married woman's view [W]
23. Announcing a Halachic ruling against cutting beard
24. *Shtreimel* (Hasidic fur hat) sale
25. *Kaporos* (ceremony of scapegoating chickens on the eve of Yom Kippur) schedule
26. Announcing a Chinese auction [KHG]
27. Urging people, "Bring your kids to shul (on the forthcoming Shevuot holy day) to hear the reading of the 10 commandments"
28. Tech class announcement
29. Ad for kosher vitamins
30. Felder for City Council
31. List of classes offered in the neighborhood
32. Ad for CD, *The Beat Goes On* (dances)
33. Chinese auction for reproductive program for infertile women

Crown Heights

1. Blood drive
2. Hanukkah extravaganza
3. Gala dinner seating plan
4. Ad for Crown Heights bungalow Colony
5. An ad for the book *Secrets of the Rebbe*
6. Inauguration of a class on Hasidism
7. Hats for sale
8. Shoes for sale at Sneaker City
9. Kehot Publications (a Lubavitcher publishing house) book sale
10. Women's study class
11. Urging readers to put up a mezuzah on the doorposts as a means for protecting the Land of Israel
12. Help us raise money
13. Welcome Moshiach (Messiah) on (the holiday of) Lag B'Omer
14. Sale on *Torat Menachem* books (twenty-seven-volume set of talks and Hasidic discourses by the Seventh Lubavitcher Rebbe)
15. Hanukkah sale, computer courses, Garden of Delights Chinese auction
16. "Kids can't resist Moshiach Times"
17. Mitzvah tank
18. Sign for the Moshiach Center
19. Tefillin warning (explaining how important it is that they be worn at daily prayers)

20. Offer of a video of the (Seventh) Rebbe
21. Urging people to come "dance and sing for Moshiach"
22. Announcing a gathering called Simchat L'Chatchila Ariber (a Lubavitcher concept of surmounting all obstacles)
23. Welcoming the rebbe's emissaries, at the Metropolitan Transit Authority bus stop

Kew Gardens Hills

1. An offer of voice lessons
2. An ad urging people to sign up for phone service that will make a donation to a yeshiva for each new customer
3. Ad for Radio Kol Haneshama, a radio channel broadcasting from Israel in Hebrew (Orthodox programming)
4. Ad for "CD Trax to Relax"
5. Synagogue talk to commemorate a *yahrzeit*
6. *Mesibat* Hanukkah party
7. An announcement (English) of a day of repentance
8. Announcing dinner on behalf of Yeshiva Torah Vadaath
9. "Jewish hottest singles" dinner party
10. Pesach Circus with Uncle Moishy [CH]
11. Rebbetzin Jungreis talk
12. Rabbis' and rebbetzin talks
13. A call for yeshiva boys to teach Russian immigrants
14. Pro Achdus [Unity] summer camp
15. Purim concert
16. Announcing a women's wig sale
17. Skulener Rebbe visit and dinner
18. Abraham Fried concert /entertainment
19. Kumzits (musical group) album sale
20. Announcing "Dr. Ben's kosher vitamins"
21. Announcing help in preparing for the New York State Regents' chemistry exam.
22. Announcing a circus and Haggadah sale for Passover
23. Announcing *sheimos* (disposal of sacred fragments)
24. Ad for reflexology
25. Announcing an Abraham Fried and Ben David concert
26. *Agunah* (chained women—i.e., unable to secure a divorce) crisis conference
27. Public gathering to honor soldier (Hebrew and English)
28. Announcing speed-dating "Date in 8"
29. Announcing a mitzvah tank in Queens
30. The Mitzvah of Nurturing Yourself
31. *Melave malke*
32. Ad for CD *The Beat Goes On* (dances) [BP]
33. Rabbi speaks about "children at risk"

34. Help with computer problems
35. B'Orech Yomim elder care talk
36. Warning on kashruth of cough medicine
37. Sale of video on Jews in the Spanish Inquisition [BP]
38. Agudah special education program [BP]
39. Shimon Kugel CD
40. HASC Fried/ Ben David concert
41. Announcing a new minyan (gathering for prayer)

Notes

Introduction

Epigraph from Marcus Lee Hansen, "The Study of Man: The Third Generation in America," *Commentary* 14 (November 1952): 496.

1. Egon Mayer, "Jewish Orthodoxy in America: Towards the Sociology of a Residual Category," *Jewish Journal of Sociology* 15 (December 1973): 151–65; Marshall Sklare, *Conservative Judaism: An American Religious Movement* (1955; reprint, New York: Schocken, 1972), 43.

2. Sklare, *Conservative Judaism*, 265–66.

3. Steven M. Cohen and Arnold M. Eisen, *The Jew Within: Self, Family, and Community in America* (Bloomington: Indiana University Press, 2000), 2, 7, 6, 37, 24. For similar attitudes and opinions, see Samuel Heilman, "Holding Firmly with an Open Hand," in *Jews in the Center: Conservative Synagogues and Their Members,* ed. Jack Wertheimer (New Brunswick, NJ: Rutgers University Press, 2000), 95–196.

4. This remains true even in their suburban outposts. See Etan Diamond, *And I Will Dwell in Their Midst: Orthodox Jews in Suburbia* (Chapel Hill: University of North Carolina Press, 2000), 24.

5. In his *Modern Yiddish-English Dictionary* (New York: Yivo and McGraw-Hill, 1968), Uriel Weinreich defines this Yiddish term as "pious" and "devout" (336). However, in colloquial parlance, because of the varying nuances of piety and devoutness within the Orthodox world—as these pages will demonstrate—the term actually denotes a pattern of behavior that in the context of a particular Orthodox community qualifies as sufficiently devout or pious. That this Yiddish term has the linguistic flexibility that allowed it to be so manipulated can be seen in the fact that a variant of it, *frumak,* Weinreich's dictionary defines as meaning "hypocritically pious," while Alexander Harkavy's *Yiddish-English Dictionary* (New York: Hebrew Publishing Company, 1898) defines the same term as "ex-

cessive piety" (278). The clear inference is that one community's *frum* individual may turn out to be another's *frumak,* and even there the distinction between what is excessive and what hypocritical piety is not always clear.

6. Samuel Heilman, *Synagogue Life: A Study in Symbolic Interaction* (1976; reprint, with new introduction and afterword, New Brunswick, NJ: Transaction Publishers, 1998), 12, 26. See also Samuel Heilman, "Frum and Frummer," *Jerusalem Post,* May 25, 2004, 13.

7. Mary Douglas, *In the Wilderness: The Doctrine of Defilement in the Book of Numbers* (Sheffield: Sheffield Press, 1993).

8. Emmanuel Sivan, "The Enclave Culture," in *Fundamentalisms Comprehended,* ed. Martin E. Marty and R. Scott Appleby (Chicago: University of Chicago Press, 1995).

9. The Hebrew term *haredi* (*haredim* in the plural) was for a time was used to denote any Jew who was punctilious about religion. But increasingly in the last fifty years it has come to designate those Jews who in their style of life, worldview, ethos, and beliefs were beyond what most people seemed to understand by *Orthodox,* a word that by itself was problematic and often exchanged for the term *religious* in English or *dati* in Hebrew. In some circles, the term *ultra-Orthodox* seemed to work, and in the English-speaking world it still serves as a shorthand marker, but (like *Orthodox*) it is a term that came from a language foreign to Jewish experience and thus could not precisely capture the essentials of the people it was meant to describe. Something more was needed. That something was *haredi,* a biblical term in its origins. Appearing in Isaiah (66:2), the term *hared,* often translated into English as "one who trembles," is used to describe one of those special sorts of people—along with the poor and those of contrite spirit—to whom, according to the prophet, the Lord will pay heed. The *haredim* are the ones to whom Isaiah (66:5) says God speaks: "Hear the word of the Lord, you who tremble [*haredim*] at His word." For more, see below and also Samuel Heilman, *Defenders of the Faith: Inside Ultraorthodox Jewry* (Berkeley: University of California Press, 1999).

10. For more on these groups, see Samuel Heilman and Menachem Friedman, "Religious Fundamentalism and Religious Jews: The Case of the 'Haredim,'" in *Fundamentalisms Observed,* ed. Martin E. Marty and R. Scott Appleby (Chicago: University of Chicago Press, 1991), 197–264.

11. Aaron Twerski, "Experiencing Golus in a Free Society—Can It Be Achieved? The Stumbling Blocks," *Jewish Observer* 13 (December 1978): 6, 7.

12. Shimon Schwab, "The Great Awakening" (1978), in *Selected Writings: A Collection of Addresses and Essays on Hashkafah, Jewish History and Contemporary Issues* (Lakewood, NJ: C.I.S. Publications, 1988), 160, 162.

13. Ibid., 162.

14. Cohen and Eisen, *Jew Within,* 12. The figure of 600,000 is an estimate based upon a variety of Jewish population surveys, about which more below.

15. Zvi Holland, "In Defense of Orthodox," *Jewish News of Greater Phoenix,* June 20, 2003.

16. For a full discussion of the demographics, see chap. 2.

17. Steven M. Cohen, "Ethnic Stability, Religious Decline," unpublished paper, Florence G. Heller/JCCA Research Center, Waltham, MA, 1998.

18. The 2000 U.S. Census, for example, reports that in the village of Kaser, an all-Vizhnitz Hasidic enclave in suburban New York, almost 88 percent of residents are native born. In the Satmar Hasidic village of Kiryas Joel the figure is an even higher 91 percent. U.S. Bureau of the Census, "Fact Sheet: Kaser Village, New York" and "Fact Sheet: Kiryas Joel Village, New York," retrieved October 28, 2005, from http://factfinder.census.gov/home/saff/main.html?_lang=en.

19. Jacob Ukeles, "A Quantitative Profile of Orthodox Jewry," paper presented at the Edah Conference, New York, February 20, 2005.

20. James Schwartz, Jeffery Scheckner, and Laurence Kotler-Berkowitz report in "U.S. Synagogue Census, 2001," *American Jewish Yearbook* (Philadelphia: American Jewish Committee, 2002), that of the 3,727 synagogues in the United States in 2001, 40 percent are Orthodox.

21. J. J. Goldberg, "America's Vanishing Jews," *Jerusalem Report,* November 5, 1992.

22. Uriel Heilman, "Whitefish Salad and Bison Beef at Annual Kosher Food Trade Show," Jewish Telegraphic Agency, November 4, 2003, retrieved October 28, 2005, from www.jta.org/page_view_story.asp?intarticleid=13410&intcategoryid=5.

23. Diamond, *And I Will Dwell,* 121, and Howard G. Goldberg, "Slaves No More to Sweet Wine," *Jerusalem Report,* April 20, 1995, 56–57.

24. *Kosher Today,* "Newspaper Archives," December 24, 2002, retrieved December 24, 2002, from www.koshertoday.com/archives_issue.asp.

25. See "The U.S. Market for Kosher Foods," April 1, 1998, retrieved September 22, 2005, from www.packagedfacts.com/pub/112882.html.

26. Actually, the kosher traveler can choose in many cases between kosher and *glatt* kosher meals and snacks.

27. Eliot Cohen, introduction to *Commentary on the American Scene: Portraits of Jewish Life in America,* ed. Eliot Cohen (New York: Knopf, 1953).

28. Lawrence Grossman, "Orthodoxy Is All the Rage," *Jewish Forward,* December 14, 2001. The Synagogue Council of America fell apart in 1994 when the Orthodox decided to pull out. "In Brief," *Washington Post,* February 27, 1999, B8.

29. Nathan Glazer, *American Judaism* (Chicago: University of Chicago Press, 1957), 147.

30. Hent de Vries, "In Media Res: Global Religion, Public Spheres, and the Task of Contemporary Comparative Religious Studies," in *Religion and Media,* ed. Hent de Vries and Samuel Weber (Stanford, CA: Stanford University Press, 2001), 3.

31. See ibid., 7, and Marty and Appleby, *Fundamentalisms Observed.*

Chapter 1. Orthodoxy in America after the Holocaust

Epigraphs from Eliezer Gershon Friedenson, *Beth Jacob Journal,* June 27, 1938, quoted in Joseph Friedenson, "Remembering the Second Siyum Hashas," *Jew-*

ish Observer 23 (April 1990), 9, and Hua-Pen, "Song of the Forsaken Wife," in *A Treasury of Chinese Literature,* trans. and ed. Ch'u Chai and Winberg Chai (New York: Appleton Century, 1965), 144.

1. This Zionist attitude was called in Hebrew *shlilat ha golah,* negating the Diaspora.

2. On the Hatzalah program, see Efraim Zuroff and Yehuda Bauer, *The Response of Orthodox Jewry in the United States to the Holocaust* (New York: Ktav, 2000), and Y. Rosenblum, *They Called Him Mike: Reb Elimelech Tress—His Era, Hatzalah, and the Building of American Orthodoxy* (New York: Mesorah Publications, 2000). On interwar Orthodoxy in America, see also Jenna Weissman Joselit, *New York's Jewish Jews* (Bloomington: Indiana University Press, 1990).

3. See chap. 2.

4. Yehuda Nir, a psychiatrist whose clientele is heavily populated by members of the Satmar Hasidic community in Brooklyn, asserts that no one he treats has not had some immediate contact with the Holocaust (Yom HaShoah address, April 29, 1992, Young Israel of Scarsdale, New York). See also William B. Helmreich, who notes in *Against All Odds: Holocaust Survivors and the Successful Lives They Made in America* (New York: Simon and Schuster, 1992), 78–79, that 41 percent of the Holocaust survivors he interviewed were Orthodox. In general, most American Orthodox Jews (and their institutions) trace their origins to the years just before or after the Second World War. On the actual numbers, see chap. 2.

5. Erik Erikson, "Identity and Uprootedness in Our Time," in *Insight and Responsibility* (New York: Norton, 1984), 85–86.

6. Arnold Van Gennep, *The Rites of Passage* (Chicago: University of Chicago Press, 1960).

7. On the origins of Orthodoxy, see Moshe Samet, "The Beginnings of Orthodoxy," *Modern Judaism* 8 (October 1988): 249–67, and Samuel Heilman, "The Many Faces of Orthodoxy, Part I," *Modern Judaism* 2 (February 1982): 23–51, and "The Many Faces of Orthodoxy, Part II," *Modern Judaism* 2 (May 1982): 171–98. There were also those who advocated the so-called historical school of Judaism that valued tradition as normative and positive but looked for ways to make changes that were in harmony with Jewish history. Conservative in their willingness to bring about that change, they were nevertheless less adamant in their attachments to tradition than Orthodoxy proved to be. See Moshe Davis, *The Emergence of Conservative Judaism: The Historical School in Nineteenth Century America* (Philadelphia: Jewish Publication Society, 1963).

8. Not only the students in these yeshivas but also their teachers, the rabbis, were aware of and influenced by the culture of the world beyond the Jewish one. See, for example, Emanuel Etkes and Shlomo Tikochinski, "Introduction," in *Yeshivot Lita, Pirkei Zichronot* [Memoirs of the Lithuanian Yeshiva], ed. Emanuel Etkes and Shlomo Tikochinski (Jerusalem: Shazar Institute, 2004), 36; B. Epstein, "The Netziv of Volozhin," in Etkes and Tikochinski, *Yeshivot Lita,* 72–73; and Shmuel Leib Citron, "The Dynastic Battles in the Volozhin Yeshiva," in Etkes and Tikochinski, *Yeshivot Lita,* 82–84.

9. *Verbesserung* literally means "improvement," which was what most of its supporters believed it promised those who embraced it.

10. See Heilman, "Many Faces of Orthodoxy, Part I," and "Many Faces of Orthodoxy, Part II."

11. Ramaz School, "Mission Statement for the Ramaz School," March 4, 1992, retrieved September 22, 2005, from www.ramaz.org/public/mission_s.cfm.

12. I thank Rabbi Shubert Spero (pers. comm., March 2004) for this insight.

13. For many central European Jews, that high culture was German. For a discussion of some of these Jews, the so-called Prague Circle of Jewish writers, see Scott Spector, *Prague Territories: National Conflict and Cultural Innovation in Franz Kafka's Fin de Siècle* (Berkeley: University of California Press, 2000), xiv, 331.

14. See Michael Silber, "The Emergence of Ultra-Orthodoxy: The Invention of a Tradition," in *The Uses of Tradition: Jewish Continuity since Emancipation,* ed. Jack Wertheimer (New York: Jewish Theological Society of America, 1992), 23–84.

15. Moshe Sheinfeld, *Diglenu,* Summer 1945, quoted and translated in Menachem Friedman, "The Haredim and the Holocaust," *Jerusalem Quarterly* 53 (Winter 1990): 95. Where Friedman has used the word *haredi* in his translation I have used the word *orthodox,* which in this context is a synonym.

16. Ibid., 96.

17. Ibid.

18. Netty Gross, "Why Did God Do This to Us?" *Jerusalem Report,* May 8, 2000.

19. See Samuel Heilman, *Portrait of American Jews: The Last Half of the Twentieth Century* (Seattle: University of Washington Press, 1995).

20. Assimilation "involves not only the acceptance of the dominant culture but also the *rejection* of the assimilating person's native culture as inferior, backward, and unworthy." J. E. Thompson and H. O. Thompson, "Teaching Ethics to Nursing Students," *Nursing Outlook* 37, no. 2 (1989): 80. See also Robert Redfield, Ralph Linton, and M. J. Herskovits, "Memorandum for the Study of Acculturation," *American Anthropologist* 38 (1936): 149–52.

21. See for example, Deborah Dash Moore, *At Home in America: Second Generation New York Jews* (New York: Columbia University Press, 1981).

22. To be sure, such behavior reflected attitudes that had begun during the modern period of Jewish emancipation and enlightenment, experienced first in German-speaking countries and then gradually throughout Europe, where Jews had gone from being barely tolerated minorities to being legal citizens. Then too they had given up, for example, Jewish languages and appearance in favor of the tongues and life patterns of the surrounding and dominant non-Jewish cultures. But the Nazis and their supporters had cut off this development, while America and Israel, which became increasingly the homes of Jews, allowed, and indeed encouraged, this acculturative transmigration.

23. The term originates in the Talmud but toward the end of the nineteenth century in eastern Europe became more widely used to refer to the way traditional Jews would live their lives (Menachem Friedman, pers. comm., January 2002).

24. There are reports of well-known Hasidic rabbis who shaved their beards and cut their earlocks and moved to Manhattan.

25. Mordechai Gifter, "A Path through the Ashes," adapted by R. Zipsiner and N. Wolpin, *Jewish Observer* 10 (June 1974), reprinted in *Jewish Observer* 22, no. 1 (1989): 82, reflecting on the comments of the Nitra Rav, who said, "For those who doubt and ask there are no answers."

26. See Efraim Zuroff and Yehuda Bauer, *The Response of Orthodox Jewry in the United States to the Holocaust* (New York: Ktav, 2000), and Friedman, "Haredim and the Holocaust," 96. See also Gross, "Why Did God Do This to Us?"

27. Lucy Dawidowicz, *The War against the Jews, 1933–1945* (New York: Bantam, 1976), 236.

28. See, for example, a 1987 letter to the editor (*London Times,* May 9, 1987), in which the Orthodox Lord Immanuel Jakobovits, then Chief Rabbi of the United Kingdom, asserted that the Nazi Holocaust was divine punishment for the apostasy of the German Jews who had founded assimilationist Reform Judaism. Moshe Sheinfeld suggested that "Zionists deliberately provoked Hitler from the 30s on, hoping for a mini-bloodbath that would spark mass emigration to Palestine." See Gross, "Why Did God Do This to Us?"

29. See, for example, below, the remarks of Rabbi Yaakov Perlow, member of the Moetzes Gedolei HaTorah of Agudath Israel of America, in "Our Generation: Churban Plus One," *Jewish Observer* 11 (June 1976): 10. See also Samuel C. Heilman, "The Ninth Siyum HaShas at Madison Square Garden: Contra-Acculturation in American Life," in *Americanization of the Jews,* ed. Norman Cohen and Robert Seltzer (New York: New York University Press, 1995), 311–38. On the role of the Temple's destruction in mourning, see also Samuel C. Heilman, *When a Jew Dies: The Ethnography of a Bereaved Son* (Berkeley: University of California Press, 2001). Whereas the Israelis had chosen to commemorate the Sho'ah by recalling the day that the Jews fought back—the start of the Warsaw Ghetto uprising (the day was officially called Yom Ha Sho'ah ve Ha Gevurah, the day of destruction and heroism), the traditionalist Orthodox chose the day when Jews recalled generations of suffering and destruction.

30. Yitzchok Hutner, "Holocaust—A Study of the Term, and the Epoch It Is Meant to Describe," trans. and ed. Chaim Feuerman and Yaakov Feitman, *Jewish Observer* 12 (October 1977): 6–12. See also Ruth Ebenstein, "Remembered through Rejection: *Yom Hashoah* in the Ashkenaz Haredi Daily Press, 1950–2000," *Israel Studies* 8, no. 3 (2003): 141–67.

31. Hutner, "Holocaust," 5.

32. Walter S. Wurzburger, "Is Modern Orthodoxy an Endangered Species?" n.d., retrieved August 7, 2005, from Orthodox Caucus Web site: www.orthodoxcaucus .org/projects/rove/wurzburger2.htm.

33. Leon Festinger, Henry Riecken, and Stanley Schachter, *When Prophecy Fails* (New York: Harper Torchbooks, 1956), 3.

34. Ibid.

35. Gross, "Why Did God Do This to Us?"

36. This included, for example, such institutions as "Make Friday Night into

Shabbat," a variety of Yeshiva University outreach programs, and the active efforts of Chabad/Lubavitch, with its "mitzvah tanks" and Chabad Houses manned by emissaries or *shluchim* whose goal was nothing short of transforming all Jews into Lubavitcher Hasidim.

37. Joel Wolowelsky, "Observing Yom HaSho'a," *Tradition* 24 (Summer 1989): 50.

38. Moshe Prager, "Kiddush Ha Hayim," quoted in Pesach Schindler, "The Hasidic Movement during the Holocaust," *Tradition* 13 (Spring 1973): 93.

39. Hillel Goldberg, "Holocaust Theology: The Survivors Statement Part II," *Tradition* 20 (Winter 1982): 347.

40. See Heilman, "Ninth Siyum HaShas."

41. Michael Wyschograd, "Auschwitz: Beginning of a New Era? Reflections on the Holocaust," *Tradition* 16 (Fall 1977): 68.

42. Perlow, "Our Generation," 10.

43. Wyschograd, "Auschwitz," 68.

44. There is even an effort in some quarters today to point out that some Hasidic rabbis took a much stronger role in the resistance to the Holocaust. See, for example, the literature on Rabbi Menachem Zemba (1882–1943), the Hasid of Gur, who is hailed as one of the inspirational voices arguing for resistance inside the Warsaw Ghetto.

45. Joel Cohn, "Kristalnacht at SAR," *Ten Da'at* 5 (Spring 1991): 42.

46. Gifter, "Path through the Ashes," 80.

47. Sigmund Freud, *Totem and Taboo,* trans. James Strachey (1950; reprint, New York: Norton, 1962), 144.

48. Ibid., 145.

49. See ibid., esp. 135–50, where Freud suggests the range of ambivalence and the various sources of guilt and longing.

50. Ibid., 143.

51. Samuel Heilman, *Defenders of the Faith: Inside Ultra-Orthodox Jewry* (Berkeley: University of California Press 1999), 272.

52. A. Scheinman, "Bikrovei Ekodeish: The Six Million 'Kedoshim,'" *Jewish Observer* 15 (September 1980): 9.

53. Goldberg, "Holocaust Theology," 347.

54. Zech. 3:2.

55. Yisrael Spiegel, "And They Have Sought out Many Devices," *Yated Ne'eman,* April 28, 2000, 5, trans. in Ruth Ebenstein, "Remembered through Rejection: Yom HaShoa in the Ashkenazi Haredi Daily Press, 1950–2000," *Israel Studies* 8, no. 3 (2003): 141.

56. Ibid.

57. Charles Liebman, "Orthodoxy in American Jewish Life," in *The Jewish Community in America,* ed. Marshall Sklare (New York: Behrman House, 1974), 48; Yaakov Weinberg, "Experiencing *Golus* in a Free Society—Can It Be Achieved? The Awareness Imperative," *Jewish Observer* 13 (December 1978): 4. The article is based on a speech given before the national convention of Agudath Israel of America.

58. The term comes from a speech by Hyman Cline transcribed in the *Mai-

monides Dinner Journal, January 7, 1945, and quoted in Seth Farber in *An American Orthodox Dreamer: Rabbi Joseph B. Soloveitchik and Boston's Maimonides School* (Boston: University Press of New England, 2004), 99. The Maimonides School is an institution of modern Orthodoxy.

59. Lawrence Kaplan, "Rabbi Isaac Hutner's 'Daat Torah Perspective' on the Holocaust: A Critical Analysis," *Tradition* 18 (Fall 1980): 247.

60. Quoted in Chaim Dov Keller, "Modern Orthodoxy: An Analysis and a Response," *Jewish Observer* 6 (June 1970): 3–14, emphasis added.

61. The quoted phrases come from Leo Jung, "What Is Orthodox Judaism?" in *The Jewish Library,* 2nd ser., ed. Leo Jung (New York: Bloch, 1930), 115, and Joseph Dov Soloveitchik, "Confrontation," *Tradition* 6, no. 2 (1964): 5–9 (originally a paper presented at the 1964 Midwinter Conference of the Rabbinical Council of America [RCA]). Although Soloveitchik's concern here was interfaith dialogue, his words reflect his attitudes about Orthodox Judaism no less. Indeed, as Seth Farber notes, "Rabbi Soloveitchik's positions regarding interdenominational cooperation and recognition resonate of his positions regarding the Catholic Church as outlined in his famous essay 'Confrontation'"; moreover, as chair of the Halacha Commission of the RCA, he discouraged interdenominational cooperation. See Seth Farber, "Reproach, Recognition and Respect: Rabbi Joseph B. Soloveitchik and Orthodoxy's Mid-century Attitude toward Non-Orthodox Denominations," in *American Jewish History* 89 (June 2001): 193 n. 21.

62. Wurzburger, "Is Modern Orthodoxy an Endangered Species?"

63. Keller, "Modern Orthodoxy," 12. Although Keller, a disenchanted modern Orthodox Jew, claims to eschew this position as fallacious, he perfectly articulates it as only a former true believer could.

64. Ramaz School, "Mission Statement."

65. The instrumentality for this was the Committee on Jewish Law and Standards, as well as a series of other commissions.

66. This was the fear of Rabbi Joseph Dov Soloveitchik, according to his daughter, and was why he took his most confrontational stance against it and its institutions. See Tovah Lichtenstein, "The Rav from a Distance: Retrospective Reflections," paper presented at the Conference Exploring the Influence of Rabbi J. B. Soloveitchik, Van Leer Jerusalem Institute, Jerusalem, December 31, 2003. It was also the expectation of Conservative Jews;: see Sklare, *Jewish Community,* 43.

67. The debate as to whether microphones could be used in synagogues on the Sabbath was an example of this. While some Orthodox synagogues accepted this technological innovation when it first became available, the embrace of it by the Conservative movement quickly resulted in even the modern Orthodox rejecting it. See Emanuel Rackman, "Orthodox Judaism Moves with the Times," *Commentary* 13 (June 1952): 545–50.

68. For more on this school of thought, see Heilman, "Many Faces of Orthodoxy, Part I," and "Many Faces of Orthodoxy, Part II."

69. Born in Lithuania, Revel was ordained at age sixteen, earned a Russian high school diploma, apparently through independent study, became involved in the Russian revolutionary movement, and following the unsuccessful revolution

of 1905 was arrested and imprisoned. Upon his release the following year, he emigrated to the United States and studied at the seminary that would become part of Yeshiva University. Later he earned a PhD from Dropsie University and became the first president of Yeshiva. Belkin, ordained at seventeen, was born in Poland, and studied in the yeshivas of Slonim and Mir. He immigrated to the United States as a young man in 1929 and later enrolled at Brown University, where he studied classics, was elected to Phi Beta Kappa, and received his doctorate in 1935. A member of the American Academy of Political and Social Science, he was Revel's successor at Yeshiva University. Lookstein, born in Russia but brought to the United States as a child, received ordination from the seminary at Yeshiva College in 1925–26. He studied at New York's City College as well as Columbia University. Although best known as a congregational rabbi at New York's Kehillath Jeschurun, he was also an adjunct professor of sociology and homiletics at Yeshiva College and later acting president of Israel's Bar Ilan University (*Encyclopedia Judaica* [Jerusalem: Keter, 1972), 11:487–88, and Aaron Rakeffet-Rothkoff, "The Torah and Rabbinics of the Early YC Years," *Commentator* [Yeshiva College], May 16, 2005). Jung was born in Moravia and was a son of a disciple of Samson Raphael Hirsch. He arrived in the United States in 1922 at age twenty-eight and served for over sixty years as rabbi at New York's Jewish Center. He "believed that America was God's instrument for leading the world through good and godliness to Jerusalem." Gershon Greenberg, review of *Reverence, Righteousness and Rahamanut: Essays in Memory of Rabbi Dr. Leo Jung, American Jewish History* 84, no. 1 (1996): 47. Berkovits was born in Romania, served in the rabbinate in Berlin, Leeds (UK), Sydney, and Boston, and became dean of the Hebrew Theological College in Chicago. Wurzburger was born in Munich in 1920 and fled to the United States in 1938, shortly after Kristallnacht, the sweeping attacks against Jews in Germany incited by the Nazis. He got a bachelor's degree at Yeshiva University, was ordained there, and got a master's and a doctorate in philosophy from Harvard.

70. Hasidic rebbes who did have to deal with laity represented a special case. They often could be far more flexible than the yeshiva heads but because of their sectarianism tended to be less engaged in modern American culture. Moreover, as charismatic leaders, they were less likely to feel the need to defer to the needs of lay followers.

71. See David Hartman "Halakhah as a Ground for Creating a Shared Spiritual Language," *Tradition* 16, no. 1 (1976), retrieved October 31, 2005, from www.lookstein.org/articles/halakhah_ground.htm.

72. Joseph Dov Soloveitchik, "Confrontation," 26.

73. See Heilman, "Constructing Orthodoxy."

74. See Jeffrey Gurock, "Resisters and Accommodators: Varieties of Orthodox Rabbis in America, 1886–1983," *American Jewish Archives* 35 (November 1983): 100–187.

75. Peter Berger and Thomas Luckmann, *The Social Construction of Reality* (New York: Anchor, 1967), 128.

76. Haym Soloveitchik (pers. comm., April 2003) has argued that the Hirschi-

ans knew what *derech eretz, kultur,* was but had a weak understanding of Torah, while the modern Orthodox in America would in time learn a great deal about Torah through the yeshivas that relocated in the New World but were in their lives after college too little touched by the riches of Western civilization.

77. David Reisman, *The Lonely Crowd* (New Haven, CT: Yale University Press, 1969), 21.

78. See, for example, Marcelle Fischler, "More Kosher Than Thou in the Five Towns," *New York Times,* Long Island Weekly, Sec. 14LI, 1.

79. Benny Kraut, "Yavneh in America: An Orthodox Judaism That Might Have Been," speech given at Queens Jewish Center, October 6, 2002.

80. Robert K. Merton, *Social Theory and Social Structure* (Glencoe, IL: Free Press, 1968).

81. Lawrence J. Kaplan, "The Dilemma of Conservative Judaism," *Commentary* 62 (November 1976): 45.

82. Joseph Dov Soloveitchik, "Confrontation," section 3.

83. Walter S. Wurzburger, "Confronting the Challenge of the Values of Modernity, " *Torah U-Madda Journal* 1 (1989): 110. The *Maggid Mishneh* is quoted there too.

84. See, for example, Lichtenstein, "The Rav from a Distance." See also Moshe Meiselman, "The Rav, Feminism and Public Policy," *Tradition* 33, no. 1 (1998): 5–30, and Lawrence Kaplan, "Revisionism and the Rav: The Struggle for the Soul of Modern Orthodoxy," *Judaism* 48 (Summer 1999): 290–311.

85. In one of the ironies of history, Rabbi Meir Twersky, grandson of Joseph B. Soloveitchik, a teacher in the seminary at Yeshiva University, has often expressed such points of view. For example, he has championed an attitude that he labels "intellectual *mesiras nefesh* [spiritual surrender]," which he describes as part of an essential process, for Orthodox Jews, of ridding themselves of the cultural biases that they have assimilated and that have caused so many problems for their faith. See his talk "Mai Chanukah?" given at Teaneck, NJ, December 17, 2000, retrieved October 28, 2005, from www.torahweb.org/torah/audio/audioFrameset.html.

86. S. C. Heilman and S. M. Cohen, *Cosmopolitans and Parochials: Modern Orthodox Jews in America* (Chicago: University of Chicago Press, 1989).

87. These tears, Haym Soloveitchik suggests, came out of their instinctive, nostalgic ties to Orthodox Judaism. See Haym Soloveitchik, "Rupture and Reconstruction: The Transformation of Contemporary Orthodoxy," *Tradition* 28 (Summer 1994): 116. Originally published as "Migration, Acculturation, and the New Role of Texts," in *Accounting for Fundamentalisms: The Dynamic Character of Movements,* ed. R. S. Appleby et al. (Chicago: University of Chicago Press, 1994), 197–235.

88. On symbolic religiosity, see H. J. Gans, "Symbolic Ethnicity and Symbolic Religiosity: Towards a Comparison of Ethnic and Religious Acculturation," *Ethnic and Racial Studies* 17 (October 1994): 577–92.

89. Charles Liebman, "Extremism as a Religious Norm," *Journal for the Scientific Study of Religion* 22 (1983): 75, and Martin E. Marty and R. Scott Appleby,

Fundamentalisms Observed (Chicago: University of Chicago Press, 1991), 817, emphasis in original.

90. The term had been gaining a greater popularity in Orthodox circles, as indicated in articles using it, such as Walter Wurzburger's "Centrist Orthodoxy: Ideology or Atmosphere," in *Journal of Jewish Thought—Jubilee Issue* (Jerusalem: Rabbinical Council of America, 1985), 67–75, and Yeshiva University President Norman Lamm's "Centrist Orthodoxy: Judaism and Moderationism, Definitions and Desideratum," in *Orthodoxy Confronts Modernity*, ed. Jonathan Sacks (Hoboken, NJ: Ktav, 1991), 48–61.

91. In truth, since our sample was not perfectly random but rather a targeted stratified one, one might argue that we found more centrists because we chose to look for them and that we may therefore have missed the growing presence of the right wing. Maybe so—but no one else had alternative data for the time, so we shall never know for certain.

92. Farber, *American Orthodox Dreamer*, 108.

93. Ibid., 137.

94. Aharon Lichtenstein, *Leaves of Faith: The World of Jewish Living* (Jersey City, NJ: Ktav, 2004), 236. I thank David Singer for calling this source to my attention.

95. *Jewish Advocate*, December 20, 1962, 10, quoted in Farber, *American Orthodox Dreamer*, 133–34.

96. Mary Douglas, *In the Wilderness: The Doctrine of Defilement in the Book of Numbers* (Sheffield: Sheffield Press, 1993), 57.

97. R. K. Merton and E. Barber, "Sociological Ambivalence," in *Sociological Theory, Values, and Sociocultural Change: Essays in Honor of Pitirim Sorokin*, ed. E. A. Tiryakian (New York: Free Press, 1963), 96.

98. Egon Mayer, *From Suburb to Shtetl: The Jews of Boro Park* (Philadelphia: Temple University Press, 1979).

99. On the impact of the schools on the children, see chap. 2.

100. Douglas, *In the Wilderness*, 46; Farber, *American Orthodox Dreamer*, 64.

101. Douglas, *In the Wilderness*, 46–47.

102. See Heilman, *Defenders of the Faith*, and also the film *Hiding and Seeking*, dir. and prod. Menachem Daum and Oren Rudavsky, 2004, which explores this attitude. (For further information, see the film's Web site at www.hidingandseeking.com.)

103. Hutner, "Holocaust," 6.

104. Moshe Feinstein, *Iggrot Moshe, Yoreh Deah* 3, #43 (March 1967), in David Ellenson, "A Jewish Legal Authority Addresses Jewish-Christian Dialogue: Two Responses of Rabbi Moshe Feinstein," *American Jewish Archives Journal* 52, nos. 1 and 2 (2000): 113–28. This attitude is echoed by Rabbi Herschel Schachter in "Am Hanivchar" [Chosen People], talk delivered May 2, 2004, at Beth Aaron Synagogue, Teaneck, NJ, audio file retrieved September 22, 2005, from www.torahweb.org/Schachter.html.

105. See Samuel G. Freedman, *Jew vs. Jew: The Struggle for the Soul of American Jewry* (New York: Simon and Schuster, 2000).

106. Douglas, *In the Wilderness,* 51.

107. See Heilman, *Portrait of American Jews.*

108. Charles S. Liebman, *The Ambivalent American Jew: Politics, Religion, and Family in American Jewish Life* (Philadelphia: Jewish Publication Society of America, 1976), 157.

109. Gregory Rodriguez, "The Lieberman Test for Multi-ethnic America," *Los Angeles Times,* September 24, 2000, op-ed page.

110. See Richard Alba, *Ethnic Identity: The Transformation of White America* (New Haven, CT: Yale University Press, 1990); and S. Lieberson and M. C. Waters, "The Ethnic Responses of Whites: What Causes Their Instability, Simplification and Inconsistency," *Social Forces* 72 (1993): 421–50.

111. Edah, "Past Events and Programs," retrieved August 7, 2005, from www .edah.org/pastevent.cfm.

112. Consider, for example, the case of the Jewish Community Council in Boston. When originally formed in 1944, the Jewish Community Council of Metropolitan Boston brought together twenty-one Jewish groups devoted to improving human relations: the American Jewish Committee, American Jewish Congress, Associated Jewish Philanthropies, Associated Synagogues, B'nai B'rith, B'rith Abraham, Combined Appeal, Jewish Labor Committee, Jewish National Workers Alliance, Jewish War Veterans, Mizrachi (Orthodox), Pioneers of Palestine, Poale Zion, Rabbinical Association, Workmen's Circle, Vaad Harabonim (which included Orthodox rabbis), Vaad Hoir, Zionist Groups, Young Israel (Orthodox), League of Jewish Women, and Council of Jewish Women. See box 1, folder: BJCC [Boston Jewish Community Council], statements of purpose and general program, Jewish Community Council of Metropolitan Boston Records, American Jewish Historical Society, Waltham, MA.

113. David Ellenson, "German Jewish Orthodoxy: Tradition in the Context of Culture," in Wertheimer, *Uses of Tradition,* 5–22.

114. See Adam Ferziger, *Exclusion and Hierarchy: Orthodoxy, Non-Observance and Modern Jewish Identity* (Philadelphia: University of Pennsylvania Press, 2005).

115. Shubert Spero, "The Logical Limits of Jewish Ecumenism," *Sh'ma* 13, no. 243 (December 10, 1982): 11.

116. I have introduced the concept of "right-wing" because these distinctions in practices and beliefs among the Orthodox were often more positions along a spectrum than mutually exclusive categories.

117. Hutner, "Holocaust," 6.

118. Weinberg, "Experiencing *Golus,*" 5.

119. Menachem Friedman, review of *Haredim Ltd.,* in *Haaretz,* September 14, 2001.

120. Similar and in some ways even more insidious dangers existed for those Orthodox Jews in Israel who were seduced out of their exile consciousness by the Zionist dream and reality (see Heilman, *Defenders of the Faith*).

121. Group Project for Holocaust Education, "In Favor of Holocaust Remembrances," *Jewish Observer* 15 (September 1980): 27.

122. See chap. 3 of this volume.

123. Quoted in Keller, "Modern Orthodoxy," 3.

124. Herschel Schachter, "The Temple and Mikdash Me'at," retrieved August 7, 2005, from www.torahweb.org/torah/special/2004/rsch_mikdash.html. On another occasion, he simply termed Christianity *avodah zarah* (idol worship). I thank Marc Shapiro for pointing this out to me.

125. Schachter, "Am Hanivchar." Schachter cited as his source for this conclusion the opening of the famous mystical text *Tanya*.

126. The case was brought in 1998 and lost on appeal in 2001. See also Gil Perl and Yaakov Weinstein, "A Parent's Guide to Orthodox Assimilation on University Campuses," October 2003, audio file retrieved October 25, 2005, from www.people.fas.harvard.edu/~perl/pgindex.html, which argues that the university is a dangerous place for Orthodox Jewish continuity.

127. Schachter, "Am Hanivchar."

128. See, for example, Robert Wuthnow, *The Restructuring of American Religion: Society and Faith since World War II* (Princeton, NJ: Princeton University Press, 1988), and Graham Murdock, "The Re-Enchantment of the World: Religion and the Transformations of Modernity," in *Rethinking Media, Religion and Culture,* ed. Stewart Hoover and Knut Lundby (Thousand Oaks, CA: Sage Publications, 1997), 91.

129. See "President Ronald Reagan on The 700 Club—September, 1985," retrieved August 7, 2005, from www.patrobertson.com/Statesman/RonaldReagan.asp.

130. "For Goodness' Sake: Religion's Role in American Life," Public Agenda Poll, November 2000, retrieved October 30, 2005, from www.publicagenda.org.

131. For example, in such matters as opposition to abortion, gay rights, and a variety of other liberal causes, these Orthodox Jews and the Haredim felt common cause with the Christian right. See James D. Hunter, *Culture Wars* (New York: Basic Books, 1991). See also the story on the Orthodox rabbi Yechiel Eckstein, founder and president of the International Fellowship of Christians and Jews, who has found a way to create common cause with Christian evangelical and fundamentalist communities. Zev Chafets, "The Rabbi Who Loved Evangelicals (and Vice-Versa)," *New York Times Magazine,* July 24, 2005, 22 ff.

Chapter 2. The Numbers

Epigraph from Rabbi Yaakov Haber, "The Strength of the Few," 2003, retrieved August 9, 2005, from www.torahweb.org/torah/2003/parsha/rhab_kitissa.html.

1. Daniel J. Elazar, "How Strong Is Orthodox Judaism—Really? The Demographic of Jewish Religious Identification," 1991, retrieved August 8, 2005, from Jerusalem Center for Public Affairs Web site, Israel: Religion and Society, Daniel Elazar Papers Index, www.jcpa.org/dje/articles2/demographics.htm.

2. Actually, as Stephen Sharot has demonstrated, many of those who immigrated to America during the late nineteenth and early twentieth centuries, during the great waves of migration, were not quite as religiously observant or attached to Jewish tradition as common wisdom has suggested. See Stephen

Sharot, "The Three-Generations Hypothesis," *British Journal of Sociology* 24 (June 1973): 151–64, and Jeffrey Gurock, "Resisters and Accommodators: Varieties of Orthodox Rabbis in America, 1886–1983," American Jewish Archives 35 (November 1983): 100–187.

3. A notable exception was a single survey in 1957 that found Jews to be about 3 percent of the population at the time. U.S. Bureau of the Census, "Current Population Survey, March 1957." See also A. Dashefksy, "Double or Nothing," *American Jewish History* 92 (March 2004): 126–28.

4. People of "Jewish birth" would be those born of a Jewish parent or a parent who had had a Jewish upbringing. These statistical interpretations come from a paper, "American Jewry by the Numbers: What Can We Learn from NJPS?" delivered by Leonard Saxe at the annual meeting of the Association for Jewish Studies, Boston, December 2003.

5. On the NJPS 2000 undercount, see "NJPS Methodological Appendix," retrieved August 9, 2005, from www.ujc.org/content_display.html?ArticleID =83786.

6. "Kiryas Joel, New York," retrieved August 8, 2005, from www.citydata .com/city/Kiryas-Joel-New-York.html, and "New Square, New York," retrieved August 8, 2005, from www.city-data.com/city/New-Square-New-York.html.

7. I thank my student Magda Doss for helping in assembling these figures from the census. See also "Lakewood, New Jersey," retrieved August 8, 2005, from www.city-data.com/city/Lakewood-New-Jersey.html.

8. Jacob Ukeles and Ronald Miller, "The Jewish Community Study of New York: 2002 Highlights," booklet, UJA Federation of New York, June 2003.

9. I thank Jacob Ukeles and Ronald Miller for this explication of their data (pers. comm., February 2005).

10. Jacob Ukeles, "The Jewish Community Study of Greater Baltimore," 1999, retrieved August 8, 2005, from baltimore.ujcfedweb.org/getfile.asp?id=10221.

11. From the 1997 Los Angeles Population Survey. See Tom Tugend, "Survey: L.A. Jews Intermarry Less Than National Rate," *Jewish Telegraphic Agency,* July 10, 1998. Many argued that this number was an undercount: see, for example, Anthony Gordon and Richard M. Horowitz, "Setting the Record Straight," *Jewish Journal of Los Angeles,* September 8, 2000, retrieved August 8, 2005, from www.jewishjournal.com/archive/09.15.00/community1.09.15.00.html.

12. The 1996 (and 2004) Jewish Community Federation/Cleveland State University Community Study puts the Orthodox population in Greater Cleveland at about 8,600. The 2001 Jewish Federation Survey of the Jews of Columbus finds about 3,300 Orthodox Jews there. In 1994 there were about 1,050 Orthodox Jews in Toledo and 300 in Youngstown. If we add the Orthodox Jews of Dayton and Akron, we get about 14,000 total in Ohio. About 8,000 Orthodox are to be found in Greater Detroit (according to the 1990 Jewish Federation Report).As of 1995 about 2,000 were Orthodox in St. Louis and vicinity. And in Milwaukee as of 2000 there were about 2,000. All of these community study statistics can be found at "Community Studies," retrieved November 1, 2005, from the Web page of the Mandell Berman Institute North American Jewish Data Bank

at the Roper Center of the University of Connecticut, www.jewishdatabank.org/community.asp.

13. This is a number based on 7 percent of the 641,000 Jews in Florida, a conservative estimate. See "Most Jewish U.S. States," 2002, retrieved August 8, 2005, from www.adherents.com/largecom/com_judaism.html#states_percent.

14. The 100,000 comes from taking 7 percent of the total number of Jews in Massachusetts, New Jersey, Connecticut, Pennsylvania, and Illinois, based on figures in the *American Jewish Yearbook, 1995* (Philadelphia: American Jewish Committee, 1995). Adjusting for an annual growth rate of just under 4 percent and working from the increase in the Orthodox figures since 1970, we can add to the 1995 and 1997 figures.

15. See NJPS 1990, which puts the figure at 63 percent. "NJPS 1990," retrieved October 30, 2005, from www.jewishdatabank.org/NJPS1990.asp.

16. "Comprehensive Study Probes NCSY Dynamic," *Jewish Action* 59, no. 2 (1998), retrieved August 8, 2005, from www.ou.org/publications/ja/5759winter/ncsy.htm.

17. On the implications of this, see chap. 3.

18. This survey was carried out by Nathalie Friedman and is reported in "Comprehensive Study."

19. See chap. 5.

20. The Torah prohibits carrying things on the Sabbath between a public domain and a private domain or for more than four cubits in a public domain. However, the Torah permits carrying within an enclosed "private" area. Public domains are typically nonresidential areas, including streets, thoroughfares, plazas, and highways. Private domains are residential areas; the term originally referred to an individual's home or apartments that were surrounded by a wall and could be deemed to be closed off from the surrounding public domains. The rabbis of the Talmud developed a means to make a larger area a private domain by surrounding it. Such an enclosure is called an *eruv*, more specifically *eruv chatzayrt*. The Hebrew word *eruv* means to mix or join together; an *eruv chatzayrot* serves to integrate a number of private and public properties into one larger private domain. Consequently, individuals within an *eruv* district are then permitted to move objects across the pre-*eruv* public domain/private domain boundary. In their effort to establish enclaves in which they can fully use public spaces as private ones, Orthodox Jews have increasingly sought to establish *eruv*s marking the boundaries of these neighborhoods. The problem is that it is impractical to build a continuous solid wall around a community. However, the rabbis noticed that doors are permitted within walls and that a doorway consists of two parts: the vertical members and the lintel on top. In fact, a wall may have quite a few doors and still be considered to enclose an area. In the limiting case, there are many doorway openings and very little of the solid wall remains. This is what happens in an *eruv*. The doorpost function is fulfilled by telephone (utility) poles (serving as vertical members), with the lintel being cables strung between the poles. The *eruv* is generally designed by encircling a community with a continuous string or wire. For further explanations, see http://shamash.org/lists/scj-faq/HTML/faq/07–09.html.

See also examples in Chicago, "Chicago Eruv Inc.," retrieved August 8, 2005, from www.geocities.com/chicagoeruv/, and Boston, "Greater Boston Eruv Corporation," August 2005, retrieved August 8, 2005, from www.bostoneruv.org/.

21. "New York Community Study Reports Findings," *Jewish Week*, June 7, 2004.

22. Conservatives were at 24 percent, Reform at 18 percent, nondenominational at 19 percent, and those calling themselves secular at 8 percent.

23. Jacob Ukeles, Pearl Beck, and Ron Miller, *The Jewish Community Study of New York 2002, Geographic Profile* (New York: UJA Federation of New York, 2004), 48.

24. Ibid., 53, 55.

25. This number is arrived at by taking 7 percent of the Jewish populations of Florida, Massachusetts, Pennsylvania, Illinois, and Connecticut, which constitutes the average number of Orthodox Jews there, and then taking 25 percent of that number, the average number of Haredim found in areas where we have data.

26. Marvin Schick, *A Census of Jewish Day Schools in the United States, 2003–2004* (New York: Avi Chai Foundation, 2005).

Chapter 3. Jewish Education as a Field of Conflict

Epigraph from Alfred North Whitehead, "The Rhythmic Claims of Freedom and Discipline," in *The Aims of Education and Other Essays* (New York: Macmillan, 1929), 49.

1. G. C. Haydu, "Psychotherapy, Enculturation and Indoctrination: Similarities and Distinctions," *T.-I.-T. Journal of Life Sciences* 3, no. 1 (1973): 25–27.

2. There is much evidence that this is the case in modern Jewish life. Thus, for example, as the 1990 National Jewish Population Survey documented, the more years of Jewish education that people born during the so-called baby-boom years had, the more likely they were to engage in Jewish religious behavior. Where that education lasted nine or more years, the increased Jewish religious behavior was striking. Whether the behavior in question was the widely practiced attending a seder (no Jewish education = 68 percent; 0 to 3 years of Jewish education = 77 percent; 4 to 8 years = 92 percent; 9 or more years = 95 percent) or the rarer attending a Purim celebration (none = 17 percent; 0 to 3 = 19 percent; 4 to 8 = 31 percent; 9+ = 49 percent), or even the rigorous using of separate dishes for milk and meat at home (none = 11 percent; 0 to 3 = 10 percent; 4 to 8 = 17 percent; 9+ = 27 percent), Jewish education clearly led to Jewish behavioral consequences and religious enculturation. See Mordecai Rimor and Elihu Katz, "Jewish Involvement of the Baby Boom Generation," booklet, Avi Chai Foundation, Jerusalem, November 1993, table 1.5, p. 7.

3. Peter Berger, Brigitte Berger, and Hansfried Kellner, *The Homeless Mind* (New York: Random House, 1973), 119.

4. J. E. Thompson and H. O. Thompson, "Teaching Ethics to Nursing Students," *Nursing Outlook* 37, no. 2 (1989): 84–88.

5. See Mary Douglas, *In the Wilderness* (New York: Oxford University Press, 2001), 54.

6. Marvin Schick, *The Effectiveness of Preparatory Tracks in Jewish Day Schools* (New York: Avi Chai Foundation, 2002), 3.

7. This was certainly the view of the rabbis and many other Jews. See Y. Amir, "Education as a Religious Deed in A. D. Gordon's Philosophy," in *Abiding Challenges: Research Perspectives on Jewish Education,* ed. Yisrael Rich and Michael Rosenak (London: Freund Publishing), 19–64.

8. Douglas, *In the Wilderness,* 46–47.

9. While many of the settlers believe that their intensified Orthodox observance requires that they attach themselves to biblical Israel to hasten the coming of the Messiah, the Lubavitchers believe that intensifying religious observance among all Jews will hasten redemption.

10. To be sure, the assumption of American multiculturalism is that all cultures are equally legitimate ways of living, while the Haredi and fundamentalist view is that only one way is truly right.

11. Samuel Heilman, "Haredim and the Public Square: The Nature of the Social Contract," in *Jewish Polity and American Civil Society: Communal Agencies and Religious Movements in the American Public Sphere,* ed. Alan Mittleman, Jonathan D. Sarna, and Robert Licht (New York: Rowman and Littlefield, 2002), 320.

12. On this concept, see Erich Rosenthal, "Acculturation without Assimilation," *American Journal of Sociology* 66 (November 1960): 275–88.

13. Berel Levy, "Forging a Jewish Nation," 2002, retrieved August 8, 2005, from the Web site of the Committee for the Advancement of Torah: www.okkosher.com/Content.asp?ID=165.

14. This attitude that put non-Jewish education on a lower ontological level had already displayed itself in some of the European yeshivas during the early years of the twentieth century. Later, in America, it was why so many yeshiva heads looked upon the idea of Yeshiva University, an institution that claimed to be both, as oxymoronic. "It isn't a yeshiva," those on the Orthodox right wing claimed, and "It isn't a university," those on the left chimed in. See Julie Wiener, Jewish Telegraphic Agency, "Yeshiva U. Confronts Fault Lines of Modern Orthodoxy," retrieved August 8, 2005, from www.jewishsf.com/content/2-0-/module/diplaystory/story_id/15764/format/print/edition_id/307/displaystory.print. On the problems with university education for the Orthodox, see Gil Perl and Yaakov Weinstein, "A Parent's Guide to Orthodox Assimilation on University Campuses," October 2003, audio file retrieved October 30, 2005, from www.people.fas.harvard.edu/~perl/pgindex.html.

15. Maimonides Mishnah Torah, Hilchot Talmud Torah 1:13. The reluctance to teach Torah to women is traced to a Mishnah in the tractate Sota 3:4. That Mishnah's main focus is the *sota,* the woman who has aroused the jealousy of her husband because she has been with another man and who must prove her innocence of adultery by the ritual of the "bitter waters" (Num. 5:26). The rules governing this cocktail that the *sota* must drink suggest that women who have been meritorious in their lives prior to their sin of adultery, which the drink supernaturally reveals and punishes, will be protected against its fatal consequences for several years. Women who know this, from their study of the Torah, will there-

fore not be overcome by the drink right away. From this the Mishnah concludes, according to ben Azzai, "It is a man's duty to teach his daughter Torah so that if she must drink, she should know that her merit will hold her punishment in abeyance." But in a counterview that gains more support (and fame), Rabbi Eliezer says, "If any man teach his daughter Torah, it is as though he taught her lewdness." That is, knowing the role that merit can play in suspending the punishments of the *sota* might lead women to become adulterous, for they are aware that with enough merit they can "hide" the evidence. From this assertion of Eliezer, based on the possible actions of learned women who are adulterous, the general principle opposing the teaching of Torah to women became accepted, especially after its codification by Maimonides in the Middle Ages, as the received tradition. Needless to say, for many modern women, including Orthodox Jewish ones, this blanket prohibition based on the possible behavior of deviants has seemed unjustified.

16. Judah ben Samuel, he-Hasid, *Sefer Hasidim* (Frankfurt: M. A. Wahrmann, 1924), 1501, 835.

17. Mordechai Eliav, "Pioneers of Modern Jewish and Religious Education for Girls: The First Schools in Germany in the 19th Century," in Rich and Rosenak, *Abiding Challenges*, 146.

18. Ibid., 150.

19. Ibid., 155.

20. Samuel Heilman, "The Many Faces of Orthodoxy, Part I," *Modern Judaism* 2 (February 1982): 23–51, and "The Many Faces of Orthodoxy, Part II," *Modern Judaism* 2 (May 1982): 171–98.

21. Eliav, "Pioneers," 155.

22. As reported by David Kranzler, the Beth Jacob Seminary in the 1930s had a two-year course of study, and its curriculum was as follows:

> Five Books of Moses: This included the study of the Five Books of Moses in the original text in its entirety with the commentary of Rashi and Rabbi Samuel Raphael Hirsch.
>
> Prophets and Hagiographica: Thirty chapters in Isaiah; selections from Jeremiah and the twelve minor prophets with special emphasis on those used as Haftorahs; fifty selected chapters from the Psalms with accompanying ethical commentaries; readings from the Megillos according to the holidays and also on a regular day-to-day basis.
>
> Prayers: Selections from prayers for the weekday, holiday, and Sabbath; ethics of the Fathers.
>
> Jewish History: From the Creation until modern times.
>
> Hebrew Grammar: Rules of vocalization, declension of nouns and conjugation of regular and irregular verbs; drill and analysis in oral and written composition and recitation of simple stories of the Bible and dictation.
>
> Jewish Law: Laws pertaining to daily living as well as those of the Jewish year, both duties and obligations of the Jewish man and in particular duties

and obligations of the Jewish woman. Some of the textbooks used were *Mesilat Yishorim,* by Rabbi Moses Chaim Luzzato; *Selected Works from Chorev; The Nineteen Letters of Ben Uziel,* by Rabbi Samson Raphael Hirsch; *The Jewish Problem* and *Traces of the Messiah,* by Dr. Isaac Breuer; *Amudai Hagolah,* by Stern.

Psychology: Psychological foundation of spirituality and the important discoveries and laws of spiritual life.

Pedagogy: History of pedagogy, biographies and selections of outstanding pedagogues, pedagogic quotations culled from the Talmud, educational psychology and methodology, special methodology to be employed in the general studies program, and special methodology for Beth Jacob schools, school health and hygiene. Texts used: Pedagogic works by Frostier, Kerschensteine, and Spranger

Polish: The studies in Polish literature, history, and geography were taught according to the prescribed course of study as set up the government.

German: Instruction in the correct oral and written use of the language. The goal of this course was to provide the teachers with the ability to read by themselves the important religious literature of Hirsch and others which was written in the German language, as well as selected classical works such as the poetry of Schiller, Goethe, *Nathan the Wise* by Lessing, Zweig, and Beer-Hoffman.

Gymnastics: The course included exercises and instruction in various games for children, outings, free-play. The exercises were held indoors in the winter and outdoors in the summer.

Handicrafts: Sewing, repairing, embroidery, knitting.

Requirements for graduation were a written lesson plan for a model lesson; a pedagogic essay or composition; and a final paper about a specified text of the Bible. See David Kranzler, "An Orthodox Revolution: The Creation and Development of the Beth Jacob Seminary for Girls," paper presented at Yad Vashem, October 11, 1999, retrieved August 8, 2005, from www.yadvashem.org.il/download/education/conf/Kranzler.pdf.

My late mother, Lucia Heilman, the daughter of a Polish Hasid, was briefly a student in Schnirer's classroom in Krakow. She reported to me that for all of this curricular innovation, the school was far from modernist in either its outlook or its practice.

23. *Encyclopedia Judaica* (Jerusalem: Keter, 1972), 16:1259.

24. Quoted in Kranzler, "Orthodox Revolution," 4. See also Deborah Weissman, "Bais Ya'akov as an Innovation in Jewish Women's Education: A Contribution to the Study of Education and Social Change," *Studies in Jewish Education* 7 (1995): 278–99.

25. In Israel these are called *midrashot,* and there are at least twenty. See Rabbanit Chana Henkin, "Women's Issues: New Conditions and New Models of Authority—the Yoatzot Halachah," retrieved August 9, 2005, from www.nismat.net/article.php?id=160&heading=0.

26. Among the best known of the former is Machon Chana, a summer program in Crown Heights, Brooklyn; see "Summer Programs," retrieved August 8,

2005, from www.machonchana.org/summer.html. Among the latter are a whole variety of local institutions, perhaps the best known being the Drisha Institute in New York (www.drisha.org/).

27. Tamar El-Or, *Educated and Ignorant: Ultraorthodox Jewish Women and Their World* (Boulder, CO: Lynne Rienner, 1994).

28. Moshe Feinstein, *Igros Moshe, Yore Deah* (responsa), *chelek* 73, *siman* 78.

29. Aaron Kotler, "Hinnukh BeYeshivot Qetanot," in vol. 3 of *Sikhot Mussar* (Lakewood, NJ: Makhon Mishnat Rabbi Aharon, 1996), 169. I am grateful to Yoel Finkelman for this reference. Apparently, this subject came up at a convention of Torah U'Mesorah (the Orthodox Jewish day school association), when Rabbi Kotler, who generally disliked the day school model, was asked about the propriety of coeducation. See Chaim I. Waxman, "American Modern Orthodoxy: Confronting Cultural Challenges," *Edah Journal* 4 (May 2004): 6, and comments of Ncoom Gilbar and Jay Bailey on the Mail.Jewish Mailing List, vol. 19, no. 86 (June 1995), retrieved October 30, 2005, from www.ottmall.com/mj_ht_arch/v19/mj_v19i86.html#CABD.

30. There are those who argue that Rabbi Joseph Soloveitchik, often cited as a champion of coeducation in Jewish study at the primary level, did so less out of conviction than out of expedience. "Don't bring a proof from Maimonides about mixed classes. The times were very different then. You have to understand, I had no choice: either have mixed classes, or there would have been no Maimonides."

31. See, for example, comments by Ari Shapiro, Mail.Jewish Mailing List, vol. 19, no. 21 (April 1995), retrieved August 8, 2005, from www.ottmall.com/mj_ht_arch/v19/mj_v19i21.html#CGH.

32. Even Haezer, *siman* 21.

33. See Ezra Kopelowitz, "Jewish Identity," in *Modern Judaism: An Oxford Guide,* ed. Nicholas de Lange and Miri Freud-Kandel (New York: Oxford University Press, 2005).

34. S. M. Breslauer, "Yeshiva Education: Reclaiming the Secular Departments," *Jewish Observer* 10 (January 1973): 13.

35. See, for example, "Question 2.18: What Is a Torah Jew?" June 2004, retrieved August 8, 2005, from www.faqs.org/faqs/judaism/FAQ/02-Who-We-Are/section-19.html.

36. Places like Hebrew Teachers College in Boston (founded in 1921), Baltimore Hebrew College (founded in 1919), and Spertus College in Chicago (founded 1924).

37. The Morasha Jewish Day School in Rancho Santa Margarita, California, bills itself this way, but it is by no means unique in this regard. See www.morasha.org.

38. Gerald Bubis, "The Costs of Jewish Living: Revisiting Jewish Involvements and Barriers," retrieved August 8, 2005, from the Chicago American Jewish Committee Web site: www.ajc-chicago.org/InTheMedia/Publications.asp?did=427. See also S. Barack Fishman, "Jewish Education and Jewish Identity among Contemporary American Jews: Suggestions from Current Research," booklet, Bureau of Jewish Education, Center for Educational Research and Evaluation, Boston, 1995, and Harold Himmelfarb, "Jewish Education for Naught: Educating the Cul-

turally Deprived Jewish Child," booklet, Synagogue Council of America, New York, 1975.

39. Lots of Talmud was taught, but also Bible, codes, and in time Hebrew language, literature, Jewish history, and even some Judaica esoterica from Kabbalah to Jewish values.

40. The reasons for this, as earlier noted, had to do with their immigrant status, their relatively poor secular educational background, and their relatively large families, among other factors.

41. Ramaz School, "Mission and Legacy," retrieved August 8, 2005, from www.ramaz.org/public/mission2.cfm.

42. Mission statement: "To produce religiously observant, educated Jews who will remain faithful to their religious beliefs, values, and practices as they take their place as contributing members of the general society, Maimonides provides its students with both an outstanding religious education and an excellent college preparatory secular education in an atmosphere that reinforces their commitment to Torah and observance of Mitzvot." Maimonides School, "Mission," retrieved August 8, 2005, from www.maimonides.org/mission.htm.

43. Joseph B. Soloveitchik, public lecture, November 15, 1971, quoted in "Quotes by the Rav," retrieved October 30, 2005, from www.rav.org/therav/quote3.htm.

44. Joseph Kaminetsky and Alexander S. Gross, "Rabbi Shraga Feivel Mendlowitz," in *Men of the Spirit,* ed. Leo Jung (New York: Kymson Publishing, 1964), 563–64. See also Samuel C. Feuerstein, "Torah Umesorah, 1944–1969: A Quarter of a Century," in *Hebrew Day School Education: An Overview,* ed. Joseph Kaminetsky (New York: Torah Umesorah, 1970), 71–72.

45. *Encyclopedia Judaica,* 6:443.

46. Chaim I. Waxman, *America's Jews in Transition* (Philadelphia: Temple University Press, 1983), 125–26. See also Waxman, "American Modern Orthodoxy," 4.

47. Walter I. Ackerman, "Strangers to Tradition: Idea and Constraint in American Jewish Education," in *Jewish Education Worldwide: Cross-Cultural Perspectives,* ed. Harold S. Himmelfarb and Sergio DellaPergolla (Lanham, MD: University Press of America, 1989), 71–116, states that the number of day schools in the 1980s (including non-Orthodox institutions) was over 550, with 86 percent or about 475 of them under Orthodox auspices.

48. Marvin Schick, *A Census of Jewish Day Schools in the United States* (New York: Avi Chai Foundation, 2000).

49. More than half of those Orthodox schools are what Schick calls immigrant/outreach and Chabad.

50. Jane Jacobs, *The Death and Life of Great American Cities* (New York: Random House, 1972).

51. Marvin Schick, "A Statement on Jewish Education," 2005, retrieved August 8, 2005, from the Chicago American Jewish Committee Web site: www.ajcchicago.org/InTheMedia/Publications.asp?did=149&pid=130.

52. Schick, *Census of Jewish Day Schools,* ii.

53. See Norman Podhoretz, *Making It* (New York: Random House, 1967).

54. Graham Murdock, "The Re-Enchantment of the World: Religion and the

Transformations of Modernity," in *Rethinking Media, Religion and Culture,* ed. Stewart Hoover and Knut Lundby (Thousand Oaks, CA: Sage Publications, 1997), 87.

55. Michael Novak, *The Rise of the Unmeltable Ethnics: Politics and Culture in the Seventies* (New York: Macmillan, 1972). That some of these "unmeltables" may in fact be melting is a matter for discussion elsewhere. See, for example, David Halle, *America's Working Man: Work, Home, and Politics among Blue-Collar Property Owners* (Chicago: University of Chicago Press, 1984).

56. Daniel Bell, "Where Are We?" *Moment,* Spring 1986, 15–22.

57. In a recent study, Steven M. Cohen, who has documented a turn toward the political right among Jews, finds that the Orthodox led this turn to the right. See: Steven M. Cohen, "Survey Sees Historic Shift to the Right," *Forward,* January 17, 2003, 1.

58. See Samuel Heilman, *Portrait of American Jews: The Last Half of the Twentieth Century* (Seattle: University of Washington Press, 1996).

59. Perl and Weinstein, "Parent's Guide," 12.

60. "Modern Orthodoxy's Ontological Predicament," 2005, retrieved August 8, 2005, from Mayim Web site (UK): www.mayim.edu/future/predicament.html.

61. Max Weber, *The Protestant Ethic and the Spirit of Capitalism,* trans. Talcott Parsons (1904; reprint, New York: Charles Scribner's Sons, 1930), 285.

62. Joseph B. Soloveitchik, lecture to the parents of Maimonides School, November 15, 1971, retrieved November 20, 2003, from www.atid.org/news/s6.htm.

63. There is a growing movement in day school circles in the last couple of years to reinsert parents into the educational process, but by now they too have moved closer to the worldview and ethos expressed in the school.

64. The words come from Rabbis Yosef Sholom Eliashiv, Aharon Yehuda Leib Shteinman, M. S. Shapira, Michel Yehuda Lefkovitz, Chaim Pinchos Scheinberg, Nissim Karelitz, Tzvi Markowitz, Chaim Kanievsky, Shmuel Auerbach, and Shlomo Wolbe, all prominent in the Haredi Orthodox community. See the language of a joint letter, "Condemnation of the Book 'The Making of a Godol'," *Dei'ah veDibur,* December 25, 2002, retrieved August 8, 2005, from www.shemayisrael.com/chareidi/archives5763/shemos/SHM63amakgodl.htm.

65. Thus, for example, while the Internet is not mentioned in the Torah, Haredi rabbis Nosson Gestetner, Yitzhak Zilberstein, and others issued a *da'as Torah* saying it is prohibited to make use of the Internet unless one needs to for making a living. See Betzalel Kahn, "Daas Torah: Do Not Use the Internet," *Dei'ah veDibur,* January 12, 2000, retrieved August 8, 2005, from http://chareidi.shemayisrael.com/archives5760/bo/BOainternt.htm.

66. Randi Barocas and Tamar Milstein, "Help Wanted," *Jewish News of Greater Phoenix,* August 14, 1998, retrieved August 8, 2005, from www.jewishaz.com/jewishnews/980814/help.shtml.

67. Rabbi Isaac Elchanan Theological Seminary (RIETS), the rabbinical seminary at Yeshiva University, had 290 students enrolled in 2002, for example, only about half of whom were expected to be ordained, and of those who graduated in the previous four years, only 79 percent were in 2002 working in Jewish pub-

lic service. Avi Robinson, "Students Choose between RIETS and Chovevei Torah," *Commentator* 67 (December 31, 2002), retrieved August 8, 2005, from http://yuweb.addr.com/v67i7/features/reits.html.

68. Edah, "Past Events and Programs," 2001, retrieved August 8, 2005, from www.edah.org/pastevent.cfm.

69. Gail Lichtman, "Shaping the Future: A Jerusalem-Based Program Hopes to Assist the Next Generation of Modern Orthodox Educators," *Jerusalem Post,* April 16, 1999.

70. See the Torah Mitzion Web site, www.torahmitzion.org/, and, for example, "Real Life Stories," retrieved August 9, 2005, from www.torahmitzion.org/pub/kol03_02_e2.pdf.

71. This was tried through an intensive training program for about twelve day school educators. See "Intensive Training Program for Day School Leadership Held at Yeshiva University," August 17, 2001, retrieved September 27, 2005, from http://129.98.201.68/news/articles/article.cfm?id=100485.

72. On the Yinglish of modern Orthodoxy, see S. C. Heilman, *The People of the Book: Drama, Fellowship, and Religion* (New Brunswick, NJ: Transaction Books, 2002), 161–202.

73. Yonoson Rosenblum, "Those Hated Chareidim," *Jewish Observer* 35 (March 2002), retrieved September 27, 2005, from www.shemayisrael.com/jewishobserver/archives/march/chareidim.htm.

74. Mordechai Willig, "Secular Studies: Are They for Everyone?" *Torah U-Madda Journal* 1 (1989): 96.

75. The modernist quotations come from Edah, "Mission Statement," retrieved August 9, 2005, from www.edah.org. The others come from Aaron Brafman, "We Are Different," *Jewish Observer* 35 (November 2002): 8.

76. See Boruch Leff, "Following the Rabbi's Lead," retrieved August 9, 2005, from www.aish.com/torahportion/kolyaakov/Following_the_Rabbis_Lead.asp.

77. Quoted in ibid., 12.

78. "The Ikkar Is Gute Midos" [The Essence Is Good Qualities], *Dei'ah ve Dibbur,* July 24, 2002, retrieved August 9, 2005, from www.shemayisrael.com/chareidi/archives5762/eikev/EKV62features.htm.

79. Marvin Schick, pers. comm., January 2003.

80. Tochnit Yud Gimmel (Thirteenth-Year Program) had its formal beginnings in 1958 with New York day school and yeshiva graduates (although there had been a plan also to have public high school graduates, who would thus get all they had missed in the way of Jewish education—but this plan failed to attract students). The first group numbered twenty-five, most of whom went either to Kerem B'Yavneh, a yeshiva near Ashdod, or to Machon Gold in Jerusalem. Alvin Schiff, "Post Yeshiva-Jewish Day High School Programs for American Students in Israel," unpublished paper, World Zionist Organization Education Department, 1999 (I thank Haim Zohar for providing me a copy of this internal report). In some cases, these first yeshiva programs were loosely connected with some religious Zionist programs that might put some young people on religious kibbutzim while others went to study Torah (I thank Sylvia Barack Fishman and Avram Abelow for their

recollections of their own experiences of this time in the early 1960s). Similar programs were established for Canadian, European, and Australian Jews.

81. The Israeli institution Machon Gold, which began as a place for men and women but after 1970 evolved into primarily a girls' seminary, actually began already in 1957 to take in foreign students (at first mainly from Latin America). Gabriel Cohn of Machon Gold, pers. comm., January 2003.

82. The idea that there were institutional solutions to the dangers of acculturation was by no means unique to these Jews. Other religious groups who were anxious about the deleterious effects of the baser qualities of Western culture were likewise occupied. The Christian right looked for schools and programs that would allow people to be "born again." Among Islamists there were efforts to avoid dangers of "westoxication," and some of those in power looked to pass laws that would, as the Iranian interior minister Ali Mohammed Besharti, explained, "immunize the people against the cultural invasion of the West." "Tehran DeTunes Western Culture," *Guardian,* April 18, 1995, 6.

83. Most colleges gladly allowed this deferment because it meant they had a student who was committed to attendance but who was given an extra year to mature in what they thought was a healthy learning environment.

84. Schiff, "Post-Yeshiva-Jewish Day High School Programs," 3–4.

85. When these programs first began accepting students, the process was run through the now-defunct Torah Education Department of the Jewish Agency.

86. Schiff, "Post Yeshiva-Jewish Day High School Programs."

87. "While American Jewish tourism to Israel is way down, and American enrollment has dropped sharply at secular institutions like Hebrew University of Jerusalem, post–high school yeshiva programs in Israel are—so far—an exception to the trend. Almost 2,400 American yeshiva and seminary students will be departing for Israel in the next month, according to Sheryl Stein, a spokeswoman for El Al Israel Airlines. The number is 'a drop' from last year, 'but not significant,' Stein said." Julie Weiner, "The Yearn to Learn," JTA News Service, August 31, 2001.

88. Schiff, "Post Yeshiva-Jewish Day High School Programs," executive summary, 4.

89. Rimor and Katz, "Jewish Involvement," table 1.8, p. 9.

90. Schiff, "Post Yeshiva-Jewish Day High School Programs," 22.

91. See Shalom Zvi Berger, "A Year of Study in an Israeli Yeshiva Program: Before and After," PhD diss., Yeshiva University, 1997.

92. It was Jewishly "protected" against defilement. For a time it was also protected from violence. When in the aftermath of the second intifada this second sort of security became more questionable, some Orthodox withdrew their children's participation for a time. However, the numbers seem to have come back up after the initial drop. Moreover, those who remained gave both themselves and their parents a kind of heroic reputation for their courage in staying, the idea of their making sacrifices for their Judaism.

93. Erving Goffman, *Asylums* (New York: Anchor, 1961), 4.

94. For an extensive discussion of this, see the chat room at www.edah.org

under the topic "The Changing Hashkafot [Outlooks] of Our Children." See also Michael Lopez-Calderon, "Our Homegrown Madrasahs," October 27, 2001, retrieved August 9, 2005, from www.dissidentvoice.org/Articles/MLMadrasah.htm.

95. Shalom Berger, pers. comm., January 2003. Chaim Waxman notes that "for example, data from Yeshivat Sha'alvim indicate that 71 of the 195 Americans who studied at the yeshiva during the years 1980–89, or 18 percent, have already gone on aliyah and are living in Israel." Chaim Waxman, "Sociological Perspectives on the Rabin Murder," *Journal of Jewish Education* 62 (1996): 30.

96. Erik Erikson, *Childhood and Society* (1950; reprint, New York: Norton, 1963), 253.

97. S. N. Eisenstadt, "Archetypal Patterns of Youth," in *The Challenge of Youth*, ed. Erik Erikson (New York: Doubleday Anchor, 1965), 32.

98. The following excerpt from a Web site specializing in matchmaking for Orthodox Jews demonstrates that this term is denotative. It says that many women who come to the site are expressing desires like this: "I am a yeshivish girl and I am looking for a typical yeshivish guy from a yeshivish family . . . a guy who is really serious about his learning. That should be his real motivation in life—learning Torah." "The Shadchan's Wife," retrieved August 9, 2005, from www.theshadchan .com/preview.html. In a burlesque of this attitude, the Bangitout.com writers (see the chapter on humor earlier in this volume) have listed among the "seven habits of highly yeshivish people" "[u]sing terms like 'Boruch Hashem,' 'Bli Eyin Harah,' 'Bisiyata Dishmaya,' 'KalVechomair,' 'No Shaiychus,' 'Shtikel,' 'Bissel,' 'Al Achas Cama v Cama,' 'Nebech,' 'Laybedik,' 'Machair,' 'SuchaYenteh,' and 'Hocker' in excess and completely out of context when answering the formal 'What's doing?' line of questioning is ideal, immediately making all subsequent forms of Loshon Harah in the conversation completely permissible and gratifying." Isaac Galena, "Seven Habits of Highly Yeshivish People," retrieved August 9, 2005, from www .bangitout.com/top2.html.

99. Eisenstadt, "Archetypal Patterns," 33–34.

100. After all, 85 percent of those enrolled in these sorts of schools by the year 2001–2 were in Haredi-sponsored institutions. See Schiff, "Post Yeshiva-Jewish Day High School Programs," 26.

101. M. L. Hansen, "The Third Generation in America," *Commentary* 14 (November 1952): 492–500.

102. Haym Soloveitchik, "Clarifications and Reply," *Torah u' Maddah Journal* 7 (January 1, 1997):145.

103. One of the most famous (or infamous, depending on one's point of view) of the manifestations of this attitude came with the challenge of the so-called "Yale five," five Orthodox students at Yale University who challenged the university's requirement that they live in the dormitories by arguing that "living with members of the opposite sex before marriage violated the standards of modesty dictated by their religion." The Yale Five brought a lawsuit against the university, asking to be exempted from the university requirement that they live on campus during their freshman and sophomore years. The position was rejected by both the university and the courts. See Eli Muller, "Orthodox Jews

Relieved by 'Yale 5' Loss," *Yale Daily News,* January 12, 2001. In another version of this response the Orthodox alumni of these yeshivas who attend the University of Pennsylvania almost universally live on particular floors of the dormitory there, a residential community that is colloquially known among them as "the ghetto."

104. Perl and Weinstein, "Parent's Guide," 11.

105. For resistance to this, see chap. 7.

106. Margaret Wolfenstein, "French Parents Take Their Children to the Park," in *Childhood in Contemporary Cultures,* ed. Margaret Mead and Martha Wolfenstein (Chicago: University of Chicago Press, 1955), 115–16.

107. The argument is made explicitly in a number of places. See, for example, Mordechai Greenberg, "Opening Remarks for Zman Elul," 1999, retrieved August 9, 2005, from the Web site of Kerem Be Yavne, one of the first Israeli yeshivas to have a program for American Jews: www.kby.org/torah/article.cfm?articleid=1019.

108. This is a famous line from Scripture. It appears in Isaiah 2:3 and Micah 4:2 and is repeated in popular liturgy and the Talmud. This argument is also articulated at the Israeli Kerem B'Yavneh Web site in remarks by Rabbi Mordechai Greenberg opening the yeshiva year. He said, "The Yeshiva [of Kerem B'Yavneh] is the ideal place for one to develop himself as part of a cohesive group. In the formative stages of the Jewish educational system, R. Yehoshua b. Gamla centralized the schools in Yerushalayim [Jerusalem], based on the verse, "Ki mitzion teitzei Torah—For from Zion the Torah will come forth, and the word of Hashem [the Lord] from Yerushalayim." Mordechai Greenberg, "Opening Remarks for Zman Elul," retrieved September 29, 2005, from www.KBY.org/torah/article .cfm?articleid=1019.

109. See, for example, Matti Wagner, "Student Came for Torah, but Found Heroin," *Jerusalem Post,* January 20, 2005. To be fair, only some yeshivas accept so-called "youth at risk" in the first place. But alcoholism and some drug use are not limited to those yeshivas.

110. Yeshivat Chovevei Torah, retrieved May 26, 2004, from www.yctorah.org/ frame.asp?go=mission.

111. Even such a classic yeshiva as Mir, founded in 1815 in what is now Belarus and relocated after World War II in Brooklyn and Jerusalem (by students who had survived the war in a temporary yeshiva in Shanghai, China), now has e-mail service. "Camp S'dei Chemed," retrieved August 9, 2005, from www.campsci.com.

112. Yaakov Perlow, "The Dangers of the Computer and the Internet," *Jewish Observer* 36 (November 2003).

113. See, for example, one sponsored by the National Council of Synagogue Youth of the Orthodox Union, as reported in "First Collegiate Kollel," *Leadership Briefing* (Orthodox Union), April/May 1999, 3, retrieved September 27, 2005, from www.ou.org/oupr/Lb/!LB-499.PDF.

114. Sponsored by Yeshiva University. See "Winter Kollel," retrieved August 9, 2005, from www.angelfire.com/dc/winterkollel/.

115. Clifford Geertz, *Local Knowledge* (New York: Basic Books, 1983), 151, 161.

116. For an interesting example, see Donald M. Nonini, "Introduction:

Transnational Migrants, Globalization Processes, and Regimes of Power and Knowledge," *Critical Asian Studies* 34 (March 2002): 3–17. Although Nonini is talking about labor migration, his conclusion that such migration moves not only people but also ideologies is no less applicable, and perhaps even more so, to the case of students like those discussed here.

117. "Iran's Youth Plot a Social Revolution," *Manchester Guardian Weekly*, September 2, 2002, 3.

Chapter 4. Reinventing Tradition

Epigraph is from Haym Soloveitchik, "Rupture and Reconstruction: The Transformation of Contemporary Orthodoxy," *Tradition* 28 (Summer 1994): 64–130.

1. Horace M. Kallen, *Cultural Pluralism and the American Idea: An Essay in Social Philosophy* (Philadelphia: University of Pennsylvania Press, 1956).

2. Ivan Marcus, *The Jewish Life Cycle* (Seattle: University of Washington Press, 2004), 8.

3. Although the phrase came from another context, the declaration by Rabbi Moses Sofer that "the new is prohibited by the Torah" became the slogan that summed up and represented this viewpoint. See S. Ehrmann, "Moses Sofer," in *Understanding Rabbinic Judaism,* ed. Jacob Neusner (New York: Ktav, 1974), 339–52.

4. Clifford Geertz, *Islam Observed* (New Haven, CT: Yale University Press, 1968).

5. See Heinrich Graetz, *Geschichte der Juden,* 2nd ed. (Leipzig: Leiner, 1878), 1:429–34, and S. C. Heilman, *The People of the Book: Drama, Fellowship, and Religion* (New Brunswick, NJ: Transaction Books, 2002).

6. See Haym Soloveitchik, "Migration, Acculturation, and the New Role of Texts," in *Accounting for Fundamentalisms: The Dynamic Character of Movements,* ed. R. S. Appleby et al. (Chicago: University of Chicago Press, 1994), 197–235, n. 4. Later published as "Rupture and Reconstruction: The Transformation of Contemporary Orthodoxy," *Tradition* 28 (Summer 1994): 64–130, with more extensive notes. The *Tradition* version is the one most commonly cited, in part because this is the preferred source for the Orthodox, who read their own literature first.

7. This is the name given to the descendants (between the twelfth and the mid–fourteenth centuries) of Rashi. They added to and reconciled his works with seeming contradictions in the Talmud, using many cross-references to similar topics in other sections of the Talmud. Various schools studied and compiled these works.

8. Haym Soloveitchik, "Religious Law and Change: The Medieval Ashkenazic Example," *AJS Review* 12 (1987): 208.

9. Soloveitchik notes, for example, that Isserles, writing in Krakow, Poland, allowed for the placing of logs on the fire by Gentiles on behalf of Jews on the Sabbath, a necessity given the cold Polish winters but a matter that other codes did not necessarily permit. But he allowed it knowing that in so doing he was not giving license to a community of Jews that was rushing to throw off Jewish

tradition and law (pers comm., January 2004). See also Jacob Katz, *The Shabbes Goy: A Study in Halakhic Flexibility* (Philadelphia: Jewish Publication Society, 1992).

10. Soloveitchik, "Religious Law," 211–12.

11. Ibid., 212.

12. For example, the seventeenth-century work by Shabbetai ben Meir Hacohen *(Shach)* and the sixteenth-century work by David ben Shmuel Halevy *(Taz)* or later the eighteenth-century *Pri Migadim,* by Joseph Teomim.

13. Soloveitchik argues that not all of these were motivated by the same desires—that, for example, the *Mishneh Berurah* was driven by a struggle against the Jewish Enlightenment while the *Arukh Ha Shulkhan* was simply setting forth the rules. Perhaps so, but in the end both, as well as these other volumes, served the same purpose: to provide a code of Jewish ritual and religious conduct in a world increasingly lacking a Jewish street that had been guided by one.

14. The connection of the prayer book, the siddur, to the codes was already established by the *Tur,* which was organized according to it.

15. Peter L. Berger, *The Heretical Imperative* (Garden City, NJ: Anchor Doubleday, 1979), 3.

16. Haym Soloveitchik, "Clarifications and Reply," *Torah U-Madda Journal* 7 (1997): 144.

17. Israel Kagan, *Likutei Halachot,* vol. 2, trans. in Chaim I. Waxman, "Toward a Sociology of Psak," *Tradition* 25 (Spring 1991): n. 11.

18. Soloveitchik, "Migration, Acculturation," 209.

19. See Isaac Chavel, "On Haym Soloveitchik's 'Rupture and Reconstruction: The Transformation of Contemporary Orthodox Society': A Response," *Torah U-Madda Journal* 7 (1997): 126.

20. Ibid., 128.

21. See Marcus, *Jewish Life Cycle,* 28.

22. Quoted in Menachem Friedman, "A Lost Tradition: How the Written Word Conquered the Living Tradition, Studies in the *Shiurim* Polemic," in *A Journey to the Halacha,* ed. Amichai Berholz (Jerusalem: Yediot Acharonot, 2003), 216.

23. This is, after all, the people of the book who turned the so-called "oral tradition" into the 1,623 pages of the Talmud.

24. See Neria Gutel, *Sefer Hishtanut Hatevaim b'Halacha* [The Book on the Change in the Natural Realm in Halacha] (Jerusalem: Sifrei Kodesh, 5755 [1995]). See also, on the matter of olives the size of eggs, Friedman, "Lost Tradition," 204. "מסורת שאבדה—כיצד ניצחה האות הכתובה את המסורת החיה—עיון בפולמוס השיעורים," עמיחי ברהולץ (עורך) *מסע אל ההלכה—עיונים בין-תחומיים בעולם החק היהודי,* ידיעות אחרונות ספרי חמר, תל-אביב 2003, pp. 196–218.

25. The idea that we have declined since the past originally seemed to refer to a spiritual or ontological decline, but starting with Rabbi Yecheskel Landau in Prague (d. 1793) and continuing even more with Karelitz, this was taken to mean as well that physically the world had diminished in size. See Friedman, "Lost Tradition," 200–203.

26. For an expression of this, see the *Lubavitch Weekly* source sheet "Sichat Hashavua Vayetze," November 15, 1991.

27. Soloveitchik, "Migration, Acculturation," 212.

28. Ibid., 200.

29. Ibid., 70–71.

30. *Puk chazi ma amach dabar* is the principle in the Talmud (B.T. Berachot 45b and Eruvin 14b and about a dozen other places) by which rabbis tried hard to justify what people did. By the eighteenth century, however, with the growing cracks in walls of tradition around the Jewish enclaves, this principle began to lose its power. This was also in part because there were no rabbis whose authority was recognized by all Jews.

31. Alfred Schutz, *Collected Papers*, vol. 2, *Studies in Social Theory*, ed. Arvid Brodersen (The Hague: Martinus Nijhoff, 1971), 300. I am applying Schutz's term to everyday *Jewish* knowledge.

32. Charles Liebman, "The Training of American Rabbis," *American Jewish Yearbook, 1968* (New York: American Jewish Committee, 1969), 106–10. See also Adam S. Ferziger, *Training American Orthodox Rabbis to Play a Role in Confronting Assimilation: Programs, Methodologies, and Directions,* Research and Position Papers (Ramat-Gan: Rappaport Center for Assimilation Research, Bar Ilan University, 2003), 22.

33. Soloveitchik, "Rupture and Reconstruction," 71.

34. For a comprehensive list of these books, see Jerusalem Books, "Table of Contents," retrieved August 10, 2005, from www.jerusalembooks.com/toc.htm. For the Artscroll phenomenon, see Jeremy Stolow, "Nation of Torah: Proselytism and the Politics of Historiography in a Religious Social Movement," PhD diss., York University, Toronto, Ontario, Canada, 2001. See also Marc Shapiro, *Saul Lieberman and the Orthodox* (Scranton, University of Scranton Press, 2006), 3–4.

35. Ferziger, *Training American Orthodox Rabbis,* 19.

Chapter 5. Machon L'Parnasa

1. U.S. Bureau of the Census, "1990 Census," retrieved October 30, 2005, from www.census.gov/main/www/cen1990.html.

2. This is in contrast to the extended yeshiva learning among Israeli Haredim that, while also part of a culture war, is more a reflection of an opposition to the social Zionist ideal of labor and a consequence of the desire to remain exempt from the Israeli requirement of universal military service. See Nurit Stadler, "Lehitparnes o Lechakot Lenais," in *Haredim Yisraelim,* ed. E. Sivan and K. Kaplan (Jerusalem: Van Leer, 2004), 32–55 [in Hebrew].

3. Yair Sheleg, *The New Religious Jews: Recent Developments among Observant Jews in Israel* (Jerusalem: Keter, 2000), 120 [in Hebrew]. See also E. Berman, "Sect, Subsidy and Sacrifice: An Economist's view of Ultra-Orthodox Jews," *Quarterly Journal of Economics* 115, no. 3 (2000): 905–53.

4. See Nurit Stadler, "Is Profane Work an Obstacle to Salvation? The Case of Ultra Orthodox (Haredi) Jews in Contemporary Israel," *Sociology of Religion* 63 (Winter 2002): 455–74.

5. Menachem Friedman, "Life Tradition and Book Tradition in the Develop-

342   NOTES TO PAGES 144–151

ment of Ultra-Orthodox Judaism," in *Judaism Viewed from Within and from Without,* ed. H. E. Goldberg (New York: State University of New York Press, 1987), 235–55.

6. Rabbi Benzion Kugler, principal of a Jerusalem yeshiva, quoted in Avi Garfinkel, "The Talmud Favors Outside Study," *Ha'aretz,* January 2, 2005.

7. *Sefer Binyan Olam,* quoted in Stadler, "Is Profane Work an Obstacle?" 5, 8.

8. See D. Spain and S. Bianchi, *Balancing Act: Motherhood, Marriage, and Employment among American Women* (New York: Russell Sage, 1996), and D. Shai, "Working Women/Cloistered Men: A Family Development Approach to Marriage Arrangements among Ultra-Orthodox Jews," *Journal of Comparative Family Studies* 33 (2002): 97–116.

9. Emile Durkheim, *The Elementary Forms of the Religious Life* (New York: Free Press, 1965), 465.

10. The term *g'machim* comes from גמ״ח, an acronym for the Hebrew phrase *gemilat chesed,* the doing of kindness, which has become the accepted term for offering free loans and support for those in need.

11. Thorstein Veblen, *The Theory of the Leisure Class* (New York: Macmillan, 1899).

12. Menachem Friedman, *Ha Chevra Ha Charedit: Mekorot, Megamot, U Tahalichim* [Haredi Society: Sources, Trends and Developments] (Jerusalem: Jerusalem Institute for Israel Studies, 1991) [in Hebrew].

13. Examples are to be found in South Bend, Indiana, Chicago, and Toronto, Canada (the latter being supported by the well-known Haredi philanthropists, the Reichman family of Olympia and York fame).

14. Veblen, *Theory of the Leisure Class,* 99.

15. Yishai Weiner, quoted in Joel Rebibo, "The Road Back from Utopia," *Azure,* no. 11 (Summer 2001): 131–68, retrieved October 30, 2005, from www.jafi.org.il/education/azure/11/11-rebibo.html.

16. See Richard Fulmer, "Becoming an Adult: Leaving Home and Staying Connected," in *The Expanded Family Life Cycle,* 3rd ed., ed. Betty Carter and Monica McGoldrick (Boston: Allyn and Bacon, 1999), 215–30.

17. Amiram Gonen, *From Yeshiva to Work: The American Experience and Lessons for Israel* (Jerusalem: Floersheimer Institute for Policy Studies, 2000), 46.

18. See Stadler, "Is Profane Work an Obstacle?" 7–8, and "Lehitparnes o Lechakot Lenais."

19. Gonen, *From Yeshiva to Work,* 48.

20. These positions are not equal in social status, nor do they offer equal pecuniary compensation.

21. Taverns, video shops, movie theaters, and beauty parlors—to offer some obvious examples.

22. See Gonen, *From Yeshiva to Work,* 19–20.

23. On the Haredi love affair with all sorts of modern gadgetry, see also Samuel Heilman, *Defenders of the Faith: Inside Ultra-Orthodox Jewry* (Berkeley: University of California Press, 1999), 95–96.

24. Sheleg, *New Religious Jews,* 144.

25. Ibid., 152.

26. Richard Devens Jr. and Chester Levine, "Occupation/Employment Projections," *Occupational Outlook Quarterly* 42 (Winter 1999–2000): 11–12.

27. See chap. 8 below. The official name of the neighborhood is Borough Park, but the spelling "Boro" has become the accepted one among the locals.

28. "Flatbush Women—Welcome," retrieved August 10, 2005, from www.touro .edu/las/programs/FlatbushWomen/.

29. "Flatbush Men—Welcome," retrieved August 10, 2005, from www.touro .edu/las/programs/FlatbushMen/.

30. There are cognate institutions to the Machon: for example, an institution called Concern, which in an earlier incarnation was called Shevet Yehuda Technical Institute. There is as well a program run by Agudath Israel of America called COPE (Career Opportunities and Preparation for Employment) that accepts students who have given a formal letter of approval for such vocational preparation from the rabbinic head of the yeshiva they attended. In Israel in 1996 an institute called the Haredi Machon for Professional Preparation offers some of the same sort of training. Among its most enthusiastic students are Haredi Jews associated with the Sephardic party, Shas. There are similar institutions emerging elsewhere, including Israel. Thus an institution in Or Yehuda, Israel, describing itself as "The Haredi Campus," advertises its capacity to "open before you the gates of *Parnasa* via courses in business administration, accounting, and so on on a one-day-a-week basis." *Sichat Hashavua,* no. 908, May 28, 2004, 4.

31. Everett Hughes, "Personality Types and the Division of Labor," in *The Sociological Eye: Selected Papers by Everett C. Hughes* (Chicago: Aldine-Atherton, 1971), 332.

32. Ibid., 334.

33. Everett C. Hughes, "Bastard Institutions," in *Sociological Eye,* 104, emphasis added.

34. Ibid., 99.

35. "Machon L'Parnassa," 2003, retrieved August 10, 2005, from www.touro .edu/Machon/.

36. These comments and others come from field notes from a series of observations and interviews carried on in the fall of 2000.

37. Gonen, *From Yeshiva to Work,* 62.

38. Ibid., 72.

39. See the controversy around Moses Mendelssohn's Bible translation and also the teaching of foreign language in the Volozhin yeshiva.

40. Shirley Jackson, *The Lottery and Other Stories* (New York: Modern Library, 2000).

41. Gonen, *From Yeshiva to Work,* 22.

42. Ibid., 66.

43. Quoted in Rebibo, "Road Back from Utopia."

44. *Shababnikes* is a Yiddishism that comes from the Israeli *Shabab,* a term originally taken from Arabic and referring to unruly youths, street people. The Haredim have appropriated this term for their own unruly young, adding the Yid-

dish suffix -*nikes* to Judaize it, arguing as well that it comes from the acronym SBB, for the biblical phrase (Eccl. 11:9) *samach bachur b'yaldutecha,* meaning "Rejoice, young man, in thy youth." See Heilman, *Defenders of the Faith,* 162.

45. The involvement of a number of these young men in Israel in Zaka, the Haredi organization that collects the body parts of the dead hurt in terrorist attacks (and now also in accidents), is an example. See Nurit Stadler, "Death, Terror and the 'True Kindness': The Case of the Haredi Disaster Victim Identification Team in Israel (ZAKA)," paper presented at the Ecole des hautes études en sciences sociales, Paris, May 19, 2004.

46. Gonen, *From Yeshiva to Work,* 38.

47. Ibid., 35.

48. Yaakov Perlow, "The Dangers of the Computer and the Internet," *Jewish Observer* 36 (November 2003).

49. See Friedman, *Haredi Society.*

50. Gonen, *From Yeshiva to Work,* 73.

51. Ibid., 73.

52. Veblen, *Theory of the Leisure Class.*

53. I wish to thank Gabriella Theiler and Kristin Insulander, two Swedish students of journalism, for these and many of the other quotations from women students at the Machon.

54. When a woman does not want to take "her place" on the bus, that is news. Just this happened on the Hasidic-owned Monsey Trails Bus Lines in 1994 when one Sima Rabinovicz, who was not really a Haredi, boarded the bus on her way home from her job as a supervisor of cardiology tests and refused to move behind a curtain during an impromptu prayer service. She sued the bus company. See Joseph Berger, "Discrimination or Discourtesy? A Commuter Won't Leave Her Bus Seat for Hasidic Prayer Meeting," *New York Times,* September 9, 1994, B1.

Six months later she won her case in court, an American and not a religious court. See Bruce Frankel, "N.Y.'s 'Jewish Rosa Parks' Wins Bus Battle," *USA Today,* March 17, 1995, 4A. However the settlement did not really change the separate seating. The decision of the court was that all parties agreed to allow the praying passengers to continue to sit separately using the dividing curtain if they, not the bus company, provided their own curtain. Nevertheless, this woman's assertiveness and her legal success undoubtedly served as a lesson for the Haredi women on the bus and in the community that they did not have to always be subservient to the desires of the men.

55. Helena Z. Lopata, *Occupation: Housewife* (New York: Oxford University Press, 1971), 65–66.

56. Letter from Judy Ostrow, "Not Just a Modern Orthodox Problem," *Jewish Press,* December 10, 2003, retrieved August 10, 2005, from www.thejewish-press.com/news_article.asp?article=3161.

57. Berel Wein, "Ultra-Orthodoxy Isn't a Problem," *Jerusalem Post,* May 27, 2004, 11.

Chapter 6. Much Truth Said in Jest

Epigraph from Sigmund Freud, "Humor," in *Collected Papers,* ed. James Strachey (New York: Basic Books, 1959), 5:220.

1. Sigmund Freud, "Humor," in *Collected Papers,* ed. James Strachey (New York: Basic Books, 1959), 5:216.

2. Erik H. Erikson, *Insight and Responsibility* (New York: Norton, 1964), 126.

3. S. C. Heilman and S. M. Cohen, *Cosmopolitans and Parochials: Modern Orthodox Jews in America* (Chicago: University of Chicago Press, 1989), 198.

4. See the discussion on the Israeli yeshiva experience in chap. 3.

5. Erving Goffman, *Encounters: Two Studies in the Sociology of Interaction* (Indianapolis: Bobbs-Merrill, 1961), 85–132.

6. For the concept of "social capital," see James S. Coleman, "Social Capital in the Creation of Human Capital," *American Journal of Sociology* 94 (1988): S95–S120, and Robert D. Putnam, "Bowling Alone: America's Declining Social Capital," *Journal of Democracy* 6 (January 1995): 65–78, esp. 66. See also Robert D. Putnam, *Bowling Alone: The Collapse and Revival of American Community* (New York: Simon and Schuster, 2000).

7. Erikson, *Insight and Responsibility,* 126.

8. Ibid., 127.

9. Freud, "Humor," 217.

10. Ibid., 218.

11. "Top Ten Ways You Know It's Time for a Vacation from the Upper West Side," June 6, 2002, retrieved August 14, 2005, from www.bangitout.com/top76.html.

12. The brothers Isaac and Seth Galena, Orthodox twenty-somethings from Philadelphia, run the Web site formally.

13. Indeed, it is also tentatively trying to build a market out of these readers, who will be sold everything from T-shirts to trips abroad and anything else these young entrepreneurs can dream up. For some of these T-shirts and lapel pins, see "Jewschool Store," retrieved August 14, 2005, from www.cafepress.com/jewschool, where one can purchase the oxymoronic "orthodox anarchist pin" or a T-shirt on which a Hasid in caftan and shtreimel packs a machine gun under the logo "Go ahead make my shabbos."

14. One of the writers for the site, Aryeh Dworken, who writes many of the music reviews, took particular pleasure (interview, June 4, 2002) in the fact that he could demonstrate in cyberspace that this was possible.

15. Interview with Seth Galena and Aryeh Dworken, June 4, 2002.

16. This may of course be the author's tongue-in-cheek meaning, a kind of reference to the narrow parochialism of Orthodoxy.

17. The Freudian interpretations of the choice of *bang* as the operative word here are unusually rich. A bang is something that resonates with aggression—guns and hammers bang—and also carries a thinly veiled reference to sexual activity, a slang use of the word. To "bang it out" also echoes the desire to straighten a dent, fix a blemish, express sexual urges. All of these underlying elements are surely part of the deep structure that sustains this site.

18. Rabbi Eitan Mayer, Assistant Rabbi, the Jewish Center, "The Big Bang at the JC," October 10, 2001, retrieved October 30, 2005, from www.bangitout.com/comments.html.

19. Interview, June 4, 2002.

20. Erik Erikson, *Childhood and Society,* 2nd ed. (New York: Norton, 1963).

21. Erving Goffman, in *The Presentation of Self in Everyday Life* (Garden City, NY: Doubleday, 1959), described this as an ongoing process negotiated anew during each encounter with other people in everyday life, while Erikson, in *Childhood and Society,* portrayed it as essentially taking place only at the transitions of eight ages in life, with everything in between being a variation of the essential features of the age around which one's life was organized at the time.

22. Erik Erikson, "Youth: Fidelity and Diversity," in *The Challenge of Youth,* ed. Erik Erikson (New York: Doubleday Anchor, 1965), 3.

23. Ibid., 3.

24. Kaspar Naegele, "Youth and Society," in Erikson, *Challenge of Youth,* 55.

25. Ibid., 69.

26. This has not always been the case. Some of the "heroes" of modern Orthodoxy have argued that there need not be conflict between "Torah," Jewish tradition, and *derech eretz,* the way of the world or common custom (see Heilman and Cohen, *Cosmopolitans and Parochials,* for a fuller discussion). These days, however, as the Haredi elements of Orthodoxy have grown more assertive and controlling, that position is not dominant.

27. Kenneth Keniston, "Social Change and Youth in America," in Erikson, *Challenge of Youth,* 193.

28. See Martin E. Marty and R. Scott Appleby, introduction to *Fundamentalisms Comprehended,* ed. Martin E. Marty and R. Scott Appleby (Chicago: University of Chicago Press, 1995).

29. On the modern Orthodox poking fun at this "chumra-of-the-week," see "The Chumra of the Week Club," retrieved August 14, 2005, from http://members.tripod.com/~jewishjokes/chmura-week-club.htm. See also Haym Soloveitchik, "Clarifications and Reply," *Torah u' Maddah Journal* 7 (January 1, 1997), 145–48, and Chaim Waxman, "Toward a Sociology of Psak," *Tradition* 25 (Spring 1991): 12–25.

30. Several Orthodox rabbis issued a spring 2004 interpretation announcing that the tap water in New York City might not be kosher because of microscopic traces of nonkosher crustacean bugs in it. See "Orthodox Jews Worry New York City's Water May Not Be Kosher," June 2004, retrieved September 28, 2005, from www.uswaternews.com/archives/arcquality/4orthjews6.html. For the debate this sparked within Orthodoxy, see "Back Row of the 'Beis," retrieved August 14, 2005, from /www.thebronsteins.com/archives/000184.html.

31. Michael Winner, "60 Ways to Appear Frum and Intellectual," retrieved August 14, 2005, from www.bangitout.com/tdb38.html.

32. In an interesting commentary on this article, the iconic illustration attached to the headline features an image of a Santa hat on a Jewish face, suggesting that the "intellectual" element (Winner's euphemism for appearing "hip") is identical with appearing as a Gentile. This oxymoronic image demon-

strates that while, as the article demonstrates, Winner may have a relatively sharp sense of what appearing *frum* entails, he betrays a curious, almost naive (parochially Jewish) notion of what appearing as an intellectual means. A review of his list suggests it means acting in a way that indicates an awareness of American popular culture and acting in a way that is typically not-*frum*, or, as the picture suggests, as Gentile.

33. For an exploration of this issue, see S. C. Heilman, "Inner and Outer Identity: Sociological Ambivalence among Orthodox Jews," *Jewish Social Studies* 39 (Summer 1977): 227–40.

34. On Yinglish as a tool of Orthodox speech, see Sol Steinmetz, "Jewish English in the United States," *American Speech* 56 (Spring 1981): 3–16.

35. Sarah Galena, "Top 10 Ways You Know You're an Observant Jew Attending a Secular College," retrieved August 14, 2005, from www.bangitout.com/top33/html.

36. Kenneth Rosen, "Top 10 Indications That You Were a 90's Yeshiva High School Punk," retrieved August 14, 2005, from www.bangitout.com/top70/html.

37. Aviva Leibtag, "The Official Modern Orthodox Quiz," retrieved August 14, 2005, from www.bangitout.com/tdb40.html.

38. For these and other lists, see "The Kosher Top Ten Archives," retrieved August 14, 2005, from www.bangitout.com/koshertopten.html.

39. Erikson, *Childhood and Society,* 263.

40. Heilman and Cohen, *Cosmopolitans and Parochials,* reports that modern Orthodox premarital physical intimacies are far more permissive than one might generally expect. That these matters are on their minds can be seen, for example, in the following schedule of study topics for a summer program geared to modern Orthodox Jewish high school seniors on their way to college:

1) Interactions w/ Non-Jews

2) Interactions w/ Non-Observant and Non-Orthodox Jews

3) Gender Issues

4) Tzniut [sexual modesty] on the college campus

5) Kol Isha [hearing the (prohibited) voice of a woman singing] and the college A Cappella group

6) Hillel—Jewish Life on campus

Yeshivat Chovevei Torah, retrieved July 2003 from www.yctorah.org/hss/sched.html.

41. See Samuel Heilman, *Defenders of the Faith: Inside Ultra-Orthodox Jewry* (Berkeley: University of California Press, 1999), 277–90.

42. Indeed, some wags have suggested that in twenty-first-century America, besides young people from conservative groups, the only young people left who actually want to get married are gay couples.

43. Dov Wasserman, "Top 42 100% Guaranteed Synagogue Pickup Lines," retrieved August 14, 2005, from www.bangitout.com/top25/html. Purim is the Jewish holiday that celebrates the Jews' deliverance from catastrophe, a rescue assisted

by the fact that a Jewish girl, Esther, was set up by her Uncle Mordecai and some curious twists of fate (the hidden hand of God, according to the rabbis) to become the wife of the Persian King Achashverosh (a great *shidduch* except that it led to a Jewish woman marrying a Gentile man).

44. The original series, now issued by Skylark Books, allowed readers to enter a mysterious cave and, by following the instructions on each page, to choose among several different adventures backward and forward in time.

45. "Top Ten Ways You Know It's Time."

46. Eli Goldman, "J-Escorts," retrieved August 14, 2005, from www.bangitout .com/tdb10.html.

47. This is a private Orthodox bus connection to an Orthodox neighborhood in Rockland County, New York.

48. The reference to "G-d," the orthography used by the Orthodox who thereby "do not use God's name in vein" either is cynical and ironic or reveals that the writer, though presenting identities of young people who are putting on their Orthodoxy like some managed impression or role display, is herself still part of the world of those who take their religious commitments seriously.

49. I thank Avram Heilman for this insight and for other helpful comments with this chapter.

50. For example, a "Shidduch Directory" in a Boro Park community newspaper whose goal is not humor but an earnest and honest listing of who is out there and available offers the following twenty descriptors of Orthodox identity (there is no key to explain the "code," so we may assume that readers understand well what each category describes).

Open-minded Bais Yaakov [an Orthodox religiously right-wing women's seminary]

Worldly Bais Yaakov

Frum with-it

Heimische [homey]

Heimische Yeshivish

Heimische Very Frum

With-it Yeshivish

Frum but not Yeshivish

American Frum

With-it Heimische

Yeshivish Litvish [Lithuanian-style]

Litvish yeshivish

Chassidish

Chassidic Lubavitch inclined

Modern orthodox

Y.U. [Yeshiva University] right [wing]

Yeshivish secular

Agudah [religiously right-wing affiliation with the Agudath Israel movement] type

Young Israel [a modern Orthodox American synagogue movement]

Queens [a borough of New York City whose Orthodox population tends to be largely modern Orthodox and religious Zionist]

51. Daniel B, "Top Ten Reasons I Am a 34-Year Old Male and Still Unmarried on the Upper West Side," retrieved August 14, 2005, from www.bangitout.com/top256.html.

52. Keniston, "Social Change," 211.

53. "Top 40 Thoughts on a Bad Date," retrieved August 14, 2005, from www.bangitout.com/top21.html.

54. Keniston, "Social Change," 212. See also Erikson, *Childhood and Society,* 254.

55. Keniston, "Social Change," 201.

56. See Goffman, *Encounters,* on this conception of alienation.

57. For more on this, see Rosen, "Top Ten Indications."

58. Keniston, "Social Change," 205.

59. David Riesman, *The Lonely Crowd: A Study of the Changing American Character* (New Haven, CT: Yale University Press, 1950).

60. Robert Wuthnow, *Sharing the Journey: Support Groups and America's New Quest for Community* (New York: Free Press, 1994), reports a rapid expansion of such support groups in the last quarter-century so that fully 40 percent of Americans claim to be currently involved in one. As such, one might suggest that in choosing to turn to the young Orthodox enclave many of these Jews are acting like the 40 percent of Americans who are turning to support groups.

61. Putnam, "Bowling Alone," 67–68.

Chapter 7. Orthodox Jewish Calls from the Walls

Epigraph from Erving Goffman, *Frame Analysis: An Essay on the Organization of Experience* (Cambridge, MA: Harvard University Press, 1974), 547.

1. Menachem Friedman, *Poster People* (Jerusalem: Jerusalem Institute for Research, forthcoming).

2. Erving Goffman, *Gender Advertisements* (New York: Harper and Row, 1979), 1.

3. Ibid., 1.

4. See Erving Goffman, *Frame Analysis: An Essay on the Organization of Experience* (Cambridge, MA: Harvard University Press, 1974), 518.

5. See Emmanuel Sivan, "The Enclave Culture," in *Fundamentalisms Comprehended,* ed. R. S. Appleby and M. Marty (Chicago: University of Chicago Press, 1995), 16. On the poster as an educational tool, see S. Duchin and G. Sherwood, "Posters as an Educational Strategy," *Journal of Continuing Education for Nurses* 21 (September–October 1990): 205–8.

6. Peter Berger, "Identity as a Problem in the Sociology of Knowledge," in *The Sociology of Knowledge: A Reader,* ed. J. E. Curtis and J. W. Petras (New York: Praeger, 1970), 376. See also Bernard Spolsky and Elana Shohamy, "Language Practice, Language Ideology and Language Policy," in *Language Policy and Pedagogy,* ed. Richard Lambert and Elana Shohamy (Philadelphia: John Benjamins, 2000), 1–42, who argue that there is a language ideology in group life that fosters consensus on what language or dialect is appropriate for what purpose.

7. See Samuel Heilman, *The People of the Book* (Chicago: University of Chicago Press, 1987), 163–76.

8. This is not unlike what, for example, Spanish speakers do in certain Latino neighborhoods. See Simeon D. Baumel, "Sacred Speakers: Language and Culture among the Ultra Orthodox in Israel" (PhD diss., Bar Ilan University, 2002), 130.

9. Joshua Fishman, "Who Speaks What Language to Whom and When," *La Linguistique* 2 (1965): 71.

10. Dell Hymes, *Foundations in Sociolinguistics: An Ethnographic Approach* (Philadelphia: University of Pennsylvania Press, 1974).

11. The Satmar community in Williamsburg has as one of its particular charity projects the collection of a blood supply for Jews who are hospitalized. According to a handbill they distribute, they provide "screened volunteers" of "all blood types," as part of a "project [that] is crucial to protect our community against unpure *[sic]* blood." While at one level this purity of blood clearly refers to a supply that is less likely to suffer such contaminations as HIV than the general blood supply—or so the community believes—at another level it is part of the focus on boundaries that is part of all enclave cultures. Hence these blood drives serve not only to collect and supply untainted blood but also to reinforce the lines between insiders and outsiders.

12. Goffman, *Gender Advertisements,* 6.

13. Notice how in figure 5 a poster (for Felder's election) is already affixed on the store door adjacent to where the woman is affixing a poster.

14. The wigs in Williamsburg tend to be the obvious peruque covered by a kerchief, while in the other neighborhoods wigs tend to be more stylish and kerchiefs are not worn except to cover one's actual hair. Hats and snoods are more common in the other three enclaves.

15. See below the discussion of the mezuzah poster found in Crown Heights in the chapter section "Mezuzah Campaign: Operation Security."

16. In Kew Gardens Hills, yards play this role.

17. Jacob Ukeles and Ronald Miller, "The Jewish Community Study of New York: 2002 Highlights," booklet, UJA Federation of New York, June 2003, 32.

18. For a full review of the beginnings of Orthodox Williamsburg, see George (Gershon) Kranzler, *Williamsburg: A Jewish Community in Transition* (New York: Feldheim, 1961).

19. These and all subsequent numbers are drawn from census figures in which data were collected for white non-Hispanics in Williamsburg who at the time these data were collected (1989) were almost exclusively Orthodox Jews. This was before the more recent influx of white non-Hispanic artists into the area.

20. Or it may suggest that the young couples that want more children move to suburban Kiryas Joel.

21. This describes a steady increase from the almost 16 percent who were on welfare in 1965 and the almost 29 percent in 1971 (*New York Times,* April 10, 1972, 22).

22. A number of Haredim have been caught up in illicit schemes for funds, including laundering drug money and illegally funneling government funds to Orthodox institutions. See, for example, "Ecstasy Trade Lures Young Hasidim into World of Crime," *Newsday,* January 16, 2001, A6; "Rabbis' Drug Charges Rock a Brooklyn Hasidic Sect: Crime, Religious Community 'Known for Kindness and Charity' is Shocked at Money Laundering Allegations," *Los Angeles Times,* June 19, 1997, 1; and "Hasidim Fight Fed Fraud Charges," *New York Daily News,* June 1, 1997, 24.

23. See, for example, the discussion of the Williamsburg people who have enrolled in courses at the Machon L'Parnasa.

24. Steven I. Weiss, "G-d Damn Hipsters," *Harper's Magazine,* March 2004, 7.

25. Henry R. Styles, *A History of the City of Brooklyn* (Brooklyn, NY: H. R. Styles, 1867), 43. See also Egon Mayer, *From Suburb to Shtetl: The Jews of Boro Park* (Philadelphia: Temple University Press, 1979), 20–23.

26. Mayer, *From Suburb to Shtetl,* 24.

27. Even the spelling that formally is "Borough Park" is more commonly in the shortened form used above.

28. To be sure, for some Jews the increase in the numbers of Orthodox in the neighborhood was repulsive and stimulated an exodus among those who embraced a more liberal Jewish atmosphere.

29. See Mayer, *From Suburb to Shtetl,* 36–58, who traces this process through much of the 1970s.

30. Ibid., 49.

31. His comments also resembled those of the Fifth Lubavitcher Rabbi, Sholem Dov Ber, who warned his followers against leaving Russia for America or the Palestine. Under the czar, he explained, Jews might die but Judaism could remain unaffected by assimilation, while in those other places Jews might be safe but Judaism would suffer from defiling cultural decline. See Aviezer Ravitsky, *Messianism, Zionism, and Jewish Religious Radicalism* (Chicago: University of Chicago Press, 1996), 193–203.

32. *Chabad* is an acronym for the Hebrew words "wisdom, understanding, and knowledge" and is used to denote the philosophy and ideology of those Hasidim who hail from Lubavitch.

33. It is about a quarter of the rate in Williamsburg and about one-seventh the rate in places like Kiryas Joel and New Square.

34. These numbers may be suspect in that some Lubavitchers may count studies at their own institutions as "college" study. In general these numbers are culled from the census data for white, non-Hispanic residents of Crown Heights.

35. Much of this information is drawn from Queens Borough Public Library publications.

36. See Samuel C. Heilman, *Portrait of American Jews: The Last Half of the Twentieth Century* (Seattle: University of Washington Press, 1990).

37. To be accurate, the increase in the Haredi proportion of Orthodoxy here is not only the result of people moving in but also a result of an ideological or behavioral shift by some of those who were modern Orthodox to their religious right.

38. In general, the American Jewish model of synagogue building, as Jonathan Sarna notes, has from as early as the colonial period been to create structures that from the exterior do not stand out from the surrounding architecture. Jonathan Sarna, *American Judaism* (New Haven, CT: Yale University Press, 2004). Where this "rule" is broken it seems the implicit message is that the Jews in question are proud to stand out. The pride may be artistic, as in the Frank Lloyd Wright–designed Beth Sholom in Elkins Park, Pennsylvania. But it may also be cultural, as in the Ohr HaChayim in Kew Gardens Hills.

39. Unlike the expressway that passes through Williamsburg and over which there are bridges, these high-speed roads have large margins and service roads that parallel them, making them far more powerful boundaries.

40. In fact, outside class, the contact between the Orthodox Jews and these other ethnics remains quite limited. A student paper examining the cafeteria documented the ways in which the room is divided in an ethnic reflection of the boundaries of the surrounding neighborhoods.

41. The 2003 New York Jewish Population Survey confirms the decline of the Jewish community in the borough of Queens, hinted at by an analysis of the 1990 and 2000 U.S. Census.

42. To be sure, the use of posters is not unique to this community. Other ethnic enclaves in New York also use these, although more for advertising than for the sort of intimate cultural and social contact that the Orthodox Jews in question do.

43. Goffman, *Frame Analysis*, 1–2.

44. To be sure, when compared with posters directed to the general American community or to any other interest, ethnic, or religious group, nearly all the posters considered in these pages may seem exquisitely parochial.

45. See the introductory chapter in this volume, as well as Heilman, *Portrait of American Jews*. This of course does not mean that every Orthodox Jew is economically less well off than all other sorts of Jews but only that as an aggregate the Orthodox are poorer.

46. Kosher food is generally more expensive than nonkosher. Housing for large families and within the area limited by access to Jewish institutions tends to cost more. Private Jewish education — day schools and yeshivas — costs more than public education.

47. On the style of mendicancy popular among the Orthodox, see S. C. Heilman, "The Gift of Alms: Face-to-Face Almsgiving among Orthodox Jews," *Urban Life and Culture* 3 (January 1975): 371–95, reprinted in *The Study of Society: An Integrated Anthology*, 4th ed., ed. Peter Rose (New York: Random House, 1977).

48. In addition to 120, as used in the Williamsburg poster, the number 18, which in Hebrew numerology is equivalent to the word for "life," or its multi-

ples, is a frequent donation amount used in Jewish and particularly Orthodox appeals.

49. Retrieved in 2001 from www.innercircleny.com.

50. The list in the Appendix is a representative collection made over the course of approximately eight months in 2000–2001.

51. About 4 percent of the Jews in Kew Gárdens Hills, 5 percent of those in Boro Park, and 7 percent of those in Crown Heights claimed Yiddish as the language spoken at home in these less insular Orthodox enclaves.

52. Annual per capita income in Kew Gardens Hills was about $18,000 with about 6 percent below the poverty level, $11,000 and 26 percent in Boro Park, and $10,000 and 25 percent in Crown Heights. The population of New York City as a whole was at $17,000 and 13 percent.

53. Sivan, "Enclave Culture," 19.

54. The use of the word *Israel* in the poster is somewhat ambiguous and can refer to Jews (as in the "children of Israel") in general and not necessarily only to the state of Israel.

55. This is a reference to Deut. 6:5.

56. Yoel Behrman, *Arum di Welt in 80 Tug* (Brooklyn: Chen Publishers, 5761 [2001]), 447.

57. Weiss, "G-d Damn Hipsters." That the artists are having an impact can also be seen in the remarkable story of a Williamsburg Hasid who for a time became a heavy metal artist. See "My Experimental Phase," *This American Life,* June 25, 2004, Episode 268, retrieved August 15, 2005, from www.thisamericanlife.org.

58. In article entitled "Beating the Brokers" that appeared in the August 21, 2002, issue of the *Village Voice,* a weekly that has as its readers many singles from Manhattan, Andrew Aber informs his readers: "Before you crawl back to your parents, discover the next Willie Bs. Try Borough Park—it's got a Hasid community, too! Only 25 minutes from the city, you can still find a studio here for $800. Borough Park also borders Sunset Park, Brooklyn, which is home to the city's second largest Chinatown, as well as a growing Mexican community." Retrieved August 15, 2005, from www.villagevoice.com/news/0234,aber,37603,1.html.

59. He won, even though the election originally scheduled for September 11 had to be postponed because of the attacks on New York that day.

60. "NJPS: Jewish Households," retrieved August 15, 2005, from the United Jewish Communities Web site: www.ujc.org/content_display.html?ArticleID=83788.

61. For a full description of this, see Samuel Heilman, *A Walker in Jerusalem* (Philadelphia: Jewish Publication Society, 1995), 167–69.

62. Jewish law demands that sacred items no longer in usable condition (prayer books or scriptural texts bearing God's name being the most common such items) be buried or else stored in a *genizah* or synagogue repository.

63. Goffman, *Frame Analysis,* esp. 44–69.

64. See Philip Rieff, *The Triumph of the Therapeutic* (Chicago: University of Chicago Press, 1966).

65. The popularity of these pseudoscientific procedures has grown among populations like the one in Kew Gardens Hills that also believe in the healing power

of religion and miracle rabbis. In other words, once a person believes that illness may be treated and cured in ways not limited to modern medicine, the door is opened to folk remedies and herbal cures, nontraditional healers, and all sorts of other therapies. These elements are missing in both the other neighborhoods thus far considered. They point to the growing presence in the neighborhood of Jews who believe in folk remedies.

66. The small number of Lubavitchers in Crown Heights is often masked by the fact that because of their outreach they have emissaries throughout the world, giving the impression that they are part of a huge worldwide network and mass movement. Calling their Crown Heights office their "worldwide headquarters" underscores this impression, which is crucial to their recruitment and outreach efforts.

67. See Philip Gourevitch, "The Crown Heights Riot and Its Aftermath," *Jewish Forward,* January 1993, retrieved August 15, 2005, from www.ex-iwp.org/docs/1993/Crown%20Heights%20Riot%20Aftermath.htm.

68. On the history of this enmity, see Jerome Mintz, *Hasidic People* (Cambridge, MA: Harvard University Press, 1992), 57–59.

69. Leon Festinger, Henry Riecken, and Stanley Schachter, *When Prophecy Fails* (New York: Harper Torchbooks, 1964), 3.

70. In a remarkable illustration of this, the documentary film *A Life Apart,* dir. and prod. Menachem Daum and Oren Rudavsky, 1997, shows the lighting of a Hanukkah menorah in Red Square, with the musical accompaniment of the former Red Army band playing, among other songs, the Chabad song "God Is One and His Name Is One."

71. This is a common term for the infants, who remain undefiled and unblemished by the seductions of the world outside Chabad. The Hebrew word is *temimim.*

72. In Lubavitch mythology this is based on the parable of a king whose son had strayed from the palace, forgotten his royal origins, and become a vagabond. The king went in search of him and, to lure him back, dressed and acted like a vagabond. Thus he managed to gain access to his son and remind him who he truly was. Jews who have strayed from the Orthodox tradition are the vagabonds, and the *shluchim* are the emissaries who act like vagabonds to bring these sons and daughters back to the royal palace of the Torah and God.

73. In many Chabad communities, these videos are viewed on the same occasions when in the past the rebbe would address them live via video feed. Indeed, there are now videos for every occasion in the Chabad calendar.

74. There were other rituals, such as getting adult men to don tefillin (phylacteries) daily and lighting a large Hanukkah menorah in public, that became part of the campaign. As for the mezuzah, Chabad made part of its goal to see to it that every mezuzah's contents were checked to be certain the handwritten parchment inside was properly inscribed. This meant that even if people had affixed a mezuzah to the doorpost the Lubavitchers had something to do; they could check to make certain it was kosher.

75. For some a trip to the rebbe's grave in Queens and the spiritual renewal they get from this pilgrimage serves, particularly when it occurs on occasions when

many other Hasidim come as well—as they do in the summer on the third of Tammuz (early in July), the anniversary of the rebbe's death.

76. He actually began singing with the then-Lubavitcher Hasid Rabbi Zalman Schachter, who later became better known for his stretching of the limits of Jewish expression in a variety of other ways beyond the musical. See "Rabbi Zalman Schachter-Shalomi," retrieved August 15, 2005, from www.jewishretreatcenter.org/ec/teachers/rabbi_zalman_schachter-shalomi.

77. For a particularly remarkable testimony to his influence, see the film *Hiding and Seeking,* dir. and prod. Menachem Daum and Oren Rudavsky, 2004. (For further information, see the film's Web site at www.hidingandseeking.com.)

78. A recent online discussion of spiritual boredom and decline at the Edah organization's Web site provides an interesting window into these feelings. See "Modern Orthodoxy: General Discussion," retrieved October 30, 2005, from www.edah.org/emazeforums/program/readForum.cfm?confID=11&formID=25.

79. See Samuel Heilman, *Synagogue Life: A Study in Symbolic Interaction,* 2nd ed. with new foreword and afterword (New Brunswick, NJ: Transaction Books, 1998).

80. Menachem Mendel Schneerson, *Toward a Meaningful Life: The Wisdom of the Rebbe Menachem Mendel Schneerson,* adapted by Simon Jacobson (New York: William Morrow, 1995).

81. Sivan, "Enclave Culture," 58.

Chapter 8. Toward a Postmodern American Orthodoxy

Epigraph from Fyodor Dostoyevsky, *The House of the Dead* (London: Penguin, 1985), 279.

1. "An Orthodox Jew grows up and believes that Eretz Yisrael and the people of Israel are one. The fulfillment of Torah is Eretz Yisrael," said David Cohen, director of Orthodox Union activities in Israel. "It's not about connection. It's who we are." See Dina Kraft, "At Orthodox Union Convention, Strong Tie to Israel Seen as Key," Jewish Telegraphic Agency, November 29, 2004, retrieved August 15, 2005, from www.jta.org/page_view_story.asp?strwebhead=Orthodox+stress+Israel+ties&intcategoryid=1&SearchOptimize=Jewish+News.

2. See S. C. Heilman and S. M. Cohen, *Cosmopolitans and Parochials: Modern Orthodox Jews in America* (Chicago: University of Chicago Press, 1989).

3. "President Bush Participates in Menorah Lighting Ceremony," December 9, 2004, retrieved October 30, 2005, from www.whitehouse.gov/news/releases/2004/12/20041209-16.v.html.

4. Reuven Ziegler, "Being Frum and Being Good," in *By His Light: Character and Values in the Service of God—Based on Addresses by Aharon Lichtenstein* (Alon Shevut: Yeshivat Har Etzion, 2002), 118–21.

5. See Eli Muller, "Orthodox Jews Relieved by 'Yale 5' Loss," *Yale Daily News,* January 12, 2001.

6. "Jewish Court Excommunicates Lieberman," CNS.com, October 24, 2000,

retrieved August 15, 2005, from www.newsmax.com/articles/?a=2000/10/23/165511.txt. See also Ari Goldman, "Observant vs. Orthodox," *Jewish Week,* August 25, 2000.

7. Samuel Blumenfeld, "Lieberman's Orthodoxy Disputed," WorldNet Daily, September 5, 2000, retrieved August 15, 2005, from www.worldnetdaily.com/news/article.asp?ARTICLE_ID=12832.

8. Avi Shafran, "We Are All Mr. Lieberman," in *Coalition* [Agudath Israel], November 14, 2000, retrieved August 15, 2005, from http://members.aol.com/LazerA/AmEchad/lieberman3.html.

9. Fyodor Dostoyevsky, *The House of the Dead* (London: Penguin, 1985), 279.

10. David Berger, *The Rebbe, the Messiah, and the Scandal of Orthodox Indifference* (New York: Littman Library, 2001).

11. Ryan Bishop, "Postmodernism," in *Encyclopedia of Cultural Anthropology,* ed. David Levinson and Melvin Ember (New York: Henry Holt, 1996), 993.

12. For an expanded discussion of these reinventions, see Samuel Heilman, *Portrait of American Jews: The Last Half of the Twentieth Century* (Seattle: University of Washington Press, 1996).

Index

Note: Page numbers in *italics* refer to illustrations.

Cyberspace, 10, 169, 345n14; and humor, 184. *See also* Internet

Da'as torah, 103, 109, 136, 137, 334n65
Daf yomi, 9, 27
Dating, 99, 199, 201, 202–4; and inter-dating, 53, 54, 99; and posters, 264, and *shidduch*, 201; and speed-dating, 310; and Talmud, 206
Day school, 8, 28, 44, 54, 72, 91–98, 102–13, 182; Brooklyn 73–74; faculty, 101; and Israel, 114; number of, 333n47; parents, 334n63; versus yeshiva, 84, 89, 100, 116, 332n29
Defenders of the faith, 86, 116, 179, 189
Demographic growth, 6, 62–77, 200
Displays, 122, 159, 192, 196–99, 204, 212, *238*, 260, 268; of counterculture, 146; versus genuineness, 198–99; and other-directedness, 209; and orthography, 348n48; of piety, 110, 119, 120, 191, 291; and symbols, 248, 260, 294
Disposable income, 245, 268–70, 353n52; and haredim, 73–74, 143,146–49, 151, 156, 225, 233, 250; and Jewish bill, 8; and Modern Orthodox, 239
Divine; anger, 25; intervention 245; punish-ment, 24, 318n28; redemption, 45; revelation, 2. *See also* G-d; God
Donors, 152, 154, 243, 245
Douglas, Mary, 3, 51, 81
Dueling cultures, 189
Dueling posters, *261*, 264–68, *266*

Early marriage, 67, 142, 144
Economic dependence: and social stability, 145
Economic pressures, 257
Edah, 55, 107
Education: as enculturation, 79, 328n2
Electronics trade, 150–51, 247
Emancipation, 18, 127–8, 317n9
Emerging power of women, 8, 176
Enclave culture breach, 167–70, 257
Enclavism, 4–6, 44, 50–52, 60, 181, 193–96, 202; and calendar, 191; and contra-acculturation, 69; and education, 78, 89, 225; and intimacy 182; and material life, 14; and mes-sianism, 233; movable enclave, 194, 289–90

Enhancing income, 146, 163
Enlightenment, 87, 123, 127–28, 317n22, 340n13
Erikson, Erik, 17, 116, 181–82, 187–88, 199, 207
Eruv, 71, 327n20
Ethnic church, 297
Exile: sense of, 57, 108, 296–98, 301, 304, 324n120
Extremism: as a religious norm, 45–46

Factors: in the move to the right, 96–122
Faculty, 96 102, 105–7, 123, 155, 160; Judaic, 96, 102, 105–12
Failed prophecy, 26
Farce: as a form of fighting back, 205–7
Feinstein, Moses, 51, 89
Feminism, 37, 54, 88, 106; and JOFA, 123
Flipping, 115, 208
Folk remedies, 353n65
Friedman, Menachem, ix, 56, 83, 211, 317n23
Frum, 2, 38, 110, 190–91, 209, 305, 346n32, 348n50; and appearance, 206–7; and books, 138; and code-switching, 192; and dating, 203–4; and frumak, 313n5; and *frum*mer, 2, 13, 115, 122, 187, 195, 198, 212, 272–73, 276–77, 298, 300, 304–5; and meditation, 198
Fundamentalism, 126; Christian, 60; Jewish, 81–82; quiescent fundamen-talism, 82
Fund-raising, 30, 59, 101, 145, 148, 178, 241–43, 245, 247–51, 266, 277, 307

Galus hanefesh, 5
Gay marriage, 97, 325n131, 347n42
G-d, 58–59, 198, 204, 348n48. *See also* Divine; God
Gender equality, 54
Gender relations, 121, 142, 168, 175, 250, 347n40; and education, 152, 155; and youth, 200
Gentiles, 51, 81,191, 253, 279, 346n32, 347n43; as author, 254; and cultural seductions, 29; distinctions from, 252; and Holocaust, 25; and Jews, 25, 32, 51, 60, 111, 252, 254, 300, 339n9; and trust, 51, 56
German Orthodoxy, 3, 18–19, 34, 55, 59, 87–89, 129; and Carlebach, 291; and Washington Heights, 108

Text:	10/13 Galliard
Display:	Galliard
Compositor:	Integrated Composition Systems